NEW LIES FOR OLD

NEW LIES
FOR OLD

The Communist Strategy of
Deception and Disinformation

ANATOLIY GOLITSYN

THE BODLEY HEAD
LONDON · SYDNEY
TORONTO

British Library Cataloguing
in Publication Data
Golitsyn, Anatoliy
New Lies for Old
1. Soviet Union — Foreign relations — 1975-
I. Title
327.47 DK274
ISBN 0-370-30805-0

© Anatoliy Golitsyn 1984
Printed and bound in the United States of America for
The Bodley Head Ltd
9 Bow Street, London WC2E 7AL

First Published in Great Britain 1984

TO THE MEMORY OF

Anna Akhmatova

CONSCIENCE AND SOUL OF RUSSIAN LITERATURE

Contents

PART ONE
The Two Methodologies

PART TWO

The Disinformation Program and Its Impact on the West

PART THREE
The Final Phase and the Western Counter-Strategy

Disengagement 363—Denial of Trade and Technology 364—Isolating Communist Parties 364—Addressing the Peoples of the Communist Bloc 365—The Next Half Century 365

Editors' Foreword

VERY RARELY disclosures of information from behind the Iron Curtain throw new light on the roots of communist thought and action and challenge accepted notions on the operation of the communist system. We believe that this book does both these things. It is nothing if not controversial. It rejects conventional views on subjects ranging from Khrushchev's overthrow to Tito's revisionism, from Dubcek's liberalism to Ceausescu's independence, and from the dissident movement to the Sino-Soviet split. The author's analysis has many obvious implications for Western policy. It will not be readily accepted by those who have for long been committed to opposing points of view. But we believe that the debates it is likely to provoke will lead to a deeper understanding of the nature of the threat from international communism and, perhaps, to a firmer determination to resist it.

The author's services to the party and the KGB and the unusually long periods he spent in study, mainly in the KGB but also with the University of Marxism-Leninism and the Diplomatic School, make the author uniquely well qualified as a citizen of the West to write about the subjects covered in this book.

He was born near Poltava, in the Ukraine, in 1926. He was thus brought up as a member of the postrevolutionary generation. From 1933 onward he lived in Moscow. He joined the communist youth movement (Komsomol) at the age of fifteen while he was a cadet in military school. He became a member of the Communist Party of the Soviet Union (CPSU) in 1945 while studying at the artillery school for officers at Odessa.

In the same year he entered military counterintelligence. On graduation from the Moscow school of military counterespionage in 1946, he joined the Soviet intelligence service. While working in its headquarters he attended evening classes at the University of Marxism-Leninism, from which he graduated in 1948. From

1948 to 1950 he studied in the counterintelligence faculty of the High Intelligence School; also, between 1949 and 1952 he completed a correspondence course with the High Diplomatic School.

In 1952 and early 1953 he was involved, with a friend, in drawing up a proposal to the Central Committee on the reorganization of Soviet intelligence. The proposal included suggestions on the strengthening of counterintelligence, on the wider use of the satellite intelligence services, and on the reintroduction of the "activist style" into intelligence work. In connection with this proposal, he attended a meeting of the Secretariat chaired by Stalin and a meeting of the Presidium chaired by Malenkov and attended by Khrushchev, Brezhnev, and Bulganin.

For three months in 1952–53 the author worked as a head of section in the department of the Soviet intelligence service responsible for counterespionage against the United States. In 1953 he was posted to Vienna, where he served for two years under cover as a member of the *apparat* of the Soviet High Commission. For the first year he worked against Russian émigrés, and for the second against British intelligence. In 1954 he was elected to be a deputy secretary of the party organization in the KGB residency in Vienna, numbering seventy officers. On return to Moscow he attended the KGB Institute, now the KGB Academy, as a full-time student for four years, graduating from there with a law degree in 1959. As a student of the institute and as a party member, he was well placed to follow the power struggle in the Soviet leadership that was reflected in secret party letters, briefings, and conferences.

From 1959 to 1960, at a time when a new long-range policy for the bloc was being formulated and the KGB was being reorganized to play its part in it, he served as a senior analyst in the NATO section of the Information Department of the Soviet intelligence service. He was then transferred to Finland, where, under cover as vice-consul in the Soviet embassy in Helsinki, he worked on counterintelligence matters until his break with the regime in December 1961.

By 1956 he was already beginning to be disillusioned with the Soviet system. The Hungarian events of that year intensified his disaffection. He concluded that the only practical way to fight the regime was from abroad and that, armed with his inside knowledge of the KGB, he would be able to do so effectively. Having reached his decision, he began systematically to elicit and commit to memory information that he thought would be relevant and valuable to the West. The adoption of the new, aggressive long-range communist policy precipitated his decision to break with the regime. He felt that the necessity of warning the West of the new dimensions of the threat that it was facing justified him in abandoning his country and facing the personal sacrifices involved. His break with the regime was a deliberate and long-premeditated political act. Immediately on his arrival in the United States, he sought to convey a warning to the highest authorities in the U.S. government on the new political dangers to the Western world stemming from the harnessing of all the political resources of the communist bloc, including its intelligence and security services, to the new long-range policy.

From 1962 onward the author devoted a large proportion of his time to the study of communist affairs as an outside observer reading both the communist and Western press. He began work on this book. While working on the book he continued to bring to the attention of American and other Western authorities his views on the issues considered in it, and in 1968 allowed American and British officials to read the manuscript as it then stood. Although the manuscript has since been enlarged to cover the events of the last decade and revised as the underlying communist strategy became clearer to the author, the substance of the argument has changed little since 1968. Owing to the length of the manuscript, a substantial part of it has been held over for publication at a later date.

With few exceptions, those Western officials who were aware of the views expressed in the manuscript, especially on the Sino-Soviet split, rejected them. In fact, over the years it became increasingly clear to the author that there was no reasonable hope of his analysis of communist affairs being seriously considered in Western official circles. At the same time, he became further convinced that events continued to confirm the validity of his analysis, that the threat from international communism was not properly understood, and that this threat would shortly enter a new and more dangerous phase. The author therefore decided to publish his work with the intention of alerting a wider sector of world public opinion to the dangers as he sees them, in the hope of stimulating a new

approach to the study of communism and of provoking a more
coherent, determined, and effective response to it by those who
remain interested in the preservation of free societies in the noncommunist world.

In order to give effect to his decision to publish, the author
asked the four of us, all former U.S. or British government officials,
for editorial advice and help. Three of us have known the author
and his views for twelve years or more. We can testify to his Sisy-
phean efforts to convince others of the validity of what he has to
say. We have the highest regard for his personal and professional
integrity. The value of his services to national security has been
officially recognized by more than one government in the West.
Despite the rejection of his views by many of our former colleagues,
we continue to believe that the contents of this book are of the
greatest importance and relevance to a proper understanding of
contemporary events. We were, therefore, more than willing to
respond to the author's requests for help in editing his manuscript
for publication, and we commend the book for the most serious
study by all who are interested in relations between the communist
and noncommunist worlds.

The preparation of the manuscript has been undertaken by the
author with the help of each of us, acting in an individual and
private capacity.

The author is a citizen of the United States of America and
an Honorary Commander of the Order of the British Empire
(CBE).

STEPHEN DE MOWBRAY
ARTHUR MARTIN
VASIA C. GMIRKIN
SCOTT MILER

Author's Note

THIS BOOK is the product of nearly twenty years of my life. It presents my convictions that, throughout that period, the West has misunderstood the nature of changes in the communist world and has been misled and outmaneuvered by communist guile. My researches have not only strengthened my belief, but have led me to a new methodology by which to analyze communist actions. This methodology takes into account the dialectical character of communist strategic thinking. It is my hope that the methodology will come to be used by students of communist affairs throughout the Western world.

I accept sole responsibility for the contents of the book. In writing it, I have received no assistance of any kind from any government or other organization. I submitted the text to the appropriate US authorities, who raised no objection to its publication on grounds of national security.

For the transliteration of Russian names I have used the system adopted by US government agencies. The transliteration of Chinese names follows the old system.

I wish to thank my friends, Stephen de Mowbray and Arthur Martin, who did the lion's share of the editing and helped me throughout with their editorial advice. I thank, too, Vasia C. Gmirkin and Scott Miler for their contributions to editing and for their editorial advice.

I am grateful to PC, PW, RH, PH, and AK for their dedication in typing the manuscript, to the wives of my friends who suffered in silence during its preparation, and especially to my wife, Svetlana, for her encouragement and her forbearance.

I wish to express my deep gratitude to two of my American friends, who will remain unnamed, for their help and their efforts in bringing my manuscript to the attention of the publishers, Dodd, Mead & Company. The publishers deserve my admiration for their grasp of the significance of the manuscript and for having the courage to publish such a controversial book. I am especially grateful to Allen Klots, of Dodd, Mead & Company, who revealed a great personal interest in the publication and also made the final editing of the manuscript.

Finally, I thank the Soviet government and party for the excellent educational facilities that made this book possible; and I thank Russian history and literature for the inspiration they gave when guiding me toward my decision of conscience to serve the people rather than the party.

ANATOLIY GOLITSYN

*Men will not receive the truth from their enemies
and it is very seldom offered to them by their friends;
on this very account I have frankly uttered it.*

Alexis de Toqueville,
DEMOCRACY IN AMERICA

New lies for old.

Attributed to Anna Akhmatova

PART ONE

The Two Methodologies

1

The Problems Facing Western Analysts

THE NONCOMMUNIST WORLD devotes considerable effort to the study of the communist world, and rightly so, since Western policy toward the communist world is based on Western assessments of the situation therein. Many institutions have sprung up in the United States, Great Britain, France, and elsewhere to study communist problems. Apart from traditional historical studies of prerevolutionary Russia and China, new specialities have been invented, such as "Sovietology" or the more limited "Kremlinology," which study the policy-making level in the Soviet Union. Analogous specialities have been established in the fields of "China-watching" and East European studies.

The results of Western studies are valid only if two sorts of difficulty are successfully overcome: the general difficulties stemming from the concern for secrecy displayed by communist regimes and the special difficulties arising from their use of disinformation. The failure of current Western studies is due in large part to the failure to appreciate the second set of difficulties.

The General Difficulties

The general difficulties and obstacles in the way of Western studies derive from the nature of communist regimes and are broadly recognized in the West. Principal among these difficulties are:

• Special measures taken to prevent leakage of secret information relating to problems of policy-making and its execution, such as the payment of a 15 percent salary supplement to KGB officers for maintaining secrecy.

• The existence of immensely powerful security service resources devoted to protecting state secrets and suppressing true freedom of expression.

• The party and state monopoly over the publishing and communications media and the dissemination of information for both internal and external consumption.

• Effective control and observation of foreign embassies, journalists, and visitors to communist countries and of their contacts in those countries.

In principle, these measures are not new; they are the concomitants of all totalitarian systems, which apply them with varying techniques and degrees of efficiency.

Although these difficulties complicate the study in the West of communist regimes and policies, they do not make it impossible. Western scholars have accumulated experience in dealing with the difficulties. The eyewitness accounts of many former inhabitants of the communist world now resident in the West have proved extremely helpful to the serious study of communist regimes and their problems in the past.[1] If these general difficulties were the only ones, Western assessments of the situation in the communist world might be more or less accurate; however, there are other, special difficulties.

The Special Difficulties: Disinformation

The special difficulties derive from the deliberate efforts of communist governments to mislead and misdirect Western studies and assessments. These deliberate efforts are known as disinformation (in Russian, *dezinformatsiya*). The *Great Soviet Encyclopaedia* says that the word is taken from two French roots, *dé(s)*, implying removal or elimination, and *information*, meaning knowledge.[2] The *GSE* defines disinformation as the dissemination through press and radio of false data with the purpose of misleading public opinion. It goes on to say that the capitalist press and radio broadly use disinformation to deceive the people of the world and to portray the new war that the Anglo-American imperialist bloc are preparing as defensive and the peaceful policy of the Soviet Union and the people's democracies as aggressive.

This would have been a broadly accurate definition of disinformation if the alleged roles of the "imperialist" and Soviet blocs had been reversed. In fact, disinformation has been used to a varying extent throughout the history of the Soviet Union.

This book is primarily concerned with the communist use of strategic disinformation. The term means a systematic effort to disseminate false information and to distort or withhold information so as to misrepresent the real situation in, and policies of, the communist world and thereby to confuse, deceive, and influence the noncommunist world, to jeopardize its policies, and to induce Western adversaries to contribute unwittingly to the achievement of communist objectives. Since 1958 a program of strategic political disinformation operations has been brought into effect. Its purpose has been to create favorable conditions for the implementation of long-range communist bloc policy, to impede the adoption of effective countermeasures or policies by the noncommunist world, and to secure strategic gains for world communism. An understanding of the disinformation program is crucial to a correct analysis of the situation in the communist world, but its existence has been either ignored or discounted in the West. An attempt will be made in this book to explain, on the basis of the author's inside information and new methodology, the role of the disinformation program and the techniques employed in it.

Disinformation in Communist Regimes

It is not only by communist governments that disinformation is practiced. Nevertheless, disinformation plays a more significant role in communist regimes than in any other type. Its role is determined by the particular ways in which communist regimes respond to crises within their systems, by the unlimited extent of communist external objectives, and by the communist capacity for executing a worldwide, long-term, offensive political strategy.

The role of disinformation in communist regimes can be clarified by comparing communist and democratic systems in the manner in which they respond to internal crises and in the nature of their external policies.

In democratic societies internal crises are usually open and limited in their extent. A democratic system allows for the absorption of the forces of popular resentment through democratic elections, judicial processes, and flexible responses in the form of negotiation and mediation. For this reason political or social protest movements do not normally lead to revolts of the entire population against the regime. Crises usually result in some readjustments in the system and may seal the fate of individual politicians, groups, or parties, but the basic stability of the system remains unaffected. This kind of flexible, democratic response could be seen in the United States during the campaign against the Vietnam War and during the Watergate crisis and in France after the events of May 1968.

In communist regimes crises are usually hidden from the outside world; because of the absence of democratic processes and the suppression of internal opposition, popular political, social, and economic discontents accumulate and threaten to develop into serious upheavals or revolts of the entire population against the system as a whole. This happened in Hungary in 1956. The manner of solving such a crisis in a communist system is normally arbitrary and authoritarian.

As far as external policies are concerned, those of noncommunist countries are normally dictated by national interest and have limited, short-term objectives. Except in time of war, they are usually defensive. Democratic governments deal directly with the governments of other countries and are constrained in their dealings with the opposition except in the event of civil war. Democratic governments tend to be either disinclined or unprepared to take advantage of crises in other countries that they may or may not regard as adversaries.

Communist external policy, on the other hand, is global, ideological, and long-range, and has the final objective of world domination. It is inherently inclined to take the initiative unless it is forced onto the defensive by an extraordinary combination of circumstances. Whatever the appearances, communist foreign policy also tends to place considerable emphasis on its dealings with the extreme left-wing opposition to the established government as well as on its dealings with the government itself. Communism is always inclined, and usually prepared, to take advantage of any crisis in a noncommunist country; it is required to do so by its long-term, unlimited objectives.

The differences between communist and noncommunist systems in their reactions to internal crises and in their external policies determine the different roles of disinformation in their respective systems. Democratic systems, being more open and therefore inherently more stable politically, do not need disinformation to hide the internal crises that occur from time to time and the means by which they are resolved. Crises become common knowledge and cannot be concealed. The Watergate crisis is a case in point. The main condition for the successful solution of such a crisis is that it should become public knowledge; therefore, there is no place for disinformation. Although democratic governments do manage news to some extent to project a better image of their performance, the use of special, clandestine methods for internal purposes is liable to be disclosed and exploited by the opposition in the next election campaign. In external policy democratic governments may practice disinformation on a limited scale in pursuit of their limited, national, and normally defensive objectives, but such disinformation tends to be on a modest scale and restricted to the military and counterintelligence fields.

In communist regimes the role of disinformation is entirely different. It is conditioned in part by the inherent instability of communist systems. The political vulnerability of communist regimes, their concern for stability, and their undemocratic methods of resolving internal crises oblige them to use disinformation on a wide scale in order to conceal and dispel the threats to their existence and to present themselves in a favorable light as stable forms of society. The internal role of disinformation is, on the one hand, to conceal the undemocratic, antinational, unlawful, and even criminal methods of resolving internal crises and, on the other, to minimize or neutralize internal antiregime activities while at the same time preventing or neutralizing any attempt from outside to foment and exploit those activities.

The special role of disinformation is enhanced by the aggressive and ambitious character of communist external policy. This aims at promoting and establishing communist regimes in noncommunist countries throughout the world by giving support to the extreme left-wing opposition, by gaining temporary political allies, by exploiting and deepening whatever internal crises may occur, and even by creating artificial crises. In order to be successful, such a policy needs a cloak or screen to mask or distort its specific objectives, tactics, and maneuvers while at the same time it creates favorable conditions in the countries concerned for the achievement of its goals. Disinformation provides this cloak or screen and also a means of exerting influence. It is the combination of aggressiveness with disinformation that gives communist policy its conspiratorial character. This combination is not a matter of speculation but an existing and constant reality in communist activity that cannot be arbitrarily ignored by Western governments and scholars without affecting the accuracy and realism of their assessments of the communist world.

The scope and scale of disinformation activity by communist regimes is virtually unlimited. There are no legal or political obstacles to disinformation operations. A police state with its centralized authority, its total control over resources, its untrammeled ability to execute maneuvers and sudden shifts in policy, and its immunity from the pressures of organized public opinion offers tremendous advantages for disinformation operations as compared with a democratic system.

Given total control over the communications media, communist governments need have no fear of adverse publicity; they can say one thing in public and do the opposite in private with complete impunity. They can also use for disinformation purposes the facilities of their intelligence and security services, which operate on a scale and with an immunity unparalleled in the West.

Given these advantages, it is not surprising that communist regimes should engage in disinformation at a state level as a significant part of their activities; they have unlimited opportunities to practice total disinformation, that is to say, to use all possible types of, and channels for, disinformation.

Communist disinformation operations are controlled at the highest level of government. They serve to support the interests of long-range policy, and their forms, patterns, and objectives are therefore determined by the nature of the policy in any given period.

In assessing the potentialities of communist strategic disinformation, it should be remembered that during the Second World War the Western allies showed themselves capable of devising ingenious and effective military and strategic deception operations. The three main conditions for the success of these operations were the existence of clearly defined and agreed allied war aims, the wartime system of press and radio censorship, and the insight the allies had gained into German intelligence, particularly through their ability to decipher German communications. In 1958–60 the communist regimes enjoyed comparable conditions and advantages in relation to the West.

2

The Patterns of Disinformation: "Weakness and Evolution"

THREE PATTERNS OF COMMUNIST STRATEGIC DISINFORMA-
TION may be distinguished: a pattern for a period in which
a specific, long-range policy is being pursued; a pattern for
a period of crisis in a communist regime or its policy; and a pattern
for a transitional period.

The "Weakness and Evolution" Pattern

The pattern of disinformation used during the implementation
of a long-range policy may be called the "weakness and evolution"
pattern, or the pattern of "calculated ideological moderation." Its
aim is to calm the fears of the adversaries of international communism by understating real communist strength and to confound
the policies of those adversaries by masking the realities of communist policy.

When following this pattern, therefore, disinformation reflects
real or imaginary weaknesses, splits, and crises in the communist
world and projects an image of evolution away from an ideological
toward a conventional, national system. The intention is that the
nations of the noncommunist world, accepting the alleged disunity
and evolution of the communist world as genuine, will fail to respond effectively to communist offensive strategy and, in their confusion, will be induced to make practical miscalculations and mistakes in their dealings with the communist world. The major role
of disinformation in the weakness and evolution pattern is to conceal

and misrepresent the real nature, objectives, tactics, and techniques of communist policy.

In order to gain and exploit temporary, tactical political allies and to avoid alarming them, efforts are made to conceal or understate the actual strength and aggressiveness of communism. Factual information favorable to communist regimes is withheld or downgraded; unfavorable information is disclosed, leaked, or invented. Given that communist, unlike democratic, governments are not concerned about their electoral prospects, they can afford to reveal true or false information unfavorable to themselves. During a period of policy implementation, real and artificial weaknesses in the system are emphasized; readjustments and solutions are presented as failures; ideological differences between communist and noncommunist systems are played down; calculated moderation in, and even some departures from, communist dogma are permitted; common features and common interests between communist and democratic systems are overemphasized or exaggerated; long-range communist objectives and coordinated action in pursuit of them are hidden. But the major feature of this pattern is the projection of alleged splits and crises in the communist world and the alleged evolution of communist states into independent, conventional nation-states motivated like any others primarily by national interests. The pattern determines the forms and means. Special disinformation operations play the leading part; propaganda is relegated to a supporting role.

The Precedent of the NEP

The weakness and evolution pattern was used successfully by Lenin in the 1920s. In 1921 Soviet Russia faced imminent collapse. Industry lay ruined by the war; agriculture was in crisis. The Russian people, disillusioned by the rigid policy of "war communism," were on the brink of revolt; the policy of terror was proving ineffective; there were peasant uprisings in Siberia and along the Volga; nationalist movements in the Ukraine, Georgia, Armenia, and Central Asia were openly proclaiming separatism and posed a serious threat to national unity; the sailors at the Kronstadt Naval Base revolted. Abroad, the hopes of world revolution had faded after communist defeats in Germany, Poland, and Hungary. The major European powers, although not united, were individually hostile to communism and to the new Soviet state; a huge Russian émigré movement, spread across Europe, was plotting the overthrow of the regime. Soviet Russia was in complete political and economic isolation.

It was in this situation, facing a highly unfavorable balance of power vis-à-vis the West, that Lenin conceived and launched a long-range policy that, over the following eight years, was to show spectacular success. It was given the deliberately misleading title of the New Economic Policy, or NEP. In fact, it ranged far beyond the economy, defining also the principal political and ideological objectives and tactics for the regime internally and externally and the strategy for the international communist movement. Within the terms of the NEP, the Soviet leaders were to eliminate separatism by creating a federation of national republics, the USSR. They were to introduce national long-term economic planning. They were to plan and build an electric power system to cover and bind together the whole country. They were to start to change the world balance of power in communist favor.

To the world at large, the NEP meant that foreign industrialists were offered concessions in Soviet industry and invited to open businesses in Soviet Russia; that Soviet industrial enterprises were to be reorganized as trusts and operated on a profit basis; that smaller enterprises and properties could be owned by cooperatives or private individuals; that money was back in use and private trade permitted; that restrictions on travel were relaxed; that émigrés were encouraged to return under amnesty, while some Soviet citizens were allowed to emigrate; and that Soviet diplomacy was seeking peaceful coexistence with the West.

The Soviet leaders saw it differently. They intended that the NEP would not only bring about economic recovery, but would also serve to prevent internal revolt, expand foreign trade, attract foreign capital and expertise, gain diplomatic recognition from noncommunist countries, prevent major conflict with the Western powers, help to exploit the contradictions in and between the capitalist countries, neutralize the émigré movement, and help to promote world revolution through the communist movement.

Lenin believed that this fundamentally aggressive and ideological policy could prove effective if it was accompanied by the systematic use of misrepresentation and deception, or, to use the current word, disinformation. The characteristics of this disinformation were an apparent moderation in communist ideology, the avoidance of references to violence in communist methods, the exaggeration of the degree of the restoration of capitalism in Soviet Russia, the use of a sober and businesslike style in diplomatic and commercial negotiations with the West, and emphasis on disarmament and peaceful coexistence. All of this was intended to induce the belief in the outside world that the communist system was weak and losing its revolutionary ardor. Left to itself, it would either disintegrate or come to terms with the capitalist system.

The Soviet security service was reorganized, renamed the OGPU, and given new political tasks. It was directed to mount disinformation and political operations. False opposition movements were set up and controlled secretly by the OGPU. They were designed to attract to their ranks genuine opponents of the regime inside and outside the country. These innocent persons could then be used by the regime in various ways. They could act as channels for disinformation; they could be blackmailed and recruited as agents; they could be arrested and given public trials. A characteristic, but not unique, example of this technique is provided by the so-called "Trust" operation.

In 1921, as the NEP was being launched, the OGPU created inside Soviet Russia a false anti-Soviet organization, the Monarchist Alliance of Central Russia. It had once been a genuine organization, founded by Czarist generals in Moscow and Leningrad but liquidated by the Soviet security service in 1919–20. Former members of this organization, among them Czarist generals and members of the old aristocracy who had come over to the Soviet side, nominally led the movement. Their new loyalty to the Soviet regime was not in doubt, for they had betrayed their former friends in the anticommunist underground. They were the Czarist generals Brusilov and Zaynchkovskiy; the Czarist military attache in Yugoslavia, General Potapov; and the Czarist transport official Yakushev. The most active agent in the Trust was a former intelligence officer of the General Staff in Czarist Russia whose many names included Opperput.

Agents of the Trust traveled abroad and established confidential contact with genuine anticommunist émigré leaders in order (ostensibly) to coordinate activity against the Soviet regime. Among the important émigrés they met were Boris Savinkov and Generals Wrangel and Kutepov.

These agents confided in their contacts that the anti-Soviet monarchist movement that they represented was now well established in Soviet Russia, had penetrated into the higher levels of the army, the security service, and even the government, and would in time take power and restore the monarchy. They convinced the émigré leaders that the regime had undergone a radical change. Communism had completely failed; ideology was dead; the present leaders had nothing in common with the fanatical revolutionaries of the past. They were nationalists at heart, and their regime was evolving into a moderate, national regime and might soon collapse. The NEP should be seen as the first important concession on the road to restoring capitalism in Russia. Soon political concessions would follow. Because of this, said the Trust agents, any intervention or gesture of hostility from the European powers or the émigré movements would be ill-advised, if not tragic, since it would only unite the Russian people around their government and so extend its survival. The European governments and the émigré leaders should put a stop to anti-Soviet terrorist activities and change their attitude from hostility toward the Soviet regime to one of passive acceptance. They should grant diplomatic recognition and increase trade. In this way they would have a better opportunity to contribute to the evolutionary process. The émigré leaders should return to Russia to make their contribution.

Naturally there were doubters among the émigrés, but the prestige of the leaders of the organization (particularly, of General Brusilov) convinced the majority. They accepted at face value the Trust's disinformation and passed it on to their influential friends in the European intelligence services. By the time it had been circulated to governments as "secret" intelligence it sounded most impressive, and when as time went on the same story was confirmed by source after source, it became "secret and reliable." The intelligence services of Europe were committed and it was unthinkable that they could all be wrong.

While the Trust was thriving the OGPU took control, wholly or partially, of two other movements calculated to influence the political climate in support of the NEP. They were the "Change of Signposts" movement and the "Eurasian" movement. The first was used by the Soviet security service to mislead émigrés and intellectuals in Europe into believing that the strength of communist ideology was on the wane and that the Soviet regime was evolving into a more moderate, national state. The movement published, with unofficial government assistance, a weekly magazine in Prague and Paris, *The Change of Signposts*, and in Berlin a paper, *On the Eve*. In 1922, at some risk, the Soviet government allowed two magazines to be published in Leningrad and Moscow, *New Russia* and *Russia*. They were intended to exert a similar influence on intellectuals inside the country.

By 1926 all publications of the Change of Signposts movement had been wound up, the movement disbanded, and some of its leaders in the Soviet Union arrested. An official Soviet publication partially confirms the exploitation of the movement and describes its end. Shortly afterward, operation Trust was terminated with the arrest of those opponents of the regime who had been unwise enough to reveal themselves as such by associating with the Trust.

To impress the Soviet people, trials of members of the opposition—some genuine, some false—were held throughout the country. Abroad, various means were used to damage, disrupt, and discredit both the émigré movements and the European intelligence services. Agents of both—some genuine, some false—were publicly tried in absentia; leaders of the émigré movements, European journalists, businessmen, diplomats, and government officials were blackmailed, on the basis of their involvement, into working for Soviet intelligence; individual émigré leaders, including Boris Savinkov and General Kutepov, and the Estonian ambassador in Moscow, Birk, were kidnapped; compromised spies were exchanged or recovered; selected persons and governments were held up to ridicule as "fools who had been deluded by the clever OGPU provocation" or were pressured or blackmailed by the threat of being discredited. For example, as late as 1944, during the Soviet occupation of Finland, Zhdanov threatened Finnish President Mannerheim that if he did not comply with Soviet demands, he would be put on public trial for his involvement in anti-Soviet activities during operation Trust and thus be squeezed out of politics.

The NEP was officially ended by Stalin in 1929 with what was called "a socialist offensive on all fronts." The concessions to foreign industrialists were canceled; private enterprise in the Soviet Union was prohibited; private property was confiscated; agriculture was collectivized; repression of political opposition was intensified. The NEP might never have been.

The Results of the NEP

Agriculture, industry, and trade all improved dramatically under the NEP. Although the NEP failed to attract large credits from the West, it brought technology and efficient new equipment. Thousands of Western technicians helped to industrialize the Soviet Union, and Western firms built essential factories there. It is fair to say that the foundations of Soviet heavy and military industry were laid in the 1920s with American, British, Czechoslovak, and, after the Treaty of Rapallo (1922), German help. Germany played an especially significant role in the Soviet militarization. According to the secret clauses of the treaty, Germans helped to build modern aviation and tank factories in the USSR. Communists spoke cynically of foreign concessionaires and businessmen as "assistants of socialism." Long-range planning and industrialization were launched. De jure recognition of the Soviet Union by the West helped the regime to neutralize internal opposition and so to stabilize itself politically. The remnants of other political parties (Socialist Revolutionaries, Mensheviks, Zionists) were suppressed, liquidated, or exiled. The peasants were pacified. The independence of the churches was broken and new, controlled "living churches" accepted the regime. The nationalist and separatist movements in Georgia, the Ukraine, Armenia, and the Asian republics were crushed and their nations fully incorporated into the federal union. No new organized political opposition to the regime emerged during the NEP. Regular purges of communist party membership kept ideological purity intact; a minority of members succumbed to the temptations of capitalism and were expelled. The party and security service gained experience in activist methods and in controlling contacts with the West. The security service began to exercise effective control over Soviet society.

The European bloc that it was anticipated would be formed against the Soviet Union did not materialize. De jure recognition was granted by all major countries except the USA. The Russian émigré movement was successfully penetrated, discredited, and left to disintegrate. The Treaty of Rapallo, signed with Germany in 1922 (the crowning achievement of Lenin's activist diplomacy), raised Soviet prestige, helped to increase Soviet military strength, precluded a united anticommunist front in Europe, and weakened the Weimar Republic.

Between 1921 and 1929 twelve new communist parties joined the Comintern, bringing the total to forty-six. By the use of legal tactics, communist parties increased their influence in trade unions and parliaments. Though the bid to form a united front with the Socialist Internationals failed, some socialist parties—the German, French, Spanish, and Czechoslovak—split under the influence of the communist approach; the left-wing groups joined communist parties or formed new ones. Valuable experience was gained by the Comintern in the simultaneous use of revolutionary as well as legal tactics, in its readiness to switch from the one to the other, and in its ability to coordinate with Soviet diplomacy. United front tactics were successfully used by the communists in Nationalist China. Mongolia became the first Soviet satellite.

The Lesson of the NEP

The disinformation of the NEP period had been successful. Seen through Western eyes, the threat of communism under the NEP seemed to have become diffused. Fear of Bolshevism waned. The position of anticommunists was undermined. Expectations of rapprochement were aroused. The Western public, reluctant to make sacrifices, urged their governments toward further accommodation with the Soviet regime. In reality, of course, the challenge of communism had been reinforced: Western expectations were later to be rudely shattered. But the communist strategists had learned the lesson that Western leaders could be deceived and induced to make mistakes in their assessments of, and policy toward, the Soviet Union. Disinformation had in fact created favorable conditions for the success of Soviet internal policy, activist diplomacy, and Comintern activity.

3

The Patterns of Disinformation:
"Facade and Strength"

IF A COMMUNIST REGIME IS IN A STATE OF CRISIS, if the regime
is weak, if its leadership is split or compromised, the logical
pattern for disinformation is to conceal the crisis and its dimensions, to attract attention to other areas and problems, and to present
the situation both domestically and to the outside world in as favorable a light as possible. This is the "facade and strength," or Potemkin
village, pattern of disinformation.[1] It has been applied in all communist countries, including, for example, China and Romania as well
as the Soviet Union.

The general pattern of disinformation determines the forms it
takes and the techniques used. In the facade and strength pattern,
information damaging to the regime is suppressed and information
favorable to it is exaggerated. The real issues are reflected vaguely,
if at all, in the press. Statistics are withheld or inflated. Propaganda
plays a leading role to the extent that it becomes in itself the
main form of disinformation. Special deceptions are carried out
to support the credibility of the propaganda. The failures and weakness of the regime are presented as its successes and strengths.
Political and ideological passivity and retreat are presented as political and ideological victories. Concern about the future is presented
as confidence. The fears of the outside world at communist strength
are deliberately aroused and the communist threat is exaggerated
out of proportion to its actual potential in order to discourage
external intervention in communist affairs.

Massive use of disinformation in accordance with this pattern
was made during Stalin's purges and during the last years of his

life. For instance, during the mass repressions of the 1930s the regime projected itself to the outside world, not without success, as a model democratic system under a strong leader. The Red Army, whose officer corps had been all but eliminated, was presented as the most powerful army in the world. In the postwar period the decline in the influence of communist ideology and the degree of popular discontent in the Soviet Union and its East European satellites were hidden; the significance of the opposition to Stalin from Zhdanov and his Leningrad group in 1948 was successfully concealed; so were tensions between the Soviets and Chinese and other communist countries. The bloc was misrepresented as a monolith. The political, military, and economic strength of the so-called monolith was grossly exaggerated in communist propaganda, the main vehicle for disinformation.

To prevent the West from detecting the depth of the internal crisis in the bloc that the propaganda was intended to conceal, contact between the communist and noncommunist worlds was reduced to the absolute minimum. Soviet and satellite citizens were prohibited from foreign travel except as members of official delegations; delegates were thoroughly checked before they left and kept under close watch while abroad. The only visitors to the bloc from noncommunist countries were communists or fellow travelers, and even they were thoroughly screened before their visits were authorized. When they arrived their itineraries were firmly supervised, with a large part of their program being devoted to visiting collective farms and factories that were organized as showplaces. Foreign diplomats and journalists were subjected to rigid restrictions; their travel was limited to a twenty-five-kilometer zone around the capital. Strict procedures for official contacts between foreign diplomats and communist officials were established; special decrees were enacted in 1946–47 defining the responsibility of Soviet officials when handling state secrets. Western contact with the man in the street hardly existed; and when it did, it was controlled. By these measures the communist countries were literally sealed off from the rest of the world.

Communist newspapers were devoid of any genuine news. Their articles were concerned only with the strength of the regime, the achievements of the leaders, and the shortcomings of the noncommunist world. Only those skilled at analyzing propaganda and disinformation could sometimes read between the lines and deduce an inkling of what was really going on.

Official Speeches and Party Documents

An example of the facade and strength pattern practiced at the time can be found in the report of the Central Committee of the CPSU to the Nineteenth Party Congress in October 1952. It dealt with the political and economic situation in the USSR and the communist bloc after the war. These are some extracts:

> The grain problem [in the Soviet Union] has been solved, solved definitely and finally.

> The achievements in all branches of the national economy have led to a further improvement in the material and cultural standards of Soviet society.

> Undeviatingly implementing the national policy of Lenin and Stalin, our Party strengthened the Soviet multi-national state, promoted friendship and co-operation between the peoples of the Soviet Union, did everything to support, ensure and encourage the efflorescence of the national cultures of the peoples of our country, and waged an uncompromising struggle against all and sundry nationalist elements. The Soviet political system, which has gone through the severe test of war and has become for the whole world an example and model of true equal rights and co-operation of nations, stands witness to the great triumph of the ideas of Lenin and Stalin on the nationality question.

> The USSR's relations with these countries [the communist satellites] are an example of entirely new relations among states, not met with before in history. They are based on the principles of equal rights, economic co-operation and respect for national independence. Faithful to its treaties of mutual assistance, the USSR is rendering, and will continue to render, assistance and support in the further consolidation and development of these countries.

This report was a travesty of the real state of affairs. What it said was the direct opposite of the truth. Those who composed it, those who approved it, and those who spoke it knew full well that it was totally false.

Special Disinformation Operations

A special Disinformation Service (Service 5) was created in 1947 as part of the Soviet intelligence service, known then as the Committee of Information (KI). It was headed by Colonel Grauehr.[2]

Special disinformation operations by communist intelligence services are never regarded as ends in themselves. They are intended to serve the ends of policy, usually by creating and shaping the conditions for its successful implementation. Since in the last years of Stalin's life there was an acute crisis in Soviet affairs and a lack of any coherent policy for resolving it, the special operations of Service 5 were limited in scope to unattributable propaganda operations designed to conceal the crisis and to justify some of the more outrageous and irrational instances of Stalin's behavior. One example was the effort to plant the suspicion that Tito and other Yugoslav leaders were long-term Western agents.

A further limiting factor on the scope of special disinformation operations was the cult of personality, which pervaded Stalin's dictatorship and forbade frankness even when it was required to give credibility to a falsehood. Two examples illustrate this. A Soviet agent was sent on a mission to the West. He was to pretend that he was a defector seeking political asylum. The host country allowed him to give a press conference, at which, not unnaturally, he criticized the Soviet regime. When Stalin read the report of the press conference, he asked who was the agent's controller, and then said: "Where did he work before he went into intelligence?" "He was a collective farmer," answered the chief of the service. "Then," said Stalin, "send him back to his kolkhoz if he cannot understand how damaging his agent's statements are. They point to our political instability."

On another occasion the Polish security service created the fiction that an underground organization in Poland, which had in fact been liquidated, was still active. They wanted to use the notional organization as a channel for political and military disinformation. When Stalin was asked to authorize the passing of this disinformation, he refused. "It gives the wrong impression of Poland's political stability," he explained.

In 1951, when Soviet intelligence was transferred from the KI (Committee of Information) to the MGB (Ministry of State Security), Service 5 became a directorate in the new KI under the Ministry of Foreign Affairs, dealing only with diplomatic disinformation. During the anti-Semitic campaign in 1951–53 Service 5 was as demoralized as the rest of the intelligence service. In fact, its head, Grauehr, went mad. He was succeeded by Ivan Ivanovich Tugarinov, who later became head of the KI.

4

The Patterns of Disinformation: Transition

THE STRUGGLE FOR POWER BETWEEN STALIN'S SUCCESSORS
lasted from Stalin's death in 1953 to Khrushchev's final victory
in June 1957. To an important extent, the struggle was not
only between rival personalities, but between rival policies. In the
absence of a settled and consistent policy, it is not surprising that
there should have been no centralized disinformation department
in Soviet intelligence during the period. Disinformation was practiced sporadically by heads of departments acting on the instructions
of the head of the service.

The aims of disinformation at this time were to conceal from
the West the dimensions of the internal crisis in the communist
world, to blur the differences in policy of the contenders for the
succession, to hide the savagery of the struggle, and to misrepresent
the process of de-Stalinization.

The successful concealment of internal crisis can be illustrated
by the handling of information on events in Georgia.

On March 5, 1956, the anniversary of Stalin's death, the first
mass disturbance happened in Tbilisi, the capital of Georgia. Large
crowds of people, especially students, gathered spontaneously for
an anti-Soviet meeting in the main square. The speakers demanded
the abolition of one-party rule, dissolution of the security service,
freedom of speech, and the independence of Georgia from the
Soviet Union. The students appealed to the crowds to join the
revolt, and many Georgians responded to the appeal. On Khrushchev's order the special troops were put on the streets, with orders
to fire on the crowds. Many were killed and wounded. Many stu-

dents were arrested. The national units of the Georgian and Arme-
nian troops in the local military district were disarmed and demobi-
lized in one night.

What happened in Georgia in the spring of 1956 can be likened
to "Bloody Sunday" (January 9, 1905), a day infamous in Russian
history when, on the orders of the Czar, a people's demonstration
was dispersed with bloodshed. In 1905 Bloody Sunday was headlined
in every newspaper in Russia, arousing mass indignation throughout
the country. In 1956 the event was ignored. Not a newspaper mentioned it. It was as if it had never happened. It still remains a
state secret that Khrushchev and Serov, the Chairman of the KGB,
rushed to Georgia to direct the suppression of the disturbance.

Georgia was completely isolated from the rest of the country.
The area, which attracts holidaymakers from all over the Soviet
Union to its famous resorts, was deserted throughout the summer
of 1956. Rigid travel control was imposed. It was explained, semioffi-
cially, that the strong nationalist feelings of the Georgians had
been upset by the condemnation of Stalin.

News of the disturbance in Georgia did later filter through to
the West, but it was interpreted as a nationalist outburst of discontent with the treatment of Stalin, not as a spontaneous demonstration against the whole Soviet system.

The Misrepresentation of De-Stalinization

As for the struggle for power, the Central Committee, the KI
under the Ministry of Foreign Affairs, and the KGB were all involved by Khrushchev in a successful disinformation operation to
misrepresent the reasons for the removal of his rivals and the real
character of his own position and policy. Since this operation involved misrepresentation of the issues involved in Stalinism and
de-Stalinization and provided part of the basic technique for the
program of strategic disinformation operations launched in 1959,
it merits detailed explanation.

To avoid misunderstanding, it is useful to begin by drawing a
distinction between anticommunism and anti-Stalinism and by defining the extent to which de-Stalinization is a genuine process.

Anticommunism

Anticommunism is not specifically linked with hostility to any individual communist leader. It means opposition to communist principles and practice; it is critical of communism in the broadest sense. It has existed in various forms inside and outside the Soviet Union since before 1917. It developed in Lenin's time, flourished under Stalin, and persisted, if less vigorously, under his successors. Within it three trends can be distinguished: a conservative trend, which is more or less rigid and consistent in its opposition; a liberal trend, which from time to time favors a degree of accommodation with communism; and a neutralist trend, particularly among non-communist neighbors of the communist bloc who try to make practical arrangements with communist regimes to secure their own survival.

Anticommunism in the intelligentsia may spring from the rejection on intellectual grounds of the dogmatic pretensions of Marxism as a philosophy. At all levels of society it is nurtured by the belief that communism is an unnatural, intolerant, and inhuman system that disregards the individual, maintains itself largely by force and terror, and pursues an aggressive ideological policy aimed at eventual domination of the world. In the past, communist theory and practice in such matters as the seizure of power, the abuse and destruction of democratic institutions, the suppression of personal liberty, and the use of terror provoked a militant response from social democrats, which led to a deepening gulf between socialist and communist parties and a split in the international labor movement.

The strength of international anticommunism has waxed and waned. The two high peaks were the Anglo-French effort to create a European anti-Soviet coalition during the civil war in Russia from 1918 to 1921, and the creation of NATO after the Second World War.

Inside and outside the Soviet Union, anticommunism has expressed itself in various forms from 1917 onward. Typical examples are found in the civil war in Russia, 1918–21; the separatist movements in the non-Russian republics; the revolts in the Caucasus and Central Asia in the 1920s; the later underground resistance movements in the Ukraine and Baltic republics; and in the activities of émigré organizations, political refugees, and those who broke with the Western communist parties.

Opposition of this kind would have existed whether or not Stalin had ever been in power, though it was strengthened and hardened by his repressive influence. In fact, so personal and despotic was Stalin's rule that, for a while, Stalinism became almost synonymous with communism, and opposition to the one became confused with opposition to the other, particularly since Stalin repressed both kinds of opposition with equal ruthlessness and severity. In the 1930s he crushed actual and imaginary opposition to himself by mass repressions, even of party members. Some of the leaders of the Third International, like Zinovyev, Bukharin, and Bela Kun, were shot. Trotskiy, who along with social democratic leaders was regarded by Stalin as being among the most dangerous enemies of the Soviet Union, was assassinated in 1940 by secret agents acting on Stalin's orders. Social democratic leaders in Eastern Europe after the Second World War were physically eliminated.

Anti-Stalinism

All anticommunists are anti-Stalinists. But the important point to note is that anti-Stalinism has traditionally been embraced by many communists who have sought not to abolish the communist system, but to strengthen and purify it by eliminating certain elements in Stalin's policy and practice. Anti-Stalinism of this type is critical of communism only in a narrow sense. It has existed in the communist movement since 1922. After Stalin's death it became an element in official party life and policy and gave rise to the genuine process of de-Stalinization.

In many respects Stalin's policy followed classical Leninist doctrine: for example, in the dictatorship of the proletariat and the communist party, industrialization, the collectivization of agriculture, the elimination of the capitalist classes, the construction of "socialism" in the Soviet Union, and in support for "socialist" revolutions abroad. But there were also departures from Leninist principles and practice in Stalin's establishment of his personal dictatorship, in his ruthless physical elimination of opposition and repression of loyal elements within the party, in the widening gulf he created between the ruling class and the underprivileged workers and collective farmers, and in the manipulation and discrediting of communist ideology.

Communist opposition to Stalin was expressed over the years:

• By Lenin, who in his testament criticized Stalin's rudeness and intolerance and suggested that he should be removed from the post of general secretary of the party.

• Publicly, in the 1920s and 1930s, by Trotskiy and his followers, who distinguished between the Leninist and Stalinist elements in Stalin's policies.

• Publicly by Tito and the Yugoslav Communist party, during and after the split with Stalin in 1948.

• Secretly by Zhdanov and his Leningrad group in 1948.

• Secretly by the Chinese Communist leaders from 1950 to 1953 and openly in 1956.

• In deeds rather than words from 1953 to 1956, and openly from 1956 onward, by the leaders of the CPSU and other communist parties.

The criticisms of these individuals and groups varied in intensity and outspokenness, but all of them remained communists in their different ways and, in particular, they all retained their loyalty to Leninism. Theirs was a true expression of de-Stalinization; that is to say, they believed in the restoration of Leninist communism without Stalinist deviations.

The dangers of Stalinism to the communist movement were ignored or overlooked in the 1930s and 1940s because of the threat of fascism and the opportunities that it provided for the formation of popular fronts with socialist parties in the 1930s and for the forging of the wartime alliance with the Western powers. But by 1953–56, the damage Stalinism had done to the communist cause was apparent. It could be seen in the following:

• The distortion, degradation, and discrediting of communist ideology. The image of Marxism as a philosophy had been tarnished in the eyes of Western intellectuals.

• Deepening discontent in the Soviet Union and its satellites, leading to explosive revolutionary situations in East Germany, Poland, and Hungary.

• The decline of communist influence and the isolation of communist parties and regimes.

• The revulsion against Stalinist communism of Western liberals who had earlier been sympathetic.

• The increased influence and prestige of anticommunism.

• Strong opposition from various religious movements, including Catholicism and Islam.

• The formation of Western military alliances, such as NATO, SEATO, and the Bagdad pact (later CENTO).

• Hostility from moderate, genuinely nonaligned national leaders of the developing countries, such as Nehru.

• Cooperation between Western democratic governments and anticommunist émigré organizations.

• Collaboration between social democratic and conservative governments and parties against the Soviet threat.

• Yugoslavia's break with the communist bloc and rapprochement with the West in the period 1948–55.

• The serious tensions between the Soviet Union and Communist China, which threatened to create a split between them in 1950–53.

• Zhdanov's opposition to Stalin.

• The major power struggle in the Soviet leadership that followed Stalin's death.

In some areas Stalinism brought together the two kinds of opposition: anticommunism and anti-Stalinism. In the case of Yugoslavia, which found itself closer to the West than to the communist bloc after 1948, they almost fused. In the present context, the most significant episode in the history of unsuccessful opposition to Stalin during his lifetime was the attempt to form a group around Zhdanov in 1948. Although it was a failure, it was known to Stalin's immediate heirs in the Soviet leadership. It was part of their accumulated store of knowledge of the various forms of opposition to communism and Stalinism and an important argument in compelling them to face the need to correct Stalinist distortions in the system if they were to avoid disaster. De-Stalinization was the obvious course, and an account must now be given of how it was put into effect after Stalin's death.

De-Stalinization in Practice

Three different phases of de-Stalinization can be distinguished: first, an initial, unrehearsed, and ill-considered but genuine de-Stalinization, carried out from 1953 to 1956 by a confused, divided, and competing leadership under pressure from the populace and in the absence of any long-range policy for the bloc; second, a setback to de-Stalinization in 1956–57, when Khrushchev was resorting to Stalinist methods to suppress revolt in Hungary and opposition to himself in order to secure his own personal preeminence; third, a cautious revival from 1958 onward of some genuine elements of de-Stalinization (for instance, the gradual release and rehabilitation of some of Stalin's victims) coupled with a calculated political exploitation of the process in which some of its elements were deliberately misrepresented.

Improvised De-Stalinization from 1953 to 1956

De-Stalinization began not, as is often assumed, with Khrushchev's secret report to the Twentieth CPSU Congress in February 1956, but immediately after Stalin's death in March 1953. Each one of the pretenders to the succession, Beriya, Malenkov, Molotov, Bulganin, and Khrushchev, was in his different way an anti-Stalinist. All of them without exception knew of the crisis in the communist system and all of them agreed on the urgent necessity of abandoning Stalinist policies. On the other hand, there was disagreement on the nature and extent of the changes needed. None of the pretenders was preeminent, none of them had worked out the details of his own policies, and—living as they had done under Stalin's shadow—no agreements on policy had been worked out among them.

The different personalities and policies of the pretenders affected the course of de-Stalinization. Beriya had in mind the deepest and most heterodox forms of change, including the abolition of collective farms. Malenkov, the most confident of the leaders in his own position, went further than the others in open condemnation of secret police methods and advocacy of concessions to popular demands. De-Stalinization was initiated not by Khrushchev, but by Malenkov, Beriya, and Molotov, who dominated the Presidium after Stalin's death.

Several steps were taken more or less immediately. The cases of certain leading personalities who had been tried and imprisoned under Stalin were reviewed. The Kremlin doctors were released. A ban on mass arrests was issued. International tension was eased by the settlement of the Korean War. Stalin's instruction of December 1952 on the reactivation of Soviet intelligence abroad was canceled, lest it should compromise the impact of the new moderation in Soviet foreign policy.

The first hint of the downgrading of Stalin's role and the admission of his mistakes was given in July 1953 in a secret party letter to the party membership informing them of Beriya's dismissal and the reasons for it. It referred to Stalin not as an outstanding leader, but simply as "Stalin, I. V.," and bracketed his name with that of Beriya, stating that Stalin's favoritism had prevented Beriya's exposure. It was the first tacit admission to the party membership of the fallibility of Stalin.

Later it became known in party circles that a discussion took place in the Presidium on Malenkov's initiative in July 1953 after Beriya's arrest. It was unanimously decided to make changes in Stalinist practices in the party and administration, although without public criticism of Stalin. In particular the Presidium recommended a reexamination and reform of the practices of the security service with the idea that, at a future date when the situation in the party and in the country had settled down, a reasonable explanation should be found for Stalin's deviations from communist principles, such as his unjustified repressions of personnel, including party members. All members of the Presidium, including Khrushchev, agreed that only Stalin and Beriya should be criticized and that there should be no admission of mistakes by other members of the Presidium.

Thus the secret report on Stalin's crimes, delivered by Khrushchev in February 1956 at the Twentieth Party Congress, which later found its way to the West but which has never been published in the Soviet Union, was in fact the consequence of a Presidium decision. The report was prepared by Pospelov, the head of the Marx-Engels-Lenin-Stalin Party Research Institute. The facts were taken from secret security service archives, and many of the ideas from accounts of Stalin's repression of the Leninist "Old Guard" found in the memoirs of former communist leaders published in the West in the 1930s, especially in those of Trotskiy. The draft of Pospelov's report was discussed and approved by the Presidium on the eve of the party congress.[1] While delivering the report, Khrushchev added some personal touches of his own.

The most important point about the report was that it prevented de-Stalinization from developing into an attack on communist principles as a whole. The changes that Beriya and Malenkov had in mind in their revisionist version of de-Stalinization might have altered the regime in principle. Furthermore, given the depth of the crisis in the communist world and the intensity of the struggle for power in the Soviet leadership, if those changes had been pursued, they might have developed a momentum of their own and brought about a radical transformation of Soviet society regardless of the wishes of their initiators and with incalculable consequences for the Soviet Union and the rest of the communist and noncommunist world. It was not without reason that Beriya was shot for being an "agent of world imperialism," and that Malenkov was dismissed as Prime Minister in 1955 for "departing from Lenin's and Stalin's theories." Their ideas had indeed threatened the regime and could have led to a situation that they would have been unable to control. By pinning the blame for all past mistakes on the misdeeds—not the theories—of one single individual, Stalin, the party leadership was able, while introducing some tactical changes, to preserve the essence of the communist regime.

Re-Stalinization

The exposure of Stalin's mistakes gave a substantial boost to anticommunism in general and to anti-Stalinist feeling in both the bloc and nonbloc communist parties. Revolts occurred in Georgia, Poland, and Hungary. The crisis in many other communist parties deepened.

Khrushchev's response was to revert to Stalinist methods. The security service was strengthened; armed force was used to crush revolt in the Soviet Union and Eastern Europe.

Khrushchev's progress toward his own form of personal dictatorship alarmed his colleagues in the leadership. Molotov and Malenkov emerged as the leaders of the opposition. At this time Molotov

was forming his own attitude and policy on de-Stalinization. He
and his supporters made it clear that they wanted to remove Khrushchev in order to secure a continuation of the de-Stalinization process
that Khrushchev had arrested. As communists they wanted to stabilize the system, and they viewed with dismay Khrushchev's establishment of his own cult of personality. It threatened their own position.
In their view his resort to a policy of repression might lead to an
even bigger explosion than the Hungarian revolt, and it completely
contradicted the course adopted after Stalin's death. Khrushchev,
in their eyes, was a new Stalin who had to be removed.

The showdown came in June 1957. With the help of the army
and the security service, Khrushchev defeated the "antiparty group"
by the narrowest of margins. Had the opposition been successful,
it would once more have opened up the possibility of a genuine
and uncontrolled process of de-Stalinization and liberalization of
the regime. Public exposure of the Stalinist methods used by Khrushchev to gain personal power, coupled with renewed denunciations
of secret police repression and a public trial of the KGB chairman,
Serov, would have led to popular demands for further changes.
Being divided, the opposition group, had it come to power, would
have been obliged to make concessions regardless of the wishes
of the individual members. An intensified power struggle would
have ensued and a new, agreed-upon, long-range policy could not
have been adopted.

Khrushchev's defeat of the opposition in June 1957 left him
in an unchallengeable position, free to reconsider the situation in
the Soviet Union and the bloc without interference from inside
the leadership. His first move was to turn the tables on the antiparty
group by falsely, but successfully, pinning the Stalinist label on
them. He managed to take for himself the credit for the exposure
of Stalin's crimes, to conceal his own use of Stalinist methods in
the pursuit of power, and to distract attention from the nature
of the opposition's charges against him. Misrepresented as a victory
over the forces of Stalinism, his defeat of the opposition was made
to look like a blessing for the Soviet public and the world at large.
Although there was some initial scepticism at home, even in a
few party organizations, both domestic and international pressures
on the government were eased.

5

The New Policy and Disinformation Strategy

K HRUSHCHEV'S VICTORY in the power struggle in June 1957 marked the beginning of the end of the crisis in world communism. It opened up a period of stability in which relations between the members of the communist bloc were to be reestablished on a new and sounder basis and in which a new long-range policy and new strategies for putting it into effect were to be worked out.

Within days of his victory, Khrushchev renewed the effort to restore party as well as state relations with the Yugoslavs, a course on which he had embarked at the time of his visit to Tito in May 1955.

Already, by June 1957, the Soviet and Chinese leaders had reached an agreed assessment of Stalin and his distortions of communist doctrine. The Chinese contribution to this assessment is to be found in two articles by Mao, which were published in the Soviet press in April and December 1956.[1] At the Eighth Chinese Communist Party (CPC) Congress in September 1956, the Chinese leaders supported the condemnation of the cult of the individual by the Twentieth CPSU Congress of February 1956.[2]

By the end of 1957 reconciliation between the leaders of all the communist states had been achieved. At a conference in Moscow in November 1957, they all agreed that Stalin had been responsible for damaging distortions of communist theory and practice. In varying degrees they had all resented Stalin's interference in their internal affairs and the rigid conformity he had demanded of them. But all (including the Yugoslavs, whose presence at the

33

conference was deliberately concealed) were prepared to cooperate
on a Leninist basis in a partnership of equals. The Soviets, in effect,
agreed to abandon their domination of the communist movement.
They even offered to forego references to their leading role in
the declaration issued after the conference was over. It was at
Chinese insistence that such references were included. The conference took an unpublicized decision to formulate a new, Leninist
program for world communism that was intended to imbue the
movement with the sense of purpose and direction it so badly
needed.[3]

The next three years were a period of intense research and consultation between the communist parties inside and outside the bloc
while the new policy and strategies were worked out.[4] The process
culminated in the Eighty-one–Party Congress held in Moscow in
November 1960. The leaders of all eighty-one parties committed
themselves to the program set out in the conference's statement,
or—as it is sometimes described—Manifesto. From that day to
this the main binding force in the communist movement, inside
and outside the bloc, has not been the diktat of the Soviet Union,
but loyalty to a common program to which the leaders of many
communist parties had made their contribution. Despite subsequent
appearances, an atmosphere of confidence was created between
the party leaders in which Soviet coercion became superfluous but
Soviet advice and help were willingly accepted.

The New Policy

In 1957, as in 1921, the communist strategists, in working out
their new program, had to take into account the political, economic,
and military weakness of the communist bloc and the unfavorable
balance of power vis-à-vis the West. Fissiparous tendencies in Hungary and elsewhere in Eastern Europe threatened the cohesion of
the bloc in 1957 as nationalist movements had threatened the unity
of Soviet Russia in 1921. The communist world faced hostility
from Western conservatives and socialists alike. Western propaganda was keeping the communist regimes under constant pressure.
The West in general was reluctant to trade with the bloc. And

the bloc faced one completely new factor—the possibility of nuclear confrontation.

Against this background, how could the communist leaders make their system more acceptable to their peoples? How were they to achieve cohesion and cooperation between the members of the bloc? And how could they advance the communist cause outside the bloc without provoking a greater degree of unity in the noncommunist world? It was clear that a reversion to the Stalinist policy of mass repression at home would fail and that traditional revolutionary tactics abroad would only intensify confrontation with the West at a time when the balance of power was unfavorable. The precedent of Lenin's NEP seemed to provide many of the answers, although, of course, the new policy would need to be far more complex and sophisticated.

The need for a new policy was felt with special keenness by the Soviet leadership. The older members, like Khrushchev, Brezhnev, Mikoyan, and Suslov, wanted to purge themselves of the taint of Stalinism and rehabilitate themselves in the eyes of history. The younger ones, like Shelepin, wanted the kudos due to innovators. All of them realized that only agreement on a long-range policy would preclude recurrent power struggles and give stability to the leadership.

The Manifesto produced by the Eighty-one–Party Congress (November 1960) clearly betrays the influence of Lenin's ideas and practice, as does Khrushchev's follow-up speech of January 6, 1961.[5] These two basic documents have continued to determine the course of communist policy to the present day. They explain in detail how the triumph of communism throughout the world is to be achieved through the consolidation of the economic, political, and military might of the communist world and the undermining of the unity and strength of the noncommunist world. The use by communist parties of a variety of violent and nonviolent tactics is specifically authorized. Peaceful coexistence is explicitly defined as "an intense form of class struggle between socialism and capitalism." The exploitation by world communism of economic, political, racial, and historical antagonisms between noncommunist countries is recommended. Support for "national liberation" movements throughout the Third World is reemphasized.

All parties, inside and outside the bloc, including the Chinese, signed the Manifesto—with the sole exception of Yugoslavia. For tactical reasons, Yugoslavia was not present at the congress but, as both Gromyko and Tito indicated publicly thereafter, Yugoslav and Soviet foreign policy coincided on many issues.

Agreement between the communist leaders on a new Leninist program for world revolution was only half the battle. A strategy was needed for putting such a program into effect at a time when the subject populations in the communist bloc were seriously alien-ated from their communist regimes and when the militarily superior Western powers were determined to resist the further spread of communism.

Some aspects of the strategy, such as united fronts with socialists in the advanced capitalist countries and support for national libera-tion movements in the Third World, were openly proclaimed. But the decision to use systematic, strategic disinformation as an essen-tial component of the strategy clearly had to be carefully concealed.

The Disadvantages of Apparent Unity

The communist strategists appreciated that the major disadvan-tage of the pursuit by all the parties of the bloc of a uniform and openly aggressive policy was that a combination of ideological zeal with monolithic unity would alarm the noncommunist world and force it into greater cohesion and possibly into a vigorous and coordinated response to the communist threat. This would lead at best to a continuation of the East-West status quo, and at worst to heavier pressure on the communist world from a West equipped with a superior nuclear arsenal.

A unified strategy would have been even more hampering to the international communist movement. Experience had shown that the activities of the Comintern were handicapped by its identi-fication as an instrument of Soviet policy. The same could be said of the Cominform, its successor. Communist parties in the noncom-munist world had failed to gain influence or, in many cases, even legal recognition because of their obvious subservience to Moscow. In 1958 more than forty parties were illegal.

From the historical experience of the Soviet Union and the bloc, the communist strategists identified the factors that had favored united Western action against communism. In the pre-NEP period, the West had felt threatened by Soviet ideology and militancy. The result was allied intervention on Russian territory. After the end of the Second World War, the threat of monolithic, Stalinist communism drove the West into military and political alliances, such as NATO, SEATO, and the Bagdad pact, and into other forms of military, political, economic, and security collaboration.

Similarly the communist strategists identified the factors that had tended to undermine unity in the Western approach to the communist world. These were moderation in official Soviet policy; emphasis on the conflicting national interests of communist countries and parties at the expense of their ideological solidarity; and the dissolution of the Comintern in 1943, which caused many Western observers to believe that worldwide communist subversion had been abandoned.

The Advantages of Apparent Disunity

Communists regard unity between the Western powers as inherently unstable; it follows from the nature of the capitalist system that, in normal circumstances, divisive considerations of national interest outweigh tendencies toward solidarity and cohesion. The communist strategists therefore reasoned that, through projecting the right image of the bloc and the communist movement, they could help to dissolve the measure of Western unity that Stalinist policies had brought into being. Moreover, they decided not to await the appearance of natural contradictions and divisions in the West, but to take active political steps to create artificially conditions in which Western economic and political unity would tend to disintegrate and which would therefore prove favorable for the implementation of their long-range bloc policy. In their view, by consistent and coordinated efforts, the countries of the bloc would be able to influence the policies and attitudes of the governments and populations of the noncommunist world in a direction favorable to themselves. They had before them the successful precedent of

Soviet policy and intelligence operations during the period of the NEP.

The naive illusions displayed in the past by the West in its attitudes and policies toward communism, the failure of the Western allies to develop a coordinated, long-range policy during their alliance with the Soviet Union in the Second World War, and the inclination of capitalist countries to pursue policies based on national interest were all taken into account in planning how to bring influence to bear on the West.

The conclusion was reached that, if the factors that had previously served to forge a degree of Western cohesion—that is, communist ideological militancy and monolithic unity—were to be perceived by the West, respectively, as moderating and disintegrating and if, despite an increase in the bloc's actual strength, an image was to be successfully projected of a bloc weakened by economic, political, and ideological disarray, then the Western response to communist policy would be feebler and less coordinated; actual Western tendencies toward disintegration might be provoked and encouraged, thereby creating conditions for a change in the balance of power in favor of the communist bloc.

In other words, common logic suggested that the bloc should proceed towards its aim of worldwide victory for communism by forging its own unity and coordinating its own policies as far as possible in secret while at the same time undermining the unity and resistance of the noncommunist world by projecting a misleading image of its own evolution, disunity, and weakness. This was in fact the hidden essence of the long-range bloc policy adopted in 1958–60 and the basis of the various strategies developed from then onward in the execution of that policy. The Eighty-one–Party Congress in Moscow, in November 1960, could well have created a new, overt central coordinating body for the international communist movement as a successor to the Comintern and Cominform, but it did not do so. Instead, it ratified the use of varying tactics by individual communist parties within the framework of the long-range policy and, in place of a controlling center, called for the coordination and synchronization of policy and tactics between bloc and nonbloc parties. Thus, while coordination was in fact improved, the decision not to create a new, overt central body, the emphasis on "polycentrism," and the use of a variety of different tactics by communist parties were designed to create an effect analogous to that created by the dissolution of the Comintern in 1943.

The Political Use of De-Stalinization

The Soviet leaders recognized that mistakes had been made in the first phase of de-Stalinization. Too many rehabilitations of Stalin's victims had been allowed too quickly; the party and the security service had been too passive in the face of the spontaneous reactions of intellectuals to the revelation of Stalin's crimes; above all, the Soviet leaders accepted that they should have consulted the parties of the other communist countries in advance. They realized that further uncontrolled measures of de-Stalinization could give rise to more revisionism and popular unrest. But they also realized that vigorous waving of the anti-Stalinist flag could help them undermine opposition at home and improve their image abroad; some of the damage done by Stalinism could be repaired.

Controlled anti-Stalinism could be used to help stabilize the regime; through propaganda emphasis on the distinctions between the new policy and Stalin's policy, some internal and external opposition could be undermined. For example, former communist party members of all ranks who had suffered repression under Stalin, or their widows and families, could be brought into active collaboration with the regime in the implementation of a Leninist policy that ostensibly repudiated Stalinism. Controlled anti-Stalinism could create favorable conditions for political and diplomatic maneuvers against noncommunist countries. It could be used to change attitudes toward communism and communist parties in the labor and social democratic movements. If the consequences of Stalinism, in the shape of personal dictatorship and the indiscriminate use of terror to suppress opposition inside and outside the party, had been fusion and alliances between the different types of opposition, it was arguable that emphasis on anti-Stalinism could lead to a weakening and disruption of such alliances. If Stalinism had led to cooperation between groups with different interests, between conservatives and social democrats in the creation of NATO, between Western capitalists and Yugoslav revisionist communists after

1948, between Russian émigrés and Western governments, anti-Stalinism could be used to weaken these ties. If Stalinism had contributed to the decline in Soviet prestige, to diplomatic failures and a loss of allies, anti-Stalinism could be used to reverse the process, to recover old allies and gain new ones among Western intellectuals, liberals, social democrats, and nationalists.

Between 1953 and 1956 genuine, improvised de-Stalinization was used to correct mistakes and improve the Soviet regime. In 1956 and 1957 notional de-Stalinization was exploited deceitfully by Khrushchev as a means of defeating his rivals while concealing the nature of his own methods. From 1958 onward calculated, deceitful use was made of notional de-Stalinization to help the new long-range policy achieve its domestic and external goals.

By 1958 the real issues involved in Stalinism, anti-Stalinism, revisionism, and national communism having been resolved, they could be revived in artificial form as "issues" allegedly causing divisions between different leaders and different parties inside and outside the bloc. Individual communist leaders or groups of leaders (all of them committed Leninists) could be projected misleadingly and in contrast with one another as "Stalinists," "neo-Stalinists," "Maoists," "dogmatists," "hard-liners," "diehards," "militants," or "conservatives" as opposed to "anti-Stalinists," "pragmatists," "revisionists," and "national," "liberal," "progressive," or "moderate" communists.

The objectives of disinformation on these "issues" can be summarized as follows:

• By the revival of dead issues and the display of apparent differences of opinion over them, to present the communist countries as in a state of disarray in accordance with the weakness and evolution pattern of disinformation.

• By projecting a false picture of nationalism and competing national interests in and between the communist regimes of the bloc, to conceal the actual unity of the bloc parties and governments in their pursuit of a common, ideological long-range policy.

• To create favorable conditions for the implementation of that policy, internally and externally.

• To provide a broad framework and convenient technique for specific disinformation operations on Soviet relations with Yugoslavia, Albania,

China, Romania, Czechoslovakia, and certain West European communist parties.

• To exploit these issues for disinformation about the alleged continuing power struggles and the unsolved succession problem, for shifts in communist domestic policy and in diplomatic tactics for implementing different phases of that policy.

Sources of Inspiration

The decision in principle to revert to the whole-scale use of strategic disinformation, taken in 1957, triggered off a spate of research into precedents and techniques. For example, the Central Committee called for secret publications on the subject held by the KGB and GRU, and in particular for a secret training manual for internal use only, written by a GRU officer, Popov, that described, in about eighty pages, the technique of disinformation, and for another manual written by Colonel Raina of the KGB entitled *On the Use of Agents of Influence.*[6]

Popov's manual defined disinformation as a means of creating favorable conditions for gaining strategic advantages over the opponent. It specified that disinformation must function in accordance with the requirements of military strategy and diplomacy, and stipulated that in all circumstances it must be subordinate to policy.

The book classified different types of disinformation as strategic, political, military, technical, economic, and diplomatic. It listed the channels through which disinformation can be disseminated as:

• The declarations and speeches of leading statesmen and officials of the originating country.
• Official government documents.
• Newspapers and other materials published in that country.
• Foreign publications inspired by agents working among foreign journalists and other experts.
• Special operations in support of disinformation.
• Agents of influence and other agents in foreign countries.

Studies of particular facets of the NEP were commissioned by the CPSU's Central Committee from 1957 onward. As well as government departments, specialized institutes of the Academy of

Sciences, such as the Institutes of Law and History, contributed. Two projects of special significance for the reintroduction of strategic disinformation were undertaken in the KGB. One was a study on the use of KGB agents of influence in the Soviet intelligentsia (meaning in this context scientists, academics, writers, musicians, artists, actors, stage and screen directors, and religious leaders); the other was on the disclosure of state secrets in the interests of policy.

Popov's manual was in fact the only available modern text dealing with strategic disinformation. Lenin left behind him no specific treatise on the subject, although his writings contain scattered references to it; deception and duplicity were essential elements in his political technique. Significantly the Soviet authorities chose to publish for the first time, between 1960 and 1965 in the fifth edition of Lenin's works, some of his documents relating to the NEP period and the use of disinformation, in particular in his correspondence with his commissar for foreign affairs, Chicherin.

In one of his letters Lenin, commenting on the draft of a statement to be made by the Soviet delegation to the Genoa conference, advised Chicherin to omit any mention of "the inevitable forced *coup d'etat* and bloody struggle" and also to omit the words "our historical concept includes the use of violent measures and the inevitability of new world wars." "These frightening words," he wrote, "should not be used because they would serve the interests of our adversaries."[7]

Chicherin responded enthusiastically to Lenin's ideas on disinformation. He wrote to him on January 20, 1922: "In case the Americans would insist on representative institutions, don't you think that, for solid compensation, we can deceive them by making a small ideological concession which would not have any practical meaning? For example, we can allow the presence of three representatives of the non-working class in the body of 2,000 members. Such a step can be presented to the Americans as a representative institution."[8]

Lenin and Chicherin were not the only sources of inspiration for the revival of strategic disinformation. The ancient Chinese treatise on strategy and deception, Sun Tzu's *The Art of War*, translated into Russian by N. I. Konrad in 1950 (shortly after the communist victory in China), was retranslated into German in

1957 by the Soviet specialist Y. I. Sidorenko, with a foreword by the Soviet military strategist and historian General Razin.[9] It was published in East Germany by the East German Ministry of Defense and was prescribed for study in East German military academies. A new translation and other studies of Sun Tzu were published in Peking in 1957 and 1958 and in Shanghai in 1959. Mao is known to have been influenced by Sun Tzu in his conduct of the civil war.

This intense official interest in Sun Tzu on the part of both the Soviets and the Chinese at the very time when the new policy and strategy were being formulated is a good indication that the Chinese probably made a positive contribution to their formulation.

The strategy of strengthening the communist bloc while presenting an appearance of communist disunity is neatly expressed in Sun Tzu's aphorisms:

• All warfare is based on deception. Therefore, when capable, feign incapacity; when active, inactivity.
• Offer the enemy a bait to lure him; feign disorder and strike him.
• One who wishes to appear to be weak in order to make his enemy arrogant must be extremely strong. Only then can he feign weakness.

To be credible and effective, a deception should accord as far as possible with the hopes and expectations of those it is intended to deceive. Since the communist strategists were aware, especially through their knowledge of the Bilderberg papers,[10] that the West half expected and ardently desired the disintegration of the communist bloc, they could anticipate that the projection to the outside world of a fictitious disintegration of the bloc would be advantageous—provided always that it was accompanied in parallel by an actual, but partially concealed, implementation of the long-range policy of strengthening the bloc and changing the world balance of power in its favor.

How, in practice, was this to be achieved? Study of the genuine Tito-Stalin split of 1948 showed that by no means all of its consequences had been adverse. Open defiance of Stalin had sent Tito's prestige soaring in his own country and throughout the world. Independence of the Soviet Union had enabled Yugoslavia to obtain

substantial economic and military assistance from the West and
to acquire the beginnings of political influence in the Third World
and with West European socialist parties. Moreover, Tito had demonstrated in 1957–58 that, despite the Western support he had
received, he remained a faithful Leninist willing to work wholeheartedly with the other leaders of the bloc.[11]

A more remote, but equally instructive, precedent was provided
by Lenin's Far Eastern policy in the 1920s. Realizing that Soviet
Russia would be overstretched in defending all her frontiers simultaneously, Lenin decided voluntarily to "sacrifice" a substantial area
in the Far East by setting up an independent "noncommunist"
buffer state, the Far Eastern Republic (DVR), in April 1920. It
was independent and noncommunist in form only, its policies being
closely coordinated from the outset with those of Soviet Russia.
Nevertheless, its existence, together with promises of economic
concessions that did not materialize, relieved the pressure from
Japanese and American interests in the area while the Soviet army
and Comintern reinforced their capacity to deal with the threat
from the White Russian émigré movement in Mongolia led by
Baron Ungern. By November 1922 Soviet influence in the area
was strong enough for the "independent" DVR to be openly incorporated into the Soviet Union as its Far Eastern region (*kray*).

The combined lessons of the DVR and the Tito-Stalin split
suggested to the communist strategists of the 1950s that spurious
splits and independence in the communist world could be used
to ease Western pressure and to obtain increased Western economic
and even military aid for individual communist countries while
the world balance of power was being shifted inconspicuously in
communist favor.

By the end of 1957 the issues that had caused actual and potential
splits in the communist world, principally Stalinist interference in
the affairs of other communist states, had been finally and decisively
resolved. Common agreement had been reached on the abandonment of Stalin's acknowledged distortions of Leninist doctrine. The
Soviet Union abided by the terms of the agreement in practical
ways, for example, by making a total declaration of its former intelligence agents in China and Eastern Europe.

The reasons for genuine splits having been removed, the way
was open for the creation of spurious splits in accordance with

Dzerzhinskiy's principle of political prophylaxis; that is, the forestalling of undesirable developments (such as splits or the growth of opposition movements) by deliberately provoking and controlling such developments through the use of secret agents, and by guiding them in directions that are either harmless or positively useful to the regime.

Khrushchev had demonstrated in 1957 how misrepresentation of the Stalinist issue could be used to his own advantage in the struggle for power. The artificial revival of the dead issues related to Stalinism was the obvious and logical means of displaying convincing but spurious differences between different communist leaders or parties.

6

The Shelepin Report
and
Changes in Organization

THE ADOPTION OF THE NEW BLOC POLICY and disinformation strategy entailed organizational changes in the Soviet Union and throughout the bloc. In the Soviet Union, as elsewhere, it was the Central Committee of the party that reorganized the intelligence and security services, the foreign ministry, and other sections of the party and government apparatus and the mass organizations so as to be able to implement the new policy. Several highly significant alterations were made to the Central Committee's own apparatus in and after 1958. A new Department of Foreign Policy was set up to supervise all government departments concerned with foreign affairs and to coordinate Soviet foreign policy with that of the other communist states. It was under Khrushchev's direct control.

A new practice was adopted in relation to the appointment of ambassadors to other communist countries. Prominent party officials, normally members of the Central Committee, were chosen to ensure that there was proper coordination of policy between parties as well as governments.

Another new department of the Central Committee, the Department of Active Operations, was introduced. Its function was to coordinate the bloc disinformation program and conduct special political and disinformation operations in support of policy. It began by holding secret briefings of senior officials of the Ministry of Foreign Affairs, the Committee of Information, and the security and intelligence services. The news agency Novosti was set up to serve the interests of this new department.

An important change was the transfer to the Central Committee apparatus of the Committee of Information, which had hitherto been subordinated to the Ministry of Foreign Affairs. One of its new functions was to prepare long-range studies and analyses for the Central Committee. Another was to establish contacts with foreign statesmen and other leading figures, either in their home countries or during their visits to the Soviet Union, and use them to influence Western governments. Its head was Georgiy Zhukov, a former agent of the Soviet intelligence service, who had many contacts among Western politicians, journalists, and cultural figures. He was himself an able journalist.

Perhaps the most significant changes of all were the appointments of Mironov and Shelepin. Mironov had been head of the Leningrad branch of the KGB. While in that post he had studied operation Trust, in which the Leningrad OGPU had played an active part. He was a friend of Brezhnev and had easy access to him. Shelepin was a friend of Mironov. It was Mironov who first drew Shelepin's attention to the role of the OGPU in the NEP period.

In 1958 Mironov and Shelepin discussed with Khrushchev and Brezhnev the idea of transforming the KGB from the typical secret political police force that it was into a flexible, sophisticated political weapon capable of playing an effective role in support of policy, as the OGPU had done during the NEP.

They were rewarded for this suggestion with posts in the Central Committee apparatus. Shelepin was made head of the Department of Party Organs and, later, chairman of the KGB; Mironov was made head of the Administrative Organs Department.

In the autumn of 1958 Mironov's and Shelepin's suggestion was discussed, in the context of the performance of the KGB and its head, General Serov, by the Presidium of the Central Committee. Serov had delivered a report to the Presidium on the work of the KGB at home and abroad, and it became the focus for sharp criticism. The leading critic was Shelepin. The KGB under Serov, he said, had become a very effective police organization that, with its widespread net of informers and agents throughout the country, had successfully detected and controlled opposition elements among the population as well as agents of Western intelligence services. It had failed, however, to influence the views of the population in favor of the regime or to prevent the growth of undesirable political trends either at home or among anticommunists abroad. He praised the recent successes of the KGB in penetrating the secrets of Western governments, but said that its role was too passive and limited in that it had done nothing to help the strategic, political, economic, and ideological struggle with the capitalist powers.

Shelepin continued that the main reason for the unsatisfactory situation in the KGB was that it had departed from the traditions and style of the OGPU, its predecessor under Lenin. The OGPU, although inexperienced, had made a greater contribution to implementing policy than any of its successors. As examples of what he meant, he referred to the Eurasian and Change of Signposts movements and the Trust. Unlike the OGPU, the KGB had degenerated into a passive, repressive organization. Its methods were self-defeating because they served only to harden opposition and damage the prestige of the regime. The KGB had failed to collaborate with the security services of the other bloc countries on political matters.

Shelepin commended Mironov's ideas and said that the KGB should be concerned with positive, creative political activity under the direction of the party leadership. A new, more important role should be given to disinformation. The Soviet Union, in common with the other communist countries, had vital internal and external intelligence assets that had been lying dormant, especially in the persons of the KGB agents among the Soviet intelligentsia.

The Presidium decided to examine the new role of the KGB at the Twenty-first–Party Congress, which was due to be held in January–February 1959. The Soviet press confirmed in general terms that this examination had taken place.

Under Mironov the Administrative Organs Department became very important. Its function was to supervise and coordinate the work of departments concerned with internal order, like the KGB, the Ministry of the Interior, the prosecutor's office, the Ministry of Justice, and the law courts. Mironov was chosen in order that he should imbue these institutions with the style and methods of Dzerzhinskiy, the OGPU's chairman in the 1920s.

Shelepin was appointed chairman of the KGB in December 1958. In May 1959 a conference of senior KGB officers was held in Moscow. It was attended by Kirichenko, representing the Presidium;

the ministers of internal affairs and defense; members of the Central Committee; and some two thousand KGB officers.

Shelepin reported to the conference on the new political tasks of the KGB.[1] Some of the more specific points in his report were as follows:

The "main enemies" of the Soviet Union were the United States, Britain, France, West Germany, Japan, and all countries of NATO and other Western-supported military alliances. (It was the first time that West Germany, Japan, and the smaller countries had been so named in KGB documents.)

The security and intelligence services of the whole bloc were to be mobilized to influence international relations in directions required by the new long-range policy and, in effect, to destabilize the "main enemies" and weaken the alliances between them.

The efforts of the KGB agents in the Soviet intelligentsia were to be redirected outward against foreigners with a view to enlisting their help in the achievement of policy objectives.

The newly established disinformation department was to work closely with all other relevant departments in the party and government apparatus throughout the country. To this end, all ministries of the Soviet Union and all first secretaries of republican and provincial party organizations were to be acquainted with the new political tasks of the KGB to enable them to give support and help when needed.

Joint political operations were to be undertaken with the security and intelligence services of all communist countries.

The report ended with the assurance that the Presidium had approved the new tasks of the KGB, attached great importance to their fulfillment, and was confident that the KGB staff would do its best to put the directive into practice.

After the conference, a number of organizational changes were made in the KGB. The counterintelligence directorate was enlarged. Its three main tasks were: to influence, pass disinformation to, and recruit as agents members of the embassies of the capitalist and Third World countries in Moscow, as well as visiting journalists, businessmen, scientists, and academics; to carry out prophylactic political operations to neutralize and then use internal political opposition, especially from nationalistic, intellectual, and religious groups; and to carry out joint political operations with the security services of the other communist countries.

Department D

When Shelepin created the new disinformation department, Department D, in January 1959, he ensured that its work would be coordinated with the other disinformation services of the party and government machine: that is, the Central Committee, the Committee of Information, the disinformation department in the Soviet Military Intelligence Service, and the two new "activist methods" departments in the KGB (one serving Shelepin himself and the other serving the counterintelligence directorate).

From the beginning Department D was subordinate to the Central Committee apparatus, which defined its requirements and objectives. It differed from the other disinformation services in that it used its own means and special channels available only to the KGB to disseminate disinformation. These channels are: secret agents at home and abroad; agents of influence abroad; penetrations of Western embassies and governments; technical and other secret means of provoking appropriate incidents or situations in support of policy—for example, border incidents, protest demonstrations, and so forth.

Department D was given access to the executive branches of government and to departments of the Central Committee to enable it to prepare and carry out operations that required the approval or support of the party leadership or the government machine. Its closest contacts with the Central Committee were Mironov's Administrative Organs Department, Ponomarev's International Department, the Department of Foreign Policy, and the Department of Active Operations; and with the Soviet government through the State Committee of Science and Technology and the planning organs. There was particularly close cooperation between the new department and the disinformation department of the Military Intelligence Service.

There were two experienced candidates for the post of head of the new department: Colonel Fedoseyev, head of the foreign intelligence faculty of the KGB Institute, who was a specialist both on internal KGB operations and on the use of émigré channels to penetrate American intelligence; and Colonel Agayants, head of the political intelligence faculty in the High Intelligence School and a specialist on the Middle East (Iran in particular) and Western Europe (France in particular). Shelepin chose Agayants.

The new department consisted at the outset of fifty to sixty experienced intelligence and counterintelligence officers. Under Colonel Agayants was Colonel Grigorenko, a specialist in counterintelligence work at home and emigration operations abroad. He had been adviser to the Hungarian security service from 1953 to 1955, and then had worked in the counterintelligence directorate in headquarters as head of the department responsible for the surveillance of immigrants and repatriates. The department was abolished when Grigorenko moved to Department D.

In the department were experts on NATO, the United States, Germany, France, Japan, and other countries; on the US intelligence services; on US, European, Asian, African, and Latin American labor; and on rocketry, aviation, and other specialized subjects. There was a specialist on Israel, Colonel Kelin, who as an officer in the security service had worked for twenty years against the Jews in Moscow. Colonel Sitnikov was the department's specialist on Germany, Austria, and NATO. Colonel Kostenko (who in the 1960s appeared in England under diplomatic cover) was its specialist on aviation. Indeed, the composition of the department made it clear that it had both political and military objectives.

A disinformation section of some twenty officers was also set up in the KGB apparatus in East Germany under Litovkin, a specialist on penetration of the West German intelligence service.

7

The New Role of Intelligence

IN OUTLINE, the new tasks for the intelligence services of the bloc, in addition to their traditional intelligence-gathering and security functions, were, first, to help to create favorable conditions for the implementation of the long-range policy by disseminating strategic disinformation on disunity in the bloc and international communist movement in accordance with the weakness and evolution pattern; second, to contribute directly to the implementation of the policy and its strategies through the use of communist bloc and Western agents of influence; and third, to contribute to a shift in the military balance of power in communist favor by helping to accelerate the bloc's military and economic development through the collection of scientific and technical intelligence from the West and through the undermining of Western military programs.

To take the last of these tasks first, it was considered by Soviet officials in 1959 that the communist bloc was lagging ten to fifteen years behind the United States, for example, in the field of military electronics. Through use of the bloc's intelligence potential, it was hoped to close the gap within five years.[1] Conversely, through the disinformation potential of the bloc's security and intelligence services, it was hoped, as Shelepin put it, to confuse and disorientate Western military programs and divert them into useless, wasteful, and extravagant fields of expenditure. With this end in view, Department D, together with the Central Committee, took part in briefing Soviet scientists for their assignments at various international conferences where they have contacts with foreign scientists.

Some of the other operations of Department D were known

in outline to the author in their early stages.

There were plans for an operation to influence the French government to leave NATO. Soviet experts were already convinced by 1959–60 that "contradictions" between the United States and France could be exploited to bring this about.[2]

A long-term plan was in preparation to discredit anticommunist American labor leaders and to influence them to change their attitude toward contact with the communist trade unions.

There was also a plan called "Actions Against American Institutions," in particular the CIA and FBI, details of which are not known to the author.

An operation, carried out soon after Department D was formed, aimed to help isolate West Germany from NATO and the Western community. Experts in Jewish affairs in Department D prepared numerous letters for their agents to send to relatives in Israel and other countries that were calculated to arouse hostility to West Germany and to give a misleading impression of political developments in the Soviet Union.

Of the greatest long-term significance was an order issued by Shelepin to Agayants at the end of 1959 to collaborate with the Central Committee's Department of Active Operations and with Albanian and Yugoslav representatives on a disinformation operation connected with the new long-range policy and relating to Soviet-Yugoslav-Albanian relations.

A number of other reflections of the adoption of the new policy and the revival of disinformation came to the author's attention in the course of his work in Soviet intelligence.

Early in 1959 a secret party letter warned party members against revealing state and party secrets.

Genuine, potential Western sources of information on the new policy were suppressed. For example, the KGB arrested a valuable American agent in the Soviet Union, Lieutenant Colonel Popov of the GRU.

Other potential openings for the West to obtain information on the policy were closed: for example, a special instruction was issued to KGB staff to step up the recruitment, compromise, and discrediting of Western scholars and experts on communist affairs visiting communist countries.

An instruction was issued to KGB staff to give details to the disinformation department of all their existing intelligence sources and channels, so that, where appropriate, they could be used for disinformation purposes.

New channels were planned and created for feeding disinformation to the West. In this context, three items deserve mention. Department D showed great interest in exploiting two special French sources belonging to Soviet counterintelligence: they asked for the controlling officer, Okulov, to be transferred to Department D. There is serious, unresolved evidence that Colonel Penkovskiy was planted on Western intelligence by the KGB. There has been publicity in the American press suggesting that an important FBI source on Soviet affairs, known as "Fedora," was under Soviet control while he was collaborating with the FBI in the 1960s.[3]

The section of the KGB's Second Chief Directorate, led by Colonel Norman Borodin and responsible for the recruitment and handling of agents among foreign correspondents in the Soviet Union, was disbanded so as to avoid the creation of a central pool of agents all taking a suspiciously similar line. The agents were handed over to the appropriate geographical sections of the KGB to ensure that their disinformation activity was closely related to the particular situation in each country or area.

Two former residents of Hitler's security service, with their nets of agents in the Ukraine, which were under KGB control, were prepared for planting on the West German intelligence service.

In 1959 the head of Soviet counterintelligence, General Gribanov, issued an instruction to his staff to prepare operations to influence Western ambassadors in Moscow, in accordance with the requirements of the new policy. Western intelligence and security services—in particular, that of the French—had occasion to investigate Gribanov's activity against their ambassadors. Gribanov also instructed members of his staff, posing as senior officials of various Soviet government departments, to establish personal contact with, and exercise political influence over, the ambassadors in Moscow of all the developing countries.

In 1960 a secret directive was issued by the KGB in Moscow to the intelligence service's representatives abroad and the security service at home on the influencing of foreign visitors to the Soviet Union, especially politicians and scholars; efforts were made to use, recruit, and discredit anticommunist politicians, journalists, scholars, and analysts of communist affairs during their visits to communist countries. For instance, an attempt was made to discredit a prominent American scholar, Professor Barghoorn, by harrassing him in Moscow in 1963. Almost every Western security service has accumulated evidence on this subject.

A special form of control over the Soviet press was established by the apparatus of the Central Committee so that the press could be used by the Central Committee and KGB for disinformation purposes. For instance, the KGB supplied Adzhubey, the chief editor of *Izvestiya*, with "controversial" material on internal conditions in the Soviet Union.

The resources of the KGBs of the national republics were brought into play; for example, in the year 1957–58 alone, the KGB of the Ukraine put up for Moscow approval 180 operational proposals for the recruitment of, or the planting of agents on, foreigners inside or outside the Soviet Union.

Direct attempts were made to exert political influence abroad. Instructions were issued to the KGB residents in Finland, Italy, and France to step up and exploit their penetration of the leadership of socialist and other political parties in order to bring about changes in the leadership and policies of those parties in accordance with the requirements of bloc policy.[4]

In Finland, in 1961, the KGB resident, Zhenikhov, was working on a plan to remove from the political scene leading anticommunist leaders of the Finnish social democratic party like Tanner and Leskinen and to replace them with Soviet agents.[5]

A KGB agent was planted on the leadership of the Swedish social democratic party.

Assassinations were not excluded in the case of anticommunists who represented an obstacle to the successful implementation of bloc policy. For example, in 1959 the KGB secretly assassinated the Ukrainian nationalist leader Stepan Bandera in West Germany. This is known thanks to the exposures of the former Soviet agent Stashinskiy, who assassinated Bandera on Shelepin's orders.

The list could be expanded. But enough has been said to indicate that the entire Soviet intelligence potential was used to carry out operations in support of the first phase of the new long-range bloc policy; the same can be said of the intelligence potential of the other countries of the communist bloc.

Since even professional analysts in the West do not always realize clearly what the intelligence potential of the communist bloc in action may amount to in terms of exercising influence favorable to the bloc, it is desirable at this point to give at least some theoretical examples.

Suppose, for instance, that a particular noncommunist country becomes the target of the bloc's intelligence potential. This would imply that all the intelligence and counterintelligence staff of all the communist countries would review all their intelligence assets and make suggestions about what could be done to bring political influence to bear on the government of the country and on its policy and diplomacy, political parties, individual leaders, press, and so forth. It would imply that all the intelligence staff of the bloc countries under diplomatic or other official cover in the country concerned, which could amount to several hundred highly trained professionals plus several hundred secret agents among the country's nationals, would all be directed to work in different ways toward one objective according to one plan. The agents would be guided not only to obtain information, but also to take certain actions or to exercise influence wherever and whenever the plan required. Their combined capacity to affect governmental, press, and public opinion could well be considerable.

The same would apply if the target was a group of noncommunist countries; or a specific problem, such as the defense program of a noncommunist country; or a particular Western attitude to the communist bloc or one of its members; or world public opinion on a particular policy; or issues such as the Vietnam War, alleged West German revanchisme, or the Middle East situation.

In his speech on January 6, 1961, Khrushchev, after alluding to the fact that "the dictatorship of the working class has emerged beyond the confines of one country and become an international force," said that "in the conditions of today, socialism is in a position to determine, in growing measure, the character, methods and trends of international relations." It was the reorientation of the Central Committee apparatus, the mass organizations, and the diplomatic, intelligence, and security services of the bloc that provided Khrushchev and his allies with the means to change the character and methods of international relations.

Some elements of the new bloc policy—like the introduction

of economic reforms in the industry and agriculture of the Soviet Union and other communist states or the emphasis on peaceful coexistence, disarmament, and the improvement of diplomatic, trade, and other relations with noncommunist countries—all of them reminiscent of the NEP period, were themselves means of misrepresenting the bloc's intentions and influencing the noncommunist world in the first phase of the policy. Even more significant, and again reminiscent of the NEP period, were the striking changes in the style, quantity, and quality of information revealed by the communist world about itself. These changes were reflected in the wider access permitted to foreign visitors to the Soviet Union and most East European countries. They coincided in time with Shelepin's report and the intensive preparation of a program of political disinformation operations. The coincidence in timing helps to explain the changes.

8

Sources of Information

PRECEDING CHAPTERS HAVE DESCRIBED IN DETAIL how the program, strategy, organization, and operational philosophy at the center of international communism developed in the period 1957 to 1960. How did it happen that the Western world almost entirely failed to detect these changes and appreciate their significance? To discover the answer, one must begin by examining the sources of information available to Western analysts.

Western Sources

The main Western sources of information on communist countries are:

- The secret agents of Western intelligence services.
- The interception and decoding of communist communications.
- The monitoring of communist embassies and officials in noncommunist countries.
- Photographic and other observations of industrial installations, missile sites, troop movements, and so forth from Western aircraft and satellites flying over communist territory.
- The monitoring of nuclear and rocket tests by technical devices.
- The personal observations of Western diplomats, journalists, and visitors in communist countries.
- Unofficial contacts in these countries of Western diplomats, journalists, and other visitors.

• Scholars working on communist affairs.

• "Internal emigrants" or well-wishers in the communist states.

• Refugees from communist countries and parties and, in particular, former officials and agents of their intelligence services.

These sources vary in their significance and reliability, in the degree of access they provide, and in the manner in which they need to be interpreted.

Because communist societies are closed societies and because their governments' aims are aggressive, it is vital for the West to have vigorous, healthy, and effective intelligence services capable of obtaining reliable secret information of a strategic nature on the internal affairs and external policies of the communist countries, on their relations with one another, and on their relations with the communist parties outside the bloc. The secret agents of Western intelligence services are potentially the most valuable sources of all, provided that they are operating in good faith and have access to information at the policy-making level. The problem is that Western intelligence services sometimes accept provocateurs as genuine agents, and provocateurs are a favored channel for passing communist disinformation.

The interception and decoding of communications can provide valuable information, provided that the possibility of disinformation is always kept in mind and properly assessed.

Likewise, the monitoring of communist embassies and officials can be valuable, but it has to be remembered that the methods used by Western counterintelligence and security services are well known and in most cases are capable of being converted by the communist bloc into channels for disinformation.

The technical monitoring of nuclear and rocket tests and the various forms of aerial reconnaissance are valuable but cannot be regarded as self-sufficient. Because of their limitations, the information they provide always needs to be evaluated in conjunction with information from other sources. All techniques have their individual limitations. The general limitation which they all share is that, even if they provide accurate information on what is present and what is happening in a particular locality, they cannot answer questions on why it is present or happening, who is responsible, and what their real intentions are. For instance, from these sources

alone, one cannot say whether the existence of troop concentrations
on the Sino-Soviet border is evidence of genuine hostility between
the two countries or evidence of joint intention on the part of
the Soviet and Chinese leaders to give the impression, for strategic
disinformation purposes, that there is hostility between them.

The personal observations of foreign diplomats, journalists, and
other visitors to communist countries are of limited value because
of the controls over their travels and their contacts. The value of
information from unofficial contacts should not be overestimated,
since the probability is that these contacts, however critical they
may be of the regime, are controlled by the security services. Given
the scale of operation of the communist security services, it is impossible for a citizen of a communist country to remain for any length
of time in unauthorized contact with a foreigner. Investigative reporting of the type so popular in the West is impossible in communist countries without at least tacit cooperation from the security
authorities.

Western academics can be extremely valuable as analysts, provided they are given accurate information. Their value as sources
is not always great, since their visits to communist countries do
not necessarily give them access to inside information, and they
are as prone as other visitors to be misled by deliberate communist
disinformation. Their visits can also be hazardous.

"Internal emigrants," or well-wishers, are those citizens of communist countries who, for political or other reasons, approach foreign diplomats or visitors or attempt to enter Western embassies
with offers of secret information. They can be valuable sources,
but the problem is that there are many obstacles in their way.
For example, the Soviet security service used to practice a provocation technique through which any well-wisher who attempted to
establish contact by telephone with the American or British embassies in Moscow would be connected with specially trained officials
of the security service. These would pose as members of the American or British embassy staffs and would arrange to meet the well-
wisher outside the embassy, with predictable consequences for the
well-wisher concerned. Many well-wishers attempted to contact
Western embassies; few succeeded. Even if they did, they were
not always trusted by the embassies because the Soviet security
services deliberately discredited this type of person by sending their

own provocateurs to embassies under the guise of well-wishers.

Past experience indicates that the most valuable information has been provided by refugees and defectors from communist countries and communist parties. The most informative have been those who occupied leading positions, such as Trotskiy, Uralov, and Kravchenko, or those who worked in organizations where policy is implemented, such as the intelligence and security services (Agabekov, Volkov, Deryabin, the Petrovs, Rastvorov, Khokhlov, and Swiatlo), military intelligence (Krivitskiy, Reiss, Guzenko, Akhmedov), the diplomatic service (Barmine, Kaznacheyev), or the armed forces (Tokayev). Important information was revealed by Yugoslav leaders during the Soviet-Yugoslav split from 1948 to 1956. Valuable information was also provided by former leading communists or communist agents, such as Souvarine, Jay Lovestone, Borkenau, Chambers, and Bentley.

The value of the information from such sources depends, of course, on the degree of their access to information, and on their education, experience, honesty, degree of emotionalism, and the completeness of their break with communism. Trotskiy's exposures were of limited value because his break was not with communism but with Stalin. The same could be said of the Yugoslav leaders. Some refugee information is affected by emotionalism. During the cold war period, some of the literature on communism published in the West was distorted for propaganda reasons and can be used only with caution.

Above all, the value of information from defectors and refugees depends on their good faith, since it is common practice for the communist security and intelligence services to send provocateurs abroad under this guise to act as channels for disinformation.

Communist Sources

The communist sources need to be treated as a separate category. They may be divided into official, unofficial, and "secret" communist sources. The official ones are:

• The published records of international conferences of communist governments and communist parties inside and outside the bloc.

• The public activities and decisions of the parties, governments, and ministries of individual communist countries.

• The public activities and speeches of communist leaders and other officials.

• The communist press: books, periodicals, and other publications.

• The official communist contacts of foreign diplomats, journalists, and other visitors.

• The public activities and decisions of communist parties in noncommunist countries.

The unofficial communist sources are:

• Unofficial speeches and off-the-record comments by communist leaders and officials.

• Unofficial contacts in communist countries of foreign diplomats, journalists, and other visitors.

• Wall posters in China and underground publications in other communist countries, such as *samizdat* in the Soviet Union.

• The books of communist scholars.

The "secret" communist sources are the occasional, often retrospective, leakages or disclosures by the communist side, sometimes in documentary form, of information that has earlier been treated as secret. These often relate to polemics between members of the communist bloc and may cover:

• Secret activities, discussions, and decisions of the leading bodies of the bloc.

• Secret activities, discussions, and decisions of the parties, governments, and ministries of individual communist countries.

• The secret activities and speeches of communist leaders and officials.

• Secret party and government documents, particularly party circulars to rank-and-file members.

The Analysis of Information from Communist Sources

The possibilities of obtaining reliable information on the communist world through communist sources should be neither ignored nor overestimated. Obviously, not all the items that appear in the communist press are false or distorted for propaganda or disinformation purposes. Though both are present to a significant degree, the communist press also reflects, to a large extent accurately, the complex life and activity of communist society. The party and the population are kept informed through the press of major party and government decisions and events; they are also mobilized and guided through the press into carrying out those decisions.

For these reasons, study of the communist press is important for the West. But the problem for Western analysts is to distinguish between the factual information and the propaganda and disinformation to be found in the press. Here certain Western tendencies tend to get in the way: the tendency to regard certain communist problems as a reflection of eternal, immutable world problems; a tendency to assume that changes in communist society are spontaneous developments; and a tendency to interpret developments in the communist world on the basis of the experience, notions, and terminology of Western systems.

Undoubtedly there are eternal and universal elements at work in communist politics (Stalin did have something in common with other tyrants who were not communists). Some developments in the communist world are spontaneous (the Hungarian revolt is a case in point) and there are some similarities between the unfolding of events in the communist and noncommunist worlds. It is more important to point out that there is also a definite ideological, political, and operational continuity in the communist movement and its regimes, the specific elements of which should not be overlooked or ignored. There is a more or less permanent set of factors that reflect the essence of communism and make it different from any other social or political system, and there are certain permanent problems with which communists deal with varying degrees of failure and success. These factors and problems are, for example, class ideology, nationalism, intrabloc and interparty relations, internationalism, revisionism, power struggles, succession in the leadership, purges, policy toward the West, party tactics, the nature of crises and failures in the communist world, and the solutions or readjustments that are applied to them. To overlook what is specifically communist in the content and handling of all these problems is to fall into error. For example, attempting to explain the purges of the 1930s in terms of Stalin's psychological makeup would be skating on the surface. No less erroneous would be the analysis in Western terms of the nationalism that undoubtedly exists in the communist world.

Even those Western experts who recognize the specific nature and continuity of communist regimes and have overcome the three tendencies mentioned above often display a fourth tendency, which is to apply stereotypes derived from the Stalin period to subsequent developments in the communist world, thereby failing to take into account the possibility of readjustments in communist regimes and the adoption of a more rational approach to the abiding problems confronting them. Historically speaking, communist ideology and practice have both shown themselves capable of flexibility and successful adaptation to circumstances: Lenin's NEP is a good example. Continuity and change are both present in the communist system; both are reflected in the communist press.

Analysis of the communist press is therefore important to an understanding of the communist world but only if it is done correctly. A knowledge of communist history and an understanding of the permanent factors and problems and the manner in which they have been tackled in different historical periods is essential. So also—and hitherto this has been almost entirely lacking in the West—is an understanding of the role and pattern of communist disinformation in a given period and the effect it has on the validity and reliability of sources.

9

The Vulnerability of Western Assessments

GIVEN THAT COMMUNIST REGIMES PRACTICE DISINFORMA-TION in time of peace on a scale unparalleled in the West, it is essential to determine the pattern of disinformation that is being followed if Western studies and assessments are to avoid serious error. Once the pattern has been established, it provides criteria for distinguishing reliable from unreliable sources and genuine information from disinformation. Determining the pattern is difficult, if not impossible, unless reliable inside information is available.

Here a distinction should be noted between the communist sources and the Western sources. All the communist sources are permanently available as natural channels for communist disinformation. Western sources are in general less available as channels, but can become so to a varying extent depending upon whether their existence is or is not known to the communist side. With communist sources the problem is to detect how they are being used for disinformation. With Western sources the problem is two-fold; to determine whether they have been compromised to the communist side, and if so, whether they are being used for disinformation purposes.

Since Western sources are in general less vulnerable than communist to exploitation for purposes of disinformation, they tend to be regarded as more reliable than the communist sources, which are completely open to exploitation. However, if Western sources are compromised (and particularly if the West does not know, or does not wish to acknowledge, that they have been compromised), they can become unreliable and even dangerous. Conversely, if the pattern of disinformation is known and if an adequate method of analysis is used, even communist sources can reveal reliable and significant information.

The ideal situation for the West is when its intelligence services have reliable sources of information at the policy-making level, when adequate methods of analysis are applied by the West to communist sources, and when the pattern of communist disinformation is known. These three factors react on one another to their mutual advantage. The inside sources provide information bearing on the adequacy of Western analysis; they also help to determine the pattern of disinformation and provide timely warning of any changes in it. The pattern of disinformation, once established, and a proper analysis of communist sources together lead to an accurate assessment of Western secret sources and to the exposure of the tainted ones among them.

The trouble is, however, that the effectiveness of Western intelligence services cannot be taken for granted. Apart from the general obstacles to the acquisition of reliable, high-level inside information on the communist world, there are special risks of reliable sources becoming compromised through their own mistakes or through communist penetration of Western intelligence services. Some Western sources—for example, listening devices—can be detected and exploited by the communist side for disinformation purposes without the Western services concerned being penetrated. But the major factor that has damaged the effectiveness of Western services has been penetration by their communist opponents; this has compromised Western sources and enabled the communist side to use them as channels for disinformation.

If Western intelligence services lose their effectiveness and themselves become channels for communist disinformation, this in turn damages Western analysis of communist sources and results in failure to detect the pattern of communist disinformation and any changes there may be in it. When all three factors—Western ability to obtain secret information, Western ability to interpret communist sources, and Western ability to understand disinformation—are themselves adversely affected by the consequences of penetration and disinformation, then the whole process of Western assessment of communist affairs is vitiated, and the real problems and real changes in the communist world cannot be distinguished from fictitious and deceptive ones. Doubtful information from official, unofficial, or "secret" communist sources confirms or is confirmed by disinformation fed through compromised Western secret sources. Information deliberately leaked by the communist side is accepted as reliable by the West. Genuine information, fortuitously received by the West, may be questioned or rejected. In this way the errors in Western assessments become not only serious, but also irreversible unless and until the pattern of disinformation is correctly established. The critical condition of the assessment process in the West is the more serious because it is unrecognized and undiagnosed.

If Western assessments of the communist world are wrong, then Western miscalculations and mistakes in policy will follow. These miscalculations and mistakes will be exploited by the communist side to their own advantage. When this happens and the Western mistakes are recognized by the public, the politicians, diplomats, and scholars associated with those mistakes are discredited and a basis is laid for the emergence of extremist bodies of opinion. The rise of McCarthyism in the United States after the failure of American postwar policy in Eastern Europe and China is an obvious example.

The Consequences of Different Patterns of Disinformation

The character of Western miscalculations depends to a large degree on the pattern of communist disinformation. During a crisis in the communist system when the facade and strength pattern of disinformation is used, the West is confused about the real situation in communist countries and fails to perceive the weakness of their regimes. A convincing, but spurious, facade of monolithic unity is built around the actual explosive realities of the communist world. Spurious though it is, the facade is liable to be taken at its face value by Western observers and even governments. Their overestimate of the strength and cohesion of the apparent monolith inhibits them from taking proper steps to exploit an actual crisis in the communist world.

The Crisis in the Bloc, 1949–56

Undoubtedly there was some realization in the West of the difficulties in the communist world in the years immediately preceding and following Stalin's death. But facade and strength disinformation successfully concealed the existence of genuine Sino-Soviet differences between 1950 and 1953; it also veiled the acuteness of the revolutionary situation in Eastern Europe. If the depth of the crisis there had been more fully appreciated in the West, a more active and helpful Western response to the events in Poland and Hungary might have been forthcoming; part or all of Eastern Europe might have been liberated altogether.

During the implementation of a long-range policy, a weakness and evolution pattern of disinformation is used. Again, the West is confused about the real strength of communist regimes and, this time, about their policies as well. A convincing picture is built up of the decline of ideology and the emergence of competing national entities in the communist world. Although this image is false and is deliberately projected by the communist regimes, it is liable to be accepted at face value by the West as an accurate reflection of spontaneously occurring political developments. On this basis the West tends to underestimate the strength and cohesion of the communist world and is encouraged to overlook the necessity for proper defensive measures. Furthermore it can be misled into taking offensive steps that unintentionally serve the ends of communist policy and provide opportunities for future exploitation by the communist side, to Western disadvantage.

Of the two patterns of disinformation, the second has potentially the more serious consequences for the West in that, if applied successfully, it can adversely affect Western offensive and defensive measures; the first inhibits Western offensive measures only and serves to harden its defense.

The Second World War

Soviet expansionism was helped by disinformation during the Second World War. Without in any way questioning the necessity of the wartime antifascist alliance between the Soviet Union and the Western allies, it is legitimate to point out that the alliance was successfully exploited by the Soviet Union to further its own political objectives. There is scope for a detailed historical study of the methods and channels used by the Soviet regime to influence and disinform the American and British governments before the Tehran and Yalta conferences about the real nature of the Soviet regime and its intentions. American and British archives should yield additional information on the influence exerted by Soviet agents in the US State Department and British Foreign Office, such as Donald Maclean and Guy Burgess.[1] Meanwhile, a few points may be made to illustrate the use of the themes of the decline of ideology, the rise in nationalist influence, and the disunity and lack of cooperation between communist parties.

During the wartime alliance ideological criticism of the United States and Great Britain virtually disappeared from the Soviet press. Revolutionary ideology, though never wholly abandoned, was soft-pedalled. Old Russian traditions were glorified; former czarist ranks and decorations were restored in the Red Army. A new respect was shown for religion; Stalin held a public audience for Russian church leaders in 1943. The common dangers confronting the Soviet Union and the West and their common interest in survival were emphasized, and described as providing a basis for future cooperation. Western statesmen and diplomats were told that a postwar liberalization of the Soviet regime and its evolution into a national, Western type of nation-state were inevitable; they were even flattered with the idea that these changes would take place under Western influence. Soviet acceptance of the Atlantic Charter in 1941 and signature of the United Nations Pact on January 1, 1942, should be seen as part of the effort to raise Western expectations of favorable developments in the Soviet Union. But the most striking and significant deception designed to mask continuing, active cooperation between communist parties and convince the Western allies that revolutionary objectives had been abandoned was the dissolution of the Comintern in May 1943, six months before the Tehran conference. Allied with this deception were the themes that the Soviet Union and the Red Army were fighting only for the liberation of Eastern Europe from fascism and had no thought of establishing communist regimes in that area.

10

Communist Intelligence Successes, Western Failures, and the Crisis in Western Studies

A T PRESENT, Western efforts to obtain secret political information on the communist world, Western attempts to analyze information from communist sources, and Western ability to distinguish between reliable and unreliable sources—between genuine information and disinformation—all appear to be suffering from at least a temporary loss of effectiveness. This state of affairs is symptomatic of the penetration of Western intelligence services by their communist opponents.

Western intelligence has not always been unsuccessful. During the post-Stalin crisis, the communist intelligence and security services were weak. More people were disposed to help the West; five officials of Soviet intelligence defected in 1954. Although the West has never fully uncovered the extent of communist intelligence penetration of its governments and societies, Western intelligence did nevertheless have some reliable sources with access to policy-making bodies in the communist countries. But as the communist world recovered from its crisis, so its intelligence and security services regained their strength and effectiveness. The effort to penetrate Western governments in general and Western intelligence and security services in particular, which had been continuous from 1917 onward, was revitalized with success. This is not the place for a detailed study of the problem; nevertheless, some examples to illustrate the argument must be given.

From his service in the NATO section of the Information Department of the KGB's First Chief Directorate in 1959–60, the author knows that at that time the Soviet and bloc intelligence services had agents in the foreign ministries of most NATO countries, not to mention those of many of the non-NATO countries. This meant that the Soviet leaders and their partners were nearly as well informed about the foreign policies of Western governments as were those governments themselves.

Symptomatic of the depth and scale of penetration were the cases of the former British Admiralty official, Vassall; the former Swedish military attaché in the Soviet Union and later in the USA, Colonel Wennerström; the former senior official in NATO head-quarters in Paris, Colonel Paques; and the forty concealed micro-phones belatedly discovered in the American Embassy in Moscow in 1964.

There is also striking public evidence of communist penetration of Western intelligence services. The British security and intelligence services, the oldest and most experienced in the West, were gravely damaged by Blunt, Philby, Blake, and others who worked for Soviet intelligence inside them for many years before being discovered.

The exposure of the Felfe ring inside the German intelligence service in 1961 showed that this service had been penetrated by the Soviets since its rebirth in 1951.

The author's detailed information on extensive Soviet penetration of French intelligence over a long period of time was passed to the appropriate French authorities, who were able to neutralize the penetration.

American intelligence suffered from Soviet penetration of allied services with which it was collaborating. In 1957–58 American intelligence lost an important secret agent in the Soviet Union, Lieutenant Colonel Popov, as a result of KGB penetration.[1]

Particularly because the problem of disinformation has not been understood, it is doubtful if adequate account has been taken of the compromise of sources resulting from known instances of communist penetration of Western intelligence.

Factors in Communist Intelligence Successes

Three main factors contribute to the successes of the communist intelligence services against the West. In the first place, they operate on a vastly greater scale. The intelligence potential of totalitarian regimes is always greater than that of democracies because they rely on secret police for their own internal stability. The determination of communist regimes to promote their system in other countries entails an expanded role for their intelligence services abroad. Accordingly, communist regimes take intelligence and security work more seriously and commit more human and financial resources to it than do democracies. In the Soviet Union staff can be trained in these subjects up to the equivalent of university degree level. They are encouraged to enlarge their networks of informers on a massive scale both inside and outside their own particular territories.

Second, communist leaders appreciate the importance of good security work to their survival and the constructive contribution that good intelligence can make to the success of their international strategy. Communist intelligence and security services are therefore free from the difficult if not impossible constraints imposed on the activities of their counterparts in democratic countries. They have an officially recognized and honored place in communist institutions. They have no problems to contend with from the press or public opinion in their own countries. They can afford to be more aggressive, especially in the recruitment of new agents.

The third, and possibly the most important, factor is that from 1958–60 onward the combined intelligence and security resources of the whole communist bloc have been committed by the communist governments to play an influential part in the implementation of the new long-range bloc policy by assuming an activist political role, which has entailed providing Western intelligence services with carefully selected "secret" information from inside the communist world.

It is an additional indication of the loss of effectiveness of Western intelligence that this change in the role of the communist intelligence services has virtually escaped attention in the West, just as did the significance of the two conferences of leading KGB officials in the Soviet Union in 1954 and 1959. There has been no sign, up to the present, of any increased awareness of the new dimension of the problem posed by the involvement of the communist intelligence services in strategic disinformation. This seems to indicate that whatever secret Western sources there may be have not reported on it.

Obsolete Western Methods of Analyzing Communist Sources

Up to now Western analysts have normally used the content method of analysis of communist sources, principally the communist press and periodicals. Since the rules were formulated by the former German communist, Borkenau, it is often known as Borkenau's method. Without questioning the intelligence or integrity of Western analysts, one must question their continuing and almost exclusive reliance on his method after the new long-range bloc policy and the systematic use of disinformation had been adopted.

The basic rules of Borkenau's method can be summed up as follows:

• Avoid being taken in by the facade of communist propaganda and strip away the empty verbiage of communist statements in order to determine the real issues and real conflicts in communist societies.

• Interpret these issues and forecast possible developments in the communist world before they become public knowledge.

• Seek clues for the interpretation of developments in the communist world in the national and local communist press in announcements of appointments or dismissals of officials and in obituary notices.

• Make detailed comparisons of the speeches of leading communists in the same country and in different countries in a search for significant differences, especially in emphasis on and approach to doctrinal problems.

• Make similar detailed comparisons between communist newspapers, other publications, and broadcasts in the same country and in different countries, with the same purpose in mind.

• Interpret current developments in the light of knowledge of old party controversies.

• Pay particular attention to struggles for personal power; trace the background and careers of party bosses and study the grouping of their followers.

This method was valid and effective for the period of Stalin's dictatorship and for the power struggle that followed his death. The elimination of the Zhdanov group by Stalin in 1948–49, the existence of Sino-Soviet differences in the Stalin period, and Khrushchev's "victory" over the majority of the Presidium in June 1957 were all susceptible to more or less accurate interpretation and assessment by these means.[2] Factionalism, policy disputes, political maneuvers, and the struggle for power were all real problems at that time, and the analysis of them on Borkenau's lines justified itself and provided a key to the understanding of the realities of the communist world and its policy.

During the initial post-Stalin period, from 1953 to 1957, the most spontaneous and uncontrolled period in communist history, there were some new developments. Genuine nationalism and revisionism took on significant proportions. Different interest groups emerged (the military, the party, and the technical administration), together with groups of Stalinists and moderates, liberals, and conservatives. These new factors were taken into account by Western analysts, who modified their technique accordingly.

However, the spontaneous period ended with the reestablishment of the authority of the communist parties in the bloc. Readjustments in the communist world reversed the original significance and meaning of the various factors studied by Western analysts. Since the latter failed to apprehend these readjustments, their method of analysis of communist sources was invalidated.

The adoption of the long-range policy firmly established the principle of collective leadership, put an end to real power struggles, provided a solution for the problem of succession in the leadership, and established a new basis for relations between the different members of the communist bloc. Whereas the methods of assessing nationalism and revisionism were relevant to the crisis period of 1953 to 1956, in which there was a loss of Soviet control over the satellites and spontaneous revolts occurred, notably in Poland and Hungary, they ceased to be relevant once the leaders of the communist parties and governments had been given tactical independence and all of them, including the Yugoslavs, had committed themselves to the new long-range bloc policy and international communist strategy. The forces of nationalism and revisionism ceased to determine communist policy anywhere; communist policy determined the use that could be made of them. It was because this fundamental change was successfully concealed from Western observers that subsequent Western analysis of Soviet-Albanian, Soviet-Yugoslav, Soviet-Romanian, Soviet-Czechoslovak, Soviet-Chinese, and Soviet-Polish relations, based on the old, obsolete methodology, became dangerously misleading.

The reestablishment of the authority of the parties put an end to the influence of the interest groups. This can be illustrated with the case of the military group. Under Stalin the military were a potentially important group because they were persecuted by him. They knew all about Stalin's methods from personal experience. For that reason an antiparty move by the military was always a possibility. During the power struggle from 1953 to 1957, party control over the Soviet military was weak, and the military played a significant role first in unseating undesirable leaders like Beriya and later, through Zhukov, in Khrushchev's "victory" over the opposition. After Zhukov's removal the military came under sounder party control and were freed from the threat of persecution. Similarly, party control over the military in China was reaffirmed from 1958 onward. The military cannot and do not make policy in either country. The "discovery" by Western analysts of a military pressure group in the Soviet Union in 1960 and the emphasis on the role of the former Chinese minister of defense, Lin Piao, were both mistaken. The military leaders, like the so-called technocrats, are all party members under the control of the party leadership. In their separate fields they are all active participants in the implementation of the long-range policy.

Once collective leadership had been established in the Soviet Union and reaffirmed in the Chinese party in 1959–60, factionalism lost its meaning. There could no longer be actual groups of Stalinists, neo-Stalinists, Khrushchevites, or Maoists, but such groups could be invented if required by policy considerations. The personality factor in the leadership of communist parties took on a new significance. A leader's personal style and idiosyncracies no longer determined communist policy; on the contrary, the long-range bloc policy began to determine the actions of the leaders and to exploit their differences in personality and style for its own purposes. Stalin used the cult of personality to establish his own personal dictatorship; Mao used it, in part, to conceal the reality of collective leadership. Since the adoption of the common long-range policy also solved the problem of succession, power struggles lost their former significance and became part of the calculated and controlled display of difference and disunity within the bloc. The existence of genuine groups of Stalinists and liberals, hard-liners, and moderates in the Soviet Union is as illusory as the existence of pro-Soviet and anti-

Soviet groups, or groups of conservatives and pragmatists in the Chinese leadership. It is true that there have been representatives of the older and younger generations in both leaderships, but attempts to find differences in the ideology or policy of the different generations cannot be substantiated by hard evidence. Both generations in both parties were, and are, equally committed to the long-range policy of 1958–60.

When there was a real power struggle in the Soviet Union, it made sense to scan the communist press for clues, hints, and significant omissions, to read veiled criticism between the lines or to seek divergences of emphasis on a given subject in different papers or by different leaders in one party or in different parties. It made sense particularly in the years before and after Stalin's death. After 1960, however, continued analysis on these lines was not only useless but positively dangerous, since the bloc's strategists knew all about the Borkenau technique and its clichés and used their knowledge in planning their strategic disinformation. They knew all the pointers on which exponents of the Borkenau method had come to rely for their insight into the workings of the communist system; they knew the fascination exercised by actual and potential splits in the communist world; they knew when and how to drop hints in the media or in private conversation suggesting apparent shifts in the balance between apparent rival groups in the leadership; they knew where and how to disclose the texts of secret speeches and discussions reflecting apparent discord between parties; and, finally, they learned how to conduct controlled public polemics between party leaders realistically enough to convince the outside world of the reality of Soviet-Albanian and Sino-Soviet hostility while at the same time preserving and strengthening unity of action within the bloc in accordance with the mutually agreed long-range policy and strategy.

The Western Failure to Detect Disinformation and Its Current Pattern

Conventional methodology tends to regard a secret source as reliable if the information it provides is broadly compatible with other information openly available; conversely, a source reporting information that conflicts with the generally accepted view of the situation in the communist world may be discounted or rejected. In the absence of disinformation, this methodology would be valid. But the Shelepin report of May 1959 marked the reintroduction of a systematic program of disinformation. It is true that in the late 1960s an increase in communist disinformation activity, mainly of a tactical nature involving the fabrication and leakage by the communist side of alleged Western documents, attracted Western attention and was reported by the CIA to the Congress of the United States. But the fact is that when Shelepin delivered his report to the KGB conference in 1959, the West apparently had no sources capable of reporting on it; its contents and implications remained unknown to, and unexplored by, any Western intelligence service until the author gave his account of them. Bearing in mind the public references to the long-range political role of the KGB at the Twenty-first CPSU Congress, the good faith of any KGB source or defector who has described the KGB conference of 1959 and Shelepin's report to it as routine is open to serious doubt.

Not only did the West lack specific information on the Shelepin report; communist use of disinformation in general has been consistently underrated in the West, and the purpose of the weakness and evolution pattern is virtually unknown.[3] If the West had been aware of the Shelepin report and had appreciated its implications, Western methodology should, and probably would, have been turned upside down; it would have been realized that a reliable source would give information conflicting with the generally accepted picture. The communist concept of total disinformation entails the use of all available channels to convey disinformation; that is to say, all the communist sources and all the Western sources except, obviously, any that are unknown to the communist side and those that, for some practical reason, are unsuitable. If the communist and Western sources reflect the same image of the communist world, it is a good indication that the Western as well as the communist sources are being used successfully for disinformation purposes.

Against the background of the superior communist security and intelligence effort and its known successes in penetrating Western intelligence services, the odds are heavily against the survival of reliable, uncompromised Western secret sources at the strategic political level in the communist world. If, despite the odds, such a source were to have survived, it should have produced information at variance with that from all other sources. At a time when the facade and strength pattern of disinformation was in use, a reliable source at the right level should have drawn attention to the existence of a critical situation in the communist world that the communist side was anxious to conceal. Conversely, after the weakness and evolution pattern had been reintroduced in 1958–60, a reliable secret source should have drawn attention, in contrast with other sources, to the underlying strength and coordination of the communist world. Because the West failed to find out about or understand communist disinformation after 1958, it failed to change its methodology; because it failed to change its methodology, it has continued to accept as genuine information from all sources, both communist and Western, reflecting disunity and disarray in the communist world. The fact that all the sources, Western and communist alike, continue to tell much the same story on this subject is a good indication that the disinformation effort has been both comprehensive and effective. The most dangerous consequence of Western failure to detect and understand communist disinformation and its patterns is that, in the absence of any correcting influence from reliable Western secret sources, the version of events transmitted through communist sources has increasingly come to be accepted as the truth. Conventional Western views on the Sino-Soviet "split," the "independence" of Romania and Yugoslavia, the "Prague spring," Eurocommunist dissidence, and other subjects discussed in Part 2 were devised for the West and communicated to it by the communist strategists.

11

Western Errors

THE FAILURE OF WESTERN INTELLIGENCE SERVICES to adapt their methodology to take into account the changes in communist policy and strategy in the period 1957–60 and the reintroduction of disinformation on the weakness and evolution pattern meant that those services lost their ability to produce or contribute to accurate and balanced assessments of the situation in the communist world; they unwittingly became vehicles for the further dissemination of disinformation deliberately fed to them by their communist opposite numbers. Since they failed to convey adequate warnings either about the mobilization of the bloc's intelligence potential for political action or about the techniques and patterns of disinformation, it is not surprising that Western diplomats, academics, and journalists should also have overlooked the calculated feeding of disinformation through the communications media and should increasingly have accepted at face value the "disclosures" made to them by communist leaders and officials in unofficial, off-the-record conversations.

Acceptance of the new brand of disinformation from 1958 onward was by no means total and immediate. Until 1961 at least, there were, broadly speaking, two schools of thought among serious Western students of communist affairs. There were those who, on the basis of their long experience and acquaintanceship with communist duplicity and deceit and their intuitive mistrust of evidence and "leakages" emanating from communist sources, adopted a sceptical attitude toward the early manifestations of divergences and splits in the communist world and warned against the uncritical acceptance of these manifestations at their face value. Scepticism about the authenticity of Sino-Soviet differences was expressed in different ways and on different grounds by, among others, W. A. Douglas Jackson, J. Burnham, J. Lovestone, Natalie Grant, Suzanne Labin, and Tibor Mende. For example, Jackson wrote: "In the latter part of 1959 and throughout 1960, as a result of different views expressed in statements issued in Peking and Moscow, the notion of a possible falling out between the two powers [gained] considerable momentum in some Western capitals. The desire to see a conflict develop between the CPR and the USSR is a legitimate one, but it may tend to blind the West to fundamental realities if undue weight is given to seemingly apparent signs of rift, when in fact nothing of a fundamental nature may exist."[1]

James Burnham pointed out in the *National Review* that the Sino-Soviet conflict seemed to be a subject of conversation much favored by communist hosts for Western statesmen and journalists during their visits to Moscow and Peking; he wondered whether statements about the Sino-Soviet dispute were a "deliberate deception by the communists or wishful thinking by non-communists, or a fusion of both."[2]

Suzanne Labin repeated in her book the opinion of a refugee from Communist China, Dr. Tang, according to whom Sino-Soviet differences stemmed from a division of labor between the USSR and China.[3]

Tibor Mende, who visited China at that time, warned against exaggerating the importance of existing differences and observed that "when China and the Soviet Union meet it is not merely to bargain, but also to concert their actions."[4]

Natalie Grant, well-versed in the history of the Trust, went further, suggesting that "a careful study of the material forming the alleged grounds for concluding that there is a serious Sino-Soviet conflict proves the absence of any objective foundation for such a belief . . . all statements regarding the existence of a serious disagreement between Moscow and Peking on foreign policy, war, peace, revolution, or attitude toward imperialism are an invention. All are the fruit of fertile imagination and unbased speculation." She also said that much of the "misinformation" on Sino-Soviet relations was communist-inspired and "reminiscent of that almost forgotten era dominated by the Institute of Pacific Relations."[5]

The opposite school of thought applied Borkenau's methods to the new situation and devoted great attention to the study of what came to be known as "symbolic," or "esoteric," evidence, which began to appear in the communist press from 1958 onward, of divergences and doctrinal disputes between different members of the communist bloc.[6] The esoteric evidence of Sino-Soviet differences was supported by various unofficial statements by Soviet and Chinese leaders, such as Khrushchev's critical remarks about the Chinese communes to the late Senator Hubert Humphrey on December 1, 1958, or Chou En-lai's "frank admissions" to Edgar Snow in the autumn of 1960.[7] Further support came from off-the-record comments by communist officials in Eastern Europe.[8]

Throughout 1960 and much of 1961, opinions fluctuated between the sceptics and the believers in the esoteric evidence. Then, at the Twenty-second CPSU Congress held in October 1961, Khrushchev delivered a public attack on the Albanian Communist party leadership and Chou En-lai, leader of the Chinese delegation, withdrew from the congress. The Soviet-Albanian dialogue had ceased to be esoteric and had become public. As the public polemics between the Soviet and the Albanian and Chinese leaders developed, retrospective accounts began to appear in the West of disputes that had allegedly occurred behind closed doors at the congress of the Romanian Communist party held in Bucharest in June 1960 and the congress of eighty-one communist parties held in Moscow in November 1960. The most notable of these disclosures were those made in Edward Crankshaw's articles in the London *Observer* for February 12 and 19, 1961, and May 6 and 20, 1962. They were followed by the publication of official documents and statements in the press of the Italian, French, Belgian, Polish, and Albanian Communist parties. This material confirmed and added to the content of the Crankshaw articles.[9]

By the end of 1962 the combination of esoteric evidence, public polemics between communist leaders, and the largely retrospective evidence of factionalism at international communist gatherings proved irresistible; acceptance of the existence of genuine splits in the communist world became almost universal. The esoteric and the unofficial evidence from communist sources had proved themselves reliable and accurate. The continuing validity of the basic premises of the old methodology had been reconfirmed and its practitioners vindicated. The ground was cut from under the sceptics' feet. Some changed their minds. Those who retained their doubts lacked solid evidence with which to back them and had no option but to keep silent. Study of the splits built up its own momentum, creating on the way a variety of personal commitments to and vested interests in the validity of an analysis that demonstrated the accelerating disintegration of the communist monolith. New students entering the field had no incentive and no basis for challenging the accepted orthodoxy or for reexamining the basic premises of the methodology or the validity of the evidence on which they were founded.

The development of splits in the communist world appeals to Western consciousness in many ways. It feeds the craving for sensationalism; it raises hopes of commercial profit; it stirs memories of past heresies and splits in the communist movement; it shows that factionalism is an element in communist as in Western politics; it supports the comforting illusion that, left to itself, the communist world will disintegrate and that the communist threat to the rest of the world will vanish; and it confirms the opinions of those who, on intellectual grounds, reject the pretensions of communist dogma to provide a unique, universal, and infallible guide to the understanding of history and the conduct of policy. Not surprisingly, therefore, evidence in official communist sources that conflicts with the image of disunity and disarray in the communist world and that points, or can be interpreted as pointing, to continuing cooperation between the Soviet Union, China, Romania, and Yugoslavia and continuing coordination in the implementation of the long-range bloc policy has been discounted or ignored. The focus of attention is almost invariably on the evidence of discord. So exciting has this evidence been and so lacking has been Western understanding of the motives and techniques of communist disinformation that less and less attention has been paid to the communist origin of the evidence. Virtually all of it has in fact been provided to the West by communist governments and parties through their press and intelligence services. Failing to take this into account, Western observers have fallen deeper and deeper into the trap that was set for them.

The present situation is reminiscent of the NEP period with one important difference: In the 1920s Western mistakes related only to Soviet Russia; now the mistakes relate to the whole communist world. Where the West should see unity and strategic coordination in the communist world, it sees only diversity and disintegration; where it should see the revival of ideology, the stabilization of communist regimes, and the reinforcement of party control, it sees the death of ideology and evolution toward or convergence with the democratic system; where it should see new communist maneuvers, it sees moderation in communist policy. Communist willingness to sign agreements with the West for tactical reasons on a deceptive basis is misinterpreted as the reassertion of great-power national interests over the pursuit of long-range ideological goals.

Two further tendencies have helped to compound the series of Western errors: the tendency to apply clichés and stereotypes derived from the study of conventional national regimes to the study of communist countries, overlooking or underestimating the ideological factor in their internal systems and their relations with one another; and the tendency toward wishful thinking.

Both tendencies favor the uncritical acceptance by the West of what communist sources, official and unofficial, say in particular about the Sino-Soviet dispute. Much of the Western literature on the subject lumps together historical evidence on rivalry between the two countries when they were governed by czars and emperors with the controversies between them in the 1920s through the 1960s—all this in an effort to substantiate the authenticity of the current dispute without any serious attempt to study the different factors in operation in different periods. The focus of Western attention is always on the split and not on the evidence from the same communist sources, scanty though it is, of continuing Sino-Soviet collaboration. Western analysts, inside and outside government, seem to be more concerned with speculation on future relations between the communist and noncommunist worlds than with critical examination of the evidence on which their interpretation of events is based.

Nationalism was an important force in communist parties during Stalin's last years and the crisis after his death. Various parties were affected by it, particularly those in Yugoslavia, Poland, Hungary, and Georgia. It is important to realize, however, that nationalist dissent in the parties at that time was a reaction to Stalin's departures from Leninist principles of internationalism. Once Stalin's practices had been condemned and the necessary readjustments had been made from 1956–57 onward in the conduct of communist affairs, particularly with regard to relations between the CPSU and other communist parties, the basis for nationalist dissent in those other parties progressively disappeared. From then on, nationalist feelings in the respective populations were a factor that the communist regimes could deal with by an agreed diversity of tactics and by the calculated projection of a false image of the national independence of communist parties. Whatever the appearances, since 1957–60 the regimes in China, Romania, Yugoslavia, and Dubcek's Czechoslovakia have not been motivated by different brands of national communism; their actions have been consistently dictated by Leninist ideology and tactics directed toward the pursuit of the long-range interests and goals of the communist bloc as a whole, to which the national interests of the peoples of the communist world are subordinated.

The fundamental Western error throughout has been to overlook the adoption of the long-range bloc policy and the role and pattern of communist disinformation. Either disinformation is not taken into account at all or it is assumed that a facade and strength pattern is being followed. In reality the weakness and evolution pattern has applied since 1958–60. Disinformation on this pattern has laid the basis for erroneous Western assessments of the communist world, which in turn have engendered mistakes in Western responses and policies. As a result the communist world has been allowed systematically to implement its long-range policy over a period of more than twenty years.

12

The New Methodology

HERE ARE TWO WAYS of analyzing and interpreting each of the major developments since 1958 in world communism described in Part 2. According to the conventional view, based on the old, obsolete methodology, each of these developments is a manifestation of the spontaneous growth of fissile tendencies in international communism. The new methodology leads to the radically different conclusion that each of them forms part of an interlocking series of strategic disinformation operations designed to implement long-range bloc policy and its strategies. The essence of the new methodology, which distinguishes it from the old, is that it takes into account the new policy and the role of disinformation.

Conventional methodology frequently attempts to analyze and interpret events in the communist world in isolation and on a year-to-year basis; communist initiatives are seen as spontaneously occurring attempts to achieve short-term objectives. But because the years 1957–60 saw a readjustment in intrabloc relations and the formulation and adoption of a new long-range policy for the bloc as a whole, a proper understanding of what occurred in those years provides the key to understanding what has happened since. The first, and basic, principle of the new methodology is that the starting point for the analysis of all subsequent events should be the period 1957–60.

Factors Underlying the New Methodology

From the account of those years already given, based largely on inside information, eight new factors can be isolated. Only if all these factors and the interaction between them are understood and taken into account together can analysis of the developments of the past twenty years yield correct results. These factors are:

• The readjustments in relations between members of the communist bloc, including Yugoslavia, from 1957 onward and the adoption of a common long-range policy.
• The settlement of the question of Stalinism.
• The establishment of collective leadership, the ending of power struggles, and the solution of the succession problem.
• The phases and long-range objectives of the policy.
• The historical experience on which the policy was based.
• The preparations made to use the party apparatus, the mass organizations, and the diplomatic, intelligence, and security services of the whole bloc for purposes of political influence and strategic disinformation.
• The adoption of a weakness and evolution pattern of disinformation.
• The new appreciation by communist strategists of the use that could be made of polemics between different members of the communist bloc.

From these new factors new analytical principles can be derived. Each factor will be considered in turn.

Before the new policy began to be formulated, and as one of the essential preconditions for its formulation, a new relationship between the regimes of the communist bloc was established in 1957. Soviet domination over the East European satellites and Stalinist attempts to interfere in Chinese and Yugoslav communist affairs were abandoned in favor of the Leninist concepts of equality and proletarian internationalism. Domination gave way to genuine partnership and mutual cooperation and coordination in pursuit of the common long-range interests and objectives of the whole of the communist bloc and movement; account was taken of the diversity of the specific national conditions within which each communist regime and party was operating.

Obsolete, conventional methodology failed to spot the significance of this change; it continued to see the Soviet party as striving, often unsuccessfully and in competition with the Chinese, to exert its influence over the other communist parties so as to ensure their conformity with the Soviet pattern. Once it is realized that, by mutual agreement between the eighty-one parties that signed the Manifesto of November 1960, diversity within the communist movement was sanctioned, it is easy to see that arguments and disputes between communists over the orthodoxy of different tactics are artificial, contrived, and calculated to serve particular strategic or tactical ends. The new methodology starts from the premise that the eighty-one parties all committed themselves to the new long-range policy and agreed to contribute toward its objectives according to the nature and scale of their resources. Furthermore, since diversity was licensed, there could be a division of labor between parties and any one of them could be allotted a special strategic role in accordance with its national specifics and Lenin's suggestion, in an earlier historical context, that "we need a great orchestra; we have to work out from experience how to allocate the parts, to give a sentimental violin to one, a terrible double-bass to another, the conductor's baton to a third."[1] The decisions of 1957–60 gave the Soviet, Chinese, Albanian, Yugoslav, Romanian, Czechoslovak, Vietnamese, and other parties their different instruments and parts to play in a symphonic score. The old methodology hears only the discordant sounds. The new methodology strives to appreciate the symphony as a whole.

The new interpretation of the evidence available from official communist sources leads to the identification of six interlocking communist strategies and illustrates the different strategic roles allotted to different communist parties within the overall design.

The congress of bloc communist parties in 1957 agreed on a common, balanced assessment of Stalin's mistakes and crimes and on the measures needed to correct them. The basis for differences between communists on the question of Stalinism and de-Stalinization was removed; the issues were settled. The old methodology took little or no account of this and continued to see them as matters in contention between different Soviet leaders and between the Soviets and the Chinese and Albanians. The new methodology sees Stalinism from 1958 onward as a dead issue that was deliberately and artificially revived and used for the projection of a false image of warring factions among the leaders of the communist bloc. An understanding of the constituent elements of de-Stalinization and the way they were exploited provides a key to the understanding of communist tactics and technique in the rest of the program of related disinformation operations dealing with, for example, the alleged conflicts between Yugoslav and Soviet "revisionism" and Chinese and Albanian "Stalinism," or the "independence" of Romania.

From 1958 onward the concept of collective leadership widened progressively to cover far more than agreement on policy between the individual members of the Presidium or Politburo. It began to embrace all those who were in a position to contribute toward the formulation of the policy and the development and application of ways and means of achieving its ends, including not only the leaders of all the bloc and some of the more important nonbloc parties, but also senior officials in the Central Committee apparatuses, the diplomatic and intelligence services, and the academies of sciences.

The settlement of the issue of Stalinism, together with the establishment of collective leadership in this sense and the downward diffusion of power and influence that it entailed, effectively removed the grounds for genuine factionalism, power struggles, and succession problems in the leadership of the bloc communist parties. Thenceforward these phenomena were available to be used as the subjects of disinformation operations in support of long-range policy, and it is in this light that the new methodology regards them. Kremlinologists and China-watchers were caught out when they continued to try to rationalize the ups and downs of Soviet and Chinese leaders by using the outdated methodology, which took no account of disinformation. According to the new methodology, promotions and demotions, purges and rehabilitations, even deaths and obituary notices of prominent communist figures—formerly significant pointers for the Borkenau method of analysis—should be examined for their relevance to communist attempts to misrepresent shifts in policy as dictated by personal rather than strategic or tactical considerations.

Conventional methodology tries to analyze developments in the situation and policies of the communist world either in terms of short-term objectives or in terms of the rival, long-range great-power national interests of the Soviet Union and China. It seldom appreciates the marked influence, especially since 1958–60, of dialectical thinking on communist policies, which frequently entail their own opposites: communist détente diplomacy, for example, implying the calculated raising of international tension over specific issues and its subsequent relaxation when specific communist objectives have been achieved; the disgrace of communist leaders, implying their later rehabilitation; the harassment or forced exile of dissidents, implying their eventual pardon or return to their homeland.

The new methodology examines current developments in relation to the objectives of the long-range policy. It sees that policy as having three phases, like its predecessor, the NEP. The first phase is the creation of favorable conditions for the implementation of the policy; the second is the exploitation of Western misunderstanding of the policy to gain specific advantages. These two phases, like the phases of an alternating current electric supply, are continuous, overlapping and interacting. The beginning of the third, and final, offensive phase is marked by a major shift in communist tactics in preparation for a comprehensive assault on the West in which the communist world, taking advantage of the West's long-term strategic errors, moves forward toward its ultimate objective of the global triumph of international communism.

In the first phase of the NEP, economic reform was used both to revive the economy and to foster the illusion that Soviet Russia had lost its revolutionary impetus. Favorable conditions were thus created for the second phase, that of stabilizing the regime and winning diplomatic recognition and economic concessions from the Western powers. The third phase began with the reversal of the economic reforms in 1929 and the launching of ideological offensives internally through the nationalization of industry and the collectivization of agriculture and externally through Comintern subversion. The success of both internal and external offensives was prejudiced by the distortions of the Stalinist regime. The corresponding first two phases of the current long-range policy have already lasted over twenty years. The final phase may be expected to begin in the early 1980s.

The intermediate objectives of the policy may be summarized as follows:

• The political stabilization and strengthening of the individual communist regimes as an essential precondition for the strengthening of the bloc as a whole.

• The correction of the economic deficiencies of the bloc through

international trade and the acquisition of credits and technology from
the industrially advanced noncommunist countries.

• The creation of the substructure for an eventual world federation
of communist states.

• The isolation of the United States from its allies and the promotion
of united action with socialists in Western Europe and Japan, with a
view to securing the dissolution of NATO and the United States–Japan
security pact and an alignment between the Soviet Union and a neutral,
preferably socialist, Western Europe and Japan against the United States.[2]

• United action with nationalist leaders in Third World countries to
eliminate Western influence from those countries as a preliminary to
their absorption into the communist bloc.

• The procurement of a decisive shift in the balance of political and
military power in favor of the communist world.

• The ideological disarmament of the West in order to create favorable
conditions for the final offensive phase of the policy and the ultimate
convergence of East and West on communist terms.

The new methodology aims to see how developments in the
communist world may relate and contribute to the achievement
of these objectives in each phase of the policy. The decisions of
November 1960 authorized the use of all forms of tactics—right
and left, legal and revolutionary, conventional and ideological—in
pursuit of communist aims. Conformity with the Soviet pattern
having ceased to be a criterion of orthodoxy, the most potent cause
of actual and potential splits in the communist world had vanished.
The new methodology therefore examines the so-called splits as a
new form of tactic and tries to see how they serve the aims of
policy. Once it is realized that licensed anti-Sovietism can in fact
yield dividends for overall communist strategy, it is easy to see
that the anti-Sovietism of leading dissidents inside the Soviet Union
and Eurocommunists outside it, like the anti-Sovietism of the Chinese, Albanian, Yugoslav, and Romanian leaders, is artificially contrived to serve the ends of long-range policy.

The old methodology takes little or no account of the history
of the NEP and other periods in which disinformation was important. It cannot therefore appreciate or illuminate the implementation of the long-range policy that was based largely on a reexamination of that history. The new methodology applies the lessons of

the NEP. The elements in it most relevant to the 1960s, and therefore most useful to the new methodology for purposes of comparison, were:

• The stabilization of the Soviet regime by the creation of spurious, controlled opposition movements and the effective use of those movements to neutralize genuine internal and external opposition.
• The creation of favorable conditions for an activist Soviet foreign policy aimed at securing diplomatic recognition by, and increased trade with, the Western powers.
• The experience of the Treaty of Rapallo, of entering into a secret political and military alliance with a capitalist state for acquiring military technology.
• The successful projection of a false image of the Far Eastern Republic (DVR) as an independent regime.
• Lenin's tactical advice to communist parties on overcoming their isolation, establishing united fronts with socialists, and increasing their influence in parliaments and trade unions.

The genuine Tito-Stalin split in 1948 provided the communist strategists ten years later with a model on which to base their planning of spurious splits in the future. The history of Soviet-Yugoslav relations from 1948 to 1955 therefore provides the new methodology with a set of criteria for judging the authenticity of subsequent splits.

The decision to use the intelligence potential of the bloc for strategic disinformation purposes, embodied in the Shelepin report in 1959 and related documents, destroys the notion, implicit in much of conventional methodology, that the communist intelligence services are engaged solely in espionage and security work. The new methodology takes into account the Shelepin report and the important role allocated to Soviet officials, trade unionists, scientists, priests, academics, artists, and other intellectuals in the implementation of policy through the exercise of political influence. The new methodology tries to see how their activities and public statements may serve the interests of policy.

To create favorable conditions for the implementation of that policy, the bloc's strategists adopted the weakness and evolution pattern of disinformation used successfully in the NEP period in the Soviet Union and extended since 1958–60 to cover the whole communist bloc. The new methodology therefore dictates that all information reaching the West on the communist world and the international communist movement, including Eurocommunism, should be assessed in relation to that pattern.

A significant contribution to the formulation of the long-range policy and disinformation technique about splits was made by the Yugoslav leader Edvard Kardelj, whose book *Socialism and War* was published shortly before the Eighty-one–Party Congress in November 1960. In it Kardelj wrote that differences of opinion between communists "are not only not harmful but are the law of progress."[3] According to Kardelj the domestic and foreign policies of the Yugoslav communist party could not be independent of the interests of socialism but could be independent of the "subjectively concocted notions"[4] of other parties, such as the CPC. One should not be content with "interpreting this or that phenomenon in the course of development by the simple repetition of stereotyped dogmatic phrases."[5] "When making an objective analysis, one should try to separate what is subjective from what is objective, that is, not allow slogans or political declarations to conceal insight into the real substance of things."[6] Tito made much the same Leninist point when he said in 1958 that "internationalism is practice— not words and propaganda."[7]

For obvious reasons Kardelj and Tito could not openly announce that spurious polemics between communist parties were thenceforward to be used as part of the technique of communist disinformation. Nevertheless, the distinction clearly drawn between the subjective nature of polemics and the objective nature of common interests and socialist solidarity expressed in unity of actions provided a theoretical basis on which the genuine polemics between Tito and Stalin could be transmuted, when required by the interests of long-range policy, into spurious polemics between communist leaders without endangering the fundamental ideological and practical unity of the communist world.

An up-to-date restatement of Kardelj's point has been made by Yuriy Krasin: "Complete unanimity can hardly be a precondition of joint action. . . . What is needed is not static, monolithic unity, but a dynamic system of views and positions marked by differences on particular issues but developing on the basis of the fundamental principles of Marxism-Leninism common to all."[8]

From such statements and their implications, five related principles can be derived. The first is not to assume that where there are polemics between communists there are necessarily divisions. The second is to assess whether or not there are any solid and consistent grounds for the existence of disputes. The third is to seek evidence of unity of actions behind the disunity of words, to look for secretly coordinated joint actions by apparent enemies or rivals. The fourth is to seek correlations in timing between outbursts of polemics and major communist initiatives or negotiations with Western powers (SALT, for instance) or meetings with Western leaders. The fifth is to assume that polemics form part of a disinformation operation and examine them to see if, regarded in that light, they could contribute toward the achievement of communist objectives. To take some obvious examples, Khrushchev's charges of Chinese warmongering and Chinese countercharges of Soviet revisionism and pacificism in the 1960s should be examined to see if they helped to build up Khrushchev's image in the West as a moderate with whom it was possible to negotiate concrete deals. Yugoslavia's continued exclusion from the communist bloc, despite Tito's secret participation in the formulation and execution of the new long-range policy, should be considered in relation to the buildup of Yugoslavia's credibility as a leader of the nonaligned movement in the Third World. Soviet attacks on conservative Western leaders in the last few years should be viewed in conjunction with Chinese efforts to cultivate closer relations with those same leaders. The escalation of Sino-Soviet hostilities in 1969–70 should be considered as intended to facilitate both the SALT talks between the Soviet Union and the United States and Chinese rapprochement with the advanced industrial nations. In short, the study of polemics, if they are read as disinformation, may throw light not on the existence of splits, but on the long-range policy and strategic interests that apparent splits are intended to promote.

The New Methodology and Western Sources

The existence of a program of disinformation operations has implications for every type of source of information on the communist world. Continued failure to take disinformation into account will lead to the continuing proliferation of errors in Western assessments of, and policy toward, the communist world. Given the communist concept of total disinformation, any Western reassessment of the situation, if it is to have meaning, should cover information from all sources, open and secret, human and technical. The assumption that if secret and open sources in general support one another, the reliability of both is confirmed should be dropped; it should be realized that the two streams of information, open and secret, may well have a common point of origin in the Central Committees and disinformation departments of the bloc parties and intelligence services. If information from Western secret sources is in line with information from open sources, including official communist sources, that alone calls the reliability of the Western secret sources into question. Those Western secret sources whose information since 1958–60 conforms with the weakness and evolution pattern need particularly careful scrutiny to see whether they have become known to the communist side through compromise or other means.

If conformity with the normal pattern of information coming from the communist world is an indication of the unreliability of sources, the converse principle is that greater weight should be given to evidence that conflicts with that pattern even if it comes only from a single source. For example, the personal observations of a Western visitor to a Chinese commune in 1961, who reported that commune dwellers were no worse off in material terms than they were before and that the Chinese people were inevitably becoming more closely identified with the communist regime, should not have been discounted on the grounds that the observations conflicted with the generally accepted opinion of the time that the situation in the communes was disastrous.[9]

Total disinformation, to be effective, necessitates the release by the communist side of a volume of accurate information about itself, including genuine secrets, in order to give credibility and weight to the disinformation it is seeking to convey. In the Stalin period the release of secret information by the communist side was impossible. With the adoption of the long-range policy and disinformation program, the position changed. The Leninist concept of primary and secondary types of sacrifice was reintroduced. The primary communist secret is the existence and nature of the long-range bloc policy and strategy and the role of disinformation. Military, scientific and technical, economic, and counterespionage secrets are secondary; they form a reservoir from which information may be drawn and given away for strategic purposes, particularly if there is some reason to think that it may already have been compromised by genuine leakages or technical means. For example, the identities of secret agents who for one reason or another are reaching the end of their usefulness to the communist side may be given away through a source in whom the communist side is seeking to establish Western confidence. The good faith of Western secret sources or of defectors from the communist side is not therefore automatically established by the fact that they produce quantities of information on military, economic, scientific and technical, or counterespionage subjects or that they give vent to spectacular denunciations of communism. A more important criterion is what they have to say on communist long-range policy and the use of disinformation. The number of communist leaders, officials, and intellectuals who have full knowledge of the scope and scale of the disinformation program is very limited, but the number who participate in one or other of its aspects is very large. Most secret sources or defectors, if they have genuinely transferred their allegiance to the West, should have something of value to say on current communist techniques in this field even if they themselves do not realize the full significance of their own knowledge.

In evaluating scientific and technical information reaching the West, due regard should be paid to the fact that Shelepin, in his May 1959 report and articles for KGB staff in *Chekist*, called for the preparation of disinformation operations designed to confuse and disorientate Western scientific, technological, and military programs; to bring about changes in Western priorities; and to involve the West in costly, wasteful, and ineffective lines of research and development. It is to be expected, therefore, that information available in the West on Soviet space projects, weapons systems, military statistics, and developments in science and technology will be found to contain an element of disinformation.

Given that a program of total disinformation is in operation and given that the communist side is well aware of Western interest in intercepting its communications, evidence derived from communist communications in plain language or weak codes and ciphers is particularly suspect; in fact, it should be treated in the same way as evidence from official communist sources. According to the Western press, some at least of the evidence on casualties in the Sino-Vietnamese "war" in 1979 fell into this category.

The New Methodology and Communist Sources

All communist sources are permanently available for use as channels for disinformation; all must conform to the current pattern if the credibility of the pattern is to be maintained. Nevertheless, it is possible to distinguish between sources that are more or less likely to be used for conveying disinformation to the West and those that are more or less likely to contain revealing information on the implementation of the long-range policy.

Official Communist Sources

Beginning with the official statements and decisions of international communist gatherings, those in the period 1957 to 1960 are of fundamental importance, not only because that was the period of the formulation and adoption of the long-range policy, but also because of the nature of the policy itself. An essential element in it was that its existence and modus operandi should not be appreciated in the West. It was to be expected, therefore, that once it had been adopted subsequent official policy statements should have been less revealing about long-range objectives and the methods of achieving them than the fundamental documents of the period of policy formation. The latter should be considered as including the documents of the congress of bloc communist parties in 1957, the Twenty-first CPSU Congress in January–February 1959, the congress of eighty-one communist parties in November 1960, and Khrushchev's strategic report of January 6, 1961.

Basing themselves largely on retrospective evidence about disagreements at the Eighty-one–Party Congress, most Western analysts concluded that the decisions of that congress represented a compromise between the positions of the various conflicting communist parties that signed the congress Manifesto with varying degrees of reluctance or commitment to abide by the congress's decisions. The conclusion was incorrect. The congress lasted several weeks. No doubt many different parties aired many different views, as they had every right to do, according to Leninist principles of democratic centralism, before the policy had been adopted. Once the discussions had concluded and the policy had been ratified by the majority decision, all parties which signed the Manifesto undertook a serious commitment to work for the implementation of the policy. Any party that had genuinely dissented from the congress's decisions would not have signed the Manifesto and would have been ostracized by the international communist movement. Any party wishing to maintain its standing in the movement must be able to demonstrate that it has made consistent efforts to put the decisions of the congress into effect. If communist parties in general did not take the decisions of the higher organs of authority seriously and strive consistently to implement them, they would not be the disciplined and effective bodies they are known to be. The element of political determinism should not be overlooked, considering that it has been revealed daily in the statements and actions of communist parties inside and outside the bloc, in the proceedings of their national party congresses during the past twenty years, and in their implementation of the policy and its concomitant strategies.

In accepting the evidence that the Eighty-one–Party Congress signified a watershed in the disunity of the communist world rather than the opposite, Western analysts, unaware of the disinformation program, made a fundamental error on which it was easy for the communist strategists to build in the development of their major strategies in Europe, the Third World, and the military and ideological fields. Largely because of this error, later "evidence" in official communist sources on communist disunity came to be almost automatically accepted in the West at its face value.

Given that the disinformation program is directed primarily (though not exclusively) at the noncommunist world, it is imperative to distinguish those communist speeches, publications, and broadcasts that are primarily intended for communist audiences from those that are primarily intended for noncommunist audiences. Obviously the second category is likely to contain more disinformation than the first. It is not possible wholly to conceal the policy and its implementation from those who are expected to carry it out. For that reason the basic decisions of the period 1958 to 1960 were published, as were the findings of the congress of communist parties in 1969, which reviewed progress in the first decade of the policy. To a greater extent than elsewhere, progress in the coordination and consolidation of the communist bloc, particularly through Comecon and the Warsaw Pact organization, is recorded in the annual supplements of the *Great Soviet Encyclopaedia* which are available only in Russian. Naturally, they do not disclose the nature of the disinformation program. Nevertheless, items are occasionally included that figure less prominently, if at all, in publications directed at the West and that call into question the depth and authenticity of splits and crises in the bloc.

In particular the *Encyclopaedia* reflects the continual exchange of visits of communist leaders and delegations between communist countries and parties that are supposed to be at odds with one another. Sometimes these meetings are publicized elsewhere in the communist press, accompanied by photographs of, for example, Brezhnev warmly embracing Dubcek, Tito, or Ceausescu. Western commentators, in their obsession with splits in the communist world, automatically assume that such meetings are held in attempts, usually unsuccessful, to resolve the differences between the parties and that the photographs are intended to mask the hostility between the leaders. They forget that in the years of the genuine Tito-Stalin split it would have been more than Tito's life was worth to have visited Moscow, and they overlook the possibility that the meetings in the 1960s and 1970s have been taking place in order to coordinate the display of bogus differences intended to serve the interests of long-range policy.

The Western scholars who devoted so much attention to esoteric evidence in the communist sources pointing to splits between the Soviet Union and China and Albania seldom seemed to realize that only a privileged few in the communist world, and mainly those concerned with policy and the disinformation program, were in a position to make detailed comparisons between the press of their own party and the press of other parties. Even if foreign newspapers or broadcasts were available, few Russians could read or understand Chinese or Albanian and not many Albanians or Chinese could read or understand Russian. Radio Moscow broadcasts in Albanian in 1960–61 may not have been audible in Albania unless retransmitted by an Albanian station. They were, however, picked up by the BBC and other interested Western organizations and circulated to Western analysts in *Summaries of World Broadcasts* and similar publications. The communist intelligence services were well aware of this, but few Western analysts spotted that some of the polemics between communist leaders may only have reached a Western audience.

In their preoccupation with finding and examining splits in the communist world, Western analysts focused all their attention on the passages in communist speeches and articles that betrayed differences in approach between different parties or different leaders. Passages dealing, for example, with communist unity and commitment to the decisions of the Eighty-one–Party Congress were ignored or written off as lip service to communist shibboleths. This is not necessarily the way in which they were read and understood by members of the communist parties concerned.

Because Western analysts have not been sufficiently on the lookout for disinformation, they have paid inadequate attention to the origin and authenticity of the texts of important communist statements and speeches, particularly in cases where more than one text has been available.

Even where disputes in the communist world are reflected in official communist publications available to the West, the perception of them by the party membership in the countries concerned is likely to be very different from the perception of them in the West. By using various devices such as those suggested above, the party leadership is in a position to project simultaneously two different images of the same "dispute." To the West, it may seem to be of profound significance; in the East, it may well be a "little local difficulty" whose consequences for the leaders of the parties concerned may be wholly beneficial. To take a concrete example. As far as the author was aware, no information or guidance was issued to CPSU members on the Soviet-Albanian dispute before the Twenty-second CPSU Congress in October 1961, when Khrushchev publicly attacked the Albanian leaders. The only knowledge that the author had of anything unusual in Soviet-Albanian relations up to that point was derived from statements by two senior colleagues in the KGB in 1959 that a disinformation operation on

Soviet-Yugoslav and Soviet-Albanian relations had been planned during 1958–59.

Unofficial Communist Sources

It is not uncommon for disclosures in the communist press about dissension in the communist world to be backed up by off-the-record remarks by communist leaders and officials to their Western counterparts and friends. Bearing in mind that the KGB and the other communist security services together can count the total numbers of their informers as literally in the millions, it is a relatively simple matter for them to control the few thousands of their citizens who are in any regular form of official or semiofficial contact with foreigners. Communist regimes are not tolerant of disclosures of information by their servants to foreigners. As Khrushchev himself put it, in repudiating the idea that he had spoken out of turn to the late Senator Hubert Humphrey in 1958 on the subject of Chinese communes: "The mere suggestion that I might have confidential contact with a man who boasts of having spent twenty years fighting communism can only give rise to laughter. Anyone who understands anything at all about politics, to say nothing of Marxism-Leninism, will realise that a confidential talk with Mr. Humphrey about the policies of communist parties and relations with our best friends, the leaders of the Communist Party of China, is inconceivable."[10] Yet many Western observers and scholars claim to have benefitted from such disclosures.

In the preface to his book The Soviet Bloc: Unity and Conflict, Zbigniew Brzezinski wrote: "I am also grateful to several officials of various communist states, for their willingness to discuss matters they should not have discussed with me." No explanation is offered in the book of the reasons why communist officials should have been willing to speak frankly to a prominent anticommunist scholar and citizen of the leading "imperialist" power, nor is any reference made in the book to the possibilities of disinformation. But if the existence of a disinformation program is taken into account, together with the controls over the communist officials in contact with foreigners, the explanation for these indiscretions is obvious. Almost all the Western commentators on the "Prague spring" of

1968 and Eurocommunism in the 1970s have shown a similar tendency to believe what they have been told by leading communist participants in the events and debates concerned.

Against the background of the methods of provocation used during the NEP period and the known facts of the intensified political use of scientists, writers, and other intellectuals by the KGB from 1959 onward, the authenticity of the form of underground literature known as *samizdat*, which made its appearance in the Soviet Union in the 1960s, must be regarded with scepticism. Its significance cannot be fully assessed unless the extent of its circulation inside the Soviet Union is known. There is no justification for assuming that because it reaches a fairly wide audience abroad, it is also widely read at home. It may be in fact that few in the Soviet Union see it other than those authorized by the KGB to do so. In short, it should be regarded as falling within the category of unofficial communist sources.

Similar considerations apply to the Chinese wall posters from which the West derived much of its knowledge of the Cultural Revolution, of power struggles in the Chinese leadership, and of the Chinese attitude to the Soviet Union, especially in 1966–70. What can be said with certainty is that wall posters would not have appeared at all in this period unless the Chinese leadership had wished them to do so and that the Chinese authorities were well aware of the attention paid to them by noncommunist diplomats, journalists, and other foreign representatives in China. This alone provides grounds for reconsidering their contents against the current pattern of communist disinformation. Their full significance cannot be judged without knowing precisely by whom they were put up and what guidance was given to party members about them through the normal channels of party communication.

"Secret" Communist Sources

The remaining category of communist sources is the leakage or disclosure, documentary or otherwise, of information on the proceedings of secret party meetings and international conferences. A conspicuous feature of the evidence on disagreements between parties at the Romanian Communist party congress in June 1960 and at the communist Eighty-one–Party Congress later in the same year is that most of it was retrospective and much of it reached the West with some delay. This is a significant factor, given the existence of a disinformation program. It is a difficult matter to stage a whole conference for disinformation purposes, but it is a simple operation to fabricate or distort the record at leisure after the conference is over and to choose appropriate channels to transmit it to the West.

To Sum Up . . .

The new methodology provides explanations for many contradictions and anomalies in the communist world on which the old methodology throws no light. It explains the confidence of the communist world and the loyalty and dedication of the vast majority of its officials. It explains the reasons for disclosures of information by the communist world about itself and relates them to the requirements of long-range policy. It explains the seeming tolerance of a totalitarian system toward dissension openly expressed by its citizens in their contacts with foreigners. It provides criteria for assessing the reliability of sources, for distinguishing genuine secret agents and defectors from provocateurs, for distinguishing genuine information from disinformation and propaganda. It provides pointers to the identification of agents of influence in the West. It suggests that disinformation, recognized as such, can provide clues to the intentions of its authors. It offers guidance on the relative importance of the official and unofficial communist sources. It diverts attention from spectacular communist polemics between parties and focuses it instead on the solid advances in the groundwork of communist cooperation and coordination. It points the way to recovery from the crisis in Western studies and assessments of communism. It could help to revive the effectiveness of Western security and intelligence services. It explains the communist victory in the Vietnam War despite the Sino-Soviet split. Above all, it explains the willingness and ability of the communist world, despite the appearance of disunity, to seize the initiative and to develop and execute its strategies in relation to the United States, the other advanced industrial countries, and the Third World in the quest for the complete and final victory of international communism.

So far, the new methodology is the methodology of a minority of one. Only time will show whether it will survive; whether it will stimulate new lines of research; whether it will replace the old, obsolete methodology; and whether it will help the West to see in a new light the real meaning and dimensions of the communist problem.

PART TWO

The Disinformation Program and Its Impact on the West

13

The First Disinformation Operation:
The Soviet-Yugoslav "Dispute" of 1958–60

THE YEARS 1958 TO 1960 were marked by spectacular polemics between the Soviet and Yugoslav leaders and their party presses, with interjections from the Albanians and Chinese. Khrushchev himself participated with vigor. In his speech to the Seventh Congress of the Bulgarian Communist Party held in Sofia on June 3, 1958, he called Yugoslav revisionism a class enemy in the pay of the imperialists and a Trojan horse in the communist movement. "Some theoreticians," he said, "exist only because of the alms they receive from imperialist countries in the form of leftover goods. . . . The revisionists are trying to bore at the revolutionary parties from within, to undermine their unity and introduce disorder and confusion in Marxist-Leninist ideology [shouts of 'They won't succeed']."[1]

The existence of a Soviet-Yugoslav dispute was, to all appearances, confirmed by the boycott of the Seventh Congress of the Yugoslav party by the communist parties of the bloc, by further Soviet criticism of the Yugoslav party's program and foreign policy, and by the exclusion of Yugoslavia from the Eighty-one–Party Congress in November 1960, which condemned revisionism. However, the true picture of Soviet-Yugoslav relations, revealed by inside information supported by much open evidence, is very different.

Yugoslavia's Final Reconciliation with the Bloc

After Stalin's death the Soviet leaders made a major effort to achieve a reconciliation with the Yugoslav leaders in order to win

Yugoslavia back from the West and return her to the communist camp. Official secret negotiations between Tito and Khrushchev in 1955 and 1956 led to a full reconciliation in state relations and a partial reconciliation in party relations, but the process of reconciliation was interrupted by the Polish and Hungarian uprisings of 1956. The initial and generally sympathetic attitude of the Yugoslav leaders toward the Poles and Hungarians during these uprisings, and Tito's attacks on such Stalinist leaders in Eastern Europe as Hoxha, contributed to the surge of nationalism and revisionism in the bloc and to Hungary's short-lived break with the Soviets. The Soviets recognized the dangers of Yugoslav revisionist influence in Eastern Europe, and therefore resumed their general criticism of Yugoslavia while continuing their efforts to split her away from the West.

Although the exchanges of criticism between the Soviets and Yugoslavs intensified immediately after the Hungarian uprising, the leaders on both sides were always careful to leave the door open for subsequent meetings and discussions. After Khrushchev had defeated the antiparty group at home in June 1957, he renewed his efforts to return Yugoslavia to the bloc. This time he was successful. A complete reconciliation between the Yugoslav leaders and the Soviet and other bloc leaders was achieved. According to TASS, Kardelj and Rankovic, while on holiday in the Crimea, visited Moscow for "comradely" meetings with Khrushchev; the Albanian leader, Hoxha; and the Bulgarian leader, Zhivkov, in July.

On August 1–2, 1957, Tito, Kardelj, and Rankovic met Khrushchev and Mikoyan in Bucharest for a confidential conference on "socialist solidarity." A statement issued after the conference affirmed their joint determination to improve relations and cooperation on a basis of equality. Moscow radio reported that agreement on "concrete forms of cooperation" had been reached. The major implication of the Soviet-Yugoslavian reconciliation was that the grounds for the continuation of their old feud vanished.

It is clear from Yugoslavia's actions in the following months that she had in fact realigned herself with the communist bloc, including China. In September 1957 there were four strong indications of this: a Yugoslav delegation led by Vukmanovic-Tempo was welcomed in Peking; Yugoslavia blocked a United Nations resolution condemning Soviet intervention in Hungary; Yugoslav representatives attended a session of Comecon; and Tito, together with Gomulka, publicly repudiated "national communism." Said Tito, "We think it wrong to isolate ourselves from the great possibilities of strengthening socialist forces throughout the world." In October the Yugoslavs honored the commitment they had made to the Soviets in 1955–56 to recognize East Germany. In June 1958 Tito tacitly assented to the execution of the former Hungarian premier, Imre Nagy, whom the Yugoslavs had earlier betrayed to the Soviets.

The Yugoslavs secretly attended the first post-Stalin conference of bloc communist parties in November 1957 and openly attended the congress of sixty-four communist parties that followed it. Significantly the Yugoslav delegation to both conferences included Kardelj, who had been a Yugoslav representative to the Cominform; Rankovic, who was responsible for the Yugoslav security service; and Vlahovic, who was responsible for relations with communist and socialist parties. At the bloc conference Stalin's mistrust of other parties and his interference in their affairs were condemned. New relations between the leaders and parties of the bloc were established, based on Leninist principles of equality and cooperation. Yugoslavia signed the Peace Manifesto of the sixty-four communist parties, but not the declaration of the bloc communist parties. The absence of Yugoslavia's signature from the bloc declaration contributed to Western acceptance of the subsequent Soviet-Yugoslav dispute as genuine. However, in his lecture at the KGB Institute in December 1957, General Kurenkov made it clear that the Yugoslavs fully agreed with the declaration but had abstained from signing it because they had reached a secret understanding with the Soviets that it would be tactically advantageous for them not to sign.

Among the decisions of the conference to which the Yugoslavs secretly gave their support was the decision to formulate a long-range policy for the bloc. The agreement that the Yugoslavs should not sign the declaration established the pattern of secrecy and deception subsequently used to conceal Yugoslav collaboration in the formulation and adoption of the long-range policy and paved the way for Yugoslav participation in a joint disinformation effort in support of that policy.

From conversations in 1959 with Colonel Grigorenko,[2] the deputy head of the KGB's disinformation department, the author learned that there were consultations and agreements between the Soviets and Yugoslavs in late 1957 and early 1958 on .political cooperation between them within the framework of the long-range policy. The agreements covered cooperation in three fields: in diplomacy, particularly with regard to Egypt and India, and Arab and Asian countries generally; in dealings with Western socialists and trade unionists; and in the field of disinformation.

According to Grigorenko, early in 1958 the Presidium of the CPSU's Central Committee had given instructions to Pushkin, the head of the party's newly created Department of Active Operations, to prepare disinformation operations on Soviet-Yugoslav relations in accordance with the requirements of bloc policy.[3] This instruction preceded the outbreak of the dispute in April 1958.

The dispute manifested itself mainly in the Soviet and Yugoslav party presses. Since in both cases the party press was under the full control of the party apparatus, such a dispute was easy to manufacture and easy to control. Nevertheless, it was clear at an early stage that, in order to capitalize on the operation and build for the future, new assets, channels, and forms of action would have to be developed in coordination with the KGB. This explains why, according to Grigorenko, the Central Committee decided to use, from the end of 1959 onward, both the Department of Active Operations and the KGB's disinformation department to widen the scope of this particular operation. As a consequence of this decision, Shelepin issued instructions that a special group should be formed in the KGB's disinformation department under Grigorenko to work in cooperation with the Department of Active Operations on the one hand and with the Yugoslav and Albanian security services on the other.

Open Evidence of Yugoslav Participation in the Formulation of the Policy

Evidence that Yugoslavia accepted the application of Lenin's concepts and the lessons of the NEP period as the basis for the new bloc policy is to be found in the speeches and writings of Tito and Kardelj during the period of the formulation of the policy (from 1958 to 1960).

So much Western attention was focused on the polemics between Tito and Khrushchev in mid-1958 that the crucial statements in Tito's speeches, which are fundamental to an understanding of the actual state of Soviet-Yugoslav relations, were overlooked. Tito frequently referred to the relevance of the NEP. For example, in his speech at Labin, Yugoslavia, on June 15, 1958, in reply to Khrushchev's criticisms of Yugoslavia for accepting American aid, Tito said: "The Americans began to furnish aid to us after 1949, (as they did to the Soviet Union in 1921 and 1922) not that socialism might win in our country . . . but because on the one hand, we were threatened with famine and, on the other hand, Yugoslavia could thus more easily fight off Stalin's pressures and preserve her independence. And if perhaps some American circles cherished other hopes, this was not our concern."[4]

Tito committed himself to a new and broader concept of socialist internationalism that served to protect and support not just the Soviet Union as in the past, but all the communist countries and parties and socialist and other progressive movements.

On relations between the socialist countries, Tito said that there was a "new confidence and sincere exchange of opinions and experiences on the basis of which broad cooperation is developing." Yugoslavia could play a more useful role outside the bloc than in it. As Tito put it in his Labin speech: "Refusal to sign the Moscow Declaration and to join the socialist camp does not mean that we are not for the greatest co-operation with all socialist countries. It means, on the contrary, that we are for such co-operation in all fields but that in the present tense international situation we believe it is more useful to follow a constructive peace policy, together with other peace-loving countries which also do not belong to either bloc, than to join the bloc and thus still more aggravate a world situation which is tense enough." In other words, by remaining formally outside the bloc, Yugoslavia could contribute more effectively to the furtherance of the objectives of the common long-range Leninist policy.

Equally illuminating on the true nature of Yugoslavia's relationship with the bloc policy is Edvard Kardelj's book *Socialism and War*, published in Belgrade in 1960 shortly before the Eighty-one–Party Congress. The book attracted the attention of Western analysts at the time because of its polemics against China. In it Kardelj gives an able exposition of the policy of "active coexistence," a concept very close to Khrushchev's "peaceful coexistence," and takes the Chinese to task for their negative attitude toward this concept and their opposition to the thesis (again propounded by Khrushchev) that war is not inevitable despite the continuing existence of imperialism. The West focused on this aspect of Kardelj's book and failed to understand the significance of his recommendation that differences between communists should be analyzed in terms of their substance, not in terms of the verbal polemics between them. The West also failed to appreciate Kardelj's numerous references to Lenin's doctrines, including clear, if not explicit, references to *Left-Wing Communism, An Infantile Disorder*, and to the experience gained during Lenin's NEP in the use of concessions, diplomatic agreements with adversaries, and various other tactics; in other words, to the same historical sources that were used during 1958–60 in the formulation of the new bloc policy and international communist strategies.

The implications of the references to Lenin by the Yugoslav leaders in defining their position cannot be ignored. They clearly establish that Tito and Kardelj regarded a return to Leninism and the use of activist diplomacy and tactics in conditions of "peaceful coexistence" as the most effective way of undermining the nations of the West and changing the world balance of power in favor of the communist countries. Their statements are not only compatible with the long-range policy; they are a clear expression of many of the most important elements in it. They are important evidence that Yugoslav policy and bloc policy as they developed between 1958 and 1960 were identical and had a common source of inspiration in the historical experience of Lenin and his NEP. They also suggest that the Yugoslav leaders made significant contributions to the long-range policy and communist strategy. The possibility should not be excluded that communist strategists from other bloc countries contributed to Kardelj's book. His and Tito's ideas were solidly based on Leninist ideological doctrine, not on the form of revisionism the Yugoslavs had practiced during the Tito-Stalin split. Their concept of active coexistence was but one of the variety of tactics, including Khrushchev's variant of "peaceful coexistence" and Mao's tactic of protracted revolutionary war, approved by the Eighty-one–Party Congress of November 1960. The fact that Tito and Kardelj were developing these ideas during 1958–60 in itself exposes the unreality of their alleged dispute with the Soviets during that same period; it confirms the validity of the inside information on secret Soviet-Yugoslav cooperation.

The tactic of publishing Kardelj's book on the eve of the Eighty-one–Party Congress, which approved the long-range bloc policy and strategy for the communist movement, recalled Lenin's tactic of publishing *Left-Wing Communism, An Infantile Disorder* on the eve of the Soviet adoption of the NEP and just prior to the adoption of new tactics by the Second Congress of the Comintern.

A vague admission of the Soviet-Yugoslav cooperation against imperialism over questions on which their positions coincided was made by Khrushchev in his report to the Twenty-first CPSU Congress in January 1959.[5] Although the official *History of the CPSU*, published in Russian in 1959, criticized the Yugoslav leaders for their refusal to attend the bloc conference in November 1957 and castigated the Yugoslav party program of 1958 as revisionist,[6] it also said that normal relations between the USSR and Yugoslavia had been restored on the CPSU's initiative and that the CPSU's policy of friendship and mutual assistance had triumphed.[7]

The reconciliation with Yugoslavia in 1957–58 went far beyond the bounds envisaged by the Soviets in 1955–56. It covered the Yugoslav leaders' relations not only with their Soviet opposite numbers, but also with the Albanians, Bulgarians, Chinese, and all the other bloc leaders. The Yugoslav leaders, in fact, voluntarily surrendered their ideological and political independence to the bloc at the conference of bloc parties in November 1957. This became possible for them because the conference adopted a resolution, which Kardelj and Rankovic no doubt helped to draft, permitting the bloc parties to pursue their own national roads to socialism, provided that they followed the basic principles of Marxist revolution and construction of socialism.

Confirmation that all the bloc parties agreed that, for tactical reasons, Yugoslavia should not sign the main declaration of the conference is provided by the fact that, after the conference was over, there was no condemnation of Yugoslavia's refusal to sign by the bloc parties either individually or collectively. Indeed, since November 1957 the real state of relations among all the leaders of the bloc has been excellent and there has been no basis for any serious disputes between them.

The true relationship between Yugoslavia and the rest of the bloc during the period 1958–60 was revealed in November 1960 when the Eighty-one–Party Congress (which continued to recognize Yugoslavia as a socialist country) publicly approved, as its most fundamental and crucial decision, a policy Manifesto that not only incorporated Tito's concept of broad international solidarity, so heavily criticized by the Soviets in 1958, but also Kardelj's recommendations on the revival of Lenin's activist policies and tactics during a period of "peaceful coexistence" and the use of the historical experience of the NEP to facilitate the construction of socialism.

There was, of course, no public recognition of the Yugoslav contribution and the authors of the Manifesto were not named. In fact the congress officially announced that the Yugoslavs did not participate in the proceedings. "Yugoslav revisionism" was condemned in general terms in the Manifesto. Nevertheless, the evidence of secret agreements entered into between Yugoslavia and the rest of the bloc in November 1957, coupled with the arguments above, points to the conclusion that Yugoslavia's apparent nonparticipation in the congress in November 1960 was again no more than a tactical maneuver. The likelihood is that Yugoslavia agreed secretly in advance to the draft resolutions of the November 1960 congress and that the bloc as a whole agreed that its interests would best be served by Yugoslavia continuing to appear to be an independent, nonbloc country.

Further Anomalies in the "Dispute"

Detailed examination of the Soviet criticisms of Yugoslavia and the course of the 1958–60 dispute against the background of the genuine Tito-Stalin split throws up a number of further points that either cast additional doubt on the authenticity of the later dispute and confirm that it was a disinformation operation or help to illustrate the disinformation technique used in it and the purposes the operation was intended to serve.

The dispute opened in the spring of 1958 with criticisms in the Soviet press of the draft of the new Yugoslav party program, which included a statement about Yugoslavia's road to socialism. In fact the statement was fully in accord with the resolutions of the November 1957 conference of bloc communist parties. Consequently, Soviet criticism of it was not only strange, inconsistent, and unjustified, but contrary to the endorsement specifically given by the bloc parties of different national roads to socialism, provided that certain basic principles, such as the leading role of the communist party, were upheld. Later on, Khrushchev and Tito directly and indirectly admitted that Soviet criticism of the Yugoslav program was unfounded. In his report to the Twenty-first CPSU Congress in January 1959, Khrushchev said: "Questions of the methods and practice of socialist construction are the domestic affair of each individual country. We have no controversy with the Yugoslav leaders on the establishing of workers' councils or other matters of their domestic affairs. When the Declaration of the Conference of the representatives of the Communist and Workers' Parties of the Socialist Countries was being signed there were no arguments and no controversies on such matters."[8] Thus Khrushchev repudiated the earlier Soviet criticisms of Yugoslavia's "road to socialism," but not before the attention of Western analysts had been successfully diverted by the polemics from what was really going on inside the bloc at that time.

Soviet criticism of Yugoslavia for failing to support socialist solidarity was equally unfounded. Yugoslavia's recognition of East Germany and expressions of solidarity with the East German Communist party and its leader, Ulbricht, demonstrated that Yugoslavia honored the promises of support that had been secretly given to the Soviets. It is noteworthy that neither the Soviets nor the Yugoslavs revealed during the 1958 polemics that they had reached this secret understanding.

Officially, the Yugoslav party congress in April 1958 was boycotted by the rest of the bloc. But the boycott was strangely incomplete because, although official party delegations from the bloc did not attend, ambassadors from the bloc countries were present as observers.

There is room for considerable doubt about the reality of the economic pressure allegedly applied by the Soviets to the Yugoslavs following the 1958 dispute. The Soviets did not cancel agreements or sever economic relations, as they did when Stalin split with Tito. Trade, technical cooperation, and cultural exchanges continued. The Soviets did not cancel their 1956 credit commitments, deny them in principle, or arbitrarily delay the fulfillment dates. Rather, they suggested that there should be discussions about delaying the fulfillment dates from 1957–64 to 1962–69 and 1963–69. In December 1958 negotiations on Soviet-Yugoslav trade began in Moscow, and in April 1959 a cultural cooperation program was signed in Belgrade. In January 1960 the Yugoslav leader Vukmanovic-Tempo met Khrushchev in Moscow. At the same time the Soviet Union and Yugoslavia signed a scientific cooperation protocol.

Criticism of Yugoslavia for lack of revolutionary ardor helped to distract attention from the active support later given by Yugoslavia to liberation movements, especially in Africa.

Criticism of Tito for accepting American aid preceded by only a matter of months Soviet attempts to obtain for themselves a two-billion-dollar credit from the United States for industrial modernization. Tito pointed out the inconsistency himself in April 1959, referring to Mikoyan's visit to the United States in the previous January.

Although Yugoslavia's position in the United Nations appeared to vacillate between support for the United States and support for the Soviet Union, on vital issues such as the German treaty (in February 1959), colonialism, disarmament, reorganization of the structure of the UN, and the seating of communist China, Yugoslavia consistently supported the Soviet position. There were therefore sound reasons for Gromyko to say that the Soviets' relations with the Yugoslavs were "good" and that, on major issues, their positions coincided.[9]

Comparison of the dispute of 1958 with the split of 1948 shows how superficial the later differences were. The 1958 dispute failed to gather momentum. There were no clear breaches in political, economic, or cultural relations. Yugoslavia was not isolated politically by the bloc. Military action was not threatened against her nor was an economic boycott imposed. There were no major changes in diplomatic representation between Yugoslavia and the rest of the bloc. Exchanges of delegations between them continued. Yugoslavia asked to be admitted to the Comecon meeting in April 1959, but was allegedly refused an invitation. Nevertheless, in the same month a program of cultural cooperation between the Soviet Union and Yugoslavia was signed in Belgrade.

Since details of protocol have often been cited by Western analysts in support of the existence of splits in the communist world, it is worth mentioning that, despite the existence of an alleged dispute, Khrushchev, while on his way to Albania, sent a greetings telegram to Tito on May 26, 1959, which Tito acknowledged on the following day.

The final inconsistency in the dispute was the manner of its ending. For no apparent reason there was a sudden improvement in Soviet-Yugoslav relations in 1960, accompanied by closer diplomatic cooperation. An open reconciliation followed in 1961. The controversial Yugoslav party program, which Khrushchev and the Soviet press had criticized so vigorously in 1958 and 1959 and which the Yugoslavs had so obstinately refused to modify, ceased to be an obstacle to good relations in 1960 and 1961.

To sum up, open, official information from communist sources confirms the validity of the inside information on secret Soviet-Yugoslav agreements and leads to the conclusion that the Soviet-Yugoslav dispute of 1958–60 was not a repetition of the genuine Tito-Stalin split, but the calculated product of a joint Soviet-Yugoslav disinformation operation in support of the long-range bloc policy to the formulation of which both sides to the dispute had made their contribution.

Once the Soviet-Yugoslav dispute of 1958–60 is seen to have been artificial and once the polemics between the leaders are recognized as having been no more than shadowboxing conducted by agreement between them for the benefit of external observers, the explanation of other aspects of the controversy becomes clear. For example, in response to Chinese attacks on Yugoslavia, the Yugoslav press criticized the Chinese communes; then, in December 1958, Khrushchev revealed to the late Senator Hubert Humphrey that there were differences between the Soviets and Chinese on the subject of the communes. The following month, in addressing the Twenty-first CPSU Congress, Khrushchev repudiated his own remarks and accused the "Yugoslav revisionists" of disseminating all sorts of inventions about differences between the CPSU and the CPC. As he put it: "And now the Yugoslav revisionists have taken this fabricator [Humphrey] unto themselves as a witness." Anticipating to some extent the argument of later chapters, this incident can be seen as a good example of disinformation technique.

First, Western interest was aroused in nonexistent Sino-Soviet differences by a statement at the highest level. Then, Khrushchev's repudiation of his own statements drew further attention to them and suggested that they must indeed have represented a serious indiscretion on his part, which he was at pains to cover up. Apart from its significance in the Sino-Soviet context, the incident provided a further artificial issue with which to fuel an agreed-upon, controlled dispute between the Soviets and Yugoslavs; it was an instance not of antagonism between them, but of cooperation in fulfillment of their secret agreement to collaborate in the disinformation field.

Objectives of the Soviet-Yugoslav Dispute of 1958–60

The first objective of staging the dispute of 1958–60 was to conceal the true degree of reconciliation between the leaders of Yugoslavia and the other bloc countries. The reasons for concealment were twofold; bearing in mind the anti-Soviet stance taken up by Yugoslavia in the last five years of Stalin's life and Yugoslav sympathy with the Polish and Hungarian rebels in 1956, a sudden, open reconciliation with Yugoslavia in 1958 could have had adverse consequences elsewhere in the bloc, which it was particularly important to avoid during the formulation of a new long-range policy. Bearing in mind also the strength of nationalist feeling in the Yugoslav population and in the Yugoslav party itself, an open surrender by the Yugoslav leaders to the bloc and to the requirements of its long-range policy could have caused them severe problems with both their followers and their opponents inside Yugoslavia.

The second major objective was to prepare the Yugoslav leaders for a special strategic role by building up their image as independents. In the advanced countries this was calculated to help the leaders to use their relations with European socialist and trade union leaders to promote the formation of united fronts between socialist and communist parties and, in the longer term, to contribute toward the dissolution of military pacts with the United States and toward the neutralization of Western Europe and Japan. In the developing countries it was calculated to gain acceptance for the Yugoslavs as genuine neutralist leaders of the nonaligned movement, which in the long run they would be able to influence and turn against the West.

Subsidiary objectives were:

• To pin the revisionist label firmly on the Yugoslav party and to identify its policies and doctrines as one extreme of a variety of different brands of communism.

• At a later stage, to project Khrushchev and the Soviet leaders as veering toward Yugoslav revisionism and thereby to assist Soviet activist, détente diplomacy in its dealings with the advanced countries.

• To gain experience, to provide support, and to create a favorable atmosphere for the development of other disinformation operations, along similar lines, on Soviet-Albanian and Sino-Soviet splits and, at a later stage, on Romanian independence.

14

The Second Disinformation Operation: The "Evolution" of the Soviet Regime, Part One: The Major Changes in the USSR

ERTAIN DEVELOPMENTS IN THE SOVIET UNION since 1958 have been widely interpreted in the West as reflecting a moderation in the rigors of communist ideology and a decline in its influence over the practical handling of affairs of state. These apparent trends are usually thought of as being associated with the growth of the Soviet Union into a great power increasingly pursuing its national interests along traditional lines and facing familiar internal political problems, in particular the emergence of a dissident movement. While it is true that changes have been made in various economic, political, diplomatic, and ideological aspects of the regime, a distinction must be made between the changes themselves and the manner in which they have been presented if the nature and purpose of disinformation about them is to be understood.

Economic Changes

From the late 1950s onward, changes in Soviet economic practice included the improvement of material incentives to production in industry and agriculture, the promotion of competition, and the broadening of the private market in the cities. Sensational evidence suggesting the revival of capitalism appeared in the Soviet press in the form of articles on the black market and on underground capitalists in the Soviet Union. The confessions of a "former Soviet underground millionaire" appeared in *Izvestiya* in 1959 or 1960.

It is true that there is and, on a varying scale, always has been a private market in the Soviet Union in which collectivized peasants and some private individuals have sold the agricultural produce grown on their lots. In the NEP period, when private ownership and private enterprise were permitted, this private market reached its postrevolutionary zenith. With the ending of the NEP and the collectivization of agriculture, it shrank to insignificant proportions. During and after the Second World War, it revived again for a short period, only to be drastically curtailed in the last years of Stalin's rule. Since his death, with the new emphasis on incentives and the abolition of deliveries of goods to the State by farmers from their private lots, the private market has once more grown in scale. It now exists in two principal forms: the main market, in the cities where collective farmers and some private individuals sell their agricultural produce; and a small black market, especially in Moscow and Leningrad, in which illegal transactions in currency and goods take place between Soviet speculators and foreign diplomats and visitors.

The growth of the main market has been strictly limited because the introduction of greater incentives for farmers and other workers was not accompanied by the legalization of private enterprises; the emphasis throughout has been on increasing production and efficiency not in private enterprises, but in collective farms and state-owned industries and trading enterprises. There can be no significant widening of the private market in healthy competition with the state sector unless private ownership and enterprise are reintroduced. The Soviet government shows no sign of doing this; on the contrary, the regime maintains its hostile attitude to private ownership and the ultimate objective of party policy is still the total extinction of the private sector.

As for the black market, it is, as foreign diplomats know, extremely limited and illegal. What is less widely known is that it is secretly controlled and actively exploited by the Anticontraband Department of the KGB. Significantly this department was created in 1959 on the lines of a similar department set up in the GPU during the NEP period. Its function is to control the activities of domestic speculators and foreign businessmen and to blackmail and recruit as agents members of the diplomatic colony and other foreign visitors who engage in illicit transactions. The head of this new department, Sergey Mikhaylovich Fedoseyev, was so successful in recruiting foreigners, including Americans, that in 1961 he was promoted to be Chief of the American Department, responsible for the recruitment of officials of the US Embassy in Moscow.

Tendencies toward private enterprise have existed in the Soviet Union since the revolution. Arrests of embezzlers and speculators who have enriched themselves at state expense have not always been reported. If in the period 1959–62 such arrests were given wide publicity, this did not indicate, as some Western observers believed and as the Soviet regime wished them to believe, that capitalism in the Soviet Union was reviving; on the contrary, it indicated that the regime was stepping up its traditional ideological policy of eliminating the "remnants of capitalism" while at the same time promoting the myth that capitalism was being restored.

Since the end of the 1950s a measure of industrial reorganization has been in progress. Greater powers of initiative have been given to local economic management without weakening central control. Local councils of people's economy have been created. The authority of economic officials has been enhanced.

In Western terminology, these officials are described as "technocrats," who are said to be increasingly taking over control. But what Western observers largely ignore is that these so-called technocrats are in reality party members who, having received industrial or other specialized training, are applying the party line in their place of work. Through them the party exercises a more efficient control over Soviet industry, which, despite the appearance of recent changes, is now more comprehensively planned and more effectively coordinated than before.

From 1962 onward there was a protracted debate in the official Soviet press on the introduction of the profit motive, on the concept of a market-regulated economy, and on the creation of a trust system in industry. The Soviet economist Professor Liberman played a prominent role in the debate.[1] According to Liberman, factories should be given no more than basic production plans, which should be based mainly on commercial orders. Within the framework of the basic plan, factories should be free to determine their own wages, costs, and profits. A proportion of the profits should be paid into an incentive fund, which would pay bonuses to managers and workers. The introduction of state trusts that would function on a profit basis was encouraged by the government. In fact some trusts of this kind were created from 1962 onward; for example, small shoe factories were combined experimentally into one complex in the firm Progress in Lvov, and other trusts were set up in Gorkiy and elsewhere.

The resemblance of these reforms to capitalism is only superficial. Their effect has been to strengthen, not to weaken, party control over industry. The fundamental differences between the Soviet and capitalist systems in their basic objectives, their principles of ownership and management, and the distribution of national income and political power remain. The emphasis in the Soviet capital investment program is still on heavy industry and especially on armaments, including military satellites and nuclear missiles.

It should be noted that the economic reforms reflected to some extent the experience of the NEP. Some of Liberman's ideas, as well as the creation of trusts in industry, were directly modeled on the NEP pattern, but in fact the changes of the 1960s were less far-reaching than those of the 1920s. Private ownership of enterprises was not reintroduced after 1960; agriculture remained collectivized. Such reforms as were carried out in the 1960s and 1970s did not signal a fundamental change in the regime; they were carefully calculated steps taken by the regime within the framework of its long-range policy. Their object was not to change the nature of the system, but to stabilize it by making the economy more efficient and party control more effective.

There are, in short, fewer objective grounds for concluding now that the economic nature of the regime has been evolving since 1960 in the direction of capitalism than there were in the NEP period. In the 1960s and 1970s, however, the same technique has been used as in the 1920s to exaggerate and misrepresent the nature of such changes as have occurred to suggest a weakening of ideological influence and a tendency toward the restoration of capitalism.

The KGB has played an active part in this misrepresentation. For example, the confessions of an underground millionaire were supplied to *Izvestiya* by the KGB at the personal instigation of Shelepin. A more widespread KGB technique has been used to influence directly the opinions of visiting Western tourists, businessmen, scholars, and correspondents. For instance, Western economists who visit the Soviet Union naturally wish to meet their Soviet colleagues. It is normal practice for the latter to clear such meetings in advance with the party and the KGB. They are then briefed on the line to be taken in "frank" discussions with their Western colleagues on the faults in the Soviet system and the direction in which it is evolving.

Given that there has been no restoration of capitalism in the Soviet Union, Chinese and Albanian charges to this effect in their polemics with the Soviet leaders in the 1960s were unfounded and can therefore be seen as part and parcel of an agreed bloc disinformation effort carried out in accordance with the long-range policy decisions reached, with Chinese and Albanian participation, in the period 1958–60.

Political Changes

Western belief in a moderation in the Soviet attitude toward internal and external political problems during the 1960s was based on various changes introduced from 1958 onward. They can be briefly listed. A new formula was evolved to replace the "dictatorship of the proletariat," in official communist language. This was the concept of the "state of the whole people."[2] Certain legal changes were made. Steps were taken ostensibly to reduce the role and influence of the security service. The All Union Ministry of Internal Affairs was abolished in 1959—but only for a short time. The Chairman of the KGB, the notorious police professional General Ivan Serov, was dismissed on December 9, 1958; he was replaced two weeks later by the former leader of the Soviet youth movement and alleged liberal Shelepin. The use of terror was reduced. It was decreed that "socialist legality" should be observed. The KGB was represented as a reformed organization, hard on the enemies of the regime but "humanistic" in its approach to the Soviet people, as was its forerunner in Dzerzhinskiy's days. Khrushchev told editors of the West German social democratic press that state security organizations were not really needed at all in the Soviet Union; they could at most be used to deal with cases of petty larceny.[3] Khrushchev and Shelepin repeatedly denied that there were political prisoners in the Soviet Union.[4] According to *Kommunist*: "The state security organs are now laying more and more emphasis on

preventive, educational work . . . they are expanding their prophylactic work."[5] This line was in sharp contrast with the earlier emphasis on repression in the work of the security services.

A more tolerant attitude was ostensibly adopted toward religion.
The Chairman of the Directorate for Affairs of the Orthodox
Church, a KGB official named G. Karpov, was replaced by Kuroye-
dov, a former secretary of a party provincial committee. More religious leaders were allowed to travel abroad.

A more liberal attitude was adopted toward writers, scientists,
and other creative workers. There were occasional, apparently independent and spontaneous, expressions of public opinion. Unofficial
critical comments about the regime were sometimes published.
While traditional socialist realism in art continued to receive official
encouragement, well-publicized exhibitions of abstract painters were
held in Moscow. They were roundly criticized by Khrushchev. As
in painting, so in literature; alongside traditional hard-line writing,
certain well-known Soviet poets and authors published controversial
material in the Soviet and foreign press. Some were harassed and
punished in consequence. A Yevtushenko poem including criticism
of Stalin was published in the Soviet Union. So was Solzhenitsyn's
One Day in the Life of Ivan Denisovich, a description of life in
a Soviet prison by an author who had himself been a prisoner
under Stalin. Works by other former prisoners, such as Dyakov
and Georgiy Shelest, appeared in the early 1960s. More Soviet
tourists traveled abroad, including writers who made critical and
controversial comments about the regime. Some were allowed to
leave the Soviet Union permanently. Within the Soviet Union
the well-known writer Kochetov emerged as the leader of the "conservative" wing of the writers' union, while the late poet Tvardovskiy, who sponsored Solzhenitsyn's writings, led the "liberals."
The liberals were joined by the poets Yevtushenko and Voznesen-
skiy, also by prominent scientists and other dissidents.

With the help of these apparently more liberal official attitudes,
the image of the Soviet Union presented to the outside world
was changed; the political fundamentals of the regime were not.
The "state of the whole people" was still a dictatorship ruled exclusively, and now more effectively, by the communist party through
the party apparatus and other organs, including the KGB. The
KGB was still one of the pillars of the strength and stability of

the regime. True anticommunist political opposition was suppressed as before, but on a selective basis. The real nature of the Soviet regime and the KGB and their intolerance of ideological opposition were demonstrated in October 1959 by the assassination in West Germany by the KGB of the Ukrainian nationalist leader Stepan Bandera. The regime was no less ruthless inside the Soviet Union when dealing with nationalist or other opposition movements. Despite Khrushchev's disclaimers, political prisoners still existed, though their numbers were reduced. Political trials were normally still held in secret.

The scale of repression cannot be judged by the show trials, which were sometimes publicized, or by information that, following the example of the 1920s, was sometimes leaked for political or tactical considerations through *samizdat* and other sources. According to Mironov, its former chairman, the KGB branch in Leningrad in 1958–59 was still arresting 35 percent of the anti-Soviet elements it detected; the other 65 percent were let off with prophylactic warnings.

Soviet intellectuals were still controlled officially through party organizations in the various institutes, academies, and writers' and other unions. Unofficially they were still controlled by the security services through secret agents. There was no free, independent, spontaneous expression of political views in the Soviet Union. Although the use of terror was diminished in comparison with Stalin's time, true reform went no further than in the thaw between 1953 and 1956.

The so-called political evolution of the regime can be understood in the light of Shelepin's secret report as the implementation of the long-range policy of stabilizing and strengthening the regime by adopting the methods used with success in the 1920s. The policy entailed not diminishing the power of the KGB, but giving it a wider, more active, sophisticated, and influential political role in shaping and conditioning the life of society. The statements by Khrushchev and others quoted above on the reduction in the KGB's importance were untrue and are in themselves evidence of the deliberate creation of a false image of Soviet society. The KGB itself participated with the party and the Soviet leadership in the creation of this false image. Prominent Soviet legal experts, including several from the KGB Institute like Professor of Law

Viktor Chikvadze, helped the Soviet leaders to formulate the new concept of the "state of the whole people." They also helped to prepare the false statements quoted above on the restricted role of the KGB and the nonexistence of political prisoners. When the puzzled staff and students at the KGB Institute (including the author) pointed out the inaccuracy of Khrushchev's remarks and asked for an explanation, they were told that such statements were required for political and tactical considerations. In fact, the statements were made in order to mask the KGB's new role.

Further evidence of the role of the KGB in shaping the new, false image of the regime, evidence that illustrates the linkage in technique between the NEP period and the 1960s, can be found in the case of Shul'gin.

Shul'gin was a former monarchist émigré leader who became a victim of the OGPU's Trust and unwittingly was used by the OGPU to influence Western views on Soviet evolution. In September 1925 he was lured by the Trust into the Soviet Union, and under Trust auspices visited Kiev, Moscow, and Leningrad, meeting the defense, foreign affairs, and finance "ministers" of the Trust's "underground organization." In 1927 he wrote a book about his visit to the Soviet Union entitled *Three Cities*. After clearance with the Trust (in effect, with the OGPU), the book was published outside the Soviet Union. One of its main themes was that foreign intervention in Soviet affairs was superfluous, since communism was a declining force.

After the Second World War Soviet security agents arrested Shul'gin in Belgrade. He was imprisoned in the Soviet Union for his involvement with the Trust in the 1920s. In 1960 he was released from prison and was used by the KGB, this time wittingly, to publish a brochure in which he stated some of the reasons for suggesting that the Soviet regime was evolving toward a more tolerant and democratic system.[6]

Changes in Diplomacy

From 1958 onward the Soviet leadership laid special emphasis on peaceful coexistence, trade and economic relations with the West, and a moderate and businesslike approach to negotiations and agreements. Soviet diplomacy entered an active phase; top-level personal diplomacy became normal practice. Khrushchev and other Soviet leaders visited the United States and France; Western leaders were invited to the Soviet Union. Approaches were made to the governments of advanced capitalist countries, including Great Britain, the United States, West Germany, France, and Japan, for the purpose of improving political, economic, and cultural relations with them. The Soviets showed interest in summit conferences and international meetings on disarmament and trade. On December 4, 1958, the Soviets issued a declaration on the cessation of nuclear tests, preceded and followed by other proposals on disarmament.[7] The Soviets expressed a desire to obtain capital equipment from the industrially advanced noncommunist world on the basis of long-term credits.[8] Countries bordering on the Soviet Union received special attention.[9] In May 1962 Khrushchev suggested a world conference on trade.

These initiatives did not represent an evolution toward a less ideological and more conventional national form of diplomacy on the part of the Soviet government. They should be compared with Soviet diplomacy under Lenin during the NEP; they were similar calculated steps taken on the basis and within the framework of a long-range ideological policy. Similar emphasis on peaceful coexistence and businesslike relations with the capitalist world and a similar use of high-level contacts with noncommunist governments can be seen in Soviet diplomacy leading up to the Genoa conference of 1922. This was a period in which Lenin himself advocated the use of moderate language, avoiding in particular words suggesting that violence and terror played any part in Soviet tactics.

The Soviet government's proposals to the UN General Assembly on full and complete disarmament and the call for a world conference on trade are even more strikingly similar to Soviet proposals in the 1920s. The so-called moderate Soviet diplomacy of the 1960s was a repetition of Lenin's activist foreign policy of gaining specific benefits for the Soviet Union by exploiting the contradictions within and between noncommunist countries.

If this historical basis for Soviet diplomacy in the 1960s is taken into account together with Lenin's pamphlet, *Left-Wing Communism, An Infantile Disorder,* it is easier to understand why the emphasis on coexistence and businesslike cooperation between states with different social systems in the 1960s was accompanied by an intensification of the ideological struggle inside and outside the Soviet Union. Khrushchev's calls for peaceful coexistence and disarmament were combined with outspoken attacks on capitalism and predictions of upheavals in the West, which were made during and after his visits to the United States in 1959 and 1960.[10] Even more important was the intensification of support for revolutionary and national liberation movements abroad, most conspicuously in Vietnam and Africa. The year 1960 saw the foundation in the Soviet Union of a new university, Lumumba University, intended for the training of revolutionary leaders for the developing countries of Africa, Asia, and Latin America.

The resemblance between Soviet initiatives in the 1920s and those in the late 1950s and early 1960s did not escape the notice of all Western analysts. For example, David M. Abshire, in his contribution to the book *Détente*, said that more striking than any adjustment currently being made to meet changing conditions was the adjustment of the NEP in the 1920s.[11]

Similarly, Lazar Pistrak, in his book *The Grand Tactician*, observed that Khrushchev had "resumed Lenin's methods of an active foreign policy and the simultaneous spreading of world-revolutionary ideas by means of unprecedented propaganda devices."[12]

A third Western observer, G. A. von Stackelberg, pointed out the inconsistency between peaceful coexistence and the foundation of a university for training revolutionary leaders for the Third World. He drew a direct comparison between Lumumba University and the Communist University of the Toilers of the East, set up almost forty years earlier under Lenin to train cadres for the Eastern Soviet republics of Turkestan, Kazakhstan, and the Caucasus. As he pointed out, it could also be compared with the Sun Yat-sen University, which trained cadres for the communist revolution in China.[13]

Despite the talk of peaceful coexistence, Soviet policy provoked or contributed to a series of crises in the decade following 1958, including the Berlin crisis of November 1958, when Khrushchev proposed to terminate the city's occupied status; the U-2 crisis in 1960, which Khrushchev used to wreck the summit conference; the Soviet decision to resume nuclear testing in 1961; the Cuban crisis of 1962; and the Middle East crisis of 1967.

Again the explanation is to be found in the experience of the NEP and the Leninist view of foreign policy as a form of ideological struggle in which both peaceful and nonpeaceful methods should be used. Peaceful coexistence was defined under Khrushchev, as it was under Lenin, as a form of class struggle between antagonistic social systems based on the active exploitation of the contradictions within and between noncommunist countries.[14]

The revival of an active Leninist foreign policy was confirmed, for example, in the Soviet military newspaper *Krasnaya Zvezda* on July 18, 1963, in an article that stated: "The Leninist foreign policy carried out by the Central Committee of the CPSU and the Soviet government is a high-principled, flexible, active policy always on the offensive. It has fully justified itself and is bearing excellent fruit. . . Communists do not keep it a secret that co-existence is necessary for world-wide victory of Marxist-Leninist ideas, that there are deep-rooted differences between the two world systems of socialism and capitalism. To solve those differences, Marxists-Leninists hold, war is not an obligatory means in economic, political and ideological struggle."

Soviet foreign policy in the 1960s was not moderate; it was more offensive than in the years preceding and following Stalin's death, when the crisis of the regime forced it onto the defensive. The notion that it was more moderate, more conventional, more nationalist, and less ideological is the product of deliberate disinformation and the systematic use of terms, such as peaceful coexistence, that are themselves intentionally misleading.

The Soviet intelligence and security services played their part in misrepresenting the nature of Soviet foreign policy, in particular by projecting and underlining the common interests between communist and noncommunist countries. The participation of prominent Soviet agents of influence in the scientific field, like Academician Topchiyev, and the role they played in Pugwash and other conferences, recall the use of the Eurasian movement by Dzerzhinskiy in the 1920s.

Chinese and Albanian accusations that the Soviet regime had departed from Leninist principles of revolutionary policy contributed to Western acceptance of the notion that this was so. Since, as this analysis has shown, the charge was without foundation and since the Chinese and Albanians were parties to the adoption of the long-range policy, their accusations should be seen as another element in a joint disinformation effort.

The Influence of Ideology

The changes in the economic, political, and diplomatic practice of the Soviet government, which have been described above, contributed to the belief in the West that the influence of ideology in the Soviet system had declined. This was not so. On the contrary, the changes and readjustments were calculated, controlled, and pragmatic. They did not touch the economic and political fundamentals of the regime; in fact, they contributed to the restoration and strengthening of ideology, as compared with the Stalin period.

Similarly a not always consistently maintained moderation in the Soviet press line on the West and continuing emphasis on common interests between the communist and noncommunist worlds did not indicate revisionism or an increase in Western or nationalist influences in the Soviet Union, but rather a tactical shift within the framework of the long-range policy.

It is true that the new, educated, postrevolutionary generation that grew up in the Soviet Union (as in Eastern Europe) presented a largely silent challenge to the basic principles of the communist system and its ideology; there was strong latent anxiety and opposition, especially among intellectuals and young people, and a genuine, deep-rooted sense of nationalism among the Russian and other peoples of the Soviet Union hostile to the regime. The hostility of the young was aggravated by the repression to which the older generation had been subjected. This genuine opposition, and the decline in the influence of ideology that reached its nadir in the immediate post-Stalin years, presented the regime with a serious problem. It could either revert to mass repression on Stalinist lines or adopt a new, more flexible Leninist approach. Stalinist methods having clearly failed, Leninist methods were the obvious choice.

The economic gap between the privileged "new class" and the workers and collective farmers was narrowed, the use of terror and repression was restricted, and more sophisticated methods were used to counter religious, nationalist, and Western influences. A more flexible, Leninist approach was adopted toward the "lost" younger generation. Using the techniques of the NEP period, the regime managed to increase its prestige, relieve the internal crisis, and neutralize actual and latent internal opposition. The only real change in the ideological substance of the regime was its increased effectiveness.

Among other factors that contributed to Western belief in the decline in the influence of ideology were, for example, the replacement of the "dictatorship of the proletariat" by the "state of the whole people"; the alleged degeneration of Soviet leaders from genuine revolutionaries into reformists and revisionists; the alleged growth of special interest groups in Soviet society, and the emergence of some kind of *embourgeoisé* middle class; the revival of de-Stalinization; the increased accessibility of Soviet scientists, writers, and other intellectual and cultural figures; the larger numbers of Soviet Jews allowed to emigrate; and Chinese and Albanian accusations of Soviet revisionism.

According to the 1961 program of the CPSU, the "dictatorship of the proletariat" (in other words, the dictatorship of the communist party) had served its purpose.[15] The "state of the whole people" was to be maintained "until the complete victory of communism." Far from indicating a weakening of ideological party control, this new formula should be seen as part of the overall attempt to broaden the political base of the party and enhance its influence by giving it a more moderate and less exclusive image. The party retained its monopoly of power, policy, and ideas. The gulf between the Soviet and noncommunist social systems in fact widened even while the myth of common interests between them was being propagated. Intolerance of any genuine, uncontrolled political opposition in the Soviet Union was and is as severe as ever. All actions inside and outside the country are carried out with direct or indirect references to the abiding principles of Leninism. Ideological and political considerations override national and economic considerations as never before. Any expectation of a genuine increase in revisionist, nationalistic, or Western influences on the regime is unrealistic, especially given present Western attitudes toward the system.

Even less well-founded is the notion that Soviet leaders and party members are less ideologically motivated than before and have abandoned revolution for reformism and revisionism. Although to some extent the adjustments after 1958 were introduced under pressure from a discontented population, among whom the influences of ideology had suffered a genuine decline, those adjustments were also in line with the ideological long-range policy objectives to which all the leaders were committed.

The up-and-coming younger generation of leaders like Shelepin, Polyanskiy, and Andropov were not and are not revisionists or "Young Turks," as some Western commentators dubbed them. Shelepin's report and the KGB activity for which he and Andropov have been responsible demonstrate that they are zealous revolutionaries who are committed to an ideological, Leninist policy and are qualified to take over the burden of power from the older generation because of their commitment to that policy and because of their achievements in implementing it. There are no liberals, moderates, or conservatives in the Soviet leadership; there are only communists whose actions are determined by the requirements of the long-range policy. They may take on a public guise of liberals or Stalinists, but only if required to do so by the Presidium of the party in the interests of that policy.

Equally unfounded is the notion that the professional strata of the Soviet Union are becoming less ideologically minded or more independent of the party. The fact is that, normally, leading officials, generals, scientists, and professional bureaucrats are party members who know that their well-being depends on their standing with the party and the government and that they would suffer if the regime were to be weakened. In general they are less sceptical about communist doctrine than they were in Stalin's years. Since arrests among them are now unusual and take place only if they participate actively in opposition to the regime, they are in fact more loyal than before. They know that the authority of the party leadership is unchallengeable. Since everything is under the control of the party, there are no divisions between the party leadership and the professionals. If the professionals play a more important role in the implementation of policy, they do so under party control. It is erroneous to suppose that the professionals in any field can be independent politically, as they are in the West. They have significant influence, but no independence. Unofficial evidence that military and economic professionals or technocrats play an independent role in the policy-making process can be discounted. If some professionals resign or express critical views in the Soviet press or in contact with foreigners, it can be assumed that they are doing so on the instructions of the party. The adjustments in economic policy were not a response to pressure from economists, technocrats, or scientists, as is sometimes supposed, but were planned and implemented on the initiative and under the control of the party apparatus acting in accordance with the requirements of its ideological long-range policy based on NEP experience. The adjustments were not intended for the enrichment of individuals or groups, but for the enrichment and stabilization of the regime and the fulfillment of communist policy. The technocrats and other professionals have not lost their ideological zeal; they remain leading party officials who have simply received new assignments from the party. If any of them depart noticeably from communist norms of life or degenerate into middle-class revisionists, they are removed from their positions and replaced. Their ideological zeal is maintained through nonviolent purges, systematic ideological education, and strict party control.

Soviet workers and collective farmers are not becoming middle-class, as some observers like to think. The improvement in the lot of rank-and-file workers is still modest. They have a long way to go yet until they reach a decent standard of living. Furthermore, in Soviet conditions the emergence of a middle class is impossible because the party has different objectives and, when necessary, intensifies the ideological struggle against middle-class philosophy and practice to exclude such developments from Soviet society.

The major party and bloc documents of lasting significance, such as the record of the CPSU's Twenty-first Party Congress, the Manifesto of November 1960, Khrushchev's report of January 6, 1961, and the 1961 program of the CPSU, confirmed the fundamental principles of the Soviet regime and its ideology, as well as the final ideological objectives of the Soviet Union and the bloc. These documents directed the communist movement to an intensification of the ideological struggle against alien ideologies domestically and externally; they called for more and better communist ideological education.

The evidence does not support the conclusion that, despite these documents, the Soviet regime has been evolving into a less ideological and more conventional national system. On the contrary, it points to a deliberate decision by the regime to pursue its acknowledged ideological goals the more effectively by distracting Western attention from them. This it has sought to do by misrepresenting tactical, pragmatic shifts in its practices as fundamental and spontaneous, thereby projecting a false image of a system evolving in a direction opposite to its declared purposes. In planning and executing this misrepresentation it has used the doctrine and historical experience of Lenin's NEP.

The Revival of De-Stalinization

Perhaps the most important technique used to project a moderate image of Soviet policy in the late 1950s and early 1960s was the revival of de-Stalinization and the related issue of "revisionism." This can be seen, for example, in the appointment of Pervukhin as Soviet ambassador to East Germany in 1958; the replacement of Serov by Shelepin as Chairman of the KGB; the renewed denunciation at the Twenty-second CPSU Congress in October 1961 of the antiparty group as Stalinists for their past role in the repressions; the revived criticism of Stalin himself for these repressions, and the removal of his body from the Lenin mausoleum; the special exploitation of the Molotov affair; and the display of differences in attitudes toward Stalin between the Soviet leaders on the one hand and the Albanians and Chinese leaders on the other.

Pervukhin had been a member of the opposition to Khrushchev in June 1957. He was therefore identifiable in the West, though wrongly, as a hard-liner. He was appointed as ambassador to East Germany at a time when the Berlin crisis of 1958 was being prepared by the bloc's strategists. His appointment can be regarded as the first calculated attempt to provide the West with a plausible explanation of an international crisis being provoked by the influence of the hard-liners within the Soviet system. In fact, the crisis was created within the framework of long-range policy and the major spokesman on it was none other than Khrushchev himself.

Serov's case was different in that he had long been a supporter of Khrushchev, but, as has already been explained, his notorious past involvement in repressions and his narrow-minded attitudes made him unsuitable for a leading role in the implementation of the new long-range policy. The background of Shelepin, a former leader of Soviet youth, provided a useful contrast, which in turn contributed to Khrushchev's and Shelepin's liberal images.

The renewed criticism at the Twenty-second Party Congress of the antiparty group of Molotov, Malenkov, Bulganin, Voroshilov, and others for their role in past repressions and of Pervukhin's "resistance to the policy of reform" were perhaps the most striking and persuasive instances of the calculated use of spurious de-Stalinization. The issues involved had been settled with the ending of the power struggle and the establishment of a homogeneous team of leaders committed to a long-range policy. The display of "differences" between moderates and Stalinists was linked with the decision of the Twenty-second Party Congress on November 1, 1961, to remove Stalin's body from the Lenin mausoleum and rebury it in the Kremlin wall. Another staged display was the conspicuous refusal by KGB bodyguards, in front of foreign diplomats and journalists, to allow Voroshilov to join other Soviet leaders on top of the Lenin mausoleum for the official parade in November 1961.

One purpose of these staged displays of de-Stalinization was to create a favorable climate for the conversion of former internal enemies of the regime into active allies in the promotion of its long-range policy. Khrushchev in person had meetings with several children of the rehabilitated officials. In the effort to involve all sectors of Soviet society with the new policy, rehabilitation was extended outside the political field. Khrushchev had a well-publicized meeting with a thief who had been released from prison. The KGB was given a special role in rehabilitating former prisoners and returning them to the party ranks. The KGB helped such people to obtain apartments and jobs through its contacts in factories and other institutions. Those who were considered suitable were recruited by the KGB for political assignments.

The explanation of the Molotov affair is more complicated and deserves detailed examination. According to official and semiofficial accounts, Molotov used his appointment as ambassador to Mongolia to establish contact with the Chinese leaders. When the Soviet leaders found out about this liaison, Molotov was recalled and appointed in 1960 to be the chief Soviet representative at the International Atomic Energy Agency (IAEA) in Austria. According to Satyukov, the chief editor of *Pravda,* and other communist leaders including Kuusinen, on the eve of the Twenty-second Party Congress in October 1961, Molotov circulated a letter to the members of the Central Committee of the CPSU criticizing the draft of the new party program as "revisionist, nonrevolutionary and pacifist."[16] Molotov allegedly knew that the Chinese leaders shared his views. Molotov was recalled from Vienna to Moscow at the time of the Twenty-second Congress, but he played no part in it. Shortly afterward he returned to Vienna, where he was said to be under house arrest. A few days later he was back in Moscow. On January 8, 1962, the Soviet foreign ministry announced that he would be returning to Vienna. Within days, this statement was withdrawn.

There are many curious anomalies in this story. Molotov was sent to Mongolia by Khrushchev to isolate him and to lower his prestige in the Soviet diplomatic service. He was kept under surveillance there by informers controlled by General Dobrynin, chief adviser to the Mongolian security service and former head of the KGB's surveillance directorate. Continuing unauthorized contact between Molotov and the Chinese would have been virtually impossible. If such contact had taken place and had been reported, it is most unlikely that Molotov would have been posted to the IAEA in Austria. Like Malenkov, Bulganin, and others, he would have been sent off to retirement in a small town in the Soviet Union. Moreover, misconduct of this kind on Molotov's part would have been made known as before to party members in a secret letter as further evidence of his antiparty behavior. This did not happen. There was no reference to Molotov, in the confidential party explanation of the decisions of the congress, containing such criticisms. Furthermore, the criticisms attributed to him look most unlikely. The draft program was based on the decisions of the Eighty-one–Party Congress of November 1960, which ratified the new, revolutionary bloc policy and strategy. For Molotov to have criticized the program on the grounds alleged would have made him a laughingstock within the communist movement.

Molotov did, however, criticize Khrushchev's policy on the eve of the Twenty-first Party Congress two years earlier, in January 1959, and this was stated in the confidential circular to party members in Moscow on the decisions of that congress signed by Vladimir Ustinov, who had become a Moscow party secretary. Molotov's criticisms were described as a mixture of dogmatism and quotations from Lenin. This episode was not mentioned by Satyukov and in fact has never been disclosed to the public by the Soviet leadership.

It is therefore reasonable to deduce that Molotov's actual criticisms in 1959 were modified and only disclosed at a time suited to meeting the needs of policy in 1961. It is also possible that use was made of Molotov in this way with his knowledge and consent; as a party member, he would have had no option but to agree.

The unusual publicity given to Molotov's movements between Moscow and Vienna may well have been intended to attract Western attention to the affair at a time of alleged Sino-Soviet differences. In this connection it should be noted that Satyukov, supported by Mikoyan and other speakers, accused Molotov of predicting political conflicts with imperialism that would mean war. Mikoyan accused Molotov of rejecting peaceful coexistence. Another party official said that Molotov was opposed to high-level diplomatic contacts between Soviet and Western leaders. Satyukov summed up with this emphatic statement: "We say to Molotov—'no!' The CPSU has done its best . . . to guarantee peace for the USSR . . . on the basis of the Leninist policy of peaceful co-existence." Clearly this exposure of Molotov's alleged warmongering could have been intended to support the moderate image of the Soviet leadership and the sincerity of their interest in peaceful coexistence and détente, in contrast with the "warmongering" of Molotov and the Chinese leadership.

Two further aspects of Satyukov's attack on Molotov should be mentioned. He accused Molotov, first, of trying to assume the role of an interpreter of Lenin, and second, of criticizing the new party program as pacifist and insufficiently revolutionary. Both these criticisms were to be used by the Soviets against the Chinese leaders, at first without naming them, but later explicitly. It can therefore be suggested that the Molotov affair was used to support the authenticity of the alleged differences between the Soviets and Chinese on the issue of peaceful coexistence.

The conspicuous revival of the de-Stalinization issue at the Twenty-second Congress and Khrushchev's public attack on the Albanians apparently angered the Chinese to such an extent that Chou En-lai, the leader of the Chinese delegation, withdrew from the congress. As has already been explained, the issues of revisionism and Stalin's distortions of communism had already been settled between the leaders of the communist bloc at the end of 1957. Because they had been settled, there was no foundation for differences between communist parties on them. The conclusion may therefore be drawn that the revival of the issues at the Twenty-second Congress was artificial and that the differences between the Soviet and the Albanian and Chinese parties on Soviet "revisionism" and Chinese and Albanian "Stalinism" were calculated and agreed within the terms and in the interests of the long-range policy.

It should be noted that one of the objects of the display of differences was to add credibility to the notion of Soviet "moderation" and to present Khrushchev as a revisionist. The conclusion that the display was staged provides another argument for regarding the notion of Soviet moderation as unfounded.

The Position of Soviet Scientists and Other Intellectuals

Extensive preparations were made by the Central Committee and the KGB in 1958–60 to use scientists, writers, and other intellectuals for political and disinformation purposes in accordance with the requirements of the new long-range policy.[17] This new approach to the intellectuals had its internal aspect; by seeking their collaboration in some form of political activity, the regime sought to forestall opposition from them. But it is with the external, strategic implications of the intellectuals' role in bringing influence to bear on Western public opinion and governments that the present chapter is concerned. Fadeyev's posthumous advice to the Central Committee to use intellectuals for exerting influence, not for spying on one another, had been well taken and was put into effect.

The use of scientists in particular as agents of influence and channels for disinformation involved certain changes in their status. The Central Committee apparatus and the Ministry of Foreign Affairs, as well as the KGB, developed closer relations with them. Many of them were given intelligence training individually and in schools. The regime, instead of keeping them in isolation at home as before, began to promote both their accessibility at home and their travels abroad with a view to widening and exploiting their contacts with Western scientists.

The complaints of Academicians Kapitsa and Sakharov and the biologist Zhores Medvedev about the difficulties encountered by Soviet scientists wishing to travel and meet their Western colleagues were incomplete, and distract attention from the real grounds for complaint by Western and Soviet scientists alike, which lie in the use of these contacts by the Central Committee and the KGB for collecting intelligence, conveying disinformation, and exercising political influence.[18] In fact, the majority of Soviet scientists lend themselves willingly to intelligence work against foreign scientists because of the opportunities it gives them to increase their knowledge and advance in their careers. Like Fadeyev, they find it in better taste to spy on foreign associates than on their Soviet friends and colleagues.

The use of Soviet scientists as agents of influence and channels for disinformation entailed changes in Soviet practice over the disclosure of secret information. Although the most significant areas, especially the process of policymaking and the technique of its implementation, remained as secret as ever, certain aspects of Soviet science and society were opened up; the obsession with secrecy appeared less total than in Stalin's days.

The greater accessibility of Soviet scientists made its own contribution to the impression of evolution in the Soviet system. More important, however, was the promotion through Soviet scientists of the notion of common interests between the Soviet Union and the West. The attendance of KGB agents, such as Academicians Topchiyev, Artobolevskiy, and Khvostov, at international scientific conferences and their role in promoting the idea of the Soviet Union's common interest with the United States in avoiding nuclear conflict deserve the closest scrutiny for the bearing they may have had on American willingness to engage in strategic arms control and disarmament negotiations with the Soviet Union and the voluntary decision by the United States in the early 1960s to surrender its nuclear superiority in the naive belief that if the Americans reduced the rate of development of their nuclear arsenal, the Soviets would do the same.

As in the case of the scientists, the KGB's use of its expanded assets among Soviet writers (especially among those with well-known names) had its internal and external aspects. Shelepin's plans to introduce false opposition on Dzerzhinskiy's lines found concrete expression in the controlled debates between the "conservative" and "liberal" writers, in which the main protagonists on both sides, Kochetov and Tvardovskiy, were collaborating with the Central Committee and the KGB. This debate, together with the general increase in East-West cultural contacts, made a useful contribution to the myth of "evolution."

Objectives of Strategic Disinformation on Soviet "Evolution" and "Moderation"

The main external objective of strategic disinformation in the early 1960s on the "evolution" and "moderation" of the Soviet regime and its "common interests" with the West was to create a suitable climate for activist, détente diplomacy by the Soviet Union and other communist states and to condition favorable, and erroneous, Western responses to communist initiatives. The five specific aims of communist diplomacy were to:

- Undermine Western unity.
- Induce the advanced industrial nations to contribute to the growth of the economic and military potential of the bloc by agreeing to increase East-West trade, grant long-term credits, and supply advanced technology.
- Distract Western attention from the growth in the military strength of the bloc and the Soviet Union in particular.
- Engage the West, especially the United States, in arms control and disarmament negotiations, with a view to swinging the military balance of power in favor of the communist bloc.
- Create favorable conditions for communist parties to form united fronts with socialists and trade unionists in the advanced countries and with nationalist movements in the developing countries.

At home the main objective of the adjustments to the regime and the exaggeration of their significance through disinformation was to create favorable conditions for the further construction of socialism and the eventual transition to communism by neutralizing internal opposition and securing a reduction in external pressure on the regime from the West.

Subsidiary objectives of the revival of de-Stalinization were to:

• Provide a foundation for open reconciliation and cooperation between the Soviet Union and Yugoslavia without revealing the full extent of Yugoslavia's membership in the bloc and commitment to its long-range policy.

• Provide grounds for Soviet-Albanian and Sino-Soviet "differences" in preparation for the pursuit of coordinated, dual foreign policies by the Soviet Union and China.

• Support further disinformation operations concerning disunity and disarray in the world communist movement ostensibly brought about by the decline in the influence of ideology and the resurgence of independent nationalist tendencies in communist parties inside and outside the bloc.

15

The Third Disinformation Operation: The Soviet-Albanian "Dispute" and "Split"

The Overt Picture of Soviet-Albanian Relations

Esoteric evidence indicated to Western observers of the communist scene that disagreements between the Soviet and Chinese and Albanian party leaders had developed by 1959 into a serious cleavage on policy issues. In 1960 the dispute came out into the open: "The first international communist confrontation where the Sino-Soviet dispute and Albanian support for China publicly emerged was at the June 5–9, 1960, meeting in Peking of the General Council of the World Federation of Trade Unions."[1]

According to evidence published in the West some time after the event, there were furious polemics, mainly between the Soviets on the one side and the Chinese and Albanians on the other, at the closed sessions of the Romanian party Congress in June 1960 and the Eighty-one–Party Congress in Moscow in November 1960. The dispute acquired the status of a split when Khrushchev denounced the Albanian leaders publicly at the Twenty-second CPSU Congress in October 1961 for their criticisms of the Soviet party program, for their dogmatic Stalinism, and for their rejection of peaceful coexistence. Chou En-lai, the leader of the Chinese delegation, withdrew from the congress as an apparent gesture of support for the Albanian position. Hoxha, while expressing through the Albanian party press his party's continuing solidarity with the CPSU, responded to the Soviet attack with bitter criticism of "Khrushchev and his group" for their public attack on the Albanian party and for their revisionism. He said that they had betrayed

Leninism; that they were restoring capitalism in the Soviet Union; that they were conducting an opportunistic policy of concessions to, and cooperation with, imperialism; and that they were conspiring with the leading revisionist, Tito. A break in Soviet-Albanian diplomatic relations followed in December 1961, and from 1962 onward Albania refused to attend Warsaw Pact and Comecon meetings. Chinese support for and alignment with the Albanian position against the Soviets can be traced back at least to 1959 and possibly even earlier in the esoteric evidence.

Inside Information and Its Interpretation

The author's information contradicts this generally accepted version of the development of Soviet-Albanian relations between 1959 and 1962. Briefly, this information was to the effect that relations between all the communist states, including Albania and China, had been normalized by the end of 1957; that the Soviets had successfully mediated in the secret reconciliation of the Yugoslav and Albanian leaders in 1957–58; and that, from late 1959, the KGB's disinformation department was actively collaborating with the Central Committee's Department of Active Operations and with the Yugoslav and Albanian security services in joint disinformation operations.

The effect of Shelepin's instructions was to make Albania a party to a triangular disinformation operation with the Soviet Union and Yugoslavia, an ingenious method of turning to the advantage of the bloc's long-range policy the earlier genuine disputes and difficulties in relations between the three countries. The strategic considerations the bloc leaders would have had in mind when planning this operation would probably have been both internal and external.

Internally both the Yugoslav and Albanian regimes would have faced major political problems if the radical step of immediately and publicly normalizing their relations had been taken by those same leaders under whom the hostilities between the parties had originated and developed. In the case of Yugoslavia it was predictable that public reconciliation would have carried with it a grave risk of factionalism within the Yugoslav party because of the strength of feeling against Albania that had built up in the Stalin period. For the Albanian leaders the problems would have been even more acute. They were the same leaders who had been responsible for executing their own Albanian colleagues, including the former minister Koci Xexe, for their pre-Yugoslav sympathies. Open reconciliation with Yugoslavia might well have released pressure for the posthumous rehabilitation of Xexe and his friends and for an admission by the leadership that they had committed crimes against loyal and innocent fellow-countrymen on Stalin's orders. In other words, there might have been a popular and inner-party reaction in Albania similar to that in Hungary which accompanied the rehabilitation of the former minister, Laszlo Rajk, in 1956. Furthermore, for strategic reasons, Yugoslavia's true role as an active participant in the formulation and execution of long-range bloc policy had to be kept a closely guarded secret known only to the inner circle of Albanian party leaders. An open Yugoslav-Albanian reconciliation could not have been fully explained to the Albanian rank and file and might well have led to a revival of genuine revisionism in the party. A disinformation operation to which both the Yugoslav and Albanian leaders were parties offered substantial advantages by providing scope for intimate secret collaboration between the party leaders in an operation of importance to the whole bloc while at the same time providing a means of delaying open acknowledgment of their secret reconciliation to the party rank and file and to the populations at large.

In the Soviet Union Khrushchev had been enlightened enough to see that the best way to solve the problem of genuine dissent from and opposition to the regime among intellectuals and victims of Stalin's persecution was to involve them actively in one or another aspect of the new long-range policy. The same principle could be applied to healing splits in the bloc and preventing their recurrence. For this reason Yugoslavia was allowed to contribute significantly to the formulation of the long-range policy and was given an important role to play in its execution. The inclusion of the Albanian leaders was the logical next step. They too could be actively involved in, and committed to, the new policy. A disinformation operation embracing a calculated, spurious dispute with the Soviet Union gave them the opportunity to project themselves to their own people and to enhance their own and their party's prestige as an independent national force robust enough to stand up to Khrushchev's bullying interference in their affairs. In addition, they were given a chance to play a strategic role in a disinformation operation to misrepresent relations between members of the bloc, and especially those between the Soviet Union and China, as degenerating into a state of rivalry and hostility, the object of the misrepresentation being to widen the openings for the bloc countries to develop their political strategies vis-à-vis the noncommunist world.

Given Albania's past alignment with Stalin in the genuine Tito-Stalin split and Western knowledge of that alignment, it would have seemed logical and convincing to make Albania a "Stalinist" country in partnership with the Chinese in a calculated and controlled dispute with the Soviets. It also served as a useful preliminary move toward a more open and official Soviet-Yugoslav alignment from 1961 onward, in apparent opposition to the Sino-Albanian partnership. The realignment of Yugoslavia with the Soviet Union after 1961 would be less likely to prejudice her independent image and her political and economic relationships with the advanced and developing countries if the Soviets themselves were to be seen by those countries as revisionists, in comparison with the militant Chinese dogmatists.

The fact that Albania was the smallest and most isolated of the communist countries made her a particularly suitable choice to be the first full member of the bloc to split away from the Soviet Union after 1958. The Soviet-Albanian "split" should in fact be regarded as a pilot project for the much more significant Sino-Soviet split, which must already have been in the preliminary stages of development. It gave the bloc strategists an opportunity to test the validity of their disinformation concepts and techniques and to examine the internal and external consequences of a spurious minor split before committing themselves finally to a spurious major split between the Soviet Union and China. If the West were to see through the Soviet-Albanian split, the minimum of political and strategic damage to the bloc would have been done. If, on the other hand, the West were to be successfully taken in by it, if there were no uncontrollable repercussions of the split elsewhere in the bloc, if it proved possible to arrange for the political and economic survival of the Albanian regime, and if the West concluded from the Soviet-Albanian split that the Eighty-one–Party

Congress in November 1960 was indeed a watershed in the disintegration of the communist monolith rather than the reverse, then there would be every justification for moving ahead with the Sino-Soviet split, to the credibility of which the Soviet-Albanian split would have made its contribution. The Sino-Soviet split would help to build up the moderate image of both the Soviet Union and Yugoslavia in the 1960s, to the advantage of their strategic political rapprochement with the advanced and developing countries. The last, but not the least significant, of the reasons for bringing the Soviet-Albanian dispute out into the open as a split would have been to provide the West with confirmation of the reliability of information on intrabloc relations derived from esoteric evidence, from retrospective leakages, from articles in the communist press, and from "secret" Western intelligence sources.

Anomalies in the "Dispute" and "Split"

Detailed examination of the origins and development of the Soviet-Albanian dispute and split, using the new methodology, brings to light a number of additional points casting doubt on the authenticity of the differences between them and confirming that the dispute was manufactured in the interests of long-range policy.

According to the esoteric evidence, the Soviet-Albanian dispute began in the very period during which the long-range policy was being formulated. Hoxha himself, and other Albanian leaders, participated in the process. In January–February 1959, Hoxha led the Albanian delegation to the Twenty-first CPSU Congress, which discussed the roughly simultaneous transition to communism in all the countries of the bloc. This entailed an attempt to level up the economics of the more backward communist countries, including Albania, at the expense of the more advanced countries, including the Soviet Union.

In May 1959 an official Chinese delegation, which included Chang Wen-tien, the deputy minister of foreign affairs, formerly a Comintern official and Chinese ambassador in Moscow, and Peng Te-huai, the minister of defense, visited Tirana. Their visit coincided with the visit of a Soviet delegation, headed by Khrushchev, that included Marshal Malinovskiy, the Soviet minister of defense.

It is generally supposed in the West either that meetings were held in an unsuccessful attempt to iron out the differences between the three countries, or that the opportunity was taken by Peng and Chang to conspire with Khrushchev against Mao. The reception Hoxha gave the delegations, the course of the negotiations, and the official communiqué issued after the meeting provided clear evidence that there were no differences between them and that their relations were extremely close. Bearing in mind also that these high-level meetings in Tirana took place at the same time as the joint Soviet-Yugoslav disinformation operation was being launched, it is more likely that the leaders discussed the development of the Albanian disinformation operation than that they discussed differences between them for which there were no solid grounds.

In the same month of May 1959, Comecon met in Tirana. The fact that the Soviet delegation was headed by Kosygin, then chief of the Soviet Planning Commission, indicates the importance of the session and gives weight to the supposition that it dealt with long-range economic planning. Despite the esoteric evidence of a Soviet-Albanian dispute, the Albanians continued to participate in both Comecon and Warsaw Pact organization meetings in 1960 and 1961 up to and including the plenary session of Comecon in Moscow in September 1961, the month before Khrushchev's first public attack on them.

Most significant of all, Hoxha was among the signatories of the Manifesto of the Eighty-one–Party Congress in November 1960. In a special resolution approving the participation of Albania in the congress, the Albanian party stated that the CPSU was "the most experienced and competent body of the international communist movement," and added that "the hopes of the imperialists, headed by the USA, to split the communist camp are doomed to failure." Hoxha's official report to the Fourth Congress of the Albanian party, published on February 14, 1961, attacked the US and NATO and was replete with praise for the Soviet Union, China, and the decisions of the Eighty-one–Party Congress; it acknowledged the "general collaboration" between Albania and the Soviet Union.

The esoteric evidence of a Soviet-Albanian dispute between 1959 and 1961, relying mainly on a detailed comparison of the Soviet, Albanian, and Chinese press during these years, was developed in the West. From this comparison different approaches by the different parties to certain issues could indeed be deduced. At the same time, it should be remembered that none but a privileged few in either the Soviet Union or Albania were able to obtain and read the press of the other country and make the sort of comparison which is the stock-in-trade of Western analysts. Given the existence of a disinformation program, the clear implication is that much of the esoteric evidence was specifically directed at Western analysts and was not intended for domestic consumption.

Nevertheless, Khrushchev's public attack on the Albanians at the Twenty-second CPSU Congress, in October 1961, seemed to most observers to confirm that the esoteric evidence had all along reflected a genuine dispute. It is interesting to note, however, that press coverage of the exchanges between Khrushchev and Hoxha varied widely in the bloc. The Soviet press did not name China or give any indications of Chinese support for Albania. Some East European party leaders openly critized Chinese support for Hoxha's position. The Chinese press refrained from editorial comment on the Kremlin but printed the Albanian attacks on Khrushchev. Press coverage of the dispute was incomplete throughout the bloc; some documents and speeches were not published, even by the Soviets or the Albanians.

In contrast, official information on Albanian attendance between 1958 and 1961 at Comecon and Warsaw Pact meetings, at the Twenty-first CPSU Congress, and at the Eighty-one–Party Congress was published at the time in the press of every communist country. Commitments by communist parties to the decisions of multilateral meetings are taken extremely seriously. The point applies as much to the Albanian commitment to the Manifesto of the Eighty-one–Party Congress as to any other. The day-to-day official evidence of continuing Albanian cooperation with the rest of the bloc in the years 1958 to 1961 should be considered as reflecting far more accurately the true state of affairs than the esoteric, unofficial, incomplete, and retrospective evidence from communist sources pointing to a dispute.

Comparison with the Tito-Stalin "Split"

In the case of the genuine Tito-Stalin split in 1948 and the continuing Soviet-Yugoslav differences in 1956 and early 1957, con-

If all the evidence given above is weighed objectively, it leads to the inescapable conclusion that, in this instance, Hoxha was telling the truth and that the Soviet-Albanian dispute and split were and are no more than the products of bloc disinformation.

Objectives of the Disinformation Operation

The objectives of this disinformation were to:

• Avoid the adverse internal consequences of an open reconciliation between the Albanian and Yugoslav leaders.

• Enhance the prestige of the Albanian leaders and their parties in the eyes of their own people as an independent, national force.

• Support the projection of Yugoslav revisionism as a Trojan horse within the communist bloc.

• Suggest that, after 1961, Khrushchev himself was under revisionist influence, and thus to build up his image as a moderate in contrast to the militant Chinese and Albanian Stalinists.

• Confirm that efforts to unite the communist bloc and movement at the Eighty-one–Party Congress in November 1960 had failed and that the bloc and movement were disintegrating over the unresolved issues of Stalinism, revisionism, national communism, and the pursuit of conflicting national interests.

• Test reactions inside and outside the bloc to a minor split before the further development of the nascent Sino-Soviet dispute.

16

The Fourth Disinformation Operation: The Sino-Soviet "Split"

CPSU-CPC Collaboration, 1944-49

Historically relations between the Soviet and Chinese Communist parties have been the subject of much confusion. To a significant extent, this was due to a wide-ranging and successful wartime and postwar disinformation effort designed to mislead the West on the nature of Chinese Communism and to conceal the steady buildup of Soviet diplomatic, intelligence, and military help to the CPC in the final years of the civil war in China. The similarities between Soviet and Chinese comments on the nature of Chinese Communism are strongly suggestive of a coordinated disinformation operation. Western journalists who visited Yenan during the war were told that the Chinese Communists were not traditional communists, but agrarian reformers who admired the West and had more in common with Christian socialism than Soviet Communism.[1] Similar remarks were made by Soviet leaders. For example, in June 1944 Stalin told Averell Harriman, then US ambassador in Moscow, that the Chinese Communists were not real, but "margarine" communists.[2] In August 1944 Molotov, then Soviet foreign minister, told Patrick Hurley and Donald Nelson, President Roosevelt's two personal representatives to Chungking, that many of the so-called Chinese Communists were simply desperately poor people who would forget this political inclination when their economic condition improved.[3] In a conversation with Harry Hopkins on May 26, 1945, Stalin made some contemptuous remarks about Mao and discounted the CPC as a serious factor in the situation;

he said he thought the Chinese Communist leaders were less capable than Chiang Kai-shek and would be unable to unite their country.[4] In the course of negotiations with Wang Shih-chieh, the Chinese foreign minister, in the summer of 1945, Stalin said that Chinese Communism did not amount to much. Assurances that Chinese Communists were not real communists were given by the Soviet leaders to Secretary of State Byrnes at Potsdam in July 1945 and to a group of American congressmen visiting Moscow in September 1945.[5]

Another indication of an agreed Sino-Soviet disinformation theme was Mao's inaccurate statement, after the dissolution of the Comintern, that China had received no assistance or advice from it since its Seventh Congress in 1935.[6]

Stalin's apparent ignorance of the situation in China was of course feigned. There was close collaboration throughout between the CPSU and the CPC; Soviet intelligence coverage of the Chinese Nationalist government and its policies was at least as good as its coverage of American and British policy.

While serving in the section of the Committee of Information that was responsible for counterintelligence work in Soviet organizations in China, Korea, and Mongolia, the author learned of a Soviet decision, taken after secret negotiations with a high-level CPC delegation to Moscow in the autumn of 1946, to step up Soviet military aid to the CPC; the Soviet general staff, military intelligence, and the Ministry of Transport were all instructed to give priority to the Chinese Communist army. In addition to the Japanese arms captured by the Soviets in Manchuria, large quantities of Soviet arms and ammunition, including American weapons received by the Soviet Union from the United States during the war, were secretly shipped by train to China between 1946 and 1949. In a lecture to students of the High Intelligence School in Balashikha in 1949, General Roshchin, the head of Soviet intelligence and Soviet ambassador in China, claimed that Soviet assistance had enabled the Chinese Communist army to swing the military balance in its favor and to launch its final and successful offensive against the Nationalist army in 1947–48.

Further assistance was sent to China through Sinkiang. Soviet control over Sinkiang had been lost in 1943 when the Governor, Sheng Shih-tsai, a Soviet agent, broke with the Soviet Union. In order to restore the situation, a revolt in the Ili region of Sinkiang was organized by Fitin from Moscow, Pitovranov from Kazakhstan, Ogol'tsov and Byzov from Uzbekistan, and Langfang and Ivanov from Outer Mongolia, all of them generals of the Soviet security and intelligence service. The revolt was successful and an independent East Turkestan Republic was proclaimed under the leadership of Saifudin, a Soviet agent. Thereafter Sinkiang was used by the Soviets as a supply route to the CPC until they had taken over complete control of the province. The camel track to Ningsia from Outer Mongolia was also used as a supply route.

A major Soviet intelligence effort went into obtaining military information on the Kuomintang army for the benefit of the CPC and into the subversion of the Nationalist administration and police. When the Soviet embassy followed the Nationalist government to Canton, it did so not, as is often supposed, to demonstrate Soviet allegiance to the Treaty of Friendship with the Nationalist government, but, according to Soviet intelligence telegrams between China and Moscow, to facilitate contact with Soviet agents in the Nationalist administration. It is worth noting that Soviet recognition of the new Chinese Communist government and the establishment of diplomatic relations with it were conducted through the head of Soviet intelligence and consul-general in Peking, Colonel Tikhvinskiy.[7] It was the same Tikhvinskiy who, in answer to Nationalist charges that the Soviets were helping the CPC, issued an official denial on behalf of the Soviet government, carried in an Associated Press dispatch datelined Peking, December 30, 1947, to the effect that "my government recognizes only one government in China—the Nationalist government—and is not supplying the communists with anything. This is a 100 percent denial." The denial was, of course, 100 percent false. It was but one aspect of a major joint Sino-Soviet intelligence and disinformation operation designed to help the CPC to power while concealing from the West that Soviet aid was being given. After his defeat Chiang Kai-shek frankly and correctly admitted that the CPC "stole intelligence from our government and at the same time closed all avenues of intelligence to the government. That was to be expected. But they went one step further by furnishing the western nations with false intelligence about the Chinese government in order to create wrong impressions of our country."[8] If the United States administration had not fallen victim to communist disinformation and had realized at the time the scope and scale of Soviet aid to Chinese Communism, more decisive American aid might have been given to the Chinese Nationalists. Even if it had failed to save China from communism, at least the reaction of American public opinion to the failure of United States policy might have been more balanced than it was in the McCarthy era.

Sino-Soviet Friction, 1950–57, and Its Removal

The changed character of Sino-Soviet relations after the CPC came to power found expression in the thirty-year Treaty of Friendship signed during Mao's state visit to Moscow in February 1950.[9] Soviet support for the "liberation" of Tibet and Taiwan was promised. Mao was told by Stalin that all Soviet intelligence work in China had ceased and that the names of former Soviet agents in China would be disclosed to the Chinese intelligence service.

Despite the success of Mao's visit, there were still unsolved problems and maladjustments in relations between the two countries. It would be quite wrong to regard China at that time as a Soviet satellite. The extent of Soviet infiltration and control over the Chinese party and government was small, compared with that over the East European satellites; it was, broadly speaking, limited to Sinkiang and Manchuria. Nevertheless, the relationship was not one of equals, and at times the Soviets continued to interfere in Chinese internal affairs, especially in Manchuria, the Liaotung peninsula, Sinkiang, and the border areas. Many Soviet agents, especially in Sinkiang, were disclosed to the CPC, among them Saifudin, who had been one of the leaders of the Soviet-organized revolt in East Turkestan in 1945. He was a member of the first government of Communist China and remained in power in Sinkiang for many years after the development of the Sino-Soviet split.

Despite Stalin's assurances, some Soviet agents in China, such as the long-standing Soviet agent in Shanghai, a Chinese citizen named Kazakov, were not declared to the Chinese. Nor were the Soviets entirely frank about properties they owned secretly in China in connection with their intelligence operations; when the Chinese caught the Soviets out, as they sometimes did, there was friction between them. Another source of tension in 1950 arose from dealings with Russian émigré groups in China. Either the Soviets highhandedly carried out arrests using local Chinese security officials without informing Peking, or the Chinese refused to carry out arrests themselves on the scale demanded by the Soviets.

A serious disagreement arose when the Soviet advisers, concerned over the unusual Nationalist background of Li K'u-nun, the head of Chinese political intelligence, demanded his dismissal. The Chinese flatly refused to comply.

Since there was no formal machinery in existence for dealing with Sino-Soviet disagreements, they showed a tendency to fester.

The most serious disagreement of all arose over the Korean War, on which Stalin embarked without having taken Mao fully into his confidence. When the war started to go badly from the communist point of view as a result of the unexpectedly prompt and effective UN intervention, the Soviets suggested that the Chinese should send troops to the aid of the North Koreans. Not surprisingly, the Chinese at first refused. Only after severe Soviet pressure had been brought to bear, culminating in a secret and personal letter from Stalin to Mao, did the Chinese agree to send "volunteers" into Korea.

The uneasiness in Sino-Soviet relations, though carefully concealed from the West, remained in being as long as Stalin was alive. As soon as he was dead, the Soviets took steps to improve matters. Settlement of the Korean War was a priority objective of Stalin's immediate successors and was first discussed with Chou En-lai when he attended Stalin's funeral. Another thorny problem, which was quickly solved, centered on Kao Kang, the unofficial "Governor of Manchuria," with whom the Soviets had maintained secret contact even during the Korean War. After Beriya's arrest, the Chinese leadership was told in confidence that Kao Kang had been one of Beriya's agents. In February 1954 the Chinese government dismissed Kao Kang "for separatist tendencies and plotting to establish an independent Kingdom of Kao Kang in Manchuria." Kao Kang was imprisoned without trial and hanged himself.

In October 1954 Khrushchev and Bulganin visited China for discussions that led to the voluntary surrender to China of all Soviet extraterritorial rights. The age-old problems of Manchuria and Sinkiang having been solved, the Sino-Soviet boundaries were then finally settled. Soviet economic and military aid to China was stepped up. On January 17, 1955, the Soviet government announced that it would assist China in setting up nuclear research establishments. Later the USSR undertook to construct a nuclear reactor in China that would be operational by March 1958.

In the intelligence field the Soviets climbed down over Li K'u-nun. Li retained his position, and the Soviet adviser who could not get on with him was replaced. The earlier decision to disclose to the Chinese all former Soviet agents in China was put fully into effect without exceptions. Among the Soviet agents thus declared to the Chinese was Soong Ch'ing-ling, the widow of Dr. Sun Yat-sen. This lady was admitted to the CPC and made an honorary President of the Chinese People's Republic shortly before her death in May 1981. She was given an impressive state funeral attended by the CPC leadership. Another declared agent was Kuo Mo-jo, the well-known poet and scientist, President of the Chinese Academy of Sciences and an active member of the World Peace Council. Probably few, if any, of the names of Soviet agents came as a surprise to the Chinese leaders, but the Soviets' evident frankness finally removed this potential source of friction. Thereafter, at Chinese request, the Soviet intelligence service sent to China a number of its leading experts on such subjects as scientific intelligence, the penetration of Western embassies in Moscow, the physical protection of nuclear and rocket installations, the production of audio-surveillance equipment, and the conduct of sabotage and assassination operations.

During the turbulent events in Eastern Europe in 1956, there were signs of a divergence between Soviet and Chinese views on Stalin. While the Chinese agreed that Stalin had made mistakes, particularly on Yugoslavia, they seemed inclined to a more balanced view of his place in history than that given in Khrushchev's report to the Twentieth Party Congress. Toward the end of October 1956, a high-level Chinese delegation paid a secret visit to Moscow, criticized the Soviet leaders for their handling of satellite affairs in general, and urged immediate Soviet military intervention in Hungary. One of the consequences of the Chinese visit was a public undertaking by the Soviet government to review the status and functions of Soviet advisers in all the countries of the bloc.

Mao and Teng Hsiao-p'ing led the Chinese delegation to the

conference of bloc leaders in Moscow in November 1957. A joint assessment of Stalin was unanimously agreed upon. Mao said that Stalin's principal mistakes were his repression of party members and a tendency towards "great-nation chauvinism." The latter had found expression in Stalin's policy in Manchuria and in the behavior of some of the Soviet advisers in China. The only criticism Mao had of the Soviet decision in 1956 to admit Stalin's mistakes was that the Soviets had failed to consult other communist parties properly in advance. Khrushchev accepted the criticism as justified. The Soviet leaders undertook not to repeat Stalin's mistakes; in particular, they agreed that repressive measures would not be taken against former members of the opposition. They were to be treated as Lenin would have treated them. This explains why Malenkov, Molotov, and Bulganin were not shot.

The status and functions of Soviet advisers, including intelligence and security advisers, was settled to Chinese satisfaction. The advisers' roles were limited to consultation and coordination. Interference in the internal administrative affairs of the Chinese services was excluded. The Soviets genuinely treated the Chinese services as equals in status, if not in experience. The Soviets had at last dealt frankly with them in declaring to them all their agents of Chinese nationality. The question of Soviet bases in China for "illegal" intelligence operations into noncommunist countries was solved. New bases for "illegals," together with the necessary support facilities, were provided to the Soviet intelligence services by the Chinese in several of their ports, including Shanghai. There were other instances of practical cooperation. At Chinese request the Soviets built a special factory to manufacture highly sensitive eavesdropping devices. Soviet advisers with experience of political intelligence work against the United States and Britain were provided. These included Colonel Smirnov, a former Soviet intelligence resident in New York, and Colonel Voronin, a former head of the British Department of Soviet Counterintelligence. At the end of 1957 the Chinese asked for an adviser on political assassinations and sabotage. The Soviets responded by sending their best man, General Vertiporokh, a former head of their own assassinations and sabotage department and former intelligence resident in Iran. Vertiporokh worked as a KGB adviser in China until his death in January 1960.

Regular personal consultation between the leaders of the Soviet and Chinese services was established. Shortly after taking over as chairman of the KGB in December 1958, Shelepin paid a visit to China, from which he returned much impressed with Chinese skill in dealing with opposition to the regime from young people, intellectuals, religious leaders, and national minorities, especially during the elimination of the "thousand weeds" in the summer of 1956. Shelepin recommended that the KGB study and learn from Chinese experience in these matters. General Sakharovskiy, the head of Soviet intelligence, paid a visit to China at about the same time as Shelepin. At the first conference of the heads of bloc security and intelligence services in Moscow in mid-1959, the Chinese were represented by the minister of public security, Lo Jui-tsin. The conference decided to put security and intelligence liaison within the bloc onto a multilateral footing, and established a joint security and intelligence coordinating center for the purpose.

Early in 1960 General Pitovranov, one of the most experienced of all KGB generals and a former deputy minister of state security, who was known to and respected by the Chinese for his wartime work against the Chinese Nationalists in Sinkiang, was appointed chief KGB adviser to China.

In 1959–60 there was a regular exchange of secret political and military intelligence between the Soviets and the Chinese. This covered in particular Western views and predictions on Sino-Soviet relations. The KGB passed on to the Chinese confidential and top secret intelligence from its sources in NATO and Western Europe. The Polish intelligence service obtained and passed on to the KGB a set of papers recording the discussions at a meeting in 1958 or 1959 of the Bilderberg group of distinguished Western statesmen and commentators concerning the possibilities of a Sino-Soviet split, the likely consequences of such a split for the communist bloc, and the ways in which it might be exploited for the benefit of the West. These were among the documents taken to China by General Sakharovskiy in person. Among other documents sent to the Chinese by the KGB were secret US State Department assessments of Sino-Soviet differences over communes and the Chinese reaction to Khrushchev's visit to the United States in 1959. A copy of a secret report delivered to NATO in 1959 by its former secretary-general, Spaak, on Sino-Soviet differences and their implications for NATO was also given to the Chinese by the KGB.

It is of course a deliberately propagated myth that the Soviet and Chinese leaders are ignorant of the situation in the outside world and incapable of understanding it even if provided by their intelligence services with texts of official Western documents. Intelligence material is in fact carefully studied, absorbed, and used in the planning of communist political strategy.

In addition to secret intelligence material, it is likely that the communist strategists would have studied books like *The Prospects for Communist China*, by Walt Rostow, which openly speculated as early as 1954 on the possibilities of the Sino-Soviet alliance breaking up.[10]

It is therefore probably no coincidence that Mikoyan, in his speech to the Twenty-first CPSU Congress in February 1959, said that Western hopes and expectations of a split were doomed,[11] a line echoed in the basic communist documents of the period— the Eighty-one–Party Manifesto of November 1960[12] and Khrushchev's strategic report of January 6, 1961.[13] The theme of unbreakable Sino-Soviet friendship was also to be found in speeches and interviews by Chou En-lai[14] and the Chinese foreign minister, Chen Yi,[15] despite the accumulating evidence of a dispute.

More than a year after the reported withdrawal of Soviet economic and technical specialists from China, in July–August 1960, at least some of the KGB advisers were still in place there. A former colleague and friend of the author who had been sent to China to advise on the physical protection of Chinese nuclear installations was still in China in November 1961, the month after Khrushchev denounced the Albanians at the Twenty-second CPSU Congress and Chou En-lai walked out in apparent protest. By way of contrast, the Soviet military, intelligence, and counterintelligence advisers were the first to leave Yugoslavia when the genuine Tito-Stalin split occurred in 1948. The intimacy of the intelligence and security connection between the Soviets and Chinese up to the end of 1961 was incompatible with a serious deterioration in their overall relations before that date.

The discrepancies between the evidence of a split and the open and inside information on continuing good relations must be viewed against the past history of intimate collaboration between the Soviet and Chinese parties in disinformation operations in 1944–49, which effectively concealed the extent of Soviet aid to the Chinese party in the final years of the civil war and successfully misrepresented Chinese Communism as a relatively harmless agrarian reform movement.

Against this background, the fact that Sino-Soviet relations in 1959–61 closely followed the pattern of Soviet-Yugoslav and Soviet-Albanian relations in the same period—a period in which the grounds for tension and splits between the members of the bloc had been removed and all members, including the Chinese, contributed to the formulation of the new policy—suggests that the Sino-Soviet dispute was, like the others, the product of bloc disinformation. The fact that China continued to send observers to meetings of Comecon and the Political Consultative Committee of the Warsaw Pact up to the end of 1961 supports this conclusion.

The Historical Evidence of Sino-Soviet Differences

Since the Sino-Soviet "split" became common knowledge, it has become fashionable, with some encouragement from Soviet and Chinese sources, to seek an explanation for it in traditional rivalries and disputes between the two countries dating back as far as the sixteenth century. It would be no more farfetched to try to explain the deterioration in Franco-American relations in the 1960s by reference to the French colonization of Louisiana. Given the nature of communist ideology, the acquisition of power by communist parties, whether in the Soviet Union, China, or elsewhere, entails in every case a radical break with a country's political traditions.[16]

It would be more relevant to seek the origin of the current split in differences between the Soviet and Chinese Communist parties since 1917. Such differences have undoubtedly existed. There were differences between the Soviet and Chinese Communists on the tactics to be used toward workers and peasants in the 1920s. Stalin was opposed to Mao's leadership of the CPC in the period 1932–35; but these were transient differences that did not prevent close cooperation between the parties in the period 1935–49. The alleged differences between them on united front tactics with the Kuomintang and in their attitudes to the Chinese Nationalist government were false differences deliberately projected by joint disinformation designed to conceal Soviet support for the

CPC, to contain the scale of American aid to the Nationalist government, and to enable the Soviets and Chinese to subvert that government the more effectively through the development of a duality in their policies toward it. Soviet military support for the CPC may well have tipped the balance in favor of the communist victory in China. After the communist victory, differences and sources of friction once more appeared between the Soviet and Chinese parties. The insensitivity of Stalin's handling of Sino-Soviet and other intrabloc relations, if it had remained uncorrected, might have led to a genuine Sino-Soviet split analogous to the split with Tito. But in fact the necessary corrective measures were taken in time. By the end of 1957 there were no outstanding differences left between the members of the bloc. It is noteworthy that the Chinese, in justifying their attitude in their polemics with the Soviet Union, did not base themselves on the real difficulties they encountered with the Soviets in the period 1949–53, but on alleged differences with Khrushchev after 1957 over issues that had in fact been settled by that date. Khrushchev's contribution to the elimination of past mistakes in Sino-Soviet relations was recognized by Mao himself in 1957.[17]

The Form of Sino-Soviet Differences

Roughly speaking, three periods can be distinguished in the development of the split: the first from 1957 to mid-1963, the second from 1963 to 1969, and the third from 1969 onward. For most of the first period official communist sources aimed at communist audiences gave no recognition to the existence of Sino-Soviet differences; on the contrary, the record of Chinese participation in the world conferences of communist parties held in Moscow in 1957 and 1960 and in the Twenty-first CPSU Congress in February 1959, and also Chinese attendance as observers at meetings of the Warsaw Pact and Comecon, all indicated continuing and even increasingly close collaboration at a high level between the Soviet and Chinese governments and parties. The same conclusion could be drawn from the exchange of delegations. In 1959 alone no less than 125 delegations visited China from the Soviet Union and Eastern Europe; over 100 Chinese delegations paid return visits.

The evidence of disagreements was to be found in unofficial communist sources: different lines on various issues in the Soviet and Chinese press, remarks by communist leaders to Western journalists and statesmen, and retrospective accounts of polemics at closed meetings of, for example, the Romanian party congress in June 1960 and the Eighty-one–Party Congress in November 1960. This unofficial evidence, much of it retrospective, pointed to a deterioration in party and diplomatic cooperation in 1959, to a termination of Soviet military and nuclear collaboration in that year, and to the cessation of Soviet economic aid to China in 1960.

From late 1961 onward indications of Sino-Soviet differences began to appear in the official communist sources. There was symbolic Chinese support for Stalin and the Albanian position when Khrushchev denounced them both at the Twenty-second CPSU Congress. Friction and competition between the Soviet and Chinese delegations at the meetings of international front organizations became conspicuous. The flow of information from official communist sources on the subject of Sino-Soviet collaboration dwindled.

During the second period of the split, the existence of differences was fully acknowledged. An ostensible attempt to settle them was made when a high-level Chinese party delegation visited Moscow for talks in July 1963. The talks apparently failed and public polemics between the parties began. Hitherto secret party letters revealing differences between the parties were disclosed in the Soviet and Chinese press. Some Chinese diplomats were expelled from the Soviet Union for distributing leaflets. China withdrew from the international front organizations. Some communist parties in the noncommunist world openly took up pro-Soviet or pro-Chinese positions; in some cases pro-Chinese splinter groups broke away from pro-Moscow parties.

In the third period, beginning roughly in 1969, the apparent deterioration in Sino-Soviet relations was expressed in actions as well as words. Troop levels were built up on the Sino-Soviet frontier. Border incidents took place between the two countries against a background of mutual accusations of "hegemonism." China began publicly and systematically to take up an opposite position to the Soviet Union on NATO, the Warsaw Pact, the EEC, détente, disarmament, European security, and many Third World issues, including Soviet intervention in Afghanistan. After the communist victory in Vietnam, the Vietnamese aligned themselves more closely with the Soviet Union. The Soviets and Chinese backed opposite sides in the conflict between rival communist factions in Kampuchea. In 1979 the Chinese "punished" the Vietnamese with a brief invasion of their territory. But, despite all the apparent violence of Chinese hostility to the Soviet Union and her close Vietnamese ally, by 1980 the split had still not led to a breach in diplomatic relations with the Soviet Union, as did the Soviet-Albanian dispute in 1961. Nor was the Sino-Soviet treaty of friendship, mutual cooperation, and assistance abrogated. Up to 1980 each side remained committed to support the other in an emergency.

From this brief outline survey of the split, it will be seen that for most of the first period there was a total conflict between the evidence from unofficial communist sources and the evidence from official communist sources supported by the author's inside information. In the second period there was a closer coincidence in the evidence from official and unofficial communist sources, although there was still a conflict between the official sources in the first period and the evidence of differences leaked retrospectively in the second period. The new methodology, taking into account the launching of a disinformation program in 1958–60 and the historical precedents on which it was based, gives greater credence to the evidence from official communist sources and calls into question the authenticity of the secret party letters and polemics published in the second period of the split.

Several inconsistencies can be pointed out. First, the official evidence of close Sino-Soviet relations was carried in the press of both countries. The Manifesto of the Eighty-one–Party Congress, in November 1960, specifically underlined that Western hopes of a split in the bloc were doomed. By signing it the Chinese specifically endorsed the tactic of peaceful coexistence as one of the options in a common long-range policy. The Chinese president, Liu Shao-chi, who led the Chinese delegation to the congress, subsequently toured the Soviet Union in the company of the Soviet president, a curious thing to do if there was a serious rift between them. Khrushchev's report of January 6, 1961, widely distributed in the Soviet Union, emphasized the closeness of Sino-Soviet relations.

Second, although the Soviet and Chinese press and radio must be regarded as official communist sources, they should also be regarded as subordinate to official sources, such as the Manifesto of the Eighty-one–Party Congress, or the decisions and declarations of Soviet and Chinese party congresses. These decisions and declarations should not be regarded as being controverted by statements in the press and radio of individual parties, especially in the light of all the evidence of a decision in 1958–60 to support the new long-range policy with a program of disinformation operations.

Third, neither the Russian nor the Chinese public was informed of the existence of a dispute before the end of 1961, and even then, up to mid-1963, only indirectly and by implication. Neither the Russian nor the Chinese public is in a position to study the press of the other country and to note the divergences between them on foreign policy or doctrinal issues. It is doubtful whether the reduction in the coverage of each other's affairs in their national presses, even if noticed, would have been accorded much significance. Furthermore, as the author can personally testify, the Soviet party was not briefed on the dispute up to the end of 1961. In contrast, as already recorded above, confidential guidance was given to the party from the beginning in the case of the genuine Tito-Stalin split in 1948.

Fourth, although it would be impossible to assess how much of the polemical material was made available and how widely it was distributed within the Soviet Union and China, it can at least be said that a proportion of the material available in and directed at the West would not have reached the Russian or Chinese public. For example, much of Novosti's material on Sino-Soviet relations was distributed in English and in magazine supplements, which may or may not have been distributed in the Soviet Union. According to the Soviet press, the Chinese distributed polemical material to communists in the Soviet Union in English, which would have been pointless if it was really aimed at a Soviet, rather than a Western, audience.[18] This, along with the esoteric evidence, supports the conclusion that the evidence of the dispute was deliberately made available to the West either directly to Western statesmen and commentators or indirectly in such a manner that Western analysts would be likely to pick it up. The question arises: Why would the Soviet and Chinese leaders deliberately draw Western attention to the existence of a dispute that they were at pains to conceal from their own parties and populations unless by so doing they could serve their mutual interests in promoting their recently agreed upon long-range policy for the bloc?

Fifth, the polemics between the Soviets and Chinese were not continuous, but intermittent. They could well have been coordinated, rather than spontaneous. In the Soviet press they began in July 1963, continued until the beginning of October, and were then dropped until April 1964. They were revived in that month with the publication of material on the meeting of the CPSU Central Committee in February 1964, allegedly because the Chinese had continued to publish polemical material despite appeals from Khrushchev and the Soviet leadership to desist.[19]

The new methodology further suggests that the Sino-Soviet hostilities of the third period, however convincing they may appear, should be reexamined to see whether they could have been staged, and if so, with what strategic object. At this stage, four general points may be made. First, frontier incidents in a remote corner of the world, like on the Ussuri river, though spectacular and convincing evidence of hostility, can very easily be staged—particularly if, as will be shown later, means of coordinating action between the two "opponents" are readily available. Second, the hostilities, like the verbal polemics, have been intermittent as well as pointless. Third, despite all the apparent violence of Chinese hostility to the Soviet Union and her close Vietnamese ally, by 1980 the split had still not led to a breach in diplomatic relations with the Soviet Union, as did the Soviet-Albanian dispute in 1961. Nor was the Sino-Soviet treaty of friendship, mutual cooperation, and assistance abrogated. Up to 1980 each side remained committed to support the other in an emergency. Fourth, the hostilities can be correlated in timing with important communist initiatives or with the opening of East-West negotiations—for example, SALT—or with the visits of Western statesmen to the Soviet Union and China. Like the verbal polemics, therefore, minor hostilities cannot be accepted as evidence of a genuine dispute, and in the light of the new methodology should be examined for the possible relevance they may have to communist political and strategic aims in furtherance of a common long-range policy. In the same light must be seen the adoption of opposing positions on international issues by the Soviet Union and China. The question must be asked whether the ultimate goal of a worldwide communist victory cannot be achieved more expeditiously by the two leading communist powers adopting dual foreign policies in apparent opposition to one another than by pursuing a single policy in open solidarity.

The Content of Sino-Soviet Differences

Differences between the Soviets and Chinese have allegedly arisen since 1958 in the ideological, economic, military, political, and diplomatic fields. To many observers it appeared that the differences stemmed from a clash of national interests between the two leading communist powers. The various types of difference must be examined in turn to see what substance, if any, there is to each of them.

Ideological Differences

Historically, as already noted, one of the first indications of the Sino-Soviet dispute was an apparent difference over the subject of the introduction of communes in China, which Khrushchev mentioned to the late Senator Humphrey in December 1958. According to some Western interpretations of communist theory, communes are the highest form of organization of socialist agriculture, and their introduction ought therefore to be preceded by industrialization and by a lower form of socialist agricultural organization, such as collective farming. The attempt to introduce communes in Soviet Russia in 1918–20 failed because the time was not yet ripe. By introducing communes before collectivization, the Chinese, according to this line of argument, were sinning against orthodoxy in two respects: They were not abiding by communist theory, and they were implicitly rejecting the Soviet model in their agricultural development. By so doing, it was argued, they had incurred Soviet displeasure. Furthermore, comparisons were drawn between the "leftist" policy of the Chinese in setting up communes and the "rightist" policy of the Soviets in permitting collective farms in 1958 to purchase state-owned farm machinery.

This reasoning was outdated. The 1957 conference of bloc communist parties reached agreements, endorsed by the Eighty-one–

Party Congress in November 1960, on the basic laws of communist development, which legitimized the Chinese course of action. As far as agriculture was concerned, the basic law was that it should be collective. The exact type of organization, whether commune or collective farm, was not specified; it was left to be determined by the specific national conditions in each country. In China the specific national conditions and problems confronting the CPC were how to break up the strong family ties in the vast mass of the Chinese peasantry; how to overcome the lack of agricultural machinery and to use mass manual labour to best advantage; and how to appropriate the land, which belonged not (as in the Soviet Union) to the state, but to the peasants. The commune provided the best solution to all three problems. In addition the Chinese leaders would undoubtedly have taken into consideration, in agreement with their Soviet colleagues, the high cost in human and material terms of Stalin's method of collectivization, the obloquy it had brought on his regime, and the impossibility of contemplating a repetition of that experience with the even greater numbers of Chinese peasants. The Chinese choice of communes was no more unorthodox than the continued existence of private agriculture in Yugoslavia, Poland, and Hungary, which was accepted by the bloc leaders as a temporary phenomenon until the specific conditions in those countries could be changed.

Scant Western attention was paid to the speech of the then Soviet ambassador to China, Yudin, in which he told the Twenty-first CPSU Congress in February 1959 that "the Chinese peasantry, in alliance with the working class, is advancing confidently and resolutely toward socialism under the leadership of the Communist party and has achieved enormous successes. The Communist Party of China—a glorious detachment of the international Communist movement—is wisely leading the Chinese people along the path of socialism, despite tremendous difficulties and constant threats and attempts at interference on the part of American imperialism."

Chinese allegations of a restoration of capitalism in the Soviet Union were unfounded. Economic reform in the Soviet Union was aimed at increasing the efficiency of the economy and improving party control over it. The impression of a return toward capitalism was deliberately fostered by disinformation for tactical and strategic purposes. The Chinese would have been aware of this. Similarly, the phrase "dictatorship of the proletariat" was dropped by the CPSU, not as the result of any dilution of the party's monopoly of control, but to widen the party's political base and to suggest an "evolution" of the regime. The notion that the Soviet regime was less ideological than the Chinese was unfounded. It is interesting to observe how the Chinese, following the Soviet example, have themselves introduced economic incentives and other elements of capitalism.

Economic Differences

The disparity in the levels of economic development between China and the Soviet Union—or, in wider terms, between the Asiatic and European communist zones—presented the communist strategists with a dilemma. In 1960 the Chinese, saddled with a backward industry, lack of capital, a population explosion, and a low level of trade with the advanced noncommunist world, could hardly expect to carry out ambitious industrialization and military programs without help from the European zone; and help from the European zone could only make a significant impact on the rate of Chinese industrial development if the European zone severely curtailed its own development programs and abandoned its aim of outstripping the level of production in the United States.

The difference in economic levels between the Soviet Union and China was a potential source of tension within the communist bloc, but it is worth noting that the problem existed at the time of the communist victory in China and did not lead to a Sino-Soviet split in the decade thereafter.

As late as October 1958, the year in which the formulation of long-range bloc policy got under way, a leading Soviet theoretician, T. A. Stepanyan, took the view that the European socialist states, led by the Soviet Union, and the Asiatic socialist states comprised "particular economic zones" and that the former, being more advanced, would be the first to "enter communism."[20] However, at the Twenty-first CPSU Congress in January–February 1959, Khrushchev in a speech that must be regarded as authoritative, overrode this view and announced that all socialist countries would achieve communism "more or less simultaneously on the basis of the planned and proportionate development" of the economy of the bloc. A month later he went on to speak of the future economic integration of a communist bloc without internal frontiers.[21] Khrushchev's points were underlined by Yudin, the Soviet ambassador to China, who referred to the socialist camp as a "single economic system" and said that the economic plans of the socialist countries would be more and more coordinated and that "the more highly developed countries will help the less developed countries in order to march in a united front towards communism at an increasingly faster pace."[22] Khrushchev referred to the "unity of the socialist camp" as one of the advantages enjoyed by the Soviet Union in its struggle to overtake the United States in economic power. Chou En-lai, who led the Chinese delegation to the congress, and Soviet Deputy Premier Mikoyan both spoke of the unbreakable friendship between the Soviet Union and China.

The period around the Twenty-first CPSU Congress was one in which there was a shift of emphasis toward long-range economic planning in Comecon. These discussions took place in the presence of Chinese observers. It seems that, at the time, a decision was taken to step up Soviet industrial aid to China. As a result of Khrushchev's visit to Peking in August 1958, the Soviet Union agreed to build forty-seven additional industrial projects in China. Chou En-lai's visit to Moscow for the Twenty-first CPSU Congress resulted in another Soviet agreement to build seventy-eight additional projects in China between 1959 and 1967 at a total cost of $1.25 billion.[23]

In July 1960 the picture of closer Sino-Soviet relations changed abruptly. The conventional view is that the Soviet Union terminated its economic aid to China, withdrew its technical and economic advisers, and took steps to curtail Sino-Soviet trade drastically. Support for this view came from reports on the departure of Soviet technicians from China (later confirmed in Sino-Soviet polemics in 1963–64), from the widely different treatment given the subject of bloc assistance to China in the Soviet and Chinese press, and from statistics on Sino-Soviet trade. There were also reports on the economic damage done to China by the cessation of Soviet economic aid, which came on top of the introduction of communes and the failure of the Great Leap Forward. Letters from the communes to the outside world and Chinese grain purchases in Australia and Canada underlined the point.

The alleged withdrawal of Soviet economic and technical specialists in July 1960 was not accompanied by, or even followed by—
at least up to the end of 1961—a withdrawal of Soviet intelligence
and security advisers.

On the evidence available, the most likely interpretation of what
occurred in mid-1960 is that a switch took place in Chinese thinking
on economic development in favor of self-reliance and concentration
on small-scale projects. As a consequence of the completion of
some projects and the cancellation of others, a proportion of the
Soviet technical experts was withdrawn from China in July 1960.
If some were replaced by Czechoslovaks and other East Europeans,
this would have been done to reinforce the impression of a split.
Soviet and East European aid continued to be given after 1960,
but on a narrower front and with a concentration on the scientific
and technical fields. It can further be surmised that these changes
took place by agreement between the Soviets and the Chinese
and that the extent and the consequences of the contraction in
Soviet economic aid were misrepresented by each side in accordance
with their common disinformation program. Apart from the wider
strategic purpose of supporting the authenticity of the split, the
publicity on the withdrawal of Soviet technicians could have been
intended, in line with historical precedent, to hide continuing Sino-
Soviet collaboration in sensitive key areas—in this case, the development of Chinese ballistic missiles and nuclear weapons.

Military Differences

It is often thought that the real nub of the Sino-Soviet split
was a decision by the Soviets in 1959 to withhold assistance to
China over nuclear weapons. According to a secret Chinese party
letter, which was made public by the Chinese on August 15, 1963,
the secret Sino-Soviet agreement on the sharing of military nuclear
secrets and the provision to the Chinese of the necessary help in
developing their own nuclear potential, which was concluded on
October 15, 1957, was broken by the Soviets on June 20, 1959.[24]

The letter is tantamount to an admission that collaboration in
the military nuclear field, up to June 1959, was close. It would

have been unconvincing to deny it, given the earlier publicity about Sino-Soviet nuclear collaboration in general.[25] But there are several anomalies in the statement that this secret agreement was repudiated by the Soviets in June 1959. The most important is that, in spite of the alleged decision and the fury it is supposed to have generated in China, the Chinese continued to be represented at meetings of the Warsaw Pact in 1960. It is difficult to believe that a Soviet decision with such profound implications would not have been reflected immediately and across the board in the field of Sino-Soviet military relations. In fact, not only did the Chinese continue to send observers to Warsaw Pact meetings for more than a year afterward, but several years of virtually open Sino-Soviet military collaboration followed over the supply of military assistance to North Vietnam. The references to Chinese military students returning from the Soviet Union in 1964–65 indicate that at least some Soviet military training continued to be given to the Chinese armed forces after the split had developed.

It is also more than surprising that if, as alleged, there was an abrupt cancellation of Soviet nuclear help to China, the Soviets should have continued to provide, and the Chinese to accept, advice on the physical protection of their nuclear installations. As already recorded, a KGB officer known to the author was still in China in November 1961, having been sent there as one of a group of Soviet advisers on nuclear security requested by the Chinese.

Sino-Soviet cooperation in the peaceful use of nuclear energy continued after June 1959. There are references in the Chinese press to a prominent Chinese scientist, Professor Wang Kan-chang, serving as vice-director of the Joint Nuclear Research Institute at Dubna, near Moscow, in April 1960.[26]

Many observers at the time believed that within the Chinese military leadership there were differences on strategy, which were associated with the Sino-Soviet split and which led to the dismissal of the Chinese defense minister, Peng Te-huai, allegedly for conspiring with the Soviet leaders against Mao. Part of this conspiracy supposedly took place during the visit of Khrushchev and Peng to Albania in May 1959, but this visit is far more easily explicable in terms of preparation for the spurious Soviet-Albanian split and the need to coordinate the replacement of Soviet by Chinese military, political, and economic support for Albania. The suggestion that Peng and other Chinese leaders were disgraced for acting as Soviet agents is inconsistent with the declaration by the Soviets to the Chinese in 1954–55 of all their intelligence assets in China and with the close Sino-Soviet intelligence relationship that persisted at least up to the end of 1961. In any case, as Edgar Snow pointed out, Peng neither led a conspiracy against Mao nor suffered arrest in 1959.[27] He was still a member of the Chinese Politburo in 1962.

Interestingly enough, there does seem to have been a genuine discussion, in China, between two schools of military thought between 1955 and 1958.[28] Settlement of the argument occurred in the same period in which many other problems were resolved in the Soviet Union and the bloc, such as the elimination of the anti-Khrushchev opposition in July 1957; the ousting of Marshal Zhukov in the following October; and the first conference of bloc parties in November, at which relations between them were normalized and the decision was taken to formulate a new long-range policy for the bloc. In his speech to the conference, Mao argued in favor of using the whole potential of the bloc, especially its nuclear missile potential, to swing the balance of power in favor of the communist world. By their own account the Chinese agreement with the Soviets on collaboration over nuclear arms dated from the end of 1957. It is tempting to suggest, therefore, that in line with the basic technique of reviving dead issues and using them for disinformation purposes the argument in the Chinese armed forces was artificially revived, together with allegations of a Khrushchev-Peng conspiracy, to support joint Sino-Soviet-Albanian disinformation on their mutual relations. Furthermore, in view of his long services to Sino-Soviet strategy, Peng would have been an obvious candidate to continue to serve in a secret Sino-Soviet or bloc policy coordinating center. His "disgrace" could have been designed to cover up a secret assignment of this kind.

In parallel with the alleged differences in the Chinese army, there were allegedly differences in the Soviet army that led to, among other changes, the dismissal of Marshal Sokolovskiy as chief of general staff in April 1960 and the dismissal in the same year of Marshal Konev as commander in chief of the Warsaw Pact forces. Sokolovskiy was replaced by Zakharov and Konev by Grechko.

If there had in fact been genuine differences in the Soviet general staff, the author would have expected to pick up some reflection of them from two former GRU officers, Bykov and Yermolayev, who served with him in the NATO section of the KGB's Information Department and kept in close touch with the general staff. If Sokolovskiy was really in disgrace in 1960, it is curious that he was chosen by the Soviet Ministry of Defense to edit a basic book on Soviet military strategy two years later.[29]

Differences in National Interest

Many factors have been cited as contributory causes of the split. The list includes the racial and cultural differences between the Russian and Chinese peoples; the Chinese population explosion; the decline in the influence of communist ideology; the reassertion of purely national interests; and hegemonism, or the desire of the Soviet and Chinese parties to dominate others.

No one could deny the existence of racial differences. The Chinese in particular have used the racial issue for political purposes.[30] But these differences did not prevent the closest possible alliance between the Soviets and Chinese between 1957 and 1959, nor were they responsible for the Sino-Soviet friction between 1949 and 1955. If they are now thought to have been important in the causation of the split, it is largely because of the evidence provided by the Soviets and Chinese themselves in the course of their polemics in the mid-1960s.

For the same reason attempts were made to reinterpret Khrushchev's virgin lands campaign of 1954–56 as inspired by Soviet concern over China's population explosion and designed to preempt any future Chinese expansion into Siberia. As Professor W. A. Douglas Jackson rightly pointed out, the motives for the campaign were domestic.[31]

Cultural differences undeniably exist, but it is interesting that cultural relations between China and the Soviet Union and Eastern Europe should have survived the Sino-Soviet split. The Chinese Friendship Association still exists in the Soviet Union and the Sino-Soviet Friendship Association still exists in China.[32] Cultural visits were exchanged at least until November 1966.[33]

National rivalry is seen by the West as the force behind the apparent struggle between the Soviets and Chinese for influence in the developing countries in Asia, Africa, and Latin America. The assertion of Chinese national interests is seen in Chinese claims on Taiwanese, Indian, and Outer Mongolian territory and in demands for revision of "unequal treaties," dating from the nineteenth century, which awarded certain Chinese territories to Russia. Soviet national self-assertiveness was seen in Soviet attempts to incite revolt in Sinkiang and among tribal groups straddling the frontier with China and in Soviet complaints about Chinese border violations, which, according to Soviet official sources, amounted to five thousand in 1962 alone. The clash of Soviet and Chinese national interests was seen in short-lived and sporadic outbreaks of border hostilities, especially on the Ussuri River, which were intensified in 1969–70. Border clashes were sometimes accompanied by Soviet and Chinese student demonstrations outside each other's embassies and in ostentatious walkouts by Soviet and Chinese representatives from international gatherings.

The manner in which the traditional problems over Manchuria and Sinkiang were solved after Stalin's death has been described, as has the normalization of relations between the members of the bloc, including the Soviet Union and China, in 1957. Khrushchev's contribution to this achievement was recognized by Mao in 1957.[34] Against this background it would have made no sense for the Soviet Union to meddle in Sinkiang. Chinese confidence that they would not attempt to do so is demonstrated by the continuance in high office in Sinkiang throughout the 1960s of a known former Soviet agent, Saifudin. Far from trying to "liberate" areas of one another's territory, the two powers cooperated in a war of national liberation in a third country, Vietnam.

Before the outbreak of the Sino-Soviet split, the border area had been converted, in Professor Jackson's words, from a zone of tension into a zone of cooperation and stabilization.[35] The split was not therefore the culmination of a continuing series of border problems; the frontier incidents cannot be seen as a cause of the dispute. In this connection attention should be drawn to articles on the border problem published in 1964–65 by Academician Khvostov, whose connection with the KGB was known to the author. Equally, anything said or written on the subject by Tikhvinskiy, the former Soviet intelligence resident in Peking and Britain, should be regarded as reflecting the communist disinformation line.

Western belief that nationalism is the driving force behind Soviet or Chinese policy fails to take into account the nature of communist theory and the distinction that must be made between the motives of a communist regime and the sentiments of the people which it controls.

In communist theory nationalism is a secondary problem. The fundamental political force is the class struggle, which is international in character. Once the "victory of the international working class" has been achieved, national differences and national sentiment will disappear. Meanwhile, the "class enemy" is not nationalism, but capitalism and its adjunct, imperialism. It is in large part because of communism's claims to an international, rather than a national, form of loyalty that it has managed to retain its appeal and its hold over its acolytes. The main point, however, is that the disinformation about the Sino-Soviet split provides a new, more effective way for fighting nationalism by investing the communist parties with a nationalist image in the eyes of their people.

Differences in Political and Diplomatic Strategy and Tactics

Marked differences have existed since 1960 in what the Soviets and Chinese have said on subjects such as détente, peaceful coexistence, and the inevitability of war. In the 1960s the Soviet press defended peaceful coexistence, the Chinese press attacked it. Under the banner of peaceful coexistence, the Soviet leaders established personal contact with Western statesmen, sought an expansion of East-West trade, and adopted a generally moderate and businesslike approach to negotiations with the West. The Chinese denounced the Soviet approach as a betrayal of Leninism and a capitulation to the forces of imperialism and capitalism. Eschewing closer contacts with the West, the Chinese advocated implacable, militant revolutionary policies toward it. Khrushchev's visit to the United States in 1959, Soviet détente with Western Europe, and the Nuclear Test Ban Treaty of 1963 all came in for their share of Chinese communist abuse. The Chinese and Soviets took diametrically opposing lines on the Sino-Indian conflict in 1959, the Cuban crisis of 1962, and other matters. In relation to the developing world, the Soviets emphasized the importance of diplomacy and economic aid; the Chinese advocated wars of national liberation.

Was there any real substance to this war of words? The thesis that war is not inevitable was formulated by Khrushchev at the Twentieth CPSU Congress in February 1956. At the time the Chinese frequently expressed their agreement with it.[36] It was only in 1960 that divergent views on the topic began to appear in the Soviet and Chinese press, to be followed by open polemics, beginning in 1963. Broadly speaking, the Soviets maintained that, although the causes of conflict between the two different social systems had not disappeared, the strength of the communist bloc was such that nuclear war, which would mean the destruction of both sides, was no longer inevitable; communists should seek the victory of their cause through peaceful coexistence and peaceful competition. The Chinese argued that the communist aim was world revolution. Communists should not fear world war because it would mean the final victory of communism, even if at the sacrifice of many million lives.

The unreality of the dispute is clear when the record of the two sides is examined. The Soviets were far from moderate in their approach to the Berlin problem from 1958 onward, in their disruption of the summit conference in 1960, in their supply of weapons to Indonesia and their resumption of nuclear testing in 1961, in their provocation of the Cuban crisis in 1962, and in their Middle Eastern policy in 1967. The Chinese were no more aggressive than this in practice. They were not even consistent in their maintenance of an aggressive posture, sometimes maintaining that they did not want world war and would fight only if attacked.[37] Indeed, without Soviet backing the Chinese were in no position in the 1960s to wage an aggressive war.

On the question of support for wars of national liberation in the developing countries, which the Chinese accused the Soviets of betraying, there was nothing to choose between the two sides in practice. Khrushchev's verbal support for this form of war was given practical expression in the foundation of Lumumba University and in support for guerrilla movements in Vietnam, the Middle East, and Africa.[38]

There was, in fact, duality both in Soviet and Chinese policies and in the interaction between them. Both countries, in different areas or at different times, used provocation and negotiation, aggressiveness and moderation. In the 1960s Chinese militancy provided a helpful backdrop to Soviet détente diplomacy; there was an apparent common interest between the Soviets and the West in confronting the "Yellow Peril" from the East. In the 1970s the roles were more or less reversed. Soviet aggressiveness in Africa, her menacing stance in Europe, her domestic neo-Stalinism, and her intervention in Afghanistan all helped to create a favorable climate for the Chinese to extend their relations with both advanced and developing countries as a potential ally against Soviet expansionism.

Differences over Tactics for Nonbloc Communist Parties

Sino-Soviet differences spilled over into questions of the tactics of the international communist movement. Despite the mutual accusations of hegemonism and despite the alignment of extremist communist groups with China and the more moderate communist parties with the Soviet Union, rivalry between the Soviets and Chinese was not carried as far as it might have been in practice. There was no serious Chinese attempt to disrupt the international communist movement. China withdrew from the international front organizations in the 1960s, but did not set up rival organizations under Chinese auspices.

The accusations of hegemonism were false. Neither the CPSU nor the CPC seeks to impose its diktat on the communist movement. Neither needs to do so. At the same time, the rejection of hegemonism in principle is not incompatible with recognition of the undeniable fact that the CPSU has the longest and widest experience in power of any communist party and is the best placed to play a leading role. It was the Chinese themselves who insisted on this point in 1957.

The Technique of the "Split"

It will be objected that, even if there is no substance to the differences that are alleged to divide the Soviets from the Chinese, it is inconceivable that they could have sustained a fictitious split for over twenty years without being found out and without doing serious damage to their own cause. If the Soviet Union and China were democracies, that would be a correct judgment; but in communist states, controls over the communications media, the discipline imposed on party members, and the influence of the intelligence and security services are combined to provide unparalleled facilities for practicing disinformation. It should not be forgotten that the closeness of CPSU-CPC relations between 1935 and 1949 was successfully concealed from the outside world. Communist victory in China was achieved more swiftly through the duality of Soviet and CPC policies toward the Nationalist government and the United States than it would have been through an outward show of solidarity between them.

The technique of the Sino-Soviet split was not developed overnight. Historical precedents drawn on in developing disinformation on false splits and secret coordination, such as Lenin's Far Eastern Republic, have already been cited in this and earlier chapters. The genuine Tito-Stalin split was also obviously of prime importance, and it is interesting to note how the published texts of the alleged secret party letters between the Soviet and Chinese parties recall the genuine party letters on the Tito-Stalin split and how the spurious allegations that Peng and Lin Piao, both Chinese ministers of defense, were Soviet agents echo the well-founded accusation that the Yugoslav chief of staff in 1948 was working for the Soviet intelligence service.

There is also a certain parallel between the Mao-Khrushchev polemics in the 1960s on the subject of peaceful coexistence and the Lenin-Trotskiy argument over the issue of war and peace after the revolution of 1917. This earlier controversy could well have been used as a model for the later polemics.

The Eighty-one–Party Congress Manifesto of November 1960, to which the CPC acknowledged its commitment, spoke of the need for "unity of will and action" of all communist parties, not for unity of words.[39] It also spoke of "solving cardinal problems of modern times *in a new way*" (author's italics). What it meant by this in practice was that centralized, Stalinist control over the movement having proved a failure, the aim of a worldwide federation of communist states would be pursued in the transitional stage by an agreed variety of different strategies and tactics to be followed by different parties, some of which would appear to be at loggerheads with one another. Traces of Chinese communist thinking about splits can be found in the Chinese press. The analogy is drawn between growth in nature, which is based on division and germination, and the development and strengthening of the communist movement through "favorable splits." The creation of two or more communist parties in one country was advocated openly.[40] One Chinese paper used the formula: "Unity, then split; new unity on a new basis—such is the dialectic of development of the communist movement." *Problems of Peace and Socialism* referred disparagingly to Ai Sy-tsi, a Chinese scholar well versed in dialectics, who developed the idea of the contradiction between the left and right legs of a person, which are mutually interdependent and move in turn when walking.[41] All of this suggests that the communist leaders had learned how to forge a new form of unity among themselves through practical collaboration in the exploitation of fictitious schismatic differences on ideology and tactics.

It would be erroneous to attempt to separate the Sino-Soviet split from the four disinformation operations already described and those that will be described in succeeding chapters. The disinformation program is an integrated whole. The Chinese have played an important part in every operation. As Chapter 22 will argue, the Sino-Soviet split is the underlying factor in all the different strategies developed in support of long-range policy.

Mutual criticism between two parties should be seen as a new way of supporting the credibility of the disinformation each is trying to spread about itself. For example, Chinese criticism of Soviet and Yugoslav revisionism, the decay of ideology, and the restoration of capitalism in the Soviet Union helped to build up the illusion that Khrushchev was truly moderate and that Tito was truly independent. The Soviet and Chinese lines on different issues should be seen as the left and right legs of a man, or better still, as the two blades of a pair of scissors, each enhancing the other's capacity to cut.

The communist strategists proceeded cautiously and pragmatically with the development of the Sino-Soviet split. The second period of open polemics was not introduced until 1963, which gave time for thorough study of the consequences of the Soviet-Yugoslav dispute of 1958–60, the Soviet-Albanian split, and the first period of the Sino-Soviet split. Even now, precedents exist for the further extension of the Sino-Soviet split that have not yet been exploited. The Soviet-Albanian split was carried to the point of a breach in diplomatic relations with the Soviet Union. The Sino-Vietnamese split was carried to the point of a major Chinese incursion into Vietnamese territory in 1979. Either of these could presage similar developments in Sino-Soviet relations.

Strategic Objectives of the "Split"

The strategic exploitation of the split will be described in Chapter 22. Its overall objective can be defined briefly as the exploitation of the scissors strategy to hasten the achievement of long-range communist goals. Duality in Sino-Soviet polemics is used to mask the nature of the goals and the degree of coordination in the communist effort to achieve them. The feigned disunity of the communist world promotes real disunity in the noncommunist world. Each blade of the communist pair of scissors makes the other more effective. The militancy of one nation helps the activist détente diplomacy of the other. Mutual charges of hegemonism help to create the right climate for one or the other to negotiate agreements with the West. False alignments, formed with third parties by each side against the other, make it easier to achieve specific communist goals, such as the acquisition of advanced technology or the negotiation of arms control agreements or communist penetration of the Arab and African states. In Western eyes the military, political, economic, and ideological threat from world communism appears diminished. In consequence Western determination to resist the advance of communism is undermined. At a later stage the communist strategists are left with the option of terminating the split and adopting the strategy of "one clenched fist."

17

The Fifth Disinformation Operation: Romanian "Independence"

BELIEF IN THE EXISTENCE OF SERIOUS DIFFERENCES between the Soviet and Romanian leaders and, consequently, in the independence of Romania is based on evidence that varies from the sensational to the insignificant.[1]

Allegedly the differences between the Soviet and Romanian parties had their roots in wartime, or even prewar, history. The difficulties were intensified in the period 1962–64, when Gheorghiu-Dej was still alive and the leading figure in the Romanian communist party and government. At that time the differences were more or less concealed from view, but from 1964 onward they came out into the open and became generally known to the West. Gheorghiu-Dej and Khrushchev were believed to be at odds. There were stories that Khrushchev had tried to unseat Gheorghiu-Dej and suggestions that Gheorghiu-Dej had played some part in securing the removal of Khrushchev in 1964. Their disagreements were said to have been based on differences of view between the Soviets and Romanians on long-term economic planning and the Soviet approach to Comecon. It was suggested that Romania's insistence on proceeding with its own speedy industrialization program had prevailed with difficulty over Soviet opposition.

Gheorghiu-Dej died in March 1965. Nicolae Ceausescu, who had for long been Gheorghiu-Dej's right-hand man, took over as first secretary of the party. Before this event, public but muted manifestations of Soviet-Romanian differences and Romanian independence were detected in the West. Examples were: Romania's refusal, in contrast with other East European communist states, to align itself with the Soviet position in the Sino-Soviet conflict; efforts by the Romanian leaders to play down the extent of Soviet influence in their country by measures such as the removal of Russian street names; publication by the Central Committee of the Romanian Communist party in April 1964 of a statement on its independence; Romanian efforts, apparently launched without the prior agreement of the bloc, to increase trade ties with Western countries, particularly France and the US, through the exchange of trade delegations; and, at a later stage, Romanian diplomatic conduct in such matters as the maintenance of diplomatic relations with Israel after 1967 and Ceausescu's involvement in the arrangements for Sadat's visit to Jerusalem in 1977, which contrasted with Soviet behavior and indicated the independence of Romanian foreign policy from that of the Soviet Union and the rest of the bloc. This impression of independence was reinforced by occasional alleged refusals on the part of the Romanians to cooperate with the Soviet Union and the bloc in joint political, economic, or military projects within Comecon and the Warsaw Pact; and the adoption of an independent position by the Romanians on Warsaw Pact intervention in Czechoslovakia in 1968.

Critical examination of these manifestations of independence against the background of the normalization of intrabloc relations in 1957 and the adoption of a long-range bloc policy and strategic disinformation program in 1958–60 shows that, as with the splits already examined, there is no substance in the alleged differences between Romania and other communist countries. The differences can be explained as the product of a bloc disinformation operation.

Special Relations between the Romanians and Soviets

As already argued, the normalization of intrabloc relations removed the grounds for splits between the members of the bloc in general. But, in the Romanian case, there were special reasons, according to inside information available to the author, why a split was an impossibility under Gheorghiu-Dej and why it is still an impossibility under the present leader, Ceausescu.

Gheorghiu-Dej was an agent of Soviet intelligence. At the time of the liberation of Romania from the fascists by Soviet troops, he was directed by the head of Soviet intelligence in Romania, Colonel Fedichkin. The Romanian Communist party was then small in relation to the social democratic party. Under Fedichkin's guidance, Gheorghiu-Dej worked on the elimination of Romanian social democratic leaders who were unreliable from a Soviet point of view and who threatened to acquire influential positions in the new Romanian government. The shedding of the blood of noncommunist Romanian politicians and the ousting of the Romanian king, actions undertaken jointly by Gheorghiu-Dej and the Soviet government, created unbreakable ties between them.

The head of Soviet intelligence in the late 1950s and 1960s, General Sakharovskiy, was chief adviser to the Romanian security service from 1949 to 1953. He was in official contact with Gheorghiu-Dej. Through Gheorghiu-Dej and his staff, Sakharovskiy carried out the Romanian purges of 1951–52 and, in particular, the arrest of Anna Pauker and other leading communists, who were accused of being Yugoslav and Zionist agents. Relations between the Soviets and Gheorghiu-Dej and other Romanian leaders were sealed with blood. If there had been any really spontaneous or uncoordinated attempt by Gheorghiu-Dej to break with the Soviet Union, the Soviet regime would have had enough evidence, including personal correspondence, to destroy him and his associates morally and politically both inside and outside their country. This fact must be kept in mind when assessing the genuineness of the later differences between the Soviets and the Romanians.

If a Soviet-Romanian split was impossible under Gheorghiu-Dej, there were even fewer grounds for expecting one under Ceausescu, who had been his right-hand man and who replaced him after his death in March 1965. As has already been explained, Stalinist "colonial" practices toward Romania and other satellites had been abandoned by the Soviet Union under Khrushchev in 1957. Soviet-Romanian party relations were normalized on a Leninist basis of equality. From 1958 to 1960 Romanian leaders played an active role in consultations between the Soviet and other bloc leaders in the Soviet Union, Romania, and elsewhere. Ceausescu, as one of the secretaries of the Central Committee of the Romanian Communist party, took part in some of these consultations. He was a member of the Romanian delegation to the Twenty-first CPSU Congress.

There was also secret collaboration between the Romanian security and intelligence services and the KGB under its chairman, Shelepin, over the preparation of joint operations in support of the bloc's long-range policy. The heads of the Romanian intelligence and security services attended the bloc conference of intelligence and security services in the Soviet Union in 1959. A new KGB chief adviser was sent to Romania in 1960. He was Colonel Skomorokhin, a specialist not on Romania, but on Western Europe and, in particular, France, who was sent to assist the Romanian services in the implementation of joint political operations.

Important evidence that Ceausescu continued to cooperate actively with the Soviet leaders within the framework of the long-range bloc policy is to be found in the Soviet press coverage of his official visit to the Soviet Union in 1964, when he was already in the process of taking over from Gheorghiu-Dej. This shows that during his four- or five-day visit to the Soviet Union he was accompanied by Shelepin in his capacity as a secretary of the Central Committee of the CPSU. Bearing in mind that it was Shelepin who, between 1958 and 1960, launched the use of disinformation in support of the long-range policy and from 1961 onward appears to have become the coordinator of its use in bloc operations, it is reasonable to conclude that the opportunity was taken to discuss with Ceausescu his role in sustaining the myth of Soviet-Romanian differences.

The "Evidence" of Soviet-Romanian Differences

The so-called evidence of differences between the Romanian and Soviet leaders in Comecon in 1962–63 cannot be taken seriously. Romania's insistence on its own speedy industrialization fitted in with the objectives of the long-range policy; hence there was no reason for the Soviets to oppose it. Against Romania's alleged opposition to the creation of the Executive Committee of Comecon and its long-range planning concepts must be set the official evidence indicating that the Romanian leadership under both Gheorghiu-Dej and Ceausescu was committed to long-term economic integration of the bloc under the auspices of Comecon and its executive committee—on which, in fact, Romania was represented.

Official records of the period 1960 to 1964 reflect close relations between the Soviet Union and Romania and an active exchange of party and governmental delegations between them, suggestive of coordination in the implementation of policy. The fact that the evidence of Soviet-Romanian differences during this period was based on esoteric and confidential sources and was in conflict with the official record of Soviet-Romanian cooperation suggests that it was the product of disinformation. The conflict between the official and esoteric evidence became especially obvious in the 1970s, when Romania, along with other members of the bloc, was involved in concrete measures of economic integration.

Among the manifestations of Romania's neutrality in the Sino-Soviet dispute were: the return of a Romanian ambassador to Albania in 1963, which was out of step with the Soviet Union and other East European communist states; the visit of the Romanian Prime Minister, Ion Gheorghe Maurer, to Peking in the spring of 1964, a year after open Soviet polemics against China had begun; and a statement by the Romanian party leadership, described below, that was interpreted in the West as a "declaration of Romanian independence."

Once it is realized that the Soviet-Albanian and Sino-Soviet splits are joint disinformation operations prepared and launched in 1958–60 with the approval of all the leaders of the bloc, it is easy to see that Romania's neutrality is a posture calculated to support the authenticity of both splits, and that Romanian independence can be misrepresented as one of their consequences.

Given that the West had accepted the authenticity of the Soviet-Albanian split, the return to Albania of a Romanian ambassador supported the myth of Romanian independence. It also had the practical advantage of providing an additional East European channel for bloc diplomatic consultation with Albania. The step may reasonably be assumed to have received the bloc's blessing in advance. Maurer's visit to Peking can be interpreted as a visit to discuss and coordinate this combination of disinformation operations with the Chinese leaders, an interpretation supported by the fact that Maurer went on from Peking to North Korea and then returned to Romania via the Soviet Union, where he presumably also had discussions.

When Maurer returned from his tour, the Romanian Communist

party's Central Committee held a week-long secret meeting, at the end of which it issued a statement on the party's attitude to the situation in the world communist movement. The statement was sixteen thousand words in length. It was given wide publicity in Romania and was immediately translated into Russian, Spanish, English, French, and German for distribution abroad. The points in it that were singled out and interpreted in the West as expressions of Romanian independence included the following:

• It is the sovereign right of each socialist state to work out, choose or change the forms and methods of socialist construction.

• The planned management of the national economy is one of the . . . inalienable attributes of the sovereignty of the socialist state.

• Communist countries should co-operate and help each other in economic matters [only on the basis of] fully equal rights, observance of national sovereignty and interests, mutual advantage and comradely assistance [mainly] through bilateral and multilateral agreements.

• The idea of a single planning body for all Comecon countries has the most serious economic and political implications.

• To hand over [the levers of management of economic and social life] to the competence of some supra-state or extra-state bodies would be to turn sovereignty into a concept without any real content.

• Romania favours the strengthening of co-operation with all "socialist" countries and achieving an "international division of labour" provided that this does not mean that the communist countries have to isolate themselves from "the general framework of world economic relations"; it is natural for communist states to "display initiative and to manifest themselves actively on the international arena."[2]

Remarks of this kind aroused lively Western interest, but it should be pointed out that other parts of the statement were more significant. There was, for example, a reaffirmation by the Romanian party leadership of their commitment to the basic decisions and objectives formulated at the Eighty-one–Party Congress in November 1960, such as the strengthening of economic cooperation between the socialist states, the emphasis on peaceful coexistence combined with support for national liberation movements, the effort to attract new members into Comecon, and the quest for the final and inevitable victory of communism throughout the world.

Western commentators overlooked the fact that statements about the maturity of the communist parties, their capacity to develop their own domestic and foreign policies, and their eagerness to take their own initiatives in the international arena were not in contradiction with the decisions of the Eighty-one–Party Congress, which specifically approved tactical flexibility in the pursuit of an activist foreign policy. The Romanian statement in fact not only does not conflict with the Eighty-one–Party Manifesto; it emphasizes the point that communist parties, in developing their own policies, should do so within the framework of the "socialist community."

The evidence used to support the notion of personal animosity between Khrushchev and Gheorghiu-Dej is both flimsy and selective. Gheorghiu-Dej's failure to attend the celebrations in Moscow in honor of Khrushchev's seventieth birthday is given more weight by Western commentators than the more significant fact that, on this same occasion, Khrushchev was awarded Romania's highest decoration. It can scarcely be argued, as Floyd attempts to do, that the level of Soviet representation at the Romanians' twentieth anniversary celebrations was downgraded if Mikoyan, at that time a member of the Presidium of the Central Committee and President of the Soviet Union, attended rather than Khrushchev, who was "not invited."[3] Against the background of the bloc's disinformation program, it is interesting to note that the "Romanians were at no pains to deny" rumors that Khrushchev had tried to remove Gheorghiu-Dej from the leadership of the Romanian party.[4]

Against the same background, Gheorghiu-Dej's visit to Tito and his well-advertised friendship with him in 1964 can be seen as a deliberate attempt to build up the image of Gheorghiu-Dej's independence in Western eyes by associating him with Tito.

The evidence of disagreements between the Soviets and Romania under Ceausescu's leadership is equally unconvincing. Insofar as it comes from the communist side in the form of official statements, these can be easily tailor-made by the party apparatus and intelligence services to suit the needs of the disinformation program.

Evidence of Romanian independence has been seen in the replacement in the 1960s of Russian street names by Romanian, and in other attempts to play down the extent of Soviet influence in Romania. But in the post-1957 atmosphere in the bloc, such measures were not grounds for disagreement with the Soviets; they would have met with the Soviets' full understanding and approval. The tactless attempts by Stalin to impose a Soviet mold on all aspects of life in the East European satellites had been rejected. Variety in the national aspects of each country had been taken into account, and communist parties had been given latitude by the Eighty-one–party Manifesto to vary their tactics in accordance with the conditions facing them. Romanian claims to be fighting Soviet interference in their country were and are no more than a pretense adopted with Soviet connivance, and are intended to invest the party and its leaders with a nationalist and independent image in the eyes of the internal and external public. Despite the development of an apparently heterodox Romanian foreign policy, the internal regime remained as rigidly orthodox and repressive as before.

That Romania increased its commercial, economic, and political ties with the West in the 1960s and 1970s is beyond question. What is questionable is whether it did so without the prior agreement of the Soviet Union and other communist states. The Comecon conference in June 1962 called for an expansion of bloc trade with the West. The Romanians have done no more than give effect to this decision. Moreover, by pretending to be acting independently and by exploiting their so-called independence while in reality acting with the bloc's connivance, they have contributed more to the achievement of the bloc's objectives of increasing trade and securing long-term credits and advanced technology from the West than they could have done by acting as an orthodox member of the bloc. To take one specific example, Romania's "independence" enabled her to import Rhodesian chrome, whether on her own or the bloc's behalf, without the bloc collectively incurring the political odium of so doing.

Romania's independent foreign policy should be regarded as a device characteristic of Lenin's activist diplomacy as exhibited in his use of the Far Eastern Republic. It offers various advantages for the bloc in the diplomatic field. For example, a communist diplomatic presence has been maintained in Israel since 1967 through the Romanian Embassy in Tel Aviv, while the bloc as a whole has gained favor with the Arab world through its severance of diplomatic links with Israel. The close coordination between the diplomacy of Romania and the other members of the bloc has gone largely unobserved.

The surest signs of disinformation in action are to be seen in the contrast between the well-advertised, superficial Romanian disagreements with Comecon and the binding effect of her continued membership in the organization and her participation, for example, in joint energy projects in Eastern Europe. Similarly, occasional well-publicized Romanian refusals to participate in military exercises should blind no one to the fact that Romania remains a member of the Warsaw Pact. The Romanians' ostensible rejection of Soviet influence must be seen alongside the continuing exchanges of friendly visits between the Soviet and Romanian leaders and the award to Ceausescu of an Order of Lenin in Moscow in January 1978.

The Motives for the Projection of Romanian "Independence"

It is not difficult to reconstruct the economic and political thinking behind the decision to misrepresent Romania as an independent member of the communist bloc, taken perhaps as early as 1958–60 when the long-range policy was being formulated. The long-range policy called for industrialization and a gradual leveling up of the economies of the entire communist bloc. The effort to swing the world balance of power in communist favor entailed nuclear armaments programs; massive conventional armed forces; a vast propaganda, intelligence, and security bureaucracy; military and economic aid to developing countries; and worldwide support for communist parties and national liberation movements. At the same time living standards in the communist world needed to be raised if further popular explosions were to be avoided. The policy as a whole could be sustained only with Western technical and economic help. That help was unlikely to be given to an apparently aggressive, monolithic communist bloc. Some inducement was needed to procure a change in Western attitudes.

The strategic-political case for presenting the bloc as disunited has already been argued. The addition of a further brand of communism, distinguishable from the Soviet, Chinese, Albanian, and Yugoslav varieties, would have recommended itself to the communist strategists because it would help to authenticate the disagreements, which had already begun to be displayed within the bloc, and would give further encouragement to Western illusions that national sentiment and national interest were achieving dominance over ideology as the driving force behind the communist world. These illusions would raise Western hopes and expectations that, with cautious and selective help and political encouragement, the fissures in the communist monolith could be gradually enlarged until the monolith disintegrated altogether.

Although a united Western world, improving the living standards of its peoples without suppressing their political freedom, sets an example for those living under communism, breeds discontent among them, and causes them to exert pressure on their leaders, the experience of the NEP had shown that the dangers to a communist system from close Western ties could be contained; efficient secret police control and ideological countermeasures were capable of neutralizing the risks of political and ideological contamination of the public from the presence of Western businessmen and experts in their midst. Western expectations of expanding Western influence in communist countries through economic links could once more be disappointed if the necessary adjustments to the communist system were to be properly calculated, controlled, and deceptively presented. Visible evidence of foreign economic support for communist regimes, far from stimulating internal opposition to them, has the opposite effect. Genuine would-be opponents of the regime can anticipate little support from Western powers committed to helping the established system. Knowing this, the communist strategists would have calculated that Western technical and economic help could safely be used to support their long-range policy. In the long run, having benefited from that help, they would hope to demonstrate to their own subjects and to the world at large the superiority of the communist system.

The Tito-Stalin split provided further precedents and lessons. Tito's defiant rejection of Soviet interference sent his prestige soaring, both at home and overseas, and won for his country generous Western military and economic aid without obliging him to abandon fundamental communist principles. After Stalin's death it was a richer and more stable Yugoslavia that was reconciled with the communist bloc.

Lenin's creation of an independent Far Eastern Republic, whose policies were closely but secretly coordinated with those of Soviet Russia, had demonstrated the advantages of using a diversity of forms in the pursuit of "activist diplomacy." Lenin had also said that "what we need is a great orchestra" with the different parties, like different instruments, playing different roles. The Yugoslavs, with their background of independence, were particularly suited for the role of developing relations with European socialists and the nonaligned developing countries. Their spurious dispute with the Soviets in 1958–60 was intended to prepare them for that role. But there would also have been arguments for using an existing member of the Warsaw Pact and Comecon to play a similarly independent role.

Several factors probably influenced the choice of Romania for the purpose. It may have been thought likely that Romania's long-standing ties with France and linguistic and cultural affinity with other Latin countries would help to ensure a favorable European response to a show of Romanian independence. The Latin background fitted Romania to play a special role in relation to the influential European communist parties in Italy, France, and Spain. But probably more important was the fact that the Romanian regime, next to the Polish and Hungarian, was the weakest and most despised by its subject population. Given Tito's experience between 1948 and 1953, it was reasonable to expect that a repeat display in public of differences with the Soviet Union—even if, on this occasion, spurious ones—would enhance the domestic and international prestige of the Romanian Communist party and its leaders; they would be able to present themselves not as Soviet puppets, but as bold, national leaders willing to challenge the authority of the Soviet Union. But the weakness of the regime and the contempt in which it was held internally meant that the appearance of a split could not be carried very far. A relaxation of internal control might have endangered the regime; hence the decision to combine, however incongruously, an apparently heterodox and independent foreign policy with a rigidly orthodox, oppressive, Brezhnev-style domestic system.

Basing themselves on the Yugoslav example, the communist strategists would have calculated correctly that Western commercial and political interests would combine in pressing for more open-handed trading policies toward Romania in the hope of weaning her further away from the bloc. Since Romanian independence was a myth, such hopes would prove illusory. Meanwhile, more liberal trading policies would certainly be of benefit to Romania and probably to the bloc as well.

Objectives of the Disinformation Operation

This disinformation serves primarily the development of Romania's special strategic role, especially in promoting, in association with Yugoslavia and the Eurocommunist parties, the idea of the dissolution of military pacts and the creation of a neutral socialist Europe. In summary form the objectives of disinformation on Romanian independence may be defined as follows:

• To support other disinformation operations on the theme of the disintegration of the bloc; to establish a new form of "independent communism" within the bloc.
• To raise the internal and international prestige of the Romanian party and its leaders.
• To enable Romania to obtain more generous Western technical and economic help.
• To allow her to take advantage on the bloc's behalf of diplomatic and commercial openings that would be closed to more orthodox communist states.
• To prepare her for a special strategic role.
• To build up Western confidence in her as a potential ally or confidant within the communist world.
• To support, at a later stage, the independence of the Eurocommunist parties.
• To prepare her, probably, for a shift to a more "liberal" domestic regime in the final phase of long-range bloc policy.

18

The Sixth Disinformation Operation:
The Alleged Recurrence of Power Struggles
In the Soviet, Chinese, and Other Parties

THE WEST HAS BEEN SEEING EVIDENCE since the early 1960s of recurrent power struggles in the leadership of the Soviet, Chinese, Yugoslav, Czechoslovak, and other parties. In the Soviet Union it has been seen in the alleged dismissal of Khrushchev in October 1964 for his policy failures and "adventurism"; in the alleged power struggle between the moderate and Stalinist factions that followed his dismissal; in Brezhnev's switch to neo-Stalinist practices since 1968 and in opposition to him from the liberals in the Soviet leadership.

In China it has been seen in the alleged struggle for power between the militant, radical, Stalinist, Maoist faction (Mao, Lin Piao, Chen Po-ta) and the moderate, pragmatist faction (Chou En-lai, Teng Hsiao-p'ing, Peng Te-huai, Peng Chen, Liu Shao-tsi, Lo Jui-tsin); in the dismissal of Teng Hsiao-p'ing, Peng Te-huai, Liu Shaochi, Peng Chen, and others; in the alleged cult of Mao; in unexplained phenomena in China, such as the activity of the Red Guards during the Cultural Revolution; and in the reemergence of pragmatists, like Teng Hsiao-ping, since Mao's death in 1976.

In Yugoslavia it has been seen in the alleged power struggle between Tito and his deputy premier and minister of the interior, Rankovic, which resulted in the ousting of Rankovic in 1966. In Czechoslovakia it has been seen in the struggle between the conservative Novotny faction and the liberal Dubcek faction, which resulted in the victory of the liberals and the alleged dismissal of Novotny in 1968.

In order to demonstrate that this semblance of recurrent power struggles is a misrepresentation of the facts directed principally at Western observers and intended to serve communist strategic purposes, the developments in these struggles in the Soviet Union and elsewhere must be examined in the light of both official and inside information about them.

Succession in the Soviet Leadership: New Stabilizing Factors

The problem of succession in the leadership of the Soviet Union and other communist countries is of great importance, since on it depends the solution of many other practical problems. The question that has to be answered is whether or not a one-party, communist, dictatorial system can settle the problem of succession without recourse to a struggle for power, as has happened in the past. Another related question is whether Khrushchev was forcibly removed in 1964 or whether, on the contrary, he succeeded in transferring his power and solving the succession problem without a crisis.

Most noncommunist observers are inclined to regard communist parties as incapable of finding a solution; they think that the recurrence of power struggles is inevitable. The most dramatic confirmation of this view was the allegedly forcible removal of Khrushchev from the Soviet leadership in 1964.[1]

The present study will attempt to distinguish between the facts surrounding Khrushchev's departure from office, the deliberate misrepresentation of them by the Soviet strategists, and the unfortunately erroneous interpretation of them by reputable Western scholars. In order to make the distinctions clear and to explain how and why the facts were misrepresented by the Soviet strategists and why reputable Western scholars continue to accept uncritically information on the continuing existence of power struggles, it is helpful to compare the succession situations of 1924 and 1953 with the events of 1960–64, using for the purpose official information as well as inside knowledge and the new methodology.

The Failure of Lenin and Stalin to Solve the Succession Problem

There are similarities between the situations in 1924 and 1953. Lenin's death in January 1924 left a political vacuum. There was no single recognized successor with a ready-made team of supporters: instead, there were several rival leaders, each with his own claim on power. The situation in the country was still critical. Lenin's adopted policy, the NEP, was still in force, but many practical problems within that policy awaited their solutions.

Stalin's death in March 1953 left an even greater political vacuum. The dictator left no designated heir, nor was there a single recognized successor with a supporting team; as in 1924, there were several leaders with rival claims on power. There was a critical situation in the Soviet Union and in other communist countries. No long-range policy had been adopted despite the need for long-term solutions to the crisis in the bloc.

All these circumstances invited succession crises. Power struggles were inevitable in both cases because of the rivalries among the new groups of leaders. The membership of the new generation in each case was fortuitous, unstable, and divided, its individual members ambitious to play a leading role and at the same time faced with the necessity of formulating a policy for the party. The critical situation in the Soviet Union in 1924 and in the bloc as a whole after 1953 demanded new solutions to burning issues. The struggle for power became at the same time a struggle for policy, which added to its bitterness. In each case the struggle ended with the elimination from political life of all but one of the contenders.

Lenin's death was not unexpected, in view of his long illness. The struggle for power began while he was still alive. Stalin took the opportunity to strengthen his position to some extent even before Lenin's death. In 1924 there was still an atmosphere of inner-party democracy. The party rank and file, as well as the party and government apparatus, participated in the struggle and exerted some influence over it, which explains why the struggle after 1924 lasted longer than that after 1953.

Lenin revealed his concern about the succession in letters to the party congress, written in December 1922 and January 1923, in which he warned against the concentration of too much power in Stalin's hands. He also warned against the possibility of a split in the leadership and the need to prevent "conflicts between small Central Committee groupings which would gravely affect the fate of the party as a whole." He advocated a dispersal of his powers not to a few leaders, but rather to an enlarged Central Committee with enhanced authority, whose membership should be increased from twenty-seven to as many as a hundred members.[2]

Of necessity, some dispersal of power did occur. Lenin's personal rule was followed for a few years by an oligarchic rule. But there were no constitutional means of deciding the succession and no provision for popular participation in the process. The problem was one for the leader of the party himself to solve; only the leader had the authority to put his recommendations into effect. The difficulty was that, although Lenin gave a theoretical solution to the succession problem, he did not solve it in practice because of his illness. Moreover, although he was worried about a split in the leadership after his death, he himself invited a power struggle in his ambiguous testament, in which he did not indicate who should be his successor. Had he not been ill, he could have made his testament effective; in the event, it was not fulfilled after his death.

Partly because Stalin needed time to take control over the government apparatus, the struggle after Lenin's death lasted until the mid-1930s, by which time all Stalin's rivals and real or possible opponents and even some of his supporters had been eliminated physically. Not infrequently, Stalin adopted the policies of his victims.

The emphasis on physical elimination was not irrational. Because the whole party apparatus was involved in the struggle and because some vestiges of inner-party democracy survived, he was obliged when removing leaders to purge all of their supporters from the party by mass repressions to forestall possible opposition from them. He dispensed with collective leadership and established his own total, personal dictatorship. This was a backward step, which weakened the communist system and gave rise to the succession crisis and many other problems. After the physical elimination of his rivals and the mass repressions of their followers, he could no longer rely on his colleagues or the party, but only on the security bureaucracy. He ruled by watching potential rivals, dividing them, and exploiting one against the other. By eliminating Zhdanov, the most promising of his possible successors, he invited a crisis in the succession. Up to his last days he ignored the problem, and his negligence left a vacuum after his sudden death that further contributed to the intensity of the ensuing struggle.[3]

Stalin's rigid personal dictatorship and his destruction of inner-party democracy meant that the party membership was not involved in the power struggle after his death; it took place only in the upper reaches of the party and government hierarchy. In 1953 the bureaucracy would have been prepared to serve any leader who was capable of taking control over it; unable to appeal directly to the party or the people, the bureaucrats had become nobodies in Stalin's final years. For these reasons the struggle after his death was relatively short and was not accompanied by mass repressions, except in the case of Beriya's supporters.

There were similarities and differences between Stalin and Khrushchev. Like Stalin, Khrushchev, after the removal of Malenkov in 1955, began as a communist dictator. He established his preeminence in 1956–57, using nonconstitutional means and tactics, and wielded his power, though not for long, in dictatorial fashion. From 1956 to 1959 he replaced Stalin's cult of personality with one of his own. The darker side of Khrushchev's career is still kept hidden from the public by the Soviet leaders.

Unlike Stalin, Khrushchev did not physically eliminate his rivals, apart from Beriya; since they had no followings, it was unnecessary. Unlike Stalin, Khrushchev, though he remained supreme, managed to establish collective leadership during his final years in power. But the most important difference between him and Stalin was that he succeeded in accomplishing the transfer of power to a successor he had chosen. The view that he shared Stalin's disregard for the succession problem is erroneous. Like Lenin, he was concerned about it. Moreover, according to the present analysis, he found what Lenin tried but failed to find—a practical solution to the problem. Probably with the help of Mao's influence, he solved it on the lines of Lenin's recommendations and by committing his followers to a long-range policy for the whole communist bloc, and in so doing he established the model for the leaders of other communist states to follow.

Khrushchev's "Removal" an Agreed Transfer of the Leadership to Brezhnev

The view that Khrushchev was removed in a palace revolt is probably mistaken; it is not supported by the available evidence. In 1964 the situation differed radically from that in 1924 or 1953.

After Khrushchev's departure from the leadership, there was no political vacuum. The same united team of active Khrushchev supporters carried on. The internal crisis of the regime and the problems of intrabloc relations had been solved. The long-range policy for the whole bloc had been adopted and was in operation. There were no grounds for expecting political crisis or power struggle.

The tragic consequences of the two previous succession crises were not lost on Khrushchev and the other Soviet leaders. Lenin's death had been followed by the liquidation of a generation of party leaders, by mass repressions in the party, and by splits in the Communist International and its affiliates. The struggle after Stalin's death had delayed the formulation of a long-range policy and threatened the continued existence of the communist bloc. It was vital that there should be no further repetition of these disasters.

In 1964 favorable conditions existed for a calculated transfer of power by Khrushchev to a leader or group of leaders of his choice because of the existence of collective leadership, as practiced under Khrushchev since 1959; the increased influence of the Central Committee and party apparatus; the absence of opposition in the leadership; the greater stability of the regime; improved relations with the leaders of other communist countries; the establishment of collective leadership in the Chinese party under Mao; and, above all, the adoption of the long-range policy. Khrushchev had a personal interest in the implementation of this policy through his successors because it was adopted during his rule and with his active participation. His role in its initiation offered him promise of greater posthumous respect and recognition than Stalin had been accorded, for all the power and glory of his reign.

In his concern for long-range policy, Khrushchev would naturally have considered the question of succession. He was in a perfect position to arrange it, since he controlled the situation in the party and the government and he had time in which to act. He had packed the Presidium and the Central Committee with his men; he had his nominees in the KGB and the army and at key points in the party and government apparatus; he retained his own leading position in the party secretariat, the Presidium, and the government. In the light of his claims to be another Lenin, it seems likely that he gave serious thought to the problem, as Lenin did in 1922–23. Following Lenin's example, he probably made recommendations to the Central Committee in the form of secret letters or speeches on the eve of the Twenty-second Party Congress.

Such indications as there are support the conclusion that he was thinking about and acting on the succession problem on the eve of his "removal." Signs of this can be detected from the Twenty-second Party Congress in October 1961 onward. Speaking about Lenin's advice on the cult of personality, he called on the party to be worthy pupils of Lenin in this matter.[4] He confirmed Stalin's mistakes and warned about the consequences of the cult of personality for leaders who forget their duties to the party.[5] According to his definition, the chief evil of the cult of personality lay in the leader's being outside the control of the party.[6] He claimed that collective leadership had been achieved and asked that his own personal role should not be emphasized.[7]

The new party statutes adopted at the congress provide that, at every regular election of the CPSU Central Committee and Presidium, not less than one quarter of the members must be new; of the central committees of the republic parties, not less than one third must be new; and of committees of other party organizations, not less than one half. The alleged purpose of these reforms was to foster "inner-party democracy." The new regulations and other decisions of the congress, which were complied with thereafter, were defined by Khrushchev as guarantees against recurrence of the cult of personality.[8] At the same time the Soviet party press recalled a quotation from Lenin stating that "the revolutionary movement cannot be stable without an organization which maintains the succession of leaders."

Two other significant decisions of the Twenty-second Congress were obviously modeled on Lenin's recommendations, namely, the increase in the membership of the Central Committee in comparison with the Twenty-first Congress from 125 to 175 members and the transfer from the Presidium of Ignatov, Furtseva, Mukhitdinov, Belyayev, and Aristov, and their replacement by new party activists in accordance with the statutes.[9]

In the author's view Khrushchev's was a short-term personal dictatorship which was replaced, wisely and in time, by collective leadership in order to avoid a succession crisis and a further struggle for power. Various new circumstances contributed toward, and conditioned, the reorganization of the system. They were:

• The condemnation of Stalin's cult of personality and the practice of physically eliminating rivals.

• The incompatibility between personal dictatorship and the active, constructive, and harmonious collaboration of a bloc of communist countries in pursuit of a common long-range policy.

• Mao's voluntary and exemplary decision in 1959 to give up all his positions of power except the leadership of the party in order to concentrate on problems of long-range policy and communist strategy.

• The concern of the bloc leaders as a whole to avoid a repetition of the painful events after 1924 and 1953.

• The personal interest of Khrushchev and Mao in avoiding subsequent condemnation of their activities resulting from a further power struggle, and hence their willingness to yield power voluntarily to the party apparatus and bureaucracy.

• The stabilizing effect of the long-range bloc policy.

Given past experience, given the establishment of collective leadership, and given these new circumstances, the bloc's leaders had already begun by 1960 to make advance arrangements within their Central Committees to ensure a smooth, timely, and peaceful transfer of power—as was the case, in the author's view, with the succession to Khrushchev in 1964.

The Western version of Khrushchev's removal was based on inadequate and unreliable evidence. The main items taken into account were that: Khrushchev was given no recognition for his services; his portraits disappeared in Moscow; his son-in-law and associate in policy, Adzhubey, was dismissed (it became known later that he had been demoted to a less important position in a Soviet newspaper); references appeared in the Soviet press to the cult of personality, which, though they did not directly mention Khrushchev's name, were interpreted in the West as a campaign of "de-Khrushchevization"; Khrushchev was allegedly living in humble obscurity with a small retinue of servants; according to unconfirmed reports, he was dismissed for nepotism at the end of an eight-hour meeting of the Presidium on the strength of a report by Suslov; he was responsible for numerous policy mistakes and failures, such as the withdrawal from Cuba, the begging of wheat from the United States, the quarrel with China, the ill-conceived decentralization of the Soviet economy, his proposed visit to West Germany, and his unsuccessful personal style of diplomacy with its mixture of insults to and cajolery of the West.

This evidence is unconvincing and contradictory. The first argument against Khrushchev's having been forcibly removed is the fact that it was his team that continued, without significant changes, to dominate the Soviet leadership. Brezhnev, who replaced him as the party leader, was his most trusted, obedient, and experienced assistant, friend, and colleague. He owed his career to Khrushchev and was a link between the Ukrainian and the Moscow party groups. Kirilenko and the former President, Podgornyy, were almost as close to Khrushchev as Brezhnev. Other faithful lieutenants and appointees of Khrushchev, like Shelepin, Biryuzov, Malinovskiy, Semichastnyy, and Patolichev, retained their key positions in the party and the government.

Even more important, two of Khrushchev's relatives continued to hold power in the leadership and government; one of them was even promoted later on. The two were Polyanskiy, who stayed on as a member of the Presidium and premier of the Russian Republic, and Marshal Grechko, who remained as first assistant of the minister of defense and chief of the Warsaw Pact forces; a few years later, he was promoted to the major post of minister of defense.[10] The fact that Khrushchev's relatives retained their key positions after his departure is inconsistent with Western belief in a palace revolution and Khrushchev's abrupt dismissal; it supports the conclusion that it was a smooth and agreed transfer of power. Furthermore, it disposes of the story that Khrushchev was dismissed for nepotism, because his relatives, apart from Adzhubey, were not affected by his loss of office. Here it is important to point out that the relationship of Grechko and Polyanskiy to Khrushchev has never been publicly revealed by Brezhnev or other party leaders. Such information is normally kept secret and is known to very few within the party.

If Khrushchev had in reality been dismissed for his cult of personality or his policy mistakes, open criticism of him could have been expected in the communist press. In fact there was very little, and such as there was was oblique and indirect. There were no revelations about his complicity in Stalin's crimes or about the ruthlessness of his struggle for power in 1955–57. There was no criticism of his "adventurist" foreign policy over the Berlin and Cuban crises or of his exploitation of Soviet writers. There was some vague criticism in the Soviet press about cult of personality and other rather minor aspects of policy, which was interpreted by Western journalists as referring to Khrushchev. Perhaps this interpretation was supported by revelations of communist officials to their Western contacts, but communists do not normally give Western diplomats or journalists the true facts of the case. There was some speculative reporting about Khrushchev's private life— his hunting, his apartments, and his villas—and there was his sensational appearance before Western journalists. Such manifestations should not be accepted at face value; they can be better understood in the context of bloc disinformation operations. Naturally there was no official recognition of Khrushchev's services to the Soviet Union, because that would have upset bloc disinformation about the recurrence of power struggles.

To sum up, there was no major convulsion before or after Khrushchev's retirement. With few exceptions there was continuity in the leadership. Above all, there was continuity in the implementation of the long-range policy that Khrushchev had initiated. The most likely explanation, therefore, is that Khrushchev's removal was a staged affair conducted with his full agreement. Furthermore, it was probably staged with the foreknowledge and agreement of the communist leaders of other countries. This would explain the well-publicized visits of Western communist leaders to Moscow after the dismissal to demand "explanations" for it and to express their high regard for Khrushchev and his policies, thereby demonstrating to the West their newly won independence of the Soviet Union.

Over the radio, in their newspapers, and in official documents, the Russian people were told that Khrushchev had resigned on grounds of age and failing health. He was born in 1894. The official version could well be near the truth. Lenin had set a precedent for retirement on grounds of health. Khrushchev wanted to go down in history as another Lenin. Like Lenin, he even went hunting in the neighborhood of Moscow after his retirement. In spite of his Stalinist background, he had made a significant contribution to the communist cause, but this contribution could not be given immediate public recognition for tactical considerations. In due course, probably after the conclusion of the long-range policy, tribute will be paid to all the leaders who were responsible for the policy, including Khrushchev, Mao, Novotny, Ulbricht, Tito, Brezhnev, Teng Hsiao-p'ing, and many others. Khrushchev would not have been a true communist if he had not agreed to such an arrangement, and no doubt he did so with his usual mocking humor.

It is interesting that Neizvestnyy, the controversial sculptor whom Khrushchev had himself criticized for abstractionism, was allowed by Soviet officialdom to design the symbolic black and white monument on Khrushchev's grave. Not many years after his death, Khrushchev's name began to reappear in the *Great Soviet Encyclopaedia*.

According to the present, new interpretation, Khrushchev's retirement, which incidentally enabled him to write his memoirs, was intended to solve the problem of succession in the Soviet Union, to rehearse the changing of the guard in accordance with his wishes, and to forestall upheavals and difficulties for the party, for the regime, and even for himself. A smooth, agreed-upon transfer of power was rendered possible by, and in itself served to guarantee, the continuity of long-range bloc policy and strategy. The new guard came from the old team of leaders committed to the same policy. Since all the leaders of the communist bloc were and are equally committed to it, none can change it arbitrarily, whether in the Soviet Union, China, Romania, or any other communist country, without facing serious opposition from the party apparatus in his own and other communist parties. Since Khrushchev's retirement was probably agreed with the leaders of the other parties, it can also be suggested that his example was followed, with local variations, in the transitions from Gheorghiu-Dej to Ceausescu in Romania, from Novotny to Dubcek to Husak in Czechoslovakia, from Gomulka to Gierek to Kania in Poland, and from Ulbricht to Honecker in East Germany; and in the transitions in China and Yugoslavia that followed Mao's and Tito's deaths.

According to this analysis Khrushchev's retirement was a successful fulfillment of Leninist ideas on the transfer of power between leaders. Since there is no solid foundation for the belief that Khrushchev was removed by power struggle, the conclusion can be drawn that, for strategic reasons, his retirement was deliberately misrepresented, partly to the inhabitants of the communist countries but mainly to the West, as part of a succession crisis analogous to those that followed Lenin's and Stalin's deaths. Similar conclusions can be drawn from so-called power struggles in the Yugoslav, Chinese, Czechoslavok, and Polish parties; in fact, all of them should be regarded as operations within the framework of the bloc disinformation program.

Objectives of Disinformation on Power Struggles

The disinformation effort to keep alive Western belief in the existence and inevitability of recurrent power struggles in the leadership of communist parties serves several purposes. There is an obvious close connection between power struggles and factionalism; neither exists without the other. Disinformation on power struggles therefore supports and complements disinformation operations based on spurious factionalism, such as those on de-Stalinization, the Soviet-Albanian and Sino-Soviet splits, and democratization in Czechoslovakia in 1968. It further serves to obscure the unity, coordination, and continuity within the bloc in pursuit of an agreed long-range policy. By creating false associations in Western minds between different communist leaders and different aspects or phases of communist policy—Khrushchev with "revisionism," Mao with "dogmatism," Teng Hsiao-p'ing with "pragmatism," Dubcek with "democratization," and Brezhnev with "neo-Stalinism"—the West can be induced to make false deductions about the mainsprings of communist policy, inaccurate predictions about its future course, and mistakes in its own responses. The West is more likely to make concessions, for example, over SALT negotiations, or the supply of high technology goods to the Soviet Union or China, if it believes that by so doing it will strengthen the hand of a "liberal" or "pragmatic" tendency or faction within the party leadership. Conversely, the West can be persuaded to attribute aggressive aspects of communist policy to the influence of hard-liners in the leadership. The disappearance from the scene of leaders thus identified can be used to promote the myth of liberalization, as was done in the case of Novotny in Czechoslovakia in 1968. Part Three will argue that similar developments may be expected in the Soviet Union and elsewhere in Eastern Europe in the final phase of long-range policy and that the succession to Brezhnev may well be exploited for the same purpose.

One further possible purpose of spurious power struggles may be suggested, that the "purging" or "disgrace" of leading communists such as Teng Hsiao-p'ing in China or Barak in Czechoslovakia, who disappeared for varying periods of time allegedly as the victims of a power struggle, may be intended to cover up their secondment to serve during their disappearance in a secret policy coordinating center somewhere in the bloc.

19

The Seventh Disinformation Operation: "Democratization" in Czechoslovakia in 1968

The Western Interpretation

As reported in the communist and Western press, the leaders of the communist party introduced certain economic and political reforms in Czechoslovakia during 1968. In the economy, greater independence was given to factory managers; the profit motive and market-orientated practices were partially reintroduced. Sensational developments occurred in the political field. Communist sources revealed that an intensive struggle was fought out in the party leadership between the conservatives, or Stalinists, led by the general-secretary, President Novotny, and the liberals, or progressives, led by the secretary of the Slovak Communist party, Dubcek. In January 1968 the liberals won and Dubcek replaced Novotny as the country's leader.

The new regime disclosed certain crimes committed by the former party leadership, denounced the cult of personality the former leaders had practiced, allegedly reduced to some degree the role of the security services, and broadened the political rights of the population. Censorship was abolished, intellectuals were given greater freedom, opportunities for foreign travel were improved, and even the possibility of permitting the formation of noncommunist political parties was discussed.

The Soviet Union, alarmed by these developments, denounced them as counterrevolutionary. In August Warsaw Pact troops invaded Czechoslovak territory without meeting resistance from the Czechoslovak army. The political situation was reversed; Dubcek and other liberals were replaced by Soviet puppets.

Western journalists, scholars, and officials, basing their interpretation largely on accounts of these events in communist sources, accepted the Czechoslovak crisis as an attempt at a spontaneous, peaceful democratic revolution. They accepted as genuine the power struggle between progressives and conservatives. They accepted Dubcek's reforms as a new brand of democratic "socialism with a human face." Indignation at the occupation of Czechoslovakia by forces of the Warsaw Pact evoked deep sympathy for Dubcek, his regime, and his new brand of socialism.

Four additional factors contributed to Western acceptance of the liberalization of the Czechoslovak regime at face value. First, the liberalization took place in a country that had had strong democratic traditions before the communist coup in February 1948, and the liberalization seemed like a revival of those traditions. Second, the Czechoslovak leaders seemed to have gone further than any other communist leaders in their criticism of the Soviet Union, in their preparedness to permit noncommunist parties, and in their denunciations of the crimes of former Soviet and Czechoslovak security officials against noncommunist statesmen, such as Jan Masaryk, the former foreign minister. Third, extreme Soviet pressure was exercised on the Dubcek regime through the Soviet press and through conspicuous movements of Warsaw Pact forces on the Polish-Czechoslovak border. Fourth, there was a close apparent parallel between events in Czechoslovakia in 1968 and those in Hungary in 1956.[1]

According to the Western interpretation of events, the overthrow of the Novotny regime by the progressives was brought about through the alliance of some liberal-minded economists and dissenting intellectuals with a few progressive communist leaders, such as Dubcek. Weak as it was, this alliance succeeded in carrying out a democratic revolution against a totalitarian regime enjoying the support of the armed forces and security services without the firing of a single shot.

Western Errors

A major error in most Western assessments of Czechoslovakia in 1968 was to consider the events of that year in isolation from the recent past. Unfortunately, failing to appreciate the changes in relations within the bloc and the adoption of the long-range policy between 1957 and 1960, they used outdated methodology in their interpretation of events. Failing also to take into account the systematic dissemination of disinformation through sources under communist control, including the communist press and communist officials and intellectuals, they placed excessive reliance on these sources.

A Reinterpretation of Czechoslovak "Democratization"

The new methodology dictates a new and opposite interpretation of Czechoslovak "democratization." It sees it not as a spontaneous development, but as a planned, controlled maneuver and rehearsal for a similar development, all to take place within the framework of the long-range policy. The major argument in favor of this view is that Czechoslovak "democratization" fitted into, and met the requirements of, communist strategy for Western Europe. A second argument is that, throughout the upheavals of 1968, Czechoslovakia remained an active member of Comecon and the Warsaw Pact.

The Czechoslovak party leaders, their security and intelligence services and the regime as a whole actively participated in the formulation, adoption, and implementation of the long-range bloc policy in the period 1958 to 1960. Novotny frequently consulted with the Soviet leaders, especially Khrushchev, in this period, and Novotny and his colleagues—notably Hendrych, the party official responsible for ideology and work with intellectuals—played a key role in the formulation of the policy in so far as it related to Czechoslovakia. A Czechoslovak party delegation led by Novotny took part in the Eighty-one–Party Congress, in Moscow in November 1960, which adopted the long-range bloc policy and strategy for the international communist movement.

There are indications that the special strategic role for Czechoslovakia had been worked out, at least in outline, by 1960 and that preparations for the maneuver began immediately thereafter. In May 1961 Dubcek visited the Soviet Union and was received by Suslov.[2] In June and July a delegation of Czechoslovak party workers led by Lenart went to the Soviet Union to study the work of the

CPSU.[3] In June 1962 Novotny led another party delegation to the Soviet Union.[4]

Coordination between the Czechoslovak, Soviet, and other bloc intelligence and security services over their political role in the implementation of the long-range bloc policy began in 1959. The minister of the interior, Barak, and other members of his ministry attended the conference of bloc security and intelligence services in Moscow in that year. Thereafter the Czechoslovak services became members of the intelligence and security coordinating center for the bloc.

From 1959 to 1968 Novotny and his minister of the interior (Barak until 1961) were actively working on the dissolution of genuine political opposition and the creation of false, controlled opposition in Czechoslovakia, on the lines introduced and practiced in the Soviet Union by Shelepin.

Dissolution of genuine opposition was tackled largely by rehabilitations and amnesties. The Novotny regime carried out amnesties in 1960, 1962, 1964, and 1965, the most extensive being the one in 1960 in which most of the "state criminals" were freed. The last amnesty, in 1968, was carried out under Dubcek, who was thus continuing a policy already established by Novotny and Barak.

The Role of Historians and Economists in "Democratization"

A close parallel developed in the period 1959 to 1968 between the approach adopted by Khrushchev and Shelepin to the use of writers, economists, historians, other intellectuals, and rehabilitated party members in activist political work and the approach adopted by the Czechoslovak leaders. The indications are that a false opposition was created in Czechoslovakia and that the struggle between alleged liberals and alleged conservatives was staged on the pattern established in the Soviet Union by Khrushchev and Shelepin.

In 1963 the Central Committee of the Czechoslovak Communist party set up two commissions of experts. One was a commission of thirty-six historians under Gustav Husak, then vice-president of the council of ministers; the other was a group of economists under Ota Sik, who later became a vice-premier in the Dubcek government. The Central Committee made the party's secret archives and statistics available to the two commissions.

The date 1963 is significant in that it was three years after the adoption of the long-range bloc policy and five years before the so-called "democratization" took place. The commissions were established in the Novotny period: Husak and Sik subsequently figured prominently in the "democratization" and its reversal. Putting these facts together, the conclusion may be drawn that the commissions were established under Novotny's leadership within the framework of the long-range policy to prepare the groundwork for the events of 1968. There is a strong pointer to Soviet-Czechoslovak coordination in the matter in that the Economic Commission was established by Novotny at Khrushchev's suggestion.[5] Soviet historians were mobilized in support of long-range policy in the Soviet Union during the same period, though in a different manner. Academician Khvostov played an important part in this activity.

The Roles of Barak and Sik

Barak's role, his dismissal in February 1962, and his rehabilitation and reappearance in 1968 can be completely reinterpreted.

Barak was minister of the interior from 1953 to 1961 and a member of the Presidium of the party from 1954 until February 1962. As minister of the interior he played an important part in the formulation of the long-range policy and was in close liaison with the chairman of the KGB, Shelepin. The chief of the KGB Institute, General Kurenkov, informed the staff and students of the KGB Institute in Moscow in 1959–60, after the return of a KGB delegation to Czechoslovakia of which he was a member, that the KGB had closer relations with the Czechoslovak security service than with any other service in the bloc.

Significantly the young technocrats and planners who became members of the Economic Commission in 1963 and played key roles in the introduction of economic reforms in 1968, including Ota Sik, were close to Barak in the late 1950s and early 1960s.[6] Given Barak's connection at the time with the planning of the long-range policy and the new role of the security and intelligence services in it, it is likely that even then the young technocrats were being prepared for their part in introducing controlled "democ-ratization."

On February 9, 1962, it was announced in the Czechoslovak press that Barak had been arrested and sentenced to fifteen years imprisonment for embezzlement of public funds. He was released in May 1968 with the explanation that the funds were not embez-zled at all but were intended for the Czechoslovak intelligence service. Barak himself indicated that his removal was due to Novot-ny's fear of being the victim of the young technocrats and economic planners by whom he, Barak, liked to be surrounded.[7]

Given Barak's involvement in long-range policy formulation in 1959 to 1961, it is likely that his arrest in February 1962 was fictitious and was used to mislead Western analysts about the true nature of his relations with technocrats like Sik. It could also have been used to fabricate for this leading secret policeman a reputation as a liberal reformer and a victim of Novotny, the better to explain his reappearance under the new regime of 1968. There was a further possible motive for the staging of Barak's arrest; in the course of compiling their damage report on the author's defection in Decem-ber 1961, the KGB would have discovered that the author was aware of the close liaison between the leaders of the KGB and of the Czechoslovak security service under Barak.

A likely speculation is that, instead of spending his time in jail from 1962 to 1968, Barak was sent secretly to Moscow to represent the Czechoslovak government in the bloc's intelligence and security coordinating center. His reappearance in Czechoslovakia in May 1968 would have been to act as a behind-the-scenes coordinator of the developments of that year. As a key man at the planning stage of those developments, he would have been needed on the spot during the crucial period of their unfolding.

Given Sik's relations with Barak and his appointment as head of the Economic Commission by the Central Committee of the party in 1963 under Novotny's leadership, his role in the introduc-tion of economic reforms, his support for Dubcek in 1968, and his participation in the Dubcek government should be regarded not as a spontaneous personal activity, but as the fulfilment of a party assignment within the framework of the long-range policy. It was probably no coincidence that his appointment in 1963 fell within the same period as the emergence in the Soviet Union of a liberal economist, Professor Liberman. Sik, in fact, became known as the "Czechoslovak Liberman."

The Role of Writers in "Democratization"

An understanding of Sik's party role in introducing economic reforms in Czechoslovakia, together with an understanding of the Soviet party's use of Tvardovskiy and Kochetov as the leaders of the "liberal" and "conservative" factions among Soviet writers, helps toward an understanding of the role of Czechoslovak writers in the "democratization" of 1968. Since Khrushchev advised the Czechoslovak party to set up an Economic Commission in 1963, it is not unlikely that he or Shelepin advised the Czechoslovak party and security service to use their writers in a controlled "liberalization" in the same way as they themselves had used Tvardovskiy and Kochetov.

Czechoslovak writers played an important part in the alleged removal of Novotny and his replacement by Dubcek. For example, at the Writers Congress in May–June 1967, the "liberal" Slovak writer Ludvik Vaculik, a member of the Central Committee, a member of the staff of *Literarni Listy*, and a confidant of Dubcek, delivered several lectures advocating more creative freedom. In a plea for "democratic socialism" he also called for an active struggle against "neo-Stalinists." The Slovak writer Mnacko attacked Novotny. Anton Liehm, one of the founders of *Literarni Noviny*, spoke against censorship and police despotism. Another writer read out to the congress Solzhenitsyn's "secret letter" against censorship.

The criticism of neo-Stalinism was convincing. But Vaculik, Klima, and Liehm, who participated in this criticism and called for democratization, were all members of the Central Committee of the party at the time. This raises at least a possibility that they were acting, like Tvardovskiy and Kochetov, on the instructions of the party. It is interesting that, three months later (in September 1967), these writers were expelled from the party "for spreading anticommunist propaganda at the Writers Congress." Knowing the methods of provocation used by communist security services, the expulsions can be interpreted as deliberate steps to build up the image of these writers as independent, spontaneous critics of the regime and genuine exponents of democratic socialism. At the same time the expulsions would have served to cover up their secret party assignments.

Some of the actions and speeches of the Czechoslovak writers—Vaculik's speech, for instance—were reminiscent of the actions and speeches of Hungarian writers in 1956. The question to be asked is whether the Czechoslovak writers' actions and speeches were truly spontaneous or whether they were deliberately modeled in advance on the Hungarian pattern by the Central Committee and its Ideological Department in preparation for the introduction of a program of controlled reform designed to stabilize the Czechoslovak regime and serve the purposes of bloc strategy in Europe.

It is interesting that in his speech Vaculik, after condemning "the first Stalinist phase" of the Czechoslovak regime, referred to the "second phase" in which democratic socialism would be realized. It is possible to detect in this a hint of forward planning. It could well be that these speeches were prepared by the writers in conjunction with the Commission of Historians set up in 1963. Vaculik himself revealed in March 1967 (two to three months before the Writers' Congress) that he had been present at a meeting of the Ideological Department of the Central Committee at which questions on freedom for creative activities were discussed.

Vaculik and other writers published a manifesto titled "Two Thousand Words" in the weekly *Literarni Listy* on June 27, 1968.[8] This later became the credo of the party "progressives" and was used by the Soviets and other "orthodox" communists to denounce them as counterrevolutionaries. Some of the statements in it reveal the kind of "democratization" the authors had in mind. While identifying themselves with the party "progressives," they called for support for the party functionaries and security organs and "respect for Czechoslovakia's treaties of friendship with its allies" (i.e., the Soviet Union and other countries of the Warsaw Pact). The following are a few quotations:

"In the first place, we will oppose the opinion, if it manifests itself, that a democratic rebirth can come without the communists or even against them; this would be not only unjust but unreasonable. . . . The communists have well-established organisations; these organisations are necessary to sustain the tendencies of progress. They have experienced functionaries and they also have in hand the controls of command. They have prepared a programme of action which has been proposed to the public. It is a programme aiming at reparation of the greatest injustices and they are the only ones in possession of such a concrete programme. . . . Let us bring the National Front back to life. . . . Let us give our support to the security agencies when they pursue criminal and common law delinquents. We have no intention of provoking anarchy or a general state of insecurity. . . . And we give to our allies the assurance that we shall respect our treaties of friendship, alliance and trade."

Seen against the background of party and security service interest in introducing and controlling a process of "democratization," these expressions of support for the party functionaries, security services, and the Warsaw Pact are clear indications of party guidance to the writers.

The "Struggle" between the Novotny "Conservatives" and the Dubcek "Progressives"

If the "liberal" economists and writers are considered the first two moving forces behind the "democratization" of 1968, the third was the alleged struggle in the party leadership between the "progressives" led by Dubcek and the "conservatives" led by Novotny, which culminated eventually in the victory of the "progressives."

Although Novotny was of the Stalinist generation and was brought up against the background of Stalin's and Gottwald's leadership of the Soviet and Czechoslovak Communist parties, he did not take over the leadership of the Czechoslovak party until after Stalin's death. And it was under his leadership, as under Khrushchev's in the Soviet Union, that an actual de-Stalinization of the Czechoslovak party took place in the period 1956–60 during which many party political prisoners were rehabilitated. It is questionable therefore whether the charges of neo-Stalinism brought against Novotny by the "progressives" were well-founded. The air of artificiality about them supports the thesis that they were contrived, within the framework of the long-range policy and disinformation program, in order to misrepresent as a spontaneous liberal upheaval what was in fact an orderly, planned, and controlled succession to a new generation of party leaders.

Similarly there are grounds for suggesting that Dubcek was chosen and groomed for the role of Novotny's leading adversary in a calculated display of internal party differences serving the same purpose. Like Novotny, although junior to him in age and rank, Dubcek was a product of the Stalinist party machine with a militant communist background. A Slovak by origin, he had intimate connections with the Soviet Union, where he lived from 1922 to 1938. In 1939 he joined the Czechoslovak Communist party, in which he rose steadily during the last fourteen years of Stalin's lifetime. In the year of Stalin's death in 1953, Dubcek became party secretary of a town in Slovakia.

According to Salomon, Dubcek loved and respected the Soviet Union.[9] Between 1955 and 1958 he studied at the High Party School, attached to the Central Committee of the CPSU, in Moscow. This school selects and trains future leaders for the CPSU and other communist parties. Dubcek was still there in 1958, the year in which the formulation of the long-range policy began. It could well be that it was in part because of his Russian background and training in this school that Dubcek was chosen and groomed by the Central Committee as the leader of the "progressives."

Dubcek was made a secretary of the Slovak Communist party and a member of the Presidium in 1963, the same year in which Sik was appointed head of the Economic Commission and Husak head of the Commission of Historians. It may therefore be surmised that Dubcek was chosen for his role in 1963.

There are a number of anomalies in the story of the "quiet revolution" that raise serious doubts about its spontaneous nature. Some of the unanswered questions are as follows:

• Why did the "conservative" majority in the Presidium vote for Dubcek and why did Novotny himself not object to Dubcek's candidacy?

• Why did the Central Committee and party machine controlled by Novotny's "conservative" supporters not prevent the replacement of Novotny by Dubcek?

• Why did neither the "conservative" military and security leaders, like the minister of defense, Lomsky, and the head of military security,

Mamula, nor the leaders of the shock troops and militia of Prague, which organized the coup d'etat in 1948, act against Dubcek if there was a genuine risk that he might turn into a Czechoslovak Imre Nagy and threaten the foundations of their regime?

• Why did Hendrych, an "ultraconservative" Novotny supporter, a frequent visitor to Moscow, the head of the party's ideological department, the controller of the country's intellectuals since 1958—in short, the Czechoslovak equivalent of Il'ichev—side with Dubcek at the secret session of the Central Committee in January 1968 that nominated Dubcek as general-secretary?

• Why did all these "conservatives" accept Dubcek without resistance when, if the revolution had been spontaneous, they would have stood to lose their heads?

• Why did not Dubcek remove key officials like Lomsky or Mamula right at the beginning in March 1968?

• Why did the press censors themselves support "democratization" and vote against the censorship?

• Why was Novotny untouched after he had lost power, if he was such a villain?

• Why did the foreign policy of Dubcek's regime follow the old, orthodox conservative line: anti-NATO, anti-USA, and anti-Israel?

• Why did the "progressive" leaders welcome the bloc's occupation troops?

Had the Dubcek regime been authentically democratic, it would have removed the orthodox party and security officials who had been responsible for past repression. In fact, only three hundred persons in the Ministry of the Interior were allegedly discharged or demoted, a mere drop in the bucket. By and large the Old Guard went unscathed. "Conservative" and "orthodox" officials and "new progressives," some of them former victims of "conservative" repression, served together in the new regime of "democratic socialism."

In fact the major change was a return to the higher ranks of government of certain rehabilitated party members, whose rehabilitation was exploited to project a new image of the communist regime. Among them were Husak, vice-premier (released in 1960); Smrkovsky, president of the National Assembly (released in 1955); and Pavel, minister of the interior (released in 1955). Their return could well have been the realization of a calculated policy of rehabilitation carried out on Soviet lines. It should be remembered in this context that both Gomulka and Kadar, who rose to be the party leaders in Poland and Hungary respectively, were rehabilitated party members.

A distinctive feature of rehabilitation in Czechoslovakia was that former communist officials were fully rehabilitated; some of the noncommunist political prisoners were not. The Rehabilitation Law adopted in June 1968 approved the review of individual cases but did not annul the courts' decisions, lest "justly sentenced, authentic counterrevolutionary elements" should be set free.

Perhaps the most convincing evidence of the essential continuity between the old and new regimes is the fact that Gottwald, who was responsible for the reign of terror from 1948 onwards—involving, according to official statistics, the confinement of one hundred and thirty thousand persons—was not denounced as a criminal by the new regime. On the contrary, Dubcek decorated the widows and orphans of martyred communist officials with the Order of Gottwald, under whose leadership their husbands and fathers had been executed. Strangely, the victims' relatives accepted these decorations.[10]

The controlled nature of "democratization" in Czechoslovakia shows up clearly when comparisons are made with Hungary in 1956. The Hungarian revolution was a popular uprising; while it lasted, it dismantled the system, the party machine, and the security services. It replaced party leaders with nonparty leaders. Some party leaders, like Imre Nagy, broke with the party and sided with the people. In Czechoslovakia, on the other hand, "democratization" was carried out by the party, hence the "quiet revolution." Basically, the party machine, the army, and the security services were untouched. There was continuity, not a fundamental break, with the previous regime. Older communist leaders were replaced by younger communist leaders, so that the party's monopoly of power and ideology was not broken. The Hungarian revolution occurred during the crisis of the communist bloc and was an expression of that crisis. The Czechoslovak revolution occurred during the period of the bloc's recovery from crisis and exemplified the bloc's long-range policy in action.

Some aspects of the Soviet reaction to events were a little strange.

Despite the exchange of criticism between the Soviet and Czecho-slovak leaders, they continued to visit one another's countries. Photographs appeared of Dubcek and Brezhnev warmly embracing one another. Nothing is known about the talks that actually took place between them, other than a few hints inspired by the communist regimes themselves. In the West this evidence of good relations between the Soviet and Czechoslovak leaders was either ignored or interpreted as a crude attempt to cover up the depth of the divisions between them. The revised interpretation of the "quiet revolution," based on the new methodology, suggests that these meetings were used for consultation and coordination of the further action to be taken by each side.

The movements of the Warsaw Pact troops on the Polish-Czechoslovak border, no doubt intended to recall events in Hungary in 1956, were too conspicuous to be accepted at face value. Their movement into Czechoslovakia was, on this analysis, an agreed measure of assistance to the regime by the bloc, as indeed the Czechoslovak party maintained at the time.[11] It was also an opportunity to season and rehearse troops from bloc countries in a "punitive" intervention in another communist country to stabilize its regime. Significantly, troops from those countries which had been most rebellious in the past (Poland, Hungary, and East Germany) were used in Czechoslovakia. But the primary purpose the intervention served was to drive home the lesson throughout Eastern Europe and the communist world that the United States and NATO were powerless to intervene and that internal opposition in Czechoslovakia or any other communist country would be crushed.

Conclusions

Given that the Czechoslovak leaders took part in the formulation of the new, long-range bloc policy between 1958 and 1960; given that their security and intelligence services were involved in the planning and preparation of activist political disinformation operations in support of this policy; given the indications that the economic reforms of Sik and others were planned from 1963 onward under the Novotny regime; given the indications that the Czechoslovak writers, in demanding "democratization," were not acting spontaneously, but in accordance with their party role under Hendrych's guidance; given the anomalies in the "democratization" process and in the alleged struggle between "progressives" and "conservatives" led respectively by Dubcek and Novotny, the inescapable conclusion is that the "quiet revolution" was a controlled operation planned and conducted by the party apparatus itself with the benefit of recent parallel Soviet experience in the preparation of a false opposition movement. It cannot, of course, be denied that some political and economic reforms were carried out in 1968, but it would be erroneous to consider them either as spontaneous or as far-reaching and democratic, as the communist leaders made them out to be. They were calculated readjustments made on the initiative and under the control of the party, which "had in hand the controls of command."[12] Goldstuecker, one of the leading figures in "democratization," put it bluntly to Salomon: "We have tried to develop an effective control of power from within our own system."[13]

The "quiet revolution" was an effective demonstration of the new, creative leading role of the party working through its economists, historians, writers, rehabilitated members, and alleged "progressives" and using the techniques of political action and disinformation. It was radically unlike the spontaneous Hungarian revolution. It represented a further stage in the extension of controlled disinformation operations throughout the bloc to serve the purposes of long-range policy and strategy. It had some purely local, Czechoslovak elements. Among these were, for example, the exposure of the Jan Masaryk affair (the whole story of which has not yet been told), the acceptance of noncommunist parties (controlled effectively by the regime), and the alleged "removal" of Novotny (more likely a natural retirement, as in Khrushchev's case, for reasons of age or health).

Communist Gains and Losses from "Democratization"

Undoubtedly the Soviet government and the bloc as a whole lost prestige through their so-called intervention in Czechoslovakia. But the immediate and future advantages in terms of long-range bloc policy and strategy definitely outweighed the losses.

Before 1968 there were acute problems in Czechoslovakia, which demanded solutions. The communist party, the regime, and its institutions were discredited and unpopular; there was a need for change in the party leadership; there was internal and external opposition to the regime; there was discontent among the intellectuals and formerly imprisoned party members; there was Slovak resentment at Czech domination; the unattractive stigma of the crushing of democracy in February 1948 still attached to communists in Western Europe and hampered their electoral collaboration with liberals and socialists.

With the help and support of the leaders of the other bloc regimes, the Czechoslovak leaders developed communist solutions to these problems through calculated and controlled "democratization." They succeeded in revitalizing the party, the regime, and its institutions and in giving them a new, more democratic image. They solved the succession problem without convulsions or a power struggle. They committed the younger party leaders to the continuation of the long-range policy and the strengthening of strategic coordination within the Warsaw Pact.[14] In the "quiet revolution" they demonstrated their long-range approach to the selection and training of future leaders and to rotation of the candidates to create a reservoir of experience. They developed their own Czechoslovak version of the disinformation on de-Stalinization and power struggles used already by the Soviet, Chinese, and Yugoslav parties. They succeeded in confusing and, partially, in neutralizing internal and external opposition to the regime.[15] They neutralized discontent among the intellectuals by involving them as collaborators in their policy. They neutralized the discontent of the imprisoned party members by rehabilitating them and giving them leading roles. They neutralized Slovak discontent by bringing forward Slovaks (Dubcek and Husak) as party leaders of Czechoslovakia and by increasing investment in the Slovak economy.

In short, the Czechoslovak communist leaders succeeded in preserving and in fact strengthening the power and effectiveness of the regime while at the same time giving it a new image. Dubcek was firmly identified at home and abroad with a new brand of "socialism with a human face," acceptable to Western social democrats and liberals.

Possible Implications of "Democratization" for the West

The Soviet, Czechoslovak, and bloc communist leaders and strategists gained valuable experience and insight into Western reactions
to "democratization" in Czechoslovakia. The Dubcek government,
communist though it was, rapidly acquired a radically new image
in the West. It was perceived not as an oppressive, totalitarian
regime, tainted by the stigma of February 1948 and deserving to
be scorned and shunned on that account, but as the harbinger of
a new era of "socialism with a human face," deserving to be encouraged and supported by all currents of opinion. The Dubcek brand
of communism deprived both conservatives and the moderate left
of the argument that the acquisition of power by communist parties
in Western Europe or elsewhere would lead automatically to the
extinction of democracy as it did in Czechoslovakia in 1948. At
the same time it provided West European communist parties in
particular with a powerful new propaganda weapon and a new basis
for establishing united fronts with socialist parties in common opposition to capitalism and conservativism. In this context it should
be remembered that the international organ of the communist
parties, *The World Marxist Review—Problems of Peace and Socialism*, is based on and is published in the Czechoslovak capital.

In the short term Dubcek's departure was a setback for West
European communist parties; under Husak, the pendulum appeared
to have swung back toward a more orthodox and traditional brand
of communism. Nevertheless, the Dubcek government aroused
great Western expectations of possible future political evolution
in Eastern Europe and the Soviet Union and the emergence of
new brands of communism. Indeed, it can be confidently expected
that the experiment will be repeated both in Czechoslovakia (with
or without Dubcek) and on a broader scale in the final stage of
the bloc's long-range policy. Future "Prague springs" could well
bring electoral victory for one or more West European communist
parties. Provided those parties conform to the Dubcek brand of
communism, there is a real danger that socialist, moderate, and
conservative opinion, failing to realize the true nature and strategic
motives of Dubcek's communism, will accept the situation with

all its attendant dangers and potential consequences.

It would be worthwhile for the West to study the scenario and techniques of the Czechoslovak experiment so as not to be taken in again as it was in 1968. The scenario could well be repeated, in essence, although with local variations. Its main constituents are therefore recapitulated here:

- A revival of de-Stalinization, together with publication abroad of the memoirs of former party and other political prisoners.
- Subsequent publication of these memoirs in the home country and of new exposures and revelations about the old regime, especially through the medium of "prison literature."
- Rehabilitation of former party leaders.
- Stories of a struggle for power behind the scenes in the party leadership, and the emergence of "progressive" and "liberal" leaders.
- A writers' congress, with demands for greater freedom and the abolition of censorship.
- Production of controversial television programs, films, and novels.
- Emphasis on "socialist legality" and "socialist democracy"; emphasis on federalism rather than on centralism (in relation to Slovakia).
- Expansion of commercial freedom and an increased role for economic and workers' councils and trade unions.
- Suppression of censorship in the press, radio, and television, with greater freedom for cultural and artistic activity.
- Formation of controlled noncommunist parties and political clubs and organizations, such as Club 231.
- Reunions of political prisoners.
- Adoption of new laws on rehabilitation.
- Controlled student demonstrations.
- Secret meetings of the Central Committee and the choice of new, "progressive" leaders.

Objectives of the "Quiet Revolution"

The staging of the "quiet revolution" and its reversal served a wide variety of strategic and tactical objectives. They can be summarized thus:

• To give a new, democratic image to the party, its institutions, and its leaders, and to increase thereby their influence, prestige, and popular appeal.

• To revitalize the party, the regime, and institutions—such as the National Front, the trade unions, press, and parliament—and to make them effective organs of power and control in the political and economic life of the country.

• To avoid a genuine crisis and popular revolt by provoking an artificial, controlled crisis through coordinated action by the party, the security services, the intellectuals, trade unions, and other mass organizations.

• To prevent the controlled crisis from becoming uncontrolled by the introduction of bloc troops into Czechoslovakia in a move planned with and agreed to in advance by the Czechoslovak leaders.

• To demonstrate the uselessness of opposition and the powerlessness of NATO and the United States to intervene.

• To provoke genuine internal and external opposition into exposing itself, and thereafter to neutralize or liquidate such opposition (the regime may well have found it convenient to get rid of a number of genuine anticommunists by allowing freedom of travel for a while).

• To rehearse the use of Warsaw Pact troops in "stabilizing" a Warsaw Pact country in case the need should arise to use them in another "independent" communist state, such as Romania, Albania, or Yugoslavia.

• To secure a smooth succession from the older to the younger generation of communist leaders.

• To ensure the unbreakable identification of the younger party leaders with, and their total personal commitment to, the long-range bloc policy initiated by the older generation.

• To provide the younger leaders with experience in handling controlled political developments.

• To increase their prestige at home and abroad as independent, national democratic leaders.

• To bridge the gap between the older and younger generations, and to appeal to the national sentiments of the younger generation in particular.

• To support and amplify bloc strategic disinformation on political evolution, the decay of ideology, the emergence of new brands of communism, and the disintergration of the bloc into independent, national regimes.

• To give the Romanian and Yugoslav regimes an opportunity to demonstrate their independence by criticizing the occupation of Czechoslovakia.

• To do the same for certain West European communist parties.

• To enable those parties to increase their electoral appeal by identifying themselves with "socialism with a human face."

• To arouse sentiment against military pacts in Europe.

• To increase pressure in the West for the convening of a conference on security in Europe, the communist interest in which is to promote the dissolution of military pacts, the creation of a neutral, socialist Europe, and the withdrawal of the American military presence.

• To provide grounds for the future discrediting of Western statesmen (especially conservatives) and of Western diplomatic and intelligence services by misleading them over "democratization" and by falsifying their assessments through the unexpected invasion of Czechoslovakia.

• To rehearse and gain experience for the repetition of "democratization" in Czechoslovakia, the Soviet Union, or elsewhere in Eastern Europe during the final phase of the long-range policy of the bloc.

20

The Second Disinformation Operation: The "Evolution" of the Soviet Regime, Part Two: The "Dissident" Movement

WESTERN HOPES AND EXPECTATIONS of liberalization in the Soviet Union, aroused by the disinformation of the early 1960s, were largely dashed by Soviet intervention in Czechoslovakia in 1968, which underlined the return to a form of neo-Stalinism in the Soviet Union associated with the leadership of Brezhnev. But this new brand of Stalinism seemed unable either to conceal or control the forces of internal opposition. The West witnessed the emergence not just of individual dissidents, but of an entire "dissident movement" with an unofficial leader in the person of Academician Andrey Sakharov and with a marked capacity to survive persecution by the regime and maintain communication with the West. The phenomenon can be understood only in the light of past history and the new methodology.

Genuine opposition to the communist system in the Soviet Union in the period 1958–60, when the new long-range policy and the KGB's new political role were being worked out, was deep-seated and intense. Dissatisfaction was widespread among workers, collective farmers, priests, and intellectuals. It was particularly strong among Ukrainian, Latvian, Lithuanian, and Jewish nationalists. The opposition rejected the Soviet regime in principle. Its members did not believe in the possibility of "evolution"; they firmly believed that freedom could come only through a new revolution, the overthrow of the regime, and the dissolution of the communist party. They did not call themselves dissidents nor were they described as such by the regime. They were known in KGB and party documents as "enemies of the people."

The KGB was capable of preventing and neutralizing contacts between the West and genuine opponents of the regime; publication of material regarded as inimical to Soviet interests was effectively suppressed. Two examples, known to the author in 1961, illustrate the point. In that year a prominent Soviet author and journalist, V. Grossman, wrote an anti-Soviet book and tried to have it published abroad. The idea conveyed by the book was that the main fault in the Soviet leadership was not the cult of Stalin, but the cult of Lenin and his works. Grossman handed his manuscript to the former Swedish ambassador and dean of the Moscow diplomatic corps, Sulman. The KGB learned of this, and a special operational group was set up on Shelepin's instructions to use any available means to recover the manuscript. The Politburo was concerned at the effect it might have on foreign communist parties if it was published abroad, especially at a time when the new long-range policy had recently been adopted. Within days the manuscript was delivered by Shelepin to the Politburo. The West knew nothing of the affair at the time.

In the same year a prominent scientist named Zagormister, a former Soviet deputy minister of geology who had access to important secret information on the status of nuclear questions in the Soviet Union, requested political asylum from the Israeli embassy in Helsinki while on a visit to Finland. His request was refused, and he was referred to the Finnish police. Through their secret sources in Finland, the KGB residency in Helsinki received a report that a prominent Soviet official had tried to defect to the West and had asked the Finnish authorities for help. The KGB intervened. Zagormister was handed over to the Soviet consul, Sergeyev, a KGB officer, who returned him to the Soviet Union in an embassy car. Zagormister was interrogated by the KGB in Moscow. He died of a heart attack when he was shown a copy of his conversation with the Finnish police. Again, nothing was known or published about this tragic incident in the Western press.

The serious challenge to the regime from the real opposition required special measures. The preparations made by the Central Committee and the KGB to deal with this and other problems have been described. They were based on the techniques of political provocation and prophylaxis used with success by Dzerzhinskiy in the 1920s.

Briefly, Dzerzhinskiy's GPU, faced with the problem of a strong internal opposition supported and exploited by émigrés and Western governments, created a false opposition movement known as the Trust, which it used to expose, confuse, and neutralize genuine internal and external opposition. By tricking the émigrés and Western intelligence services into supporting the Trust, they effectively isolated the genuine internal opposition from the outside world. Furthermore, the successful projection through the Trust of a false image of the Soviet regime in evolution toward a more conventional national European system helped the Soviet leaders to achieve their diplomatic aims, such as recognition by and closer relations with the major European powers and China, the acquisition of Western economic expertise, and, through the Treaty of Rapallo, the supply of military aid by Germany.

Applying the new methodology to the emergence of the present dissident movement means taking into account:

• All the evidence of a return to Dzerzhinskiy's techniques of political provocation and disinformation, following the weakness and evolution pattern and, in particular, the known advocacy of such methods by Mironov and Shelepin.

• The specific instructions given by Mironov and Shelepin to the KGB in 1959 to use its expanded intelligence potential among scientists, writers, and other intellectuals for political purposes and to prepare political operations and experiments aimed at dissolving internal opposition in the Soviet Union.

• The strategic role played by KGB agents of influence among Soviet scientists in the 1960s in promoting the idea of common interests between the Soviet Union and the United States.

• The debate in the 1960s between "liberal" and "conservative" writers inspired and controlled by the KGB through its agents Tvardovskiy and Kochetov.

• The known assets of the KGB among scientists, writers, and other intellectuals in 1960 and the likelihood of their further expansion since then.

• The prominence of scientists and writers in the dissident movement.

If all these factors are kept in mind, there can be no reasonable doubt that the dissident movement as a whole is a KGB-controlled false opposition movement analogous to the Trust and that many of its leading members are active and willing collaborators with the Central Committee and the KGB. Only if this interpretation is accepted is it possible to explain why a totalitarian, neo-Stalinist regime should allow a degree of Western contact with, and freedom of movement to, prominent "opposition" figures. It is, of course, more than likely that some of the individual rank and file dissidents are honest people who have become involved in the movement without realizing how they will be exploited and eventually victimized. The movement would not be fulfilling its internal function if it did not succeed in attracting innocents.

The main apparent purpose of the movement is to strive for democratization, human rights, and the fulfillment of the Helsinki agreements. The overall impression created in the West is that of a deep-rooted, spontaneous struggle between the regime's conservative supporters and liberal scientists, writers, and other intellectuals. Intense Western indignation, sympathy, and support are naturally aroused by news that "dissidents" like Sakharov are being harrassed, arrested, and sentenced to imprisonment or exile without trial. Emotions are further heightened by the deliberately engineered connection between the problems of Soviet dissidents and those of Soviet Jews. It is perhaps the emotionialism of the West's response that clouds perception of the fact that much of Western knowledge of the dissident movement is acquired by courtesy of the Soviet authorities.

The growth of the dissident movement is often seen as one of the fruits of East-West détente in the 1960s. Despite the present apparent persecution of dissidents, long-term Western hopes and expectations of a future liberalization of the Soviet regime have come to be pinned on the eventual success of their "heroic struggle." In fact both the dissident movement and the conspicuous harrassment of it by the Soviet authorities are largely artificial, and both form part of the deliberate stage-setting for the final phase of long-range bloc policy. This may be expected to begin soon after Brezhnev's disappearance from the political scene, and is likely to include a spurious liberalization of the regime rendered plausible by the "rehabilitation" of the present dissident leaders.

The parallel between the dissident movement and the Trust is not of course exact. World conditions changed profoundly in the fifty years between them. In the 1920s Lenin, Dzerzhinskiy, and the GPU were fighting for the survival of communism in one country. In the 1960s and 1970s dissidence of different kinds came to be exploited throughout the communist bloc, conspicuously in Czechoslovakia in 1968. Dissident movements are discernible elsewhere in Eastern Europe and even in China.

The present chapter will be confined to an examination of the unofficial dissident leader, Sakharov, now living in internal exile in the city of Gor'kiy.

Sakharov

Sakharov is a scientist of distinction whose past services to the Soviet regime in the development of nuclear weapons are officially recognized. As one of the chief scientific advisers to the Soviet government, he would have had access to the most sensitive nuclear secrets and an insight into Soviet strategy and Soviet relations in the nuclear field with other communist states, including China. It is inconceivable that, if he were seriously at odds with the regime and therefore a security risk, he would have been given the opportunities he has had to maintain contact with Western friends and colleagues. Even from his "exile" in Gor'kiy, he is able to convey his views to the West through intermediaries and correspondence. The only conclusion consistent with these facts is that Sakharov is still a loyal servant of his regime, whose role is now that of a senior disinformation spokesman for the Soviet strategists.

The theme of "common interests" between East and West, developed by Soviet agents of influence in the 1960s, was expanded after 1968, most notably in Sakharov's writings, into the concept of "convergence" between the communist and noncommunist systems.

Before examining Sakharov's statements, brief reference must be made to the Change of Signposts movements described above. The adherents of this movement asserted that the Soviet regime was evolving from an ideological into a conventional, national, capitalistic state. Therefore, they argued, White Russian émigrés should not struggle against the Soviet regime, but should cooperate with it in order to encourage the development of these trends. The movement had a significant effect both on the émigrés and on the Western governments with which they were in touch, and it created favorable conditions for the regime to win Western diplomatic recognition and economic help. But the adherents of the Change of Signposts movement were mistaken. Diplomatic recognition and economic help did not result in the evolution of the Soviet Union into a conventional, capitalistic, national state. On the contrary, the Soviet regime emerged from the 1920s stronger, more aggressive, and more ideological than before. The adherents of the Change of Signposts movement were exposed as bankrupt prophets.

Western convergence theorists are unwittingly and naively accepting basically the same disinformation message as the former adherents of the Change of Signposts movement, namely that the influence of communist ideology is in decline, that communist regimes are coming closer to the Western model, and that there are serious possibilities of further changes in them that will prove favorable to Western interests.

In the 1920s the message was conveyed by the regime through the émigré movement: from 1958 onward, Soviet scientists were used. In the 1920s the message emphasized the natural tendency of the Soviet regime to move away from ideology toward a capitalist system. In the 1960s the arguments were rather different. Exponents of convergence argued that, under the influence of the technological revolution, the Soviet Union was developing structural similarities with the West; these structural similarities provided a basis for asserting the existence of common interests between the different systems. Further grounds for asserting the existence of common interests stemmed from the development of nuclear weapons and the necessity of avoiding East-West nuclear conflict. Also, it was argued in the 1960s that the existence of Sino-Soviet differences and Soviet moderation in comparison with Chinese communist militancy created a common interest between the Soviet Union and the West in resisting the "Yellow Peril" from the East.

Since the notion of genuine evolution in the communist world is unfounded, there are no grounds for asserting that it is converging with the West. And since alleged Sino-Soviet differences are also the product of joint Sino-Soviet disinformation, there is no basis for asserting the existence of common interests between the West and either the Soviet Union or China against the other. The notions of convergence and common interests have both been shaped by communist disinformation in the interests of long-range communist policy. Western convergence theories are themselves built largely on the acceptance at face value of communist disinformation.

Western desire for convergence between the communist and noncommunist systems, is, by and large, sincere. There is genuine, intense, and legitimate concern about the avoidance of an East-West nuclear conflict. There is therefore a Western predisposition to accept the authenticity of Sakharov's dissent as expressed, for example, in his treatise, allegedly circulated privately in the Soviet Union and published unofficially in the West under the title *Progress, Coexistence, and Intellectual Freedom*, and in the later book *Sakharov Speaks*.[1] Acceptance of spurious notions of convergence has in fact been widespread in the West. Acceptance of the authenticity of fabricated Sino-Soviet disagreements has been almost universal. The false notions inspired by these deceptions aroused expectations among Western policymakers and the general public of a serious improvement in relations between the Soviet Union and the West in the 1960s and China and the West in the 1970s. Whether Western exponents of convergence realized it or not— and most did not—their attitudes were shaped by the bloc and its disinformation effort, whose main objective was to create favorable conditions for the achievement of the strategic objectives of the bloc's long-range policy.

The main lines of Sakharov's reasoning on convergence are set out in *Convergence of Communism and Capitalism—The Soviet View* and in *Sakharov Speaks*.[2] In them Sakharov is concerned about the annihilation of humanity, and therefore offers a "better alternative." Then he divides present and future world developments into several overlapping stages. In the first stage, "a growing ideological struggle in the socialist countries between Stalinist and Maoist forces, on the one hand, and the realistic forces of leftist Leninist Communist (and leftist Westerners), on the other, will lead to a deep ideological split on an international, national and intraparty scale." According to Sakharov, "In the Soviet Union and other socialist countries, this process will lead first to a multi-party system (here and there) and to acute ideological struggle and discussions, and then to the ideological victory of the realists, affirming the policy of increasing peaceful co-existence, strengthening democracy, and expanding economic reforms (1960–1980)."[3] The dates "reflect the most optimistic unrolling of events."

Sakharov continues, "In the second stage, persistent demands for social progress and peaceful co-existence in the United States and other capitalist countries, and pressure exerted by the example of the socialist countries and by internal progressive forces (the working class and the intelligentsia), will lead to the victory of the leftist reformist wing of the bourgeoisie, which will begin to implement a programme of rapprochement (convergence) with socialism, i.e., social progress, peaceful co-existence, and collaboration with socialism on a world scale and changes in the structure of ownership. This phase includes an expanded role for the intelligentsia and an attack on the forces of racism and militarism (1972–85).

"In the third stage, the Soviet Union and the United States, having overcome their alienation, solve the problem of saving the poorer half of the world. . . . At the same time disarmament will proceed (1972–90).

"In the fourth stage, the socialist convergence will reduce differences in social structure, promote intellectual freedom, science, and economic progress, and lead to the creation of a world government and the smoothing of national contradictions (1980–2000)."[4]

There can be no criticism of Sakharov for his concern over the possibility of nuclear conflict. What is disturbing is that his reasoning on convergence goes further than the Western theories. He envisages convergence on communist terms at the expense of the West. From his reasoning it is obvious that he accepts the Sino-Soviet split as genuine in itself and as a genuine catalyst for the realignment of world forces.

To understand the true meaning of Sakharov's statements, his role must be examined in the light of Shelepin's report and the long-range policy adopted in 1958–60, the period in which Sakharov began to emerge as a public figure in the Soviet Union. As a leading spokesman of the so-called dissident movement, he has all the appearances of a political provocateur. If he were a genuine dissenter, he would not have had the opportunities he has had to make contact with Western friends and colleagues. Furthermore, as an academician working in the nuclear field, he would have enjoyed access at the policymaking level to debates on nuclear strategy at the time when the new long-range policy and the use of disinformation were being launched. He would have known the true state of Sino-Soviet relations in the nuclear, as in other, fields. Given the all-embracing character of the disinformation program, any pronouncement by a Soviet scientist on strategic issues must be regarded as having been made on the regime's instructions.

Moreover, Sakharov would have known that liberalization in the Soviet Union would eventually come not in the way he suggests, as a spontaneous development, but in accordance with a blueprint worked out carefully in advance by the regime. If he had been a genuine dissenter, he would have exposed the truth. That he has not done so points to the conclusion that he is acting secretly as a spokesman for the regime chosen for the task because of the natural strength of his appeal to Western scientists and liberals.

Sakharov predicts changes in the Soviet Union and other socialist countries. These changes will be revealed in the appearance of a "multiparty system here and there" and in ideological discussions between "Stalinists" and "realists," or "Leninists." In this struggle Sakharov predicts victory for the realists (the Leninists) who, according to him, will affirm the "policy of increasing peaceful coexistence, strengthening democracy, and expanding economic reforms." These future changes in the Soviet system are seen by Sakharov as a continuation of present political developments and economic reforms.

Reading Sakharov's predictions as the product of Soviet disinformation, the conclusion can be drawn that some of his pronouncements reflect the possible future course of communist actions and their timing. Further political and economic reforms are therefore to be expected in the bloc, and they will again be used for disinformation purposes. These reforms will display an alleged "increase in democracy" and other superficial resemblances to Western systems and will be accompanied by further demonstrations of alleged Sino-Soviet conflict. From 1980 onward an "expansion of democracy" and the appearance of a so-called multiparty system can be expected in the Soviet Union and elsewhere in the bloc. This would be the logical continuation and culmination of the disinformation of the two previous decades and would represent the implementation inside the bloc of the final phase of the long-range policy. In this phase some of the current "dissidents" and "liberals," like

Sakharov himself in the Soviet Union and Dubcek in Czechoslovakia—leaders who are allegedly persecuted by their regimes—can
be expected to become the leaders of new "democratic parties"
in their countries. Naturally they will remain under the secret guidance and control of their communist parties, and their emergence
as the leaders of new parties will be regarded in the West as sensational new evidence of a true liberalization of communist regimes
and as a new basis for the practical realization of convergence
between the two systems, as predicted by Sakharov.

Reading Sakharov's writings as disinformation and decoding his
messages in that light, it can be predicted that the communist
bloc will go further in its exploitation of the fictitious Sino-Soviet
split, carrying it forward to a formal (but fictitious) break in diplomatic relations and more impressive hostilities than have so far
occurred on the Sino-Soviet borders. This may well generate realignments of international forces that will be detrimental to Western
interests and favorable to the long-range policy of the bloc.

Sakharov predicts changes in the West, particularly in the United
States, "under pressure of the socialist states and the internal, progressive forces" in the US and other Western countries. "The
leftist reformist wing of the bourgeoisie" will win and will "begin
to implement a program of rapprochement (convergence)" with
socialism. Social progress and changes in the structure of ownership
will be introduced. A "leftist reformist" element will also start
collaboration with socialism on a world scale. Forced changes in
the political and military structure will occur. During the second
phase (1972–85), the role of the intelligentsia will be expanded
and "an attack on the forces of racism and militarism" will be
made.

Again, reading Sakharov's predictions as disinformation, it can
be deduced that the bloc and its political and ideological allies
plan actions in the future to secure actual changes in the West
of a kind that Sakharov describes. The purpose of these actions
will be to achieve political systems in the West approaching closer
to the communist model. The changes planned for the communist
system will be deceptive and fictitious; those planned for the West
will be real and actual. That is the meaning of convergence in
communist language.

It is noticeable and disturbing that Sakharov, a so-called dissident

Soviet intellectual, in his references to US "racism and militarism" not only uses the normal language of communist propagandists in referring to the present American system, but identifies himself with the substance of long-range communist projections for the exploitation of these issues and appears to be working for their fulfillment.

The most striking point about Sakharov's reasoning is his choice of dates, namely 1960–80, when he predicts the expansion of political democracy and economic reform in the socialist countries; and 1972–85, when he predicts forced changes in the US political and military structure.[5] That is to say, his dates roughly coincide with the dates of the adoption of the new long-range bloc policy in 1958–60 and the date for the inception of its final phase, roughly in 1980. This is no fortuitous coincidence, since Sakharov, the secret spokesman of the communist strategists and the secret advocate of their long-range policy, is seeking to inspire and to promote trends in Western thinking on convergence that will coincide with their designs. Read as disinformation and decoded, his predictions of convergence are predictions of the victory of the long-range policy of the bloc and the surrender of the West with the minimum of resistance. That is the true meaning of his "most optimistic unrolling of events."

In essence, Sakharov's concept of convergence predicts the very outcome for the West about which the author of this book wishes to convey a warning. Sakharov sees the outcome as "optimistic" and the result of spontaneous developments like the Sino-Soviet split and "political and economic reforms" in communist countries. He desires this outcome. The purpose of this book is to explain its dangers for the West because it would not be spontaneous; it would be the result of the implementation of the 1958–60 bloc policy in which calculated use is made of fictitious splits and fraudulent evolution and reform promoted with the witting or unwitting help of Soviet scientists and intellectuals like Sakharov and others.

The official communist attitude toward convergence theories is described in *Convergence of Communism and Capitalism—The Soviet View*. According to this book the Soviets attack convergence theories as expressed both by Western experts and by Sakharov. The Soviet leaders describe convergence as an "insidious form of Western subversion" and as a "new 'positive' form of anti-communism."

The Soviets say that the dissemination of ideas of convergence is elevated by the Western countries "to the level of government policy." In the Soviet view, convergence theories have two aims: One is to "renovate" capitalism; the second is to portray "a softening or weakening of communism." In other words, the Soviets see the first aim as to defend capitalism and the second as an effort to subvert communism. The Soviets single out for criticism theories of "bridge-building" and theories of "industrial" and "post-industrial" society and their proponents, Fourastie, Aron, Galbraith, Marcuse, Kahn, Brzezinski, Leonhard, Bell, and others. Bell is singled out for his theories on the similarities in the changes in the armed forces of opposing systems under the influence of the scientific-technological revolution. The Soviets show concern at the effects of convergence theories on Soviet youth and scientists and other intellectuals. Sakharov is given as an example of someone who has fallen under the spell of Western convergence theories and has later "advanced his own theories of rapprochement between the two systems." Another physicist, Kapitsa, is mentioned as someone who "subscribed to a number of the views voiced by Sakharov."[6]

There is a chapter in *Convergence of Communism and Capitalism—The Soviet View* with the intriguing title "Moscow's Use of Convergence for Its Own Ends." The authors say that the Soviet leaders find the concept of convergence useful as the point of departure "for the 'rejuvenation' of ideological education in the Soviet Union." Party workers concerned with doctrine and ideology are urged to refute "the new myths of imperialist propaganda" and to raise "to higher levels understanding of the 'richness and eternal validity' of Marxism-Leninism." The authors say that convergence theories provide a "foil against which to stimulate and add . . . zest" to Soviet ideological campaigns. More importantly, they provide "a cutting edge" to Moscow's contention that "the USSR continues under siege by an implacable and dangerous enemy despite the Soviet claims that 'capitalist encirclement' is a thing of the past and . . . that the balance of world forces has irrevocably shifted in favor of the USSR."

American propaganda and intelligence agencies and the US embassy in Moscow have all been attacked by the KGB in the Soviet press for spreading ideas on convergence and for using tourism and scientific and technological exchanges for the purpose of subverting Soviet citizens, especially scientists and young people. This "threat" to the security of the Soviet system has been exploited to justify the intensification by the regime of its controls over Soviet society. The Soviet attack on convergence has been linked with the attacks on Ukrainian nationalists, Zionists, and religious groups in the Soviet Union and abroad. According to the authors, Soviet analysts distinguish, among the proponents of convergence theories, between "enemies," who use the concept of convergence for subversive purposes, and "idealists," who include prominent scientists, partisans of peace, and "opponents of militarism." The "idealists," among whom Professor Galbraith figures prominently, are seen by the Soviets as "offering promising targets" for Soviet influence.

Since the authors of *Convergence of Communism and Capitalism—The Soviet View* do not take into account either the use made of disinformation in the past or the adoption of the new bloc policy in 1958–60 or the new political and disinformation role assigned to Soviet scientists at that time, their explanation of the use of convergence theories in current Soviet policy is incomplete. The real meaning of attacks on convergence by the Soviet leaders can be understood more fully in the light of the historical background, the analysis of Sakharov's statements on convergence given above, and the conclusion that he acts as a channel for Soviet disinformation and influence.

From the mid-1960s onward the communist regimes stepped up the ideological indoctrination of their own populations in preparation for entry into the final phase of policy in about 1980. There was a renewed campaign of ideological and militaristic indoctrination in the Soviet Union in 1966–67 at the same time as, and similar in content to, the Cultural Revolution in China and the attack on "counterrevolution" in Czechoslovakia in 1968. While intensifying their own program of indoctrination, the communist leaders sought to protect their populations from the negative influence of Western ideas and the spillover of their own disinformation. In helping to shape Western convergence theories, they had cast a potential boomerang against the West and took steps to prevent it rebounding on their own people. At the same time, it offered them good opportunities "to expose and attack the ideological subversion and tricks of Western propaganda." There was nothing new in this technique. It was a typical instance of political provocation. At the same time as the ideas of the Change of Signposts movement were shaped by Soviet disinformation in the 1920s, they were attacked by Soviet propagandists as a Western ideological subversion. The movement was actively exploited for the suppression of internal opposition. The difference between then and now is in the broader scope and greater sophistication of such provocations and the fact that they are practiced by the whole communist bloc.

Soviet attacks on convergence, therefore, have, first, a defensive and domestic purpose. Second, they serve the strategic objectives of foreign policy. They help to build up belief in these theories in the West as a sound and effective weapon for dealing with the communist challenge. The communist strategists hope and expect that their criticisms of convergence will be interpreted in the West as evidence of their own concern at the efficacy and impact of such theories on their own regimes and on their scientists in particular. They intend that such criticisms should induce Western propagandists to continue and intensify their efforts to advance convergence theories rather than divert their efforts to less irrational and potentially more dangerous themes.

Third, Soviet criticism of Sakharov and convergence may be seen as a Soviet effort to build up the credibility in the West of Sakharov and his like as genuine opponents and martyrs of the current Soviet system who are expressing genuine dissent. By disguising convergence as an "opposition" doctrine, the Soviets can gain greater strategic impact in the West for their concept of convergence—that is to say, to have convergence on their terms.

In the light of the 1958–60 bloc policy and the use of disinformation to support it, it can be seen that notions of common interest and convergence have not developed spontaneously in the West, but are the reflections and results of communist disinformation operations whose influence has unwittingly been absorbed by Western exponents of these ideas. Convergence theories are unrealistic because they lack foundations. The impressions that the influence of ideology is declining, that the Soviet Union is evolving from an ideological into a conventional national state, that there is a struggle between the Soviet Union and Communist China, and that the communist bloc is disintegrating are all false. These impressions are the product of bloc disinformation operations that have successfully hidden the true situation. Since 1958–60, communist ideology in the communist countries has been revived, restored, and intensified; the communist bureaucracy has been given a new, constructive purpose; real and effective, but secret, coordination between the communist countries, especially between the Soviet Union and China, has been practiced on the basis of the long-range policy. Whether intended to or not, Western convergence theories effectively contribute to the successful fulfillment of this policy. They promote détente, and thereby help the communist bloc to acquire advanced technology from the West and to shift the balance of power in communist favor. They provide an unsound basis for a rational Western response to the increasing communist political and military threat. They promote the political and ideological disarmament of the West. They divert Western diplomatic effort from the reinforcement of Western anticommunist alliances toward illusory and unrealistic realignments with one or another communist state. They create exaggerated expectations in the West about the possibilities of accommodation with the communist world. They are laying a basis for destroying Western morale and public confidence in those Western statesmen, diplomats, and academics who have expounded theories based on common interests and convergence and who will be exposed as bankrupt prophets when the notion of convergence is exploded. Such has been the success of the spurious notion of convergence in the present phase of long-range policy that new Sakharovs and new variations of convergence theory may confidently be expected to appear in the third and final phase.

Objectives of Disinformation on "Dissidence"

The creation of a false, controlled opposition movement like the dissident movement serves internal and external strategic purposes. Internally it provides a vehicle for the eventual false liberalization of a communist regime; it provokes some would-be opposition elements to expose themselves to counteraction, and others are driven to conformity or despair. Externally, "dissidents" can act as vehicles for a variety of disinformation themes on the subject of the evolution of the communist system. A well-advertised wave of persecution of dissidents, partly genuine and partly spurious, generates Western sympathy for, and vulnerable alignments with, those who are secret creatures of the regime. It sets the scene for an eventual dramatic "liberalization" of the system by heightening the contrast between neo-Stalinism and future "socialism with a human face." It creates a cadre of figures who are well known in the West and who can be used in the future as the leaders and supporters of a "multiparty system" under communism. "Dissident" trade unions and intellectuals can be used to promote solidarity with their Western counterparts and engage them in joint campaigns for disarmament and the reform of Western "military-industrial complexes." In the long run the Western individuals and groups involved will face the choice of admitting that their support for dissidents was mistaken or accepting that communism has undergone a radical change, making "convergence" an acceptable, and perhaps desirable, prospect.

21

The Eighth Disinformation Operation: Continuing Eruocommunist Contacts with the Soviets— The New Interpretation of Eurocommunism

IN THE MID-1970s a display of polemics between the CPSU on the one hand and the French, Italian, Spanish, and to a lesser extent, the British Communist parties on the other seemed to indicate the emergence of a new brand of communism in Western Europe whose salient characteristic was independence of the Soviet Union. The new tendency came to be known as Eurocommunism.

The idea that Eurocommunism is a tactical and deceptive device adopted by the major West European communist parties to improve their electoral fortunes has already found expression in the West, notably in the paper *The Soviet Union and "Eurocommunism,"* by the distinguished British scholar Professor Leonard Schapiro.[1] Schapiro's paper also argues that, since Eurocommunism helps West European communist parties electorally, it serves the long-term interests of the Soviet Union. By drawing attention to this fact, the paper makes a valuable contribution. Nevertheless, since it is based on the old methodology, it accepts the differences between the CPSU and the Eurocommunist parties as genuine and continues to see the CPSU as striving vainly to reassert its hegemony over the European parties concerned. Analysis of Eurocommunism in the light of the new methodology strongly suggests that this is not so, that the phenomenon represents a further extension of the strategic disinformation program from bloc to nonbloc parties and follows a pattern similar to earlier operations emphasising the national independence of certain bloc parties. If so, several nonbloc communist party leaders have been made full partners in a disinformation operation in support of long-range communist policy and international strategy. The new analysis of Eurocommunism, unlike the old, illuminates the role that Eurocommunism may be expected to play in the final phase of the policy in the 1980s when "democratization," on the pattern of Czechoslovakia in 1968, is likely to be introduced on a broader scale in Eastern Europe.

The Manifestations of Eurocommunism

The principal manifestations of Eurocommunism are set out in some detail in Schapiro's paper. The characteristic tendencies exhibited by Eurocommunist parties may be summarized as follows:

- A desire to demonstrate their emancipation from Soviet domination.
- A critical approach toward certain Soviet repressive policies, in particular violations of human rights and harassment of dissidents in the Soviet Union and Eastern Europe.
- Rejection of the view that "proletarian internationalism" means that the state interests of the Soviet Union have priority over the interests of the international revolutionary communist movement.
- Assertion of the right of communist parties to follow their own revolutionary policies even when they run counter to the Soviet Union's pursuit of détente and economic links with the United States and Western Europe.
- Rejection of the view attributed to the CPSU that unity between communists and socialists is only possible if socialists renounce their adherence to "class collaboration": that is, for practical purposes, if they become communists.
- Refusal to accede to alleged Soviet demands that they should denounce the Chinese.
- Suggestions that an electoral victory by a communist party in Western Europe would be contrary to Soviet interests.
- The abandonment of the quest for "dictatorship of the proletariat."
- The apparent evolution of Eurocommunist parties into responsible national parties that, in contrast with the CPSU, accept existing parliamentary institutions and embrace humanistic and democratic principles including the preservation of "bourgeois freedoms" within a pluralist society.
- Condemnation of the use of terrorism by the radical left.

• Absence of the leaders of Eurocommunist parties from, or their non-participation in, international gatherings organised by the CPSU.

• Restrictions on the participation of Soviet representatives at Eurocommunist gatherings.

• Rejection of existing military blocs and espousal of the concept of a neutral, socialist Europe.

• The development of links with the Yugoslav and Romanian parties.

• The formation within some of the Eurocommunist parties of orthodox splinter groups loyal to Moscow.

Since there has been some variation in the manner and extent to which these general characteristics have been exhibited by the parties concerned, some of the main points made by each of them individually must be briefly mentioned.

The French Party

In May 1975 the party produced, in a "Declaration of Freedoms," a disguised attack on Soviet restrictions on civil liberties. On September 4, 1975, *L'Humanité* insisted that the party was committed to Western-style democracy. The following January the French communist leader Marchais said that his party's divergences with the CPSU over "socialist democracy" were so deep that he could not meet Brezhnev; he did not attend the CPSU congress in the following month, although his party was represented. Kirilenko, who attended the French party congress shortly afterward representing the CPSU, was denied the customary right to speak. In April 1976 the leading French communist Kanapa criticized the Soviet Union for praising President Giscard's policy at a time when the French party was fighting it. In May, when asked what he would do about French nuclear missile submarines, Marchais refused to comment. For the previous twenty-two years his party had continuously condemned the concept of nuclear deterrence. In January 1977 the Soviet periodical *Novoye Vremya* launched an attack on Jean Elleinstein, the deputy director of the party's research center. Elleinstein, who had previously written an anti-Stalinist history of the Soviet Union, published a new book, *Le P.C.*, in Paris in 1976 in which he said that there had been no liberty in the Soviet Union after 1922; he regretted that his own party had not followed the Yugoslav example and had been slow in criticizing the lack of freedom in the Soviet Union. Marchais did not attend the sixtieth anniversary celebrations in Moscow in November 1977, but sent a representative.

The Italian Party

In March 1975 Berlinguer criticized the pro-Moscow Portuguese Communist party for its undemocratic line at the time of the abortive right-wing countercoup in March 1975. In August, in reply to an article by Konstantin Zarodov, the editor of the *World Marxist Review,* implying criticism of the Italian party for seeking political alliances rather than insurrection, *L'Unità* said that the modern Italian situation called for an interweaving of democracy, socialism, and liberty. In February 1976 Berlinguer said he wanted to see a socialist society that guaranteed individual as well as collective rights. He also said that his party was committed to Italy's existing "international alliance." Four months later he said more specifically that Italy should stay in the Atlantic Alliance, which guaranteed "socialism in liberty, socialism of a pluralist sort."

The Spanish Party

In February 1976 the Spanish communist leader Carrillo absented himself from the Twenty-fifth CPSU Congress. In the following January the Spanish party weekly *Mundo Obrero* attacked East European governments for their repression of "dissidents." In April 1977 Carrillo published a book, *Eurocommunismo y Estado,* in which he maintained that, after sixty years of existence, the Soviet Union was still not a "workers' democracy." He advocated a pluralist society with "bourgeois freedoms" and a neutral, socialist Europe independent of either of the two military blocs. He is also on record as saying that United States bases would have to remain in Spain as long as Soviet troops remained in Eastern Europe. The book was anathematized in *Novoye Vremya* in June and July

1977. In response, Dolores Ibarruri ("La Pasionaria"), the veteran Spanish communist who, together with seven other communist leaders, had recently returned from many years of exile in the Soviet Union, proposed a resolution rejecting Soviet criticisms of the party; it was unanimously approved at an enlarged plenum of the party's central committee. The resolution supported Eurocommunism as the only way forward in the advanced countries. Carrillo attended the sixtieth anniversary celebrations in Moscow in November 1977, but was not invited to speak. He complained about this to Western correspondents. In April 1978 the Spanish party dropped the term "Leninist" from its title and incurred criticism in *Pravda* for so doing.

The British Party

In March 1976 the British communist leader McLennan told the Twenty-fifth CPSU Congress that his party was working for a type of socialism "which would guarantee personal freedom, plurality of parties, independence of trade unions, religious freedom, freedom of research [and of] cultural, artistic and scientific activities." In an article in the *Morning Star* in the following July, McLennan aligned himself with the Eurocommunist parties to the extent of denying that there was any single leading communist party and stating that each party should work out its own policy in its own country; no one else could do this for them. In November the revised "British Road to Socialism" was adopted as the party program; it advocated close cooperation between the Communist and Labour parties. In 1976 a group of hard-line opponents of Eurocommunism, under Sid French, broke away from the party to form the "New Communist Party."

Joint Statements

To some extent Eurocommunist ideas were developed by the Eurocommunist parties in open coordination with one another. For example, in November 1975 the French and Italian parties issued a joint statement after meetings in Rome supporting "bourgeois liberties, the plurality of political parties, the right to existence and activity of opposition parties and alternation between the majority and minority." Joint statements were made later by the Italian and Spanish and by the Spanish and French parties that dropped the commitment to the "dictatorship of the proletariat" from their programs. (The French party found it necessary to issue this statement despite the fact that it had not used the term since 1966.) In March 1977 Marchais, Berlinguer, and Carrillo held a Eurocommunist summit in Madrid that endorsed Soviet foreign policy objectives but pledged the participants domestically "to work within the framework of political and social forces and to respect, guarantee and develop all individual and collective freedoms."

The Soviet Attitude

Between 1974 and 1977 various articles by Ponomarev, head of the International Department of the CPSU; Zagladin, his deputy; Zarodov, the editor of the *World Marxist Review*; and others contained veiled and open criticism of "modern compromisers" and "bourgeois ideologists," meaning in fact Eurocommunists.[2]

An article in the CPSU organ *Partiynaya Zhizn'* (no. 4, 1974), described in Schapiro's paper as probably the first direct Soviet attack on a West European communist party, criticized the leading Spanish communist ideologist Azcárate for alleging that there was a contradiction between the state interests of the socialist countries and the interests of the revolutionary movement. He was further denounced for alleging that peaceful coexistence helps to perpetuate the status quo, for refusing to recognize that it serves better than cold war to create favorable conditions for revolution, for criticizing the Soviet Union, for opposing the projected international communist conference on the grounds that it might lead to the setting up of a new organizational center, and for stressing the independence of individual communist parties rather than the overriding importance of "proletarian internationalism."

On January 26, 1977, TASS dismissed Elleinstein's criticisms of violations of human rights in the Soviet Union as anticommunist propaganda. The Eurocommunist concept of a neutral, socialist Europe was implicitly rejected in the Soviet journal *Novoye Vremya*; the Soviets insisted in 1975 and 1976 that communist parties should characterize NATO as aggressive and the Warsaw Pact as defensive.

The Yugoslavs and Romanians

To some extent, the Yugoslavs and Romanians identified themselves with the Eurocommunists. For example, it is alleged that in the course of discussions in 1974 and 1975 on the convening of an international communist conference the Yugoslavs, followed by a number of West European communist parties, raised a number of questions about "proletarian internationalism." In the same period Romania openly defended the right of communist parties to independence. In 1975 both Yugoslavia and Romania backed the concept of a neutral, socialist Europe, opposed military blocs in general, and refused to characterize NATO as aggressive and the Warsaw Pact as defensive. The Romanian and Spanish parties in particular enjoyed close relations.

The New Analysis

There are various similarities between Eurocommunism and the disinformation operations already described which support the conclusion that it is a logical extension of the disinformation program intended to meet the requirements of communist strategy for Europe. These similarities can be seen:

• In the manner in which the alleged differences between the Soviet and Eurocommunist parties became known to the West.
• In the fact that these differences are based on the artificial revival of issues settled between the communist leaders in 1957–60 and are inconsistent with the evidence of the adoption of a long-range communist policy and strategy.
• In the exploitation of these issues to project a false image of the evolution of the Eurocommunist parties into independent, national parties with a view to promoting the success of their tactics, namely, forming united fronts with socialist and other parties.
• In the numerous inconsistencies in the arguments and polemics used

by Eurocommunist leaders in different contexts; and in the contrasts between their words and their deeds, especially in their continuing contacts
with Soviet and other bloc leaders which are evidence not of disputes,
but of collaboration in a joint strategy.

The Emergence of Eurocommunism

The evolution of the Eurocommunist parties toward "independence" followed the adoption of the long-range policy. The Eurocommunist parties were among the eighty-one parties that signed
the Manifesto of November 1960. When the Sino-Soviet split developed publicly in 1963, these parties, while avoiding condemnation
of the Chinese, aligned themselves informally with Moscow, thereby
identifying themselves with the moderate brand of Soviet communism rather than the militant, doctrinaire Chinese brand. In so
doing they boosted the moderate image they needed to play their
part in overall communist strategy for Europe, which entailed the
pursuit of united fronts with socialist parties. In 1965 and 1967
the Eurocommunist parties attended international communist conferences at Prague and Karlovy Vary in Czechoslovakia. In 1968,
in contrast with their supine behavior over the Soviet intervention
in Hungary in 1956, they publicly expressed their disapproval of
the Warsaw Pact intervention in Czechoslovakia, thereby demonstrating their independence of the Soviet Union. In the light of
their attendance at the Prague and Karlovy Vary conferences, it
is likely that the Eurocommunist parties' alignment with the Dubcek regime was planned and agreed to in advance as part of communist strategy for Western Europe. Allegedly the disagreements between the Soviet and Eurocommunist parties were discussed at
the world conference of communist parties in 1969. It was at this
conference that there was "the first clear indication that the CPSU
could no longer assert its traditional hegemony over the world communist movement."[3]

As in the case of the alleged differences between communist
parties of the bloc, this "indication," and others which followed
it up to 1973, came from veiled or oblique mutual criticism in
the party newspapers or from retrospective revelations by communists about debates between parties carried on behind closed doors.

Early in 1974 came the direct CPSU attack on Azcárate, followed by open polemics in the press of the CPSU and the Eurocommunist parties and retrospective evidence of disagreements at international communist gatherings in Warsaw in 1974 and Budapest in 1975, and to a lesser extent in Tihany (Hungary) in 1976. Finally, at the meeting of European communist parties in East Berlin in June 1976, "the full measure of the conflict between the CPSU and the 'Eurocommunist' parties . . . was brought into the open."[4] The validity of the earlier evidence of disagreements was confirmed. As in the previous disinformation operations, the original evidence and the confirmation of disagreements came from communist sources.

The Revival of Dead Issues

Among the issues that allegedly divided the Eurocommunist parties from the CPSU were the continued attempts by the Soviets to dominate other communist parties, to insist that they should faithfully copy the Soviet example, and to demand that, in the name of international proletarian solidarity, priority should be given by all communist parties to defending the interests of the Soviet Union. These issues were in fact settled in 1957, largely on Soviet initiative. Stalinist attempts to dominate other parties were rejected and condemned. Relations between parties, inside and outside the bloc, were reestablished on a Leninist basis of equality, trust, cooperation, and joint participation in the effort to achieve communist objectives.

The Eurocommunist parties attended the international meetings between 1957 and 1960 at which these issues were thrashed out and settled. All of them, by signing the Eighty-one–party Manifesto, committed themselves to the long-range policy and strategy that had been worked out with their active help.

Against this background it is easy to see that the revival by the Eurocommunists in the 1970s of the dead issue of the Stalinist concept of relations between communist parties was artificial, calculated, contrived, and agreed with the Soviets for the purposes of strategic disinformation in the same way as other dead issues were revived in other disinformation operations.

Exploitation of the "Independent" Image of Eurocommunist Parties

The revival of dead issues helped to promote the idea that the Eurocommunist parties were independent of the CPSU. The same purpose was served by suggesting that there were disagreements with the Soviet Union over the pursuit of united front tactics, especially by the Italian party, and that there was a conflict between the interests of Soviet diplomacy in improving relations with European governments and the interests of communist parties in acquiring power by legal means. Both suggestions were false, but both helped to emphasize Eurocommunist independence of the Soviet Union.

United front tactics were among the variety of tactics approved by the Eighty-one–Party Congress of November 1960. In his report of January 6, 1961, Khrushchev called on the communist parties to "synchronize their watches." Three months later, Suslov, a major communist strategist, led the Soviet delegation to the Sixth Italian Party Congress. There he urged the adoption of a moderate policy to achieve a broad, national democratic front. There was, of course, nothing new or unorthodox about united front tactics. They were specifically approved by the Comintern as long ago as 1935.

Equally there was and is no conflict between Soviet détente diplomacy and communist party activity. Friendly relations between the Soviet and Western governments favor the growth of Western communist parties. Détente diplomacy and united front tactics are complementary elements in a single communist strategy. Détente creates favorable conditions for the formation of united fronts. Ponomarev, head of the CPSU's International Department, made the point clearly in 1974 when he wrote that détente had the effect of neutralizing anticommunism within the social democratic parties, of undermining the militaristic preparations of the imperialist powers, and of strengthening the "realistically minded elements within the bourgeois camp."[5]

The harassment of dissidents in the Soviet Union and the denunciations of it by Eurocommunists are both calculated tactics. The conspicuous harassment of dissidents has its own strategic purpose, discussed elsewhere. Criticism of it by the Eurocommunists helps them to establish their credentials as genuine converts to democratic principles.

The Inconsistencies in Eurocommunism

There are numerous contradictions and inconsistencies in the statements and actions of "Eurocommunist" leaders. As observers like Schapiro have pointed out, the alleged conversion of Eurocommunists to democratic principles is inconsistent with the revolutionary programs they continue to advocate and the means by which they seek to implement them. Schapiro's paper quotes some telling statements by Eurocommunists on the use of force. For example, the Spanish delegate at the Tihany conference in May 1976, when asked whether the Spanish working class would have to resort to revolutionary violence, said that "abolishing a regime even by democratic means implies the use of force." Carrillo wrote in his book: "The new ideas also mean that the party is not an army, although it is able to become one if historical conditions, the violence of the ruling classes, leave no alternative." In addition he mentioned that party control over the communications media is an essential requirement, which gives some idea of the kind of democracy he had in mind. Schapiro's paper also quotes a report in the London *Daily Telegraph* of January 26, 1976, that Spanish communists had been trained in the Soviet Union and were being trained in Romania in the techniques of urban guerrilla warfare.

Even in Britain the party's aim of a "revolutionary transition to Socialism" is to be achieved by a combination of a legislative program with "mass extraparliamentary struggles" and the use of force against anyone in the right wing who attempts a coup d'état.

The theme can perhaps be developed further in the case of Italy with the suggestion that the denunciation by the Italian party of the violence of the radical left is yet another deceptive tactic. In a paper titled *Terrorism: International Dimensions*, by Paul Wilkinson, attention is drawn to the Soviet interest in direct or indirect support of terrorist movements.[6] There is a strong possibility that terrorism in Italy is backed and supported by international communism in parallel and in coordination with the use of legal, electoral, and parliamentary tactics by the Italian communist party. The object of violence is to create chaos and anarchy, to impose additional strains on ruling democratic parties, to eliminate their ablest leaders, to force them to resort to undemocratic measures, and to demonstrate to the public their inability to maintain law and order, leaving the field open to the legal communist party to present itself as the only effective alternative force.

Doctrinal justification for the use of terrorism is to be found in *Left-Wing Communism—An Infantile Disorder*, in which Lenin wrote: "All these fields of social life are . . . filled with inflammable material and offer . . . many excuses for [starting] conflicts and crises, for aggravating the class struggle. We do not and cannot know which spark out of the mass of sparks which are presently being strewn in every country under the influence of the worldwide economic and political crisis will prove to be capable of setting the fire alight, in the sense of . . . rousing the masses and we are obliged therefore with our communist principles to set about 'working over' every possible, even the oldest [and] apparently most hopeless field of action, since we otherwise will not be equal to the task, will not be thorough, will not possess every type of weapon. . . ." More specific was Shelepin's instruction to the Soviet intelligence service in 1959 to the effect that the service and its "illegals" should prepare and carry out operations that would destabilize the main Western countries and create chaos, which could be exploited by the local communist parties to their advantage.

Schapiro's paper rightly concludes that no rupture between Moscow and a Eurocommunist party has taken place and none is likely. Despite the polemics, the Eurocommunist parties have continued by and large to give their support to Soviet foreign policy objectives. In the same way the Soviet Union and the communist bloc in general have continued to support the international communist movement, including the Eurocommunist parties, in innumerable practical ways. As Schapiro points out, there is no substantial evidence that there has been any disruption of the banking and commercial channels through which the Eurocommunist parties have traditionally been financed from Moscow. Since the mutual criticisms between the Soviet and Eurocommunist parties are mutually agreed upon between the leaders, there is no reason why the Soviets should wish to disrupt these channels. Nor, since all the eighty-one parties that signed the Manifesto of November 1960 are pursuing a common long-range policy, is there any need for Moscow to seek to attach strings to whatever financial or other aid it gives them.

The anomalies in the adoption of Eurocommunism by Spanish communist leaders of the Stalinist generation, like Carrillo and

Ibarruri, are striking. At the enlarged Spanish party plenum in 1977 the resolution endorsing Eurocommunism was proposed by none other than Ibarruri, who had spent much of her life in the Soviet Union, who had lost a son at Stalingrad, who had been eulogized in *Novoye Vremya* in May 1977, and who had earlier described Eurocommunism as "nonsense." A few months after the plenum, she was back in Moscow for the sixtieth anniversary celebrations. The anomaly can be explained if it is remembered that she also was an active participant in the formulation of the long-range policy in 1957–60.

The enthusiastic support given to Eurocommunism by the Romanian party is not a little curious, given the espousal of "democratic liberties" by the Eurocommunists and the repressive internal practices of the Romanian regime. No less odd, in conventional terms, was the apparently cordial meeting between Tito and Brezhnev on the eve of the European communist conference in East Berlin in June 1976 and the award of a Soviet decoration to Tito during a visit to Moscow in the following year despite his support of Eurocommunism.[7] The anomalies disappear if Eurocommunism is seen as a further strategic disinformation operation. Carrillo's declarations of independence of the Soviet Union are then seen to be as spurious as the Romanians' and modeled on them. Both the Romanian and Yugoslav leaders have had an important role to play in supporting and coordinating the Eurocommunist movement. If accurate, the report on Romanian training of Spanish communists in urban guerrilla warfare is a further illustration of Romania's role in a coordinated bloc effort to assist the Eurocommunist parties.

Continuing Eurocommunist Contacts with the Soviets

The development of "differences" between the CPSU and the Eurocommunist parties has not, except in a few well-publicized instances, impeded the normal exchanges of visits between Soviet and Eurocommunist party delegations. Berlinguer attended the Twenty-fifth CPSU Congress in March 1976. He returned to Moscow for the sixtieth anniversary celebrations in November 1977 and was received in private audience by Brezhnev despite his commitment to pluralist democracy and the acceptance of continuing Italian membership in NATO.

Although Carrillo absented himself from the Twenty-fifth CPSU Congress, Ibarruri attended it. After the publication of Carrillo's book in April 1977, a CPSU delegation, led by the editor of *Pravda*, visited him, allegedly to work out some sort of truce. Carrillo was not afraid to return to Moscow for the sixtieth anniversary celebrations in November. The fact that he was present at the celebrations of the party he was purporting to criticize carries far more weight than his well-publicized complaints to Western journalists that he was not allowed to speak. Ibarruri spent a vacation in the Soviet Union in February 1979.

Marchais, the leader of the French party, stayed away from both the Twenty-fifth CPSU Congress and the sixtieth anniversary celebrations in November 1977, but on both occasions his party was represented, and at the European communist conference in East Berlin in June 1976 Marchais was present in person. In the course of 1977 the alliance between the French communist and socialist parties foundered as a result of communist intransigence. On October 2, *Pravda* published an article that was extravagant in its praise of Marchais's policy. Thereafter Marchais increasingly withdrew from the Eurocommunist camp to the extent of aligning the French party with the Soviet intervention in Afghanistan at the end of 1979.

The ease and impunity with which Marchais has been able to lead the French party into and out of Eurocommunism is one of the more startling incongruities pointing to the contrived nature of the movement. Various explanations have been put forward: One is that the CPSU opposed the French party's electoral alliance with the socialists all along and that when Marchais, presumably acting independently, saw fit to break off the alliance, the Soviets were ready to welcome him back into the fold; other explanations suggest that from late 1977 onward the Soviets belatedly used either financial or blackmail pressure to bring Marchais back to heel. Both these explanations are based on an outdated model of the relationship between the leaders of the CPSU and other communist parties; both imply the existence of centrifugal forces in the movement that disappeared with the adoption of the common long-range policy in 1957–60. This provided a firm ideological foundation for a disciplined, coordinated Leninist revolutionary movement experienced enough to be able to reap the strategic and tactical advantages to be gained from a display of spurious differences. The new methodology sees the termination of the alliance with the socialists in France as a temporary measure decided on jointly between the Soviet and French communist leaders in the interests of communist strategy for Europe as a whole. The decision may well be related to the timing of the beginning of the final phase of long-range policy, when all the elements in communist strategy for Europe will be brought into play together. The present interpretation perhaps provides an explanation of the fact that, despite the breakup of the alliance, communist ministers were included in the government formed after the elections in 1981.

The New Interpretation of Eurocommunism

Since the adoption of the long-range policy in 1960, a series of regional communist conferences can be traced that dealt with communist strategy in Europe. Of particular importance were those in Prague and Moscow in October 1965 and in Karlovy Vary in 1967, the year before the Prague spring. The Eurocommunist parties were represented at these conferences, which discussed the parties' appeal to socialist, Catholic, and other Christian forces and the creation of a Europe free of military blocs.[8] In other words, the parties were seeking to broaden the basis of their united front tactics, and at the same time were echoing the call for a Europe free of military blocs issued at the bloc summit conference in Bucharest the year before. The carefully prepared "Prague spring" of the following year, the deliberate association of the West European communist parties with it, and their criticism of the Warsaw Pact intervention helped the European parties to shed the stigma that was attached to them as a result of the events in Czechoslovakia in 1948 and Hungary in 1956; it gave a powerful boost to their pursuit of united front tactics.

What was new in this situation was not the use of united front tactics (the 1965 Prague conference was held in celebration of the thirtieth anniversary of the adoption of united front tactics by the Comintern), but the coordinated support given to them by bloc strategic disinformation on Czechoslovak "democratiza-tion."

If the systematic disinformation about differences between the leaders of different communist parties is stripped away, the pattern of coordination between them in knitting together the various strands in their common strategy for Europe becomes clear. A series of preparatory conferences was held before the meeting of European communist parties in East Berlin in June 1976. The series included a preparatory session in Budapest in December 1974 and a conference at Tihany in May 1976. Devlin noted that after the Budapest meeting "a curtain of official secrecy descended over the proceedings."[9] But a detailed account of the Tihany meeting was eventually published four months later in *Problems of Peace and Socialism*. The account reflected very little discussion of "Euro-communist" issues. The closing speech was delivered by Zarodov, who "argued at length the strength which derives from unity and coordination of revolutionary action—a view with which the over-whelming majority of the parties represented agreed."[10] The old methodology assumes (and has assumed since 1960) that the differ-ences between communist parties are real and that the talk of coordination between them is so much bluster intended to cover up the differences. The new methodology argues that the differences are spurious and are designed to cover up the coordination, which is real and which includes agreement to "disagree" for tactical and strategic purposes.

As Tito and Kardelj put it, it is actions, not words, that count; or, as Rumyantsev wrote in *Problems of Peace and Socialism*, state-ments should be evaluated in terms of "class analysis."[11] The polem-ics between the Soviet and Eurocommunist leaders should therefore be read not as propaganda, but as disinformation intended to help the achievement of strategic or tactical objectives. The point can be illustrated by Berlinguer's statement on television, which was broadcast five days before the elections in June 1976, that Italy should stay in the Atlantic Alliance. The pattern shows up clearly in the Spanish case also. The Eurocommunist summit meeting of French, Italian, and Spanish leaders was held in Madrid in March 1977. One month later the decision was taken to legalize the Spanish party, and in the same month Carrillo published *Eurocommunismo y Estado*. Two months later elections were held for the new Spanish

Chamber of Deputies. If the Spaniards went further in their "anti-Sovietism" than the other Eurocommunist parties, this was because they had been deeply compromised by their treatment of socialists, anarchists, and others during the Spanish Civil War and needed urgently to refurbish their image if they were to acquire legal status, gain representation in parliament, and successfully pursue an alliance with the socialists.

Confirmation of the tactical nature of protestations by Eurocommunists of their conversion to democracy is to be found in a speech made in February 1976 by Dorofeyev, a leading Soviet expert on Italian affairs. Dorofeyev justified the Italian party's advocacy of certain specific freedoms on the grounds that it was intended solely as a means of winning over the Italian petty bourgeoisie. He explained that in reality the proletariat interpreted freedom quite differently from its temporary allies, and that consequently there was no need to be alarmed by changes of this kind in the programs of communist parties, which maintained a consistently revolutionary position.[12]

Lenin advised the use of moderate language to avoid frightening the bourgeoisie. It was with such considerations in mind that Eurocommunist parties dropped the "dictatorship of the proletariat," and in the case of the Spanish party, even the word "Leninist" from its title. In dropping the "dictatorship of the proletariat," the Eurocommunist parties were following the example of the CPSU, which did so in 1961, also to improve its image.

The Possible Adverse Effects on International Communism

Real disputes between the leaders of bloc and nonbloc parties would have a damaging effect on the international communist movement. Active collaboration between them in a disinformation operation based on false disputes serves to cement their working relationships; they can but enjoy together their success in fooling outside observers.

Given that dissident movements in the communist bloc are under the control of the security services, neither the movements themselves nor Eurocommunist support for them represent any threat to the security of communist regimes. Potential adverse effects of

Eurocommunist ideas on the membership of bloc parties that are not privy to disinformation operations are no doubt neutralized by secret party letters and briefings. As far as the East European general public is concerned, it can be protected from contamination by a combination of press censorship, intensified ideological work, and the dismissal of allegations of violations of human rights as Western bourgeois propaganda. In any case, given that the Eurocommunist dispute is a planned and controlled dispute, the appearance of adverse effects on either side of the iron curtain can be swiftly countered by damping down or dropping the dispute altogether.

Senior members of the Eurocommunist parties no doubt appreciate the concrete tactical and strategic dividends to be derived from the exchange of criticism with the Soviet Union and realize that no sacrifice of communist principles is entailed. Nevertheless, the formation of a few pro-Moscow splinter groups might be held to be damaging to the Eurocommunist parties. Taking a long-term view, this is not necessarily so and the arguments that follow apply equally to the formation of pro-Chinese splinter groups as a result of the Sino-Soviet split.

In some cases the formation of splinter groups may have been controlled. For example, the expulsion from the Spanish party in 1970 of a group of Stalinists who later formed the Spanish Communist Workers Party under Enrique Lister might have been part of the forward planning for Eurocommunism. In other cases splinter groups may have resulted from the spontaneous reaction of hardcore rank and file elements who were not initiated into high-level communist strategy. Such groups tend to contain the more militant strain of revolutionary. Even if they are involved in more or less violent disputes with one another or with the principal communist party, they remain under the influence of one or another member of the communist bloc, and not of any pro-Western or social democratic party. They provide a reserve of organized militants whose hour may come with a future shift in the communist line and the abandonment of parliamentary united front tactics.

For Soviet leaders, untroubled as they are by electoral considerations, the temporary loss to Soviet international prestige entailed by Eurocommunist criticisms of their system is a small price to pay for the actual and potential strategic and tactical gains stemming from the improvement in the image and influence of the European communist parties.

Implications for Western Propaganda

The identification of Eurocommunism as a disinformation operation has obvious implications for Western policies and propaganda concerned with communism. Ideas of exacerbating friction between the leaders of the bloc and Eurocommunist parties are self-defeating because there is no real friction. Western anticommunists who align themselves with Eurocommunists in support of East European "dissidents" are playing into their enemy's hands; they are falling for a communist provocation. The vulnerability of these alignments will be exposed when "liberalization" occurs in Eastern Europe in the final phase of long-range policy. Meanwhile, they confer greater respectability on Eurocommunists. Western anticommunist policies and propaganda can only recover their effectiveness if they are based on a correct understanding of the origins, nature, and objectives of the long-range policy and strategy and the disinformation techniques used in their implementation.

Conclusion

By 1969 the bloc strategists had had a decade of experience in controlling and exploiting artificial disputes between the leaders of certain of the bloc parties. They had also had the experience of a controlled experiment in "democratization" in Czechoslovakia. They had seen how the West had been taken in by each of their disinformation operations in turn. They had seen how the image of West European communist parties had been improved by their association with the Dubcek brand of communism and by their "independent" stand on Warsaw Pact intervention in Czechoslovakia in August 1968. Although the Dubcek experiment had been brought to an end, there had been time for an assessment of its potential as a means of influencing Western attitudes to communism. The effect had been profound. It therefore made sense in the 1970s to explore the potential of artificial disputes with European communist parties to improve their future prospects. Such disputes, in the form of Eurocommunism, could be fitted into the pattern of the other disinformation operations. Eurocommunism could be supported by Romania and Yugoslavia, the "independent" communist states, and attacked both by the Soviets and Chinese. Mutual criticisms between the Soviets and Eurocommunists would help to dispel fears of the introduction of a Soviet system into Western Europe and confirm the sincerity of the Eurocommunists conversion to democratic principles. Chinese accusations that Eurocommunists were falling under social democratic influence could further the illusion that this was so. With their credentials thus improved, the Eurocommunist parties would stand to gain new allies among the working classes, the social democrats, the petty bourgeoisie, the intelligentsia, the churches, and the armed forces and thus be able to play a more influential role in overall communist strategy in Europe. Like Czechoslovak democratization, Eurocommunism should be viewed as an experiment and rehearsal for the final phase of policy. Its potential has not yet been fully realized.

Objectives of Eurocommunism

The extension of already proven disinformation techniques into Western Europe to suggest the evolution of the Eurocommunist parties into liberalized, independent, responsible national parties was intended to:

• Conceal the coordination between the Eurocommunist parties and the bloc in the pursuit of a common strategy for Europe.
• Suggest further disintegration in the international communist movement, and therefore a diminution in its threat to the noncommunist world.
• Improve the capacity of the Eurocommunist parties to achieve influence and power legally through united front tactics.
• Prepare the ground, in coordination with bloc policy in general, for an eventual "liberalization" in the Soviet Union and Eastern Europe and a major drive to promote the dissolution of NATO and the Warsaw Pact and the withdrawal of the American military presence from a neutral, socialist Europe.

—————————————————————————————

The Role of Disinformation and Intelligence Potential in the Realization of the Communist Strategies

THE DISINFORMATION PROGRAM has played a significant role in the successful realization of the communist strategies. A study of the available communist and Western evidence reveals the existence of at least six interlocking strategies for the furtherance of communism along the lines dictated by this long-range policy. The first strategy relates to the activities of communist parties in the advanced industrial countries. Its essence is the use of various tactics, such as Eurocommunism, the deliberate display of an image of a responsible, independent party to establish unity of action with social democrats and Catholics in Europe and to create a neutral socialist Europe tilted toward the communist side. The strategy envisages three periods. In the first period the communists seek temporary allies among the social democrats, the trade unionists, and the Catholics, including the moderates and the conservatives who could be brought into play against any alliance with the United States. In the second period the conservatives are eliminated and the social democrats become the principal allies in a neutral socialist Europe. In the final period the communists take the necessary steps for the complete takeover.

The second strategy deals with the communist effort to establish unity of action with the developing countries of Asia, Africa, and Latin America. Its essence is the use of various tactics, including the support of the national liberation movements by the USSR and other communist countries and capitalizing on the late Tito's influence in the nonaligned movement, which has served to lessen Western influence in these areas.

The third strategy is concerned with the effort to reverse the military balance of power, which in 1960 was tilted heavily in favor of the West. The essence of this strategy is revealed by a number of communist actions, including diplomatic negotiations, like SALT; a Chinese effort to make a false military alliance with the United States; efforts to increase Soviet military potential, involving the United States in an unpopular war like that in Vietnam; antimilitary campaigns in Western Europe; and terrorist acts against US military officials.

The fourth strategy deals with the undermining of the ideological resistance of the noncommunist world to the advance of communism. Its essence is not in the use of propaganda and the preaching of ideology, but by concrete actions and deeds, including calculated anti-Sovietism.

Underlying all of these strategies is the fifth strategy, that of the disinformation program. The most important element of this program is the calculated Sino-Soviet split, which has enabled the two communist powers to pursue successfully the scissors strategy, that is, having complementary dual foreign policies, the close coordination of which is concealed from the West and which has thus far escaped detection by the West. It is this scissors strategy that has contributed significantly to all the other strategies.

Although the communists have achieved unity of action with some Arab and African states and have generated antimilitary campaigns in Western Europe, they have failed to reach the majority of social democrats, the free trade unions, and the Catholics there. They were also unsuccessful in the United States largely because of the strong anticommunist position of the American labor movement under the late George Meany. The formation of united fronts in Latin America as a whole has been inhibited by the strength of military influence in the continent.

The Major Strategy

The sixth strategy, however, is the most significant. This strategy, which has been in preparation by the bloc for the past twenty years, deals with the solutions of the remaining problems with the unity of action and has a crucial role in the final phase of the long-range policy. This last strategy relates to the consistent effort to bring about a political and economic consolidation of individual communist regimes, the construction of so-called mature communist societies, and the preparation of a semblance of democratization in order to provide, in Togliatti's words, support for the communists outside the bloc in realization of the major strategies. In essence this strategy involves the interaction of the following factors:

1. The development of an effective political, economic, diplomatic, and military substructure under which the communists can continue to coordinate their policies and actions on a bilateral basis through a system of friendship treaties. This substructure would not be affected by the formal dissolution of the Warsaw Pact. A significant role in this coordination will rest with the party apparatuses, especially with the departments responsible for relations with the bloc countries.

2. The making of creative ideological readjustments and the revitalization of the communist parties and the mass organizations, including the trade unions and the youth and intellectual organizations. Further, the broadening of the political base of the parties and the development of the mass organizations into effective substructures of the parties. Such changes will make possible the introduction of controlled political opposition, which will provide the basically totalitarian regimes with a convincing impression of a fundamental change and a semblance of democracy. For example, within a twenty-year period the communist parties of the USSR and China almost doubled their memberships to seventeen million and thirty-six million respectively. In China this was accomplished during and after the Cultural Revolution. A major role in this revitalization was played by the ideological commissions and the cultural departments of the parties.

3. The preparation of a false opposition, during the introduction of controlled democratization in the communist regimes, for the purpose of creating a favorable condition for unity of action with the social democrats, the free trade unions, and with the Catholics against NATO and the US military-industrial complex. This preparation was revealed by the reorganization and reorientation of the KGB and the security services of the bloc countries, as ordered by Shelepin. The rationale was to coordinate their joint efforts and to introduce a false, controlled opposition along the lines of the Soviet experience with the false anticommunist organization Trust during the NEP under Lenin. Shelepin specifically ordered that agents of influence be used among prominent writers, scientists, trade unionists, nationalists, and religious leaders. He emphasized

the need to use agents of influence among the heads of the various religions, including the head of the Russian Orthodox church and the Moslem leaders in Soviet Central Asia, for political objectives. A significant and active role in such preparations is played by the administrative departments of the communist parties, which supervise the activities of the security services.

4. The development of an effective strategic coordination between the ministries of foreign affairs, ambassadors, communist parties, and mass organizations of the communist countries within the bloc and also of the communist parties outside the bloc. A significant role in such coordination belongs to the party departments of international relations and to communist diplomats. This explains why some communist ministers, such as those from Romania, Hungary, and Bulgaria, were in the past the heads of such departments. A significant role in such coordination, specifically for the realization of the strategy in Western Europe, rests with the Soviet Committee for European Security, headed by party official V. Shitikov. This committee was created in June 1971 for better coordination between the Soviet mass organizations in the struggle for the realization of a collective European security. The development and realization of the strategy is revealed by the numerous conferences of communist parties, especially in Moscow and Prague in 1965, and the high-level meetings of communist leaders with Brezhnev in the Crimea during the 1970s.

The study of available evidence leads to the conclusion that the Czechoslovakian democratization in 1968 was a rehearsal of this strategy to see how this scenario can work in practice and to test the Western reaction to it.

The Disinformation and Strategic Role of Yugoslavia

The new methodology makes it possible to see how the so-called independence of Yugoslavia has enabled her to play a leading part in promoting the success of communist Third World strategy. Yugoslavia was well qualified to bring her influence to bear in organizing the Third World, reorientating it toward socialism, and forging it into a weapon for use against the West. It was Tito who drew Khrushchev's attention to the political potentialities of friendship and cooperation with such leaders as Nasser, Nehru, and Sukarno. The reconciliation between Yugoslavia and the other communist countries and Yugoslavia's contribution and commitment to the long-range policy of 1958–60 were successfully concealed by disinformation. They have remained hidden for the past twenty years, despite the vast amount of evidence that can be interpreted as indicating the fulfillment by Yugoslavia of a strategic role in coordination with the other members of the communist bloc—above all, with those in Africa, Asia, and the United Nations.

Yugoslav influence inside and outside the nonaligned movement was acceptable to the neutralist and nationalist Third World leaders largely because they saw Yugoslavia, like themselves, as independent and, unlike the great powers, disinterested in dominating and controlling them. The Yugoslav brand of communism seemed more flexible and adaptable than the Soviet or Chinese version. Moreover, the penetration of Yugoslav ideas into the Third World was accomplished not through the traditional activities of a tightly knit communist party, but through personal influence and such mass organizations as the Socialist Alliance of the Working People of Yugoslavia and the Yugoslav trade unions.

On important issues, Tito's line was consistently anti-Western and helpful to the fulfillment of long-range communist policy. He took up an anti-American position in the Cuban crisis of 1962. He followed the pro-Arab communist line in 1967 and broke off diplomatic relations with Israel. He worked hard to persuade the nonaligned nations to follow suit. In 1973 eighteen African states broke off relations with Israel. Tito followed the communist line on the recognition of East Germany and influenced many Arab and African states in the same direction. He mobilized the nonaligned nations in condemning American intervention in Vietnam. He criticized American behavior over the civil war in Angola in 1975, and for a while the Ford Administration reconsidered its attempts to improve relations with Yugoslavia.

Tito was critical of Cuban actions in Africa and of Soviet intervention in Afghanistan, but many of his criticisms were muted and none led to any effective action. Tito and his Yugoslav colleagues can take a major share of the credit for the swing in the United Nations' balance, over the last twenty years, against the West and in favor of the communist bloc. A further point, with important implications for the final phase of long-range communist policy, is that Tito succeeded in winning the support and solidarity of many European and Japanese socialists for Third World national liberation movements.

To sum up, Yugoslav actions from 1958 to 1980 were closely coordinated with the Soviet Union and, latterly, with China. Through the use of disinformation on Yugoslav independence, which was accepted equally by the Third World and the West, Yugoslavia was able to play a major strategic role on Leninist lines in promoting united action with the Third World countries, in reorientating them toward socialism, and in converting them into allies of communism against the West. Tito well deserved the Order of Lenin he was awarded in 1979. He is dead, but his policies continue.

Because of Western failure to see through disinformation, including the violent Chinese and Albanian attacks on Tito for acting as an agent of United States imperialism in Africa, the United States and her allies have continued to regard Yugoslavia as an asset for the West and a moderating force in the newly independent countries; they have continued to accord her favorable treatment. But Yugoslav influence is dangerous. Already the groundwork has been laid for coordinated action between the communist bloc, the Third World, and many European and Japanese socialists. Without realizing the effect on its own fate, much of the Third World is ready to act as the most effective ally of the communist strategists in their offensive against the advanced countries in the final phase of policy.

Sino-Soviet Disinformation and the Cultural Revolution: A New Interpretation

Soviet denunciation of the Cultural Revolution as anti-Marxist and antisocialist helped to conceal its true meaning as part of the process of Chinese communist reconstruction. At the same time the Chinese leaders were able to exploit their alleged differences with the Soviets to rally the party and the masses behind them, during their most vulnerable period, by hoisting the flag of Chinese nationalism. In this they were repeating Stalin's exploitation of "capitalist encirclement of the Soviet Union" in the 1920s and 1930s to rally the Russian people to the Soviet regime. The difference in the Chinese case was that, deliberately deceiving their own population and the outside world, the Chinese included the Soviet Union among the "imperialist powers" attempting to encircle China. In so doing, they served their own interests in strengthening and stabilizing their regimes; at the same time, they served the strategic interests of long-range bloc policy.

Turmoil there undoubtedly was during the Cultural Revolution, but in the light of the new methodology, the facts are capable of a new interpretation. The Cultural Revolution was a part—and a very significant part—of the wider process of the communist reconstruction of Chinese society. It followed, as the next logical step, the reconstruction of Chinese agriculture. The newly established material basis of Chinese society required an appropriate Marxist political and ideological superstructure. For this reason, Mao called it "the great *proletarian* cultural revolution."

Apart from causing widespread economic dislocation, the creation of communes and the switch in priority back from industry to agriculture exposed the inadequacy of the structure and character of the existing party and its mass organizations. These were based mainly in the cities, whereas the real Chinese masses were in the countryside—hence the drive to send intellectuals to the villages. The ideological level of the party was too low and the tendency toward rigid, bureaucratic inertia was unacceptable. The decision was therefore taken to regroup the most highly indoctrinated and militant elements of the old party and youth organization into an alternative structure relying largely on the army and Ministry of Public Security to provide the necessary element of control and to prevent the situation from getting out of hand. The appearance of "political departments," detachments of Red Guards, and "revolutionary committees" was not spontaneous; it was instigated by the Central Committee. Not until essential preparations had been made on this basis for the introduction of an alternative power structure was the Cultural Revolution launched. With an alternative power structure in being, it was possible to abolish large parts of the existing party organization below the Central Committee level while huge numbers of party officials were being reindoctrinated. Meanwhile the alternative organization, drawn largely from the younger generation, set about its task of increasing its ties with, and influence over, the masses in order to fire them with revolutionary ardor and commit them to the policies of communist reconstruction. The Cultural Revolution was initiated by the plenum of the Central Committee in August 1966 and was guided and directed by the Central Committee throughout. That it was a revolution controlled from above was shown by its temporary interruption for the spring sowing season in 1967 and the simultaneous resumption of classes in schools on the Central Committee's instructions. The revolution, being ideological, was naturally directed by the Central Committee's ideologists, led by Chen Po-ta and Mao himself. By April 1969 sufficient progress had been made for the Cultural Revolution proper to be damped down by the Ninth Party Congress.

Although the turmoil died away, many of the processes begun before and during the Cultural Revolution continued. If the essence of the Cultural Revolution period from 1966 to 1969 was the creation of new organs of power and the attack by the "leftists" on the "rightists," then the essence of the following three years was the reabsorption of the older, reeducated party officials into the new organs of power and the attack on leftists, initially begun with the support of the army, which was then itself brought under firmer party control. The first signs of détente with the West began to appear. In the next three years, from 1973 to 1976, under the alleged guidance of the "Gang of Four," the process of reeducation continued. But now it was a more specific process of ideological and political preparation of the reconstructed party, government apparatus, and mass organizations for the new situation entailed by a shift to activist, détente diplomacy. With the death of Mao and the return of the "pragmatists" to power, full-scale, activist détente diplomacy was launched on Soviet lines with the aim of using economic, financial, and technological help from the noncommunist world to accelerate China's economic and military development. China was ready to play her full part in long-range bloc policy. She sought to align herself especially with conservatives in the advanced countries and Islamic regimes in the Third World, in order the more effectively to carry out the Sino-Soviet scissors strategy.

As in other communist countries, the process of communist reconstruction in China has been accompanied by the introduction of new, and the revival of old, techniques. In China's case the aims were to revitalize the communist party, to broaden its political base, to commit the younger generation to ideological objectives, to reeducate the older generation of party members, to control and neutralize internal opposition, to revitalize the state apparatus and armed services, and to prepare China as a whole for its part in the implementation internally and externally of long-range bloc policy. The techniques of political activism, provocation, disinformation, and political prophylaxis, which have been described in detail in the case of the Soviet Union, have all been used effectively in China. The alleged struggles for power in China between leftists and rightists, dogmatists and pragmatists, are as unreal as the struggles between Stalinists and anti-Stalinists in the Soviet Union.

Cooperation within the leadership to create the illusion of struggles between themselves or between the party and the army helps to forestall the threat of real struggles within the leadership or of tendencies to "putschism" in the army. It gives the party ideologists material to train party officials in fighting undesirable tendencies while at the same time preparing them for radical shifts in policy. The violence of the shifts in the Chinese line is a technique borrowed from that used by Stalin at the end of the NEP period. Stalin's shifts from left to right and back again were used to forge the party into a hardened instrument obedient to his will. The difference lies in the fact that Stalin used the technique to establish his personal dictatorship and the factionalism was real; the Chinese leadership used it to increase the effectiveness of the party as a whole and the factionalism in the leadership was faked. The recent reassessment and partial downgrading of Mao in China presents parallels with de-Stalinization in the Soviet Union and is designed in part to forestall the emergence in the future of any tendencies toward personal dictatorship in the CPC.

The formation of the Red Guards recalls the use of Komsomol activists in the Soviet Union during Stalin's collectivization of agriculture in the 1930s. The technique of using wall posters by the regime seems to have been borrowed from their use by the genuine opposition in 1956–57.

The Cultural Revolution and the whole process of Chinese communist reconstruction have followed Lenin's precepts on overcoming "infantile disorder" and isolation of the party from the masses. The reeducation of cadres and the restructuring of the party and its youth and trade union organizations were necessary both to achieve these aims and to prepare the Chinese system for activist détente with the West as the long-range policy unfolded.

Despite the alleged destruction of the party in the Cultural Revolution, in fact it strengthened itself. The Chinese trade union, youth, and women's organizations have resumed their activities.

As a result of stabilization and the reinforcement of the party and its mass organizations, the Chinese, like other communist states after 1960, were enabled to introduce NEP-style measures, including some of the appurtenances of democracy, such as wall posters; trials; the release of market forces; and the relaxation of controls over religion, intellectual life, working conditions in factories, and property ownership. "Dissidents" began to appear, on the Soviet pattern. Broader contacts were allowed with the West and more attention was paid to the overseas Chinese, whose relatives in China are said to number 12 million.

Sino-Soviet Duality and Communist Strategy in the Third World

Seen in the light of the new methodology, the Chinese effort in the Third World is complementary to that of the other communist states and an important element in communist strategy as a whole.

The character of the Chinese effort in the Third World from 1958 onward was dictated by China's historical background and current capacities. China had been freed from colonial oppression by a prolonged liberation struggle with Japan. The Chinese party had learned how to exploit conditions of military conflict to deepen its influence and win power. As a rule, Chinese and Soviet efforts can be seen in terms not of rivalry, but of a coordinated division of labor that has brought dividends for the common strategy.

Where a serious dispute exists between two Third World countries, a pattern in Soviet and Chinese policies can be discerned in which the Soviet Union and China take up opposite sides and adopt a clearcut duality in their policies. The Soviet Union seeks to build up its influence with one party to the dispute and China with the other. The classic example of this pattern is to be seen in the case of India and Pakistan.

The Sino-Indian conflict of 1962 was provoked by the Chinese. The Soviets took a broadly anti-Chinese and pro-Indian line that gained them goodwill in India. At the time of the outbreak of open Sino-Soviet party polemics in 1963, an Indian army and air force mission visited the Soviet Union. In the following year the Indian defense minister went to Moscow to discuss Soviet-Indian military cooperation. Further exchanges of military delegations took place in 1967 and 1968. In the mid-1960s regular consultations on problems of mutual interest were instituted between the Soviet and Indian foreign ministries.[1] The United States held India responsible for the Indo-Pakistani conflict in 1971 and terminated military aid to India. The Soviets called for a cessation of the conflict but nevertheless gave the Indians moral support, for which Mrs. Gandhi expressed her gratitude. A treaty of friendship was signed between the Soviet Union and India in August 1971. An influx of Soviet visitors followed. In October Firyubin went to India, interestingly enough in the same month as Tito. He was followed in the next three months by the chief of Soviet military aviation, Kutakhov, and the deputy foreign minister, V. V. Kuznetsov. In December Mrs. Gandhi condemned American policy in Vietnam.[2] In 1973 an agreement was signed for cooperation between Gosplan, the Soviet planning agency, and the Indian planning commission.[3]

Largely because of skillful Soviet exploitation of the conflict between India and Pakistan, by the mid-1970s the trend toward closer Soviet-Indian relations had become virtually irreversible. The Desai government was unable to stem the tide. Relations were further cemented by Brezhnev's visit and talks with Mrs. Gandhi in 1981.

While the Soviets were strengthening their hold in India, the Chinese were doing the same in Pakistan, using the same techniques of exchanges of visits and military delegations, especially during the years 1962–67. When the United States ceased military aid to Pakistan in 1967, the Chinese stepped theirs up. In 1968 President Yahya Khan and his foreign minister visited China. Further cooperation developed. In 1970 Kuo Mo-jo visited Pakistan. Pakistan was sufficiently close to China to be used as an intermediary in arranging the visit of Kissinger to China in 1971. Bhutto was received by Mao in 1972 after the further conflict with India and the formation of Bangladesh. The conflict resulted in Pakistan's departure from the British Commonwealth and SEATO. Further high-level exchanges of visits continued between Pakistan and China, regardless of changes in the Pakistani government.

As in the case of Soviet influence in India, Chinese influence in Pakistan is creating conditions for an alliance between them and for an eventual communist takeover. A situation already exists that can be further exploited by calculated and coordinated Soviet and Chinese moves, for example, in connection with the Soviet intervention in Afghanistan.

The recent Chinese moderation is intended to help build up the new image of respectability required by the Chinese for their détente diplomacy vis-à-vis the advanced industrial, as well as Third World, countries. It is also consistent with the emerging pattern of Sino-Soviet duality; while the Soviet Union builds up united fronts with nationalists against the United States, China seeks to ensnare the United States and other conservative countries, including the Asian and African states, in artificial, treacherous alliances with herself and her associates, ostensibly against the Soviet Union. In this way China seeks to enter her enemies' camp not merely unopposed, but welcomed as an ally against Soviet expansionism and equipped with Western arms.

In the present phase of policy, neither the Soviet Union nor China puts local communist parties in general in the forefront as strategic weapons. When the objective of isolating the United States from the Third World has been achieved, local communist parties will come into their own and accounts will be settled with nationalists who have suppressed them in the past.

Sino-Soviet Duality and Military Strategy

The new methodology illuminates the contribution to the success of communist strategies made by the division of labor between the Soviets and Chinese and the coordinated duality of their policies.

In the early years of détente, paraphrasing Lenin's words, the Chinese were given a "terrible double bass" to play in contrast with the Soviets' "sentimental violin." While the Soviets were emphasising détente and peaceful coexistence and taking up high-level contacts with American and European leaders, the Chinese advocated militant and violent revolution. Marked divergences appeared in the treatment in the Soviet and Chinese press of Khrushchev's visit to the United States in 1959. In February 1960, three months before the abortive summit meeting in Paris, the Chinese delegate at the Warsaw Pact conference criticized the Soviets for their rapprochement with the "imperialists," who had refused to make concessions on Berlin. On the eve of Khrushchev's meeting with the French President in April 1960, the Chinese press resumed its criticism of the Yugoslav "revisionists" and published articles calling for a militant, revolutionary approach to world problems while the Soviet press continued to emphasize moderation and peaceful coexistence.

Further divergences appeared in Soviet and Chinese handling of the Cuban and Sino-Indian crises in 1962, but perhaps the most striking instance of duality in the early 1960s occurred during the Soviet-American-British negotiations on the Atomic Test Ban Treaty in 1963. The arrival in Moscow of the Anglo-American delegation that was to conduct those negotiations was immediately preceded by the arrival of a Chinese delegation that was to conduct party negotiations with the CPSU. Soviet warmth toward the Western delegations contrasted sharply with their coolness toward the Chinese. Progress on the test ban talks was accompanied by the apparent failure of the Sino-Soviet negotiations. The signature of the test ban treaty was followed by interruption of the Sino-Soviet talks, attacks in the Chinese press on Soviet policy in the test ban negotiations, and open polemics between the Soviet and Chinese parties. A further eruption of Sino-Soviet polemics occurred before the Soviet-American negotiations on a nuclear nonproliferation treaty in 1966–67.

Subsequent events have shown just how little foundation there was for Chinese accusations that the Soviets had capitulated to Western imperialism in the 1960s and had sacrificed "socialist solidarity" and support for revolutionary struggle on the altar of peaceful coexistence.[4] The effect of these Chinese accusations at the time was to promote Western illusions about Soviet moderation, and thus to create favorable conditions for the success of Soviet activist diplomacy toward the United States and European NATO powers. In contrast with the implacable Chinese dogmatists, the Soviets appeared cautious, reasonable, nonideological, pragmatic communists with whom it was possible to negotiate a deal. Furthermore, they appeared sincere in their claim to have a common interest with the West in restraining Chinese influence.

Sino-Soviet duality produced the effect on the West that the communist strategists intended. It seems safe to say that it brought them substantial dividends. For example, had it not been for General de Gaulle's belief in the sincerity of Soviet interest in détente and his confidence in the authenticity of the Sino-Soviet split, it is more than doubtful that he would have gone as far as he did in his dealings with the Soviet Union, his recognition of Communist China, and his withdrawal of France from its military commitments to NATO.

From 1958 to 1969, despite all the sound and fury, China, by comparison with the Soviet Union, was passive diplomatically in relation to the Western powers. The contrast was only natural. The Soviet Union was already a military superpower engaged in strategic competition with the United States and NATO. The Soviets had a solid background of experience in dealing with the Western powers and a well-trained staff to carry out their policies. China was militarily insignificant, unrecognized by the United States and many other countries and short of trained and indoctrinated diplomatic staff. The onset of the Cultural Revolution brought a further retreat into diplomatic isolation.

In 1969 all this began to change. With the completion of the Cultural Revolution, China reemerged onto the international scene. Chinese activist détente diplomacy was launched. Trade, and especially the acquisition of advanced technology, bulked large among the obvious Chinese motives. In January 1969 a special West German ambassador, Egon Bahr, was invited to conduct trade negotiations in Shanghai. Exchanges of visits between Chinese and Western statesmen and military leaders became commonplace. A drive to obtain diplomatic recognition soon brought results. By 1970 it had been granted by fifty-five countries. On October 25, 1971, Communist China was seated in the United Nations; by 1973, it had diplomatic relations with ninety-one countries. In February 1972, after two preparatory visits by Kissinger (carried out initially in great secrecy and without consultation with the Japanese, the most directly concerned of America's close allies), President Nixon visited China. He was followed by the British foreign secretary, Douglas-Home; by President Pompidou of France in 1973; and by the West German chancellor, Schmidt, in 1975. The German and British conservative opposition leaders, Strauss and Thatcher, visited in 1975 and 1977 respectively, and the British foreign secretary, Crosland, in 1976. In return Chinese ministerial visits were paid to the United States and Europe, culminating in Teng Hsiao-p'ing's visit to the United States and Japan and Chairman Hua's journey through Europe in 1979. In the same year the U.S. President's national security adviser, Brzezinski, visited China, followed in the aftermath of Soviet intervention in Afghanistan by the defense secretary, Brown. The exchanges of visits between China and the United States, Western Europe, and Japan reflected not only the development of trade with, and credits for, China, but also the transfer of Western technology for China's industrial modernization and rearmament.

Three points about Chinese activist diplomacy deserve to be singled out for special emphasis. First, it has been continuously and consistently maintained throughout the 1970s despite the death of Mao in 1976. Chairman Hua said as much himself, on December 25, 1976, when he undertook that China would carry out the directives worked out by Chairman Mao.[5] Second, a preeminent role has been played by Teng Hsiao-p'ing, under Mao's guidance one of the principal Chinese architects of the long-range policy of 1958–60. Third, a noticeable feature of the Chinese choice of Western leaders suitable for cultivation, more readily explained in terms of strategy than ideological affinity, has been the proportion of conservatives among them. Some of them—Strauss, Brzezinski, and Thatcher, for example—were singled out as targets for personal attacks by the Soviets, attacks that did nothing to harm their relations with the Chinese.

At the same time as the Chinese were embarking on a policy of détente, the Soviets were building on the successes of their activist diplomacy in the earlier 1960s. Their efforts followed the three principal directions described above: SALT talks with the United States, CSCE in Europe, and closer bilateral relationships with certain European powers. Also, at the same time, the West began to realize that the Soviet Union had taken advantage of détente to build up its military strength.

Seen in the light of the new methodology, the stepping-up of Sino-Soviet border hostilities in 1969 and 1970 was not fortuitous; neither was the adoption by the Soviets and Chinese of diametrically opposite positions on many other issues. Duality in Sino-Soviet policies served to provide a favorable background for the launching and conduct of both the SALT negotiations and Chinese activist détente diplomacy. As far as CSCE was concerned, it was noticeable that the Chinese, while condemning the Soviets for their part in organizing the Helsinki conferences, nevertheless lent their support to the concept of a Western Europe "independent of the two superpowers," in other words, to the intermediate aim of overall communist strategy for Europe.

As the 1970s wore on and as Soviet aggressiveness became more apparent in Europe, Africa, and finally Afghanistan, China began to look attractive as a potential ally for the West. The common interest between the Soviet Union and the West in resisting Chinese militancy in the 1960s had been superseded by a common interest between China and the West in resisting Soviet expansionism in the 1970s. West European and Japanese capitalists tumbled over one another to build up China's economic and military potential, egged on by anti-Soviet conservative Western politicians and experts on defense. Alliance with China seemed to offer the best hope of redressing the growing military imbalance between the Soviet Union and the West, especially in Europe. The United States has been more and more disposed to "play the China card." The relationship with Communist China, initiated under Nixon and Kissinger and developed under Carter and Brzezinski, was carried to the point of military cooperation, under Reagan and Haig, with the intention of building up China as a counterweight to the Soviet Union. Both in relation to the Soviets in the 1960s and to the Chinese in the 1970s and 1980s, the West has forgotten the error of the German General Staff in helping to rearm the Soviet Union after the Treaty of Rapallo in 1922. The Sino-Soviet scissors strategy has not been recognized for what it is.

In short, first the Soviet Union and then China carried out the classical strategic precept of seeking to enter the enemy's camp unopposed and, if possible, welcomed by him. As Sun Tzu said: "To subdue the enemy without fighting is the acme of skill."[6]

Fighting between communist states is generally regarded as conclusive evidence of a split between them. But it should be remembered that the conflicts in the Sino-Soviet and Sino-Vietnamese border areas have taken place in the presence of few, if any, Western observers. Border incidents are easily staged and open radio communication about them can be used in support of their authenticity. Joint exercises can be made to look very much like battles. Even if genuine damage and casualties are caused, incidents are still open to more than one interpretation. Apparent fighting between communist states can contribute to such specific communist strategic objectives as promoting agreements and false alignments between communist and noncommunist states. For example, the Sino-Vietnamese "war"—and fears that it might spread—intensified Western pressure on the United States to conclude the SALT II agreement with the Soviet Union and helped make China look attractive as a potential Western ally against the Soviet Union.

Sino-Soviet Duality and the Revolutionary Movement

The Sino-Soviet split did not in general have the effect that might have been expected of splitting the nonbloc communist parties down the middle nor has it reduced their influence. Most of the West European parties became more active and remained broadly in alignment with the Soviets. Their association with Soviet "moderation" helped their images and improved their chances of success with united-front tactics. The Italian party was far more influential in 1980 than it had been in 1960. In France the socialist-communist alliance came closer to an electoral victory in 1974 than at any moment since the Second World War. Insofar as pro-Chinese splinter groups broke away from main-line communist parties, as in Belgium, for example, it was in general advantageous to long-range communist strategy. A calculated shedding of the most radical and violent revolutionary elements helped the communist parties to improve their images as respectable democratic parties and potential allies of socialist, Christian, and other progressive groups.

The Japanese party tried to take advantage of the Sino-Soviet split to broaden its political influence.

Chinese militancy and Sino-Soviet duality opened up possibilities of united action between pro-Chinese and other extreme-left factions, especially Trotskyites. In June 1963, coinciding with the outbreak of open polemics between the Soviet and Chinese parties, the Trotskyite Fourth International, in a special resolution, approved "the historic task of joining the Chinese and fighting for the creation of a united front between the Fourth International and the Chinese comrades."

In 1967 the Fourth International declared itself in favor of accelerating the revolutionary armed struggle of the masses in the main bases of capitalism. The majority supported Mao. A minority group, critical of some of Mao's ideas, proposed a more flexible line in fighting communist parties.

The Ninth Congress of the Fourth International was held at Rimini in April 1969. It discussed tactics in Latin America. The European section of the majority group held a conference in October 1969 and decided to cease attempts to penetrate communist parties and to create "independent revolutionary" parties. In the same month a congress of the minority group in Vienna approved the actions of splinter groups in the communist movement. At the same time it condemned refusal by these splinter groups to cooperate with the Soviet Union in support of the liberation struggle in Vietnam. Also in 1969, as the movement for CSCE was gathering momentum, Trotskyite meetings in protest against NATO were held in England, Denmark, Japan, and Australia.

The information publicly available is insufficient to allow judgment on the degree to which the activities of extreme-left radical groups have been successfully coordinated under Chinese or Soviet influence. But the rivalry, and sometimes even violence, between these groups and the main-line communist parties should not be allowed to obscure the extent to which the activities of all of them have served the aims of long-range communist strategy and might serve so even more in critical situations in the future. Ponomarev, while describing some of the elements of the New Left in 1971 as "adventurist," concluded that "to neglect this segment of the mass movement would mean to weaken the stress of the anti-imperialist struggle and hinder the creation of a united front against monopolistic capitalism."[7] Broadly speaking, since the adoption of the long-range policy and the development of Sino-Soviet duality, both the moderate communist parties and the radical, revolutionary, and terrorist groups have succeeded in gathering strength, often at the expense of genuine left-wing and democratic socialist movements.

In the early 1960s the international front organizations provided a convenient forum for the experimental airing of Sino-Soviet "differences." The repudiation of radical Chinese positions by these organizations helped make them less disreputable and, at the same time, apparently confirmed the authenticity of the Sino-Soviet dispute. When in the mid-1960s the Chinese finally withdrew from the front organizations, they made no serious attempt to disrupt them or to form rival counterparts of their own. The Chinese withdrawal seems to have been entirely logical. In part, it may have been dictated by the Cultural Revolution. It was no doubt also motivated by a desire neither to split nor to demoralize the organizations as they geared themselves up for their strategic role. It also left the Chinese free to pursue unorthodox tactics, including friendly relationships with conservative governments, without risk of compromising and confusing the faithful in the front organizations' ranks.

The Advantages of Sino-Soviet Duality

To sum up, the coordinated duality of Soviet and Chinese policies offers a number of advantages for communist strategy. It enables the communist bloc to retain the initiative, to open up new possibilities for maneuver, and to induce erroneous responses from its opponents. Where there are conflicts in the outside world, it enables the two communist partners, by taking opposite sides, to strengthen communist influence simultaneously over both parties to the dispute. It enables one partner to operate effectively in areas from which the other is excluded or deliberately excludes itself for tactical reasons. It facilitates a division of labor between the two partners and enables one to take unorthodox or provocative action without compromising the other. In the longer run, through enabling the Chinese to express hostility to the Soviet Union and emphasize their concern with Chinese national interests, it may well help China to appeal more effectively to the overseas Chinese. Finally, it offers possibilities of inducing conservatives in both advanced and Third World countries to compromise themselves by entering in good faith into treacherous alliances and alignments through which they can be discredited in the final phase of policy. As a strategic weapon, duality may prove itself to be more effective than either war or the export of revolution.

The Intelligence Potential and Agents of Influence

The implementation of the disinformation program can be fully understood only if one takes into account the use by the communists of their intelligence potential, especially agents of influence both in the West and in the communist bloc. Because precise information is normally lacking, surveys of communist influence in particular countries or areas seldom take into account the assets of the communist intelligence services. From his service in Finland at the time of the launching of the long-range policy, the author knows that these assets can prove to be a major factor in the internal political situation of a noncommunist country; they can contribute effectively to the furtherance of communist strategy.

In the 1950s and 1960s the Soviet government, acting largely through the Soviet intelligence service, exercised great pressure on the older anticommunist generation of Finnish social democratic leaders, especially Tanner, a true socialist and strong anticommunist who stoutly resisted Soviet pressure.

According to Zhenikhov, the KGB resident in Helsinki in 1960, Soviet intelligence, with the active help of Khrushchev and other members of the Presidium, succeeded in the 1950s in recruiting a prominent Finnish social democrat. His KGB cryptonym was "Leader." Zhenikhov was one of the KGB officers who maintained contact with him. At the KGB's suggestion, Leader argued in favor of a change in the social democratic attitude toward cooperation with the Soviet Union. Eventually, in 1959, he split away from the social democratic party and formed his own party. The KGB provided him with guidance on the political attitudes and policies of this party.

Other important recruitments were made in the social democratic leadership, and the agents concerned were used in intrigues against

Tanner and Leskinen, but their identities are not known to the author. There were also successful Soviet efforts to recruit Finnish trade union leaders.

In a conversation with the author, which took place in 1960, on the subject of removing anticommunists from the social democratic leadership, Zhenikhov said that it might be necessary to eliminate Leskinen physically by poisoning him. Zhenikhov said that he had an agent in the leadership of the Finnish conservative party who was in close touch with Leskinen and through whom the assassination could be arranged.

Until the late 1950s Soviet intelligence made use of agents in the Finnish Communist party, including Pessi and Herta Kuusinen, a communist member of parliament. In the period 1957–60, when the long-range policy was being formulated, the use by the KGB of agents in local communist parties was abandoned. At the same time secret cooperation between the leaders of the CPSU and local communist parties was strengthened, the KGB acting under the guidance of the Central Committee when necessary to facilitate this cooperation. In the Finnish case, special groups were set up in the central committees of the Soviet and Finnish parties to handle the practicalities of coordination; the KGB resident in Helsinki acted as the link between the two groups. When Khrushchev visited Finland, Herta Kuusinen was invited by the KGB resident to the Soviet Embassy, where Khrushchev discussed with her the political lines her parliamentary statements should follow.

The KGB and its residents in Finland, Kotov and Zhenikhov, played an important secret role through their agents in the election and formation of a series of Finnish governments. The KGB secretly coordinated the joint efforts of its agents and the Finnish Communist party to muster support for those candidates who found favor with the Soviet Union and to mount campaigns against those who did not. Among the Soviet agents so used was the leader of the Swedish People's party, who was handled by Zegal and Zhenikhov. The main aim of these activities was to secure the election of a prominent Finnish leader, a KGB agent of long standing, whose cryptonym was "Timo."

Timo was recruited by Soviet intelligence in 1948, at which time he was a minister. The recruitment was achieved by a rank and file intelligence officer, a Soviet Finn from Karelia, who was serving under cover as second secretary in the Soviet embassy in Helsinki. This officer developed a close social relationship with Timo, which involved drinking bouts and saunas. He succeeded in persuading him that, in return for his collaboration with Soviet intelligence, the Soviets would forget the repressive action he had taken against communists in the past while serving as a high official and would use all their influence to build him up into a major political figure.

The KGB resident at the time, Mikhail Kotov, sent Timo's re-cruiter back to Karelia and took for himself the credit for this spectacular success. From late in 1948 or early in 1949, Kotov in person maintained contact with Timo. Soviet intelligence kept their side of the bargain and threw all their weight behind his political career. Eventually Timo achieved a high office and remained in it until recently.

Soviet help for him took various forms, including diplomatic support for his policies, indirect financial support for his electoral campaigns, advice on the courses he should pursue, and help in undermining rival candidates. In 1961 agent Leader, acting on KGB instructions, declared himself as a candidate for a high office in order, at a later stage, to transfer his supporters' votes to Timo.

Timo, for his part, acted as a classic Soviet agent of influence. He promoted in his party those whom the Soviets wished to see promoted and, when possible, discussed his political appointments and decisions in advance with Soviet intelligence. For example, the Soviet government was consulted through the KGB in advance about his visit to the United States in 1961. He kept the KGB fully informed on his discussions with other Scandinavian leaders. On KGB advice he created his own secret intelligence service under Vilkuna, another Soviet agent. Timo used the service to bolster his own power, and he shared its product with the KGB, which received all reports from Finnish ambassadors and military attachés abroad and secret information from other departments of the Fin-nish government. Timo, on KGB instructions, recommended the appointments of KGB agents as ambassadors to Moscow and other important posts. In 1960 and 1961 Zhenikhov discussed with Timo the holding of the Eighth World Festival of Youth in Finland in 1962. Timo promised to help arrange this, despite fierce opposition from large sections of the Finnish public.

Meetings between Zhenikhov and Timo took place at his brother's farm or in the Soviet embassy. When official receptions were held at the embassy, a special room was prepared in which private conversations with Timo could take place. Soviet government leaders, including Krushchev and Brezhnev, were fully aware of Timo's relationship with the KGB; when conversations and negotiations with Soviet leaders took place during his visits to Moscow, Kotov and Zhenikhov would act as interpreters and advisers. Zhenikhov often used to boast that he would get Timo secretly awarded the Order of Lenin.[8]

Friction between Zhenikhov and Zakharov, the ambassador to Finland, over who should be responsible for maintaining and directing relations with Timo generated so much heat that both were summoned to appear before the Central Committee. The Central Committee's eventual decision was that Zhenikhov should remain the principal contact with Timo but that the ambassador should have the right to be consulted and to be present at meetings at which certain political matters were discussed. Zhenikhov and Zakharov were warned by the Central Committee that if there were any further squabbles between them, both would be recalled to Moscow.

In 1961 it was planned that Vladimirov should take over as KGB resident from Zhenikhov and should assume responsibility for relations with Timo and for intelligence work in Finnish political parties in general.

Kotov made a successful career in Soviet intelligence on the strength of his service in Finland. From being a Scandinavian specialist, he rose to the higher echelons of the KGB. Not long after Timo was appointed to a high office, Kotov was promoted to be a deputy chief of Soviet intelligence with responsibility for Austria and West Germany. In 1959 or 1960 he was summoned to a meeting of the Presidium at which Khrushchev congratulated him on his success in Finland and instructed him to apply his experience in Austria and Germany with a view to influencing the leaders of those countries in the direction of closer relations and eventual alliance with the Soviet Union.

This illustration shows that the role of the KGB in what is now known as Finlandization can be a significant one. For the present purpose, it is more germane to see how, through agents of influence like Timo, the Soviets have been able to promote the strategy for Europe since 1958–60.

Herta Kuusinen played an important role in the Scandinavian consultative body known as the Northern Council in promoting the idea of a nuclear-free zone in Scandinavia. She was also active in the 1960s in the Women's International Democratic Federation (WIDF) and became its chairman.

By June 1963 pro-Soviet influence in the social democratic party had reached a level at which Tanner, true to his anticommunist convictions, felt unable to accept the party chairmanship. According to the press, his successors, Paasio and Koivisto, developed close relations with both the Soviet government and party. In 1964 Simonen took over the leadership of the Social Democratic Union of Workers and Small Agrarians (SDS). In June there were negotiations on a reconciliation of this splinter group with the main social democratic party. In September Simonen led a delegation to the Soviet Union that was received by Brezhnev and Andropov.[9]

In 1967 Paasio, as chairman of the social democrats, and Simonen, as chairman of the SDS, both supported Timo for a high office. Paasio also came out against the US bombing of North Vietnam.

In 1968 Timo was reappointed to his high office. In May 1968 a delegation led by Paasio visited the Soviet Union for party negotiations with the CPSU and met Brezhnev, Suslov, and Ponomarev. The delegation "highly esteemed the foreign policy carried out by the CPSU."

Representatives of both the social democratic party and SDS demanded the cessation of American bombing in Vietnam and agreed on the convening of a European conference on security. In June 1968 a conference of delegates from fifteen countries took place in Helsinki; it concerned the recognition of East Germany and the implications this would have for European security. In the same month Timo paid an unofficial visit to the Soviet Union. In October–November 1968 Koivisto, who had taken over the post of Prime Minister, paid a visit to Moscow. In connection with the possible extension of NATO to cover "gray areas," Koivisto remarked in November 1968 that Finland "had no enemies from whom to expect an invasion." The Great Soviet Encyclopaedia recorded in 1969 that the Finnish social democratic party fully cooperated on foreign policy with the Soviet Union.[10]

Perhaps Timo's greatest single service to communist strategy will turn out to be the help he gave in convening CSCE in Helsinki. In 1969 the Finnish government agreed to act as host. During 1970 a Finnish ambassador was given a special assignment to visit the United States and Europe. In November of that year the Finnish government addressed a note to thirty-five countries proposing a preparatory meeting on European security. In December the Soviet Union agreed to the proposal. Similar agreement was expressed by all the East European states including Yugoslavia but not Albania.

It is of particular interest that Timo visited the Soviet Union twice in 1970. In between the two visits to the Soviet Union he visited the United States and discussed European security and the Middle East question. During his second visit to the Soviet Union he said that the Soviet-Finnish Friendship Treaty of 1948 was of extreme significance for Finland, and he agreed to help prolong it for a further twenty years.

The strategic role of the communist intelligence potential in Finland is known to the author in some detail up to the end of 1961 because he worked there. He also knows in general terms that similar activities were conducted in other European countries by KGB residents like Krokhin and Rogov (whose real name is Tsimbal) in France; Fedichkin, Orlov, and Gorshkov in Italy; and Korovin (an alias of General Rodin) in Britain. In West Germany the KGB was particularly active and successful in blackmailing and recruiting two categories of politicians and officials: those who had bad records from the Nazi period and those who were known, from KGB penetration of other Western intelligence services, to be working as agents for one or another of the Western powers. The exposure in April 1974 of Gunther Guillaume as an East German agent, which led to Brandt's resignation as Chancellor, showed how far communist intelligence penetration had reached in West Germany. The author reported in 1962 that, in the previous September while serving in the KGB residency in Helsinki, he had read a highly classified circular letter from KGB headquarters to residencies abroad describing successful recruitments of important new agents in recent years, which should be emulated. One case, which was given as "an example of a well-carried-out recruitment," illustrates the "false flag" recruitment technique.

The circular said that in one of its residencies the KGB had an agent. He was a very dependable, active agent who had been working for the KGB for many years and who had at one time been a minister in his country. He still had entrée into political circles in that country and in particular was sufficiently close to the American and British ambassadors for both of them to visit him at home. His KGB controller asked him if he knew anyone who could be recruited in the prime minister's office. The agent replied that he did have a friend there, but that it would be difficult to approach him because he was a man of pro-Western views. It was therefore decided that, since the man knew that the agent was on friendly terms with the American and British ambassadors, the agent would ask him, ostensibly on behalf of one of them, for information on the prime minister's conversations. The agent did so, and his friend agreed to supply information. In due course he accepted money in return. The circular said that in this way the residency had gained a new and valuable agent who began systematically to give information on the Prime Minister and his running of the country.

The normal practice in such a case would be for the KGB to take over direct contact with an agent recruited under a false flag once he had been "sucked in," but the circular did not say whether this had been done in this case. As far as the author knows, the agent and his friend have never been identified.

At the end of 1961 the KGB was planning yet more active use of high-level agents of influence to manipulate world public opinion and the policies of individual governments. The KGB residencies abroad were instructed in 1961 to encourage its agents to attend the World Disarmament Conference in Moscow in 1962. No doubt the same instructions were repeated for other world peace congresses in the 1960s and 1970s.

For Western security services, preoccupied in the main with conventional espionage, subversion, and law enforcement questions, the high-level agent of influence presents new and complex problems. Nevertheless, an understanding of communist strategy can help to throw new light on the significance of contacts made by communist embassies in the West and of visits by prominent Western citizens to the communist bloc.

Undoubtedly the bloc countries applied their intelligence potential to the service of communist strategy in the Third World as elsewhere. The author's information on the subject is fragmentary because the development of this potential was still in the early stages when he broke with the Soviet regime.

Some general indications of the way in which things were moving were, for example, the creation of new African and Latin American departments in the KGB; the instruction to Soviet counterintelligence to establish direct personal contact with all Third World ambassadors in Moscow; the more intensive use, on Shelepin's instructions, of agents of influence for political purposes; and the use of antiimperialist sentiment as the basis for recruiting agents. An additional general point is that KGB deputy residents with specific responsibility for Third World operations were appointed to important KGB residencies in the advanced countries, such as in the Washington and New York residencies.

A KGB training manual that the author read in the late 1950s mentioned three specific cases, without giving full details. The first related to the president of a developing country who was recruited on a visit to the Soviet Union. Exceptionally, this recruitment was based partly on an indirect form of blackmail. The president was a homosexual. In approaching him the KGB claimed to have information that a worldwide criminal organization had plans to blackmail him. The KGB offered to help him to avoid the blackmail in return for his cooperation against the imperialist powers. The president agreed to the proposal. The second case related to an Indian ambassador in Moscow, who performed important services for the KGB in exerting influence over other ambassadors in Moscow. The third case concerned an Indonesian ambassador in Moscow who was recruited.

The training manual described two different ways in which information obtained from the penetration of Western intelligence services could be exploited. One was the doubling of Western agents whom the KGB had identified by penetration. The manual referred to a minister or deputy minister of internal affairs of an African country who was known from the penetration of British intelligence to be a British agent and who was blackmailed and recruited by the KGB on that basis. The alternative form of exploitation was to supply information to Third World leaders with whom the Soviets had close relations on the identities of Western agents in their countries. Information of this kind was given to Nasser in the late 1950s.

The author learned of two specific recruitments from a former colleague, Sergey Antonov. In 1958 or 1959 Antonov, who was then KGB deputy resident at the United Nations in New York, recruited an important African personality. On the strength of this recruitment Antonov was appointed head of the KGB's new African Department in 1960. Vladimir Grusha, an official of the American Department, recruited, in about 1957, a high-level Indonesian diplomat in the US. For this reason Grusha, although a member of the American Department, was posted as deputy resident in Indonesia in 1958 or 1959.

Viktor Zegal, an official of the KGB residency in Helsinki, told the author that he had recruited a Brazilian diplomat in Finland in 1961. The agent's cryptonym was "Pedro."

While the author was working in the NATO section of the Information Department, the KGB obtained a memorandum written for NATO by a prominent Western Arabist on the use of Arab nationalism to divide the Arab world. The document was passed on to the Soviet leadership.

In 1960 the KGB's decoding service broke the code used by the Turkish ambassador in Moscow and systematically read the messages passing between him and the Turkish Foreign Ministry. The traffic was known as "Turkish Notebook."

Mikhail Tkach was a former Soviet military intelligence officer who spoke good Persian and English and had worked under cover as consul-general in Iran, where he was known for his skill in recruiting Iranian officials. In 1956 Tkach joined the KGB. In 1960, on Shelepin's instructions, he was appointed head of the international department of the Soviet trade union organization in order to reorientate it for political use, especially against the Third World. Tkach told the author that all the officials of this department were members of the KGB. This gives some indication of the importance attached to the recruitment of foreign trade union officials, especially those from the Third World.

That the security and intelligence potential of the Soviet national republics was used in the interests of long-range policy is indicated by the appointment in the 1970s of Aliyev as first secretary of the party's Central Committee in Azerbaydzhan.[11] He was once head of the counter-intelligence department of the KGB branch in Azerbaydzhan, and after 1961 became chairman of the branch. His promotion can be explained only by the success of the KGB branch under his leadership in fulfilling party tasks. After he was made first secretary he became active in the Third World; he has visited various Arab and African countries.

There is evidence of advice and help being given by the Soviet Union and other members of the communist bloc to friendly countries and liberation movements on intelligence, security, and guerrilla warfare. Recipients since 1960 have included Cuba, Ghana (up to 1966), and other African states.

Strategic Exploitation of KGB Agents among Prominent Soviet Intellectuals and Religious Leaders

The KGB, and its departments that are responsible for work among Soviet scientists and writers and foreign delegations and visitors to the USSR, are involved in an active effort to influence prominent foreign visitors along desirable foreign strategy lines. Especially exploited are prominent personalities who are members of the Soviet Peace Committee; the Committee for Solidarity with African and Asian Countries; Soviet Friendship societies; the State Committee of Science and Technology; the State Committee for Cultural Ties; and the Institute of USA and Canadian Studies, led by G. Arbatov.

A special word needs to be said on the exploitation of religion and leading churchmen in the communist world for strategic political purposes.

In November–December 1960 the Patriarch of All Russia, Aleksiy, an old KGB agent, accompanied by Metropolitan Nikodim, head of the Russian Orthodox Church's International Department, and Professor Uspenskiy of the Leningrad Faculty of Theology and an active member of the Soviet Peace Committee, toured the Middle East in an aircraft provided by the Soviet government.[12] In the course of the tour Patriarch Aleksiy and the Syrian patriarch issued an official communiqué that stated: "Our standpoint of Christian love compels us to condemn everything which incites hatred among peoples and impels mankind toward a new world war and

. . . to bless any attempts aimed at creating peace between peoples and nations. . . . We resolutely condemn any manifestation of colonialism as foreign to the spirit and the letter of the law of God."[13]

The real identity of Metropolitan Nikodim is an interesting question. According to official sources he was appointed head of the International Department of the Russian Orthodox church in 1960, having served from 1957 to 1959 as a priest in the Russian Orthodox church in Jerusalem. A colleague of the author's at the KGB Institute named Lapshin was appointed, on graduation from the Institute, to the religious section of the KGB's Émigré Department, where he was working in 1960. Lapshin told the author that the KGB had succeeded in placing the deputy head of the Émigré Department who was responsible for religious affairs, under cover as head of the International Department of the Russian Orthodox church. The KGB officer concerned, who used the name Viryukin in the KGB, had served as a priest in Jerusalem in 1957–58. He had earlier made a significant contribution to the KGB's penetration of the church and the persecution of its priests. He had been transferred abroad to specialize in other churches, using his KGB connections and facilities for political purposes. Lapshin himself was being prepared to serve in the United States under cover as the editor of a religious publication. His mission was probably cancelled because the author's connection with Lapshin would have been known to the KGB. Metropolitan Nikolay Krutitskiy, whom Nikodim replaced as head of the International Department, though a true priest, was an old KGB agent. His replacement by Nikodim may well have been due to the fact that Krutitskiy's association with the KGB was exposed by the former Soviet intelligence officer Deryabin in 1957.

The Christian Peace Conference, composed of East European church leaders, dates from the period of the formulation of the long-range policy. It has played an active part in influencing Western churches in the interests of that policy.

The Second All Christian Congress in Defense of Peace, held in Prague in June–July 1964, attracted one thousand delegates, including representatives of Buddhism and Islam as well as the Orthodox, Catholic, and the Anglican and other Protestant churches. The introductory speech was made by Gromadka of

Czechoslovakia, the president of the Christian Peace Conference. Speakers from the Third World included one from Madagascar and one from Uruguay. The congress appealed to all Christians for disarmament, independence, and the eradication of hunger.

In November–December 1964 the Seventh General Conference of the International Brotherhood of Buddhists, held in India, was attended by Buddhists from the Soviet Union. Mongolian, as well as Soviet, Buddhists went to a Buddhist conference in Ceylon in 1969. It was decided to hold a forum of Asian Buddhists in June 1970 to discuss the "struggle for peace" and support for North Vietnam.[14] The forum took place in Mongolia.[15] Two months later a Central Buddhist Monastery and a Buddhist Institute were opened in Ulan Bator.

In March 1965 the First Conference of Muslims of Asia and Africa was held in Bandoeng. Thirty-five countries were represented. The Mufti of Central Asia and Kazakhstan, Babakhanov, led the Soviet delegation. The conference discussed the use of Muslim proselytizing societies as weapons against imperialism. The need to harness Islam to the service of the revolution has been openly discussed by communist strategists. Based on Soviet experience in Central Asia, the problem of achieving this is considered difficult but soluble.[16]

The Christian Peace Conference held a seminar in Sofia in June 1976 to discuss the outcome of CSCE in Helsinki and its significance for the Third World. The main reports were introduced by Professor Bognar, the head of the Research Institute of World Economy of Budapest University; by Dr. Kutsenkov, deputy director of the Institute of International Labor Movements of the Soviet Academy of Sciences; and by professors from India and Puerto Rico. The theme of the seminar was that the Third World, which had been exploited by imperialism in the past, should welcome the Helsinki conference and recognize the need for cooperation in the European collective security process. Dynamic steps should be taken to ensure military détente and disarmament, which would allow Europe to contribute to the new economic order. Helsinki had not destroyed the forces opposed to détente or frustrated their anticommunist purposes. Further efforts were necessary to prevent new forms of psychological warfare by the "enemies of peace."[17]

The seminar was followed by discussions in Moscow between

Metropolitan Nikodim and delegations from Pax Christi and churches in Italy, Holland, Belgium, and West Germany. The subject was "East and West now and tomorrow from the Christian point of view." The meeting welcomed the Helsinki agreements and underlined the importance of the Nuclear Nonproliferation Treaty and the negotiations in Vienna for troop reductions in Central Europe. The secretary of the International Department of the Russian church, Buyevskiy, drew a distinction between communist and Western aid to the Third World by maintaining that communist aid was given to develop Third World economies toward independence. The Soviet Professor Osipov said that East-West collaboration resulting from Helsinki would allow the diversion of military budgets to the development of the Third World. He drew attention to the importance of the UN General Assembly's call in 1974 for a new economic order.

The *Great Soviet Encyclopaedia* recorded that by 1972 the World Council of Churches had been converted from a "pro-Western" to a "progressive" orientation in its policies on peace, disarmament, and related matters. Assiduous advocacy by the Christian Peace Conference and others of the view that Christianity and communism were natural allies in support of the national liberation movement induced the World Council of Churches to provide funds for African guerrilla movements, including the Rhodesian Patriotic Front, believed to be responsible for a massacre of British missionaries in 1978.

The Fifth General Conference of Buddhists for Peace was held in Ulan Bator in July 1979. The Patriarch of All Russia, Pimen, sent a message to his "dear, fellow friends of peace" wishing them success. In the previous month he had received the Dalai Lama, who was in Moscow on his way to Ulan Bator and no doubt shared with him his experience of peace conferences. The Patriarch's message to the conference was conveyed by Metropolitan Nikodim's successor, Metropolitan Yuvenaliy, who had acted as chairman of an All-World Conference held in Moscow in 1977, on "religious leaders for peace, disarmament, and just relations between peoples." Yuvenaliy advocated signature of the SALT II treaty and the opening of negotiations on SALT III, arguing that only détente could bring peace to the whole world, including Asia.[18]

The Evidence of Overall Coordination Between the Communist Governments and Parties

Coordination within the Bloc

The revival after 1958 of an overt central body analogous to the Comintern or Cominform to coordinate the communist bloc and movement would have been incompatible with the long-range policy and strategy. There is, however, significant inside and open information on the strengthening since 1959 of the coordinating machinery of the bloc. The establishment in 1959 of a secret coordinating center for the bloc's intelligence and security services has been described already. In addition, as Khrushchev put it in October 1961, it had become the "practice to hold periodic exchanges of views among the heads of parties and governments on major economic and political problems. The collective agencies of the socialist states—the Warsaw Treaty Organization and the Council for Mutual Economic Aid—have grown stronger."[1] The Political Consultative Committee of the Warsaw Pact was activated at about this time. In 1969 a committee of ministers of defense was added, and in 1976 a committee of foreign ministers. In Comecon a Permanent Executive Committee was established at the vice-premier level in 1963.

No less important than this supranational and governmental coordinating machinery is the wide range of multilateral and bilateral forms of contact at different levels between the leaders of the bloc and nonbloc parties and their party apparatuses. A systematic reading of official communist sources, especially the *Great Soviet Encyclopaedia*, shows the scope and scale of both governmental and party contacts. All of these provide opportunities for the communist leaders and their experts in various fields to exchange information, opinions, and accounts of their experiences in implementing the policy and strategy and to discuss and decide on new initiatives and tactics.

The possibility that, in addition to these acknowledged forms of contact, there is a secret policy coordinating center for the bloc is discussed below.

Before considering the main open forms of coordination, attention should be drawn to a general point made in the *Encyclopaedia* regarding various forms of contact. According to this source the Twenty-second CPSU Congress in October 1961 determined the "most appropriate forms of contact between parties in present conditions."[2] Chou En-lai was present at this congress. If his ostentatious walkout is discounted as part of a disinformation operation, the implication is that the Chinese took part in determining what form future contacts between parties should take. In the following year the *Encyclopaedia* stated that "in modern conditions the cooperation of communist parties finds expression in bilateral and multilateral contacts . . . in meetings between party leaders and in the participation of communist party delegations in the work of party congresses."[3] The recognition by the *Encyclopaedia* of bilateral forms of contact as well as attendance at congresses is significant in that it legitimizes the continuation of bilateral contacts with the Chinese by the Soviets and others after the Chinese withdrawal from multilateral bloc organizations. Elsewhere, the *Encyclopaedia* emphasized the importance of conferences for the "working out of agreements on joint actions for the implementation of the general line of policy." Use of the expression "general line of policy" is as near as the *Encyclopaedia* gets to an admission of the existence of a common long-range policy.

Summit Meetings

In May 1958 the first of a series of summits of first secretaries of the bloc parties and heads of the bloc governments devoted to the economic integration of the European communist countries was held in Moscow. The summits on the same subject in 1961,

1962, and 1963 were held under Comecon auspices.

The Moscow summit of August 1961, which dealt with the conclusion of the German treaty, was in the form of a meeting of the Political Consultative Committee of the Warsaw Pact. It subsequently became normal, but not invariable, practice to hold meetings of the Political Consultative Committee at or near first secretary level. For example, the Soviet delegation to the meeting of the committee in January 1965 included Brezhnev, Kosygin, Gromyko, Malinovskiy, and Andropov. It dealt with the subject of security in Europe and discussed the convening of a European conference on security and a world conference on disarmament.[4] The meeting of July 1966, held in Bucharest, was at summit level. It pursued the subject of security in Europe and called for troop withdrawals and the dissolution of NATO and the Warsaw Pact.[5] Subsequent meetings at summit level included those held in Sofia (March 1968), which issued a declaration on Vietnam; in the Soviet Union (August 1970); in Prague (January 1972); in Warsaw (April 1974); and in Moscow (November 1978).[6] The 1970 summit in Moscow was attended by a particularly strong Romanian delegation, including Ceausescu, Maurer, Niculescu-Mizil, and Manescu. Those in Prague and Warsaw discussed European problems. The *Encyclopaedia* noted that in 1970 the question of raising the level of effectiveness of cooperation between communist parties was central to the communist system. Their efforts in economic policy, ideology, and the strengthening of defense were closely coordinated.[7] Other summits were held independently of either Comecon or Warsaw Pact organizations; for example, one was held in Moscow in June 1967 and another in Budapest in the following month. These two meetings discussed the Israeli-Arab war, expressed solidarity with the Arab world, and demanded the withdrawal of Israeli troops. As the *Encyclopaedia* puts it: "These meetings provided an opportunity to work out a single position and joint political and diplomatic actions." Two summits were held on international ideological questions: one in Moscow (December 1973) and one in Prague (March 1975). They discussed the direction that should be taken by ideological cooperation "in conditions of deepening détente."[8] The political and military leaders of the Warsaw Pact countries met in Warsaw in May 1980.

In addition to formal summit meetings, a series of informal summer gatherings of communist leaders have been held in the Crimea. References can be found to such meetings in 1971, 1972, 1973, 1976, 1977, and 1978, and probably to one held in 1974. As the *Encyclopaedia* for 1974 states: "The Crimean meetings have become a tradition. The leaders keep each other informed and narrow down their positions in the political, economic, and ideological fields."[9] In 1975 the *Encyclopaedia* said that the meetings had become the forum at which the international situation is assessed, common tasks are discussed, and the strategy of joint actions is developed. Thanks to the Crimean meetings, the cooperation between communist countries has become closer."[10]

According to *Pravda* (March 20, 1981), it was noted at the Twenty-sixth CPSU Congress that, during the past years, thirty-seven friendly meetings at the summit level had taken place in the Crimea. The future development of relations between the fraternal parties and countries, key problems of world politics, and tasks for the future were discussed at these meetings.

A second new type of high-level gathering made its appearance in the 1970s. In September–October 1975, in January 1976, and in March 1977, there were conferences of the second secretaries of the central committees held in Moscow, Warsaw, and Sofia respectively. Deputy heads of government were included in the first of these conferences, which dealt with economic cooperation.[11] The second and third both dealt with ideological questions in a period of détente. The Warsaw meeting related to Europe in particular.[12] Cuba, as well as Romania and Czechoslovakia, was mentioned as being represented at the Warsaw and Sofia meetings.

One meeting of the Warsaw Pact Political Consultative Committee that does not appear to have been held at first or second secretary level is nevertheless worthy of note. It took place in Bucharest, the capital of supposedly independent Romania, in November 1976. Its agenda covered the deepening political and military cooperation between members of the Pact. In order to perfect the mechanism of political cooperation within the framework of the Warsaw Pact, a committee of ministers of foreign affairs, together with a combined secretariat, was established as an organ of the Political Consultative Committee.[13]

Coordination through Diplomatic Channels

With the adoption of the long-range policy, diplomatic representation within the bloc became a permanent form of political coordination among its members. This statement is supported by the fact that an unusually large number of new ambassadors were appointed between bloc countries in the period 1960–62. New Soviet ambassadors were appointed in 1960 to Bulgaria, Czechoslovakia, Cuba, and Hungary; in 1961 to Mongolia, Romania, Yugoslavia, and Albania; in 1962 to Cuba, Yugoslavia, and East Germany. The Romanians, Hungarians, Mongolians, and Cubans appointed new ambassadors to the Soviet Union in 1960; the Yugoslavs in 1961; the Chinese in 1962; and the Czechoslovaks in 1963.

The status of Soviet ambassadors changed at the same time. There are indications[14] that Soviet ambassadors to other bloc countries were made responsible for coordinating all aspects of long-range policy within the countries of their accreditation. Soviet ambassadors are carefully chosen so as to ensure that their background and experience fit them for the specific tasks they will have to perform. Because of their coordinating function, almost all Soviet ambassadors within the bloc since 1960 have been members of the Central Committee of the CPSU. In this context it is worth remembering Tito's complaint in 1948 that the Yugoslavs could not be expected to reveal secret party information to Soviet representatives who did not have that status. It is also interesting to note that no distinction seems to be made between the status of Soviet ambassadors in "dissenting" bloc countries, such as China and Romania, and "orthodox" countries, such as Hungary and Bulgaria. For example, the Soviet ambassador to Romania from 1965 to 1971 was Basov, a Central Committee member. The Soviet press indicated in July 1966 that he was a member of the Soviet delegation to the Comecon meeting in Bucharest; the delegation included Brezhnev and Kosygin.

Of special interest are the Soviet ambassadors to China. From 1959 to 1965 the post was held by Chervonenko. It is noteworthy that Chervonenko, who was appointed in the period in which China was actively participating in the formulation of the long-range policy, should have been kept in Peking for the first five years of the split. It is even more remarkable in the light of his background. From 1951 onward he was a senior party theoretician and official in the Ukraine; from 1956 to 1959, he was secretary of the central committee of the Ukrainian party. As such, he was a close friend and confidant of Khrushchev. He went to Peking and remained there as a leading political and party figure, not as a career diplomat; his posting indicated the close political and party relations between the Soviet Union and China. His subsequent career is of equal interest. In 1965 he was transferred from Peking to Prague, where he remained until 1973, a period spanning both the preparation for and the aftermath of the "Prague spring." In 1973 he moved to Paris, in time for the development of Eurocommunism and other elements of the bloc's strategy for Europe. He has been awarded two Orders of Lenin.

In Peking he was succeeded by Lapin, who served there from 1965 to 1970. Lapin was elected a member of the Central Committee at the Twenty-third CPSU Congress in 1966. As chief editor of broadcasts from 1944 to 1953, he became an expert on the censorship and manipulation of news. He went on to become minister of foreign affairs for the Russian Republic from 1960 to 1962 and deputy to Gromyko from 1962 to 1965.[15]

Lapin's successor was Tolstikov, a prominent party official. From 1952 onward he was active in party work in Leningrad and rose to be first secretary of the Leningrad provincial committee, one of the most important party posts in the Soviet Union, and one once held by Zhdanov. Tolstikov has been a member of the CPSU Central Committee since 1961.

Shcherbakov, who took over from Tolstikov in Peking in 1978, worked in the Central Committee apparatus from 1949 to 1963 and from 1974 to 1978. He has been a member of the Central Revision Committee of the CPSU since 1966. He was minister at the Soviet embassy in Peking in 1963–64, crucial years in the development of the Sino-Soviet split. From 1964 to 1974 he was Soviet ambassador to Vietnam.

The successive postings to China of these four very senior Soviet party officials is incompatible with the deterioration in Sino-Soviet party relations that is alleged to have taken place.

The continuity of Soviet and Chinese foreign policy is further symbolized by the continuance in office as the ministers of foreign affairs in their respective countries of Gromyko from 1957 to the present day and of Chen Yi from 1958 to 1971.

Bilateral Coordination within the Bloc

Even if bilateral coordination is considered a less perfect form of coordination within the communist world than multilateral, it is still officially recognized. There is abundant, openly available evidence of the continuity from 1958 to the present day of bilateral exchanges of visits between party and government leaders of the Soviet Union and other communist countries, including China, Romania, Czechoslovakia, Yugoslavia, and Cuba, countries which, at one time or another, have allegedly been estranged to some degree from the Soviets.[16]

For the duration of the genuine Tito-Stalin split, it would have been more than Tito's life was worth for him to have attempted to visit the Soviet Union; but since 1961, Tito, until his death, and other Yugoslav leaders have been almost annual visitors. Khrushchev, Brezhnev, Kosygin, and Gromyko in their turn have been to Yugoslavia. Tito and his subordinates have traveled often to other communist countries, including, from 1970 on, China. Tito's death did not destroy the pattern; in April 1982 Gromyko visited Yugoslavia and the Yugoslav defense minister visited Moscow despite alleged differences over Afghanistan and Poland.

In the case of Romania, some of Ceausescu's many visits to the Soviet Union have been well publicized. Western commentators, under the influence of disinformation, have almost always assumed that these visits were made in an attempt to resolve the differences between the Soviet and Romanian leaders. But the evidence of Romania's participation in Warsaw Pact, Comecon, Crimean, and other multilateral and bilateral meetings within the bloc far outweighs the occasional evidence of her nonparticipation and is inconsistent with the existence of serious differences. It points to the conclusion that, when Ceausescu met Brezhnev, it was not to be reprimanded by him, but to work out in practical terms how the fiction of Romanian independence could best be maintained and exploited in the interests of long-range policy.

Similarly, the scale of the evidence of Czechoslovak contact with

the Soviet Union, bilaterally and multilaterally, in summit, Warsaw
Pact, and Comecon meetings before, during, and after the events
of 1968 supports the conclusion that the Czechoslovak crisis was
a planned and coordinated operation. For example, in March 1968
Czechoslovak representatives informed a summit meeting of several
bloc countries in Dresden, called to discuss political and economic
unity through Comecon and bilateral contacts, that the decisions
of the January plenum were aimed at the "realization of the line
of the Thirteenth Party Congress" and that they were sure that
the leadership of the party would secure the further development
of 'socialism.' "[17]

Chinese party and government leaders played an important part
in the formulation of the long-range policy from 1958 to 1960.
As observers they attended Comecon meetings until late in 1961,
and also attended the early meetings of the Political Consultative
Committee of the Warsaw Pact.[18] It was at these meetings that
the foundations of future coordination in the bloc were laid. Even
in 1961, continued Chinese participation in multilateral gatherings
of this kind was an anomaly. For them to have continued to attend
such gatherings would have put the Sino-Soviet disinformation operation at serious risk. Less conspicuous bilateral Sino-Soviet contacts
of one kind or another have continued almost without interruption
throughout the split. They are capable of two interpretations. For
example, conventional methodology sees the meetings of the Sino-
Soviet border commission as vain attempts to resolve frontier dispute. The new methodology sees them as providing convenient
cover for coordinating policy and planning, for staging and exploiting spurious frontier incidents, and for other forms of Sino-Soviet
squabbling. The same point applies to the joint Sino-Soviet commission on navigation. The exchanges of trade delegations could equally
provide cover for contacts of a political nature. Suggestive scraps
of information can be gleaned from the *Great Soviet Encyclopaedia*.
For example:

• In April 1961 a Chinese trade delegation to Moscow was received
by Khrushchev.
• In 1962 Chinese party delegations attended party congresses in Eastern Europe.
• In January 1963 a delegation from the Supreme Soviet, led by Andro-

pov, at that time the secretary of the central committee responsible for bloc countries, visited China.

• From July 5 to July 20, 1963, there were meetings in Moscow between the leading strategists of the CPSU and CPC. The Chinese delegation was led by the general secretary, Teng Hsiao-p'ing, and the CPSU delegation included Suslov, V. Grishin, Andropov, Il'ichev, Ponomarev, Satyukov, and Chervonenko. The Chinese delegation was received by the CPSU Central Committee. The presence in Moscow of the Chinese delegation coincided with the negotiation of the Test Ban Treaty. The meetings between the delegations were interrupted, but there was an agreement that they should be resumed later.[19]

• In October 1964 there was a meeting of the Sino-Soviet railway commission in Khabarovsk.

• In the same month Soviet, Romanian, Cuban, and other delegations attended the celebrations of the Chinese revolution: the Soviet delegation was led by V. Grishin, candidate member of the Presidium and chairman of the Soviet trade union organization.[20]

• From November 5 to November 14, 1964, a party and government delegation led by Chou En-lai was in the Soviet Union; it had meetings with Brezhnev, Andropov, Kosygin, Podgornyy, Gromyko, and others and signed an agreement.[21] The reference to Gromyko's presence indicates that the meeting dealt with the coordination of foreign policy.

• On February 5–6 and 10–11, 1965, a Soviet delegation led by Kosygin stopped over in China on its way to and from Vietnam for negotiations with Chinese leaders, including Mao.[22]

• On January 7 and 13–14, 1966, Shelepin visited China on the way to and from Vietnam. It may or may not be a coincidence that Brezhnev was in Mongolia from January 11 to January 17.[23]

• In June 1966 Chou En-lai visited Albania and led a delegation to Romania for talks with the Romanian leaders.

• From June 19 to August 8, 1969, the Sino-Soviet joint commission on navigation in the Amur Basin held its fifteenth session and reached an agreement. No dates were given for the first fourteen sessions.

• In September 1969 Romanian leaders visited Peking; on September 11, Kosygin met Chou En-lai in Peking; on October 20, Sino-Soviet negotiations took place in Peking on problems of mutual interest.[24] The Soviet delegation was led by the first deputy minister of foreign affairs, V. V. Kuznetsov.[25] Kuznetsov remained in China until June 13, 1970.[26]

• On August 15, 1970, the deputy minister for foreign affairs, Il'ichev, arrived in Peking as head of a Soviet government delegation for negotiations with the Chinese.[27]

• Between July and December 1970 sixteen Sino-Soviet negotiating sessions were held on the settlement of border questions.

• In August and September 1970 negotiations on Sino-Soviet border trade were held in Khabarovsk.[28]

• On November 18, 1970, the new Soviet ambassador, Tolstikov, had a meeting with Chou En-lai.

• In 1971 the negotiations on border questions continued; from June to August a Chinese deputy minister was in the Soviet Union as head of a trade delegation negotiating deliveries; a trade agreement was signed in Moscow.

• In 1972 the Sino-Soviet negotiations on border questions did not advance "because of China's negative position"; in June a Soviet trade delegation led by I. Grishin visited China.

• In 1973 negotiations on border questions continued at the deputy minister of foreign affairs level.

• In February and March a session of the joint Sino-Soviet commission was held.[29]

• In 1974 the negotiations on border questions by the deputy ministers of foreign affairs continued.

• In February 1974 direct flights from Moscow to China were started.

• In February–March 1974 a session of the joint Sino-Soviet commission on navigation was held.

• On June 25, 1974, a Soviet delegation led by Deputy Minister Il'ichev arrived in China for negotiations on border questions.[30]

• On November 12, 1975, Deputy Minister Il'ichev arrived in Peking for negotiations on border questions.[31]

• In September 1976 the CPSU Central Committee sent its condolences on Mao's death; Gromyko and Mazurov, both members of the Politburo, called at the Chinese embassy.

• On November 29, 1976, Deputy Minister Il'ichev arrived in China; negotiations on border questions continued in Peking until February 1977.[32]

• From July to October, 1977, the joint Sino-Soviet mixed commission on navigation resumed its sessions after a two-year interruption.

• On July 20–28, 1977, a Chinese government trade delegation, led by the deputy minister of foreign trade, visited the Soviet Union and was received by Patolichev.[33]

• In April 1978 Il'ichev arrived in Peking to resume negotiations. Talks were held in Moscow from September 29 to November 30, 1979, between Il'ichev and the Chinese deputy foreign minister, Wang You-ping. They were to take up "broad questions of political and economic relations," other than border disputes. According to TASS, it was agreed that the talks should continue in Peking. Gromyko met Wang in December.[34]

• Early in 1981 China and the Soviet Union renewed an accord on navigation rights in the Amur River; this was at the twenty-third session of a series of negotiations begun in 1951.

• In March 1982 three Chinese experts visited Moscow to study Soviet management techniques and were received by the deputy chairman of the Soviet State Planning Committee.[35]

This list of bilateral contacts is obviously incomplete. Even so, no comparable list of bilateral Soviet-Yugoslav contacts could be drawn up for the period of the genuine Tito-Stalin split. For a substantial fraction of the period covered, the Soviet Union was represented in China by a deputy minister as well as by a leading party official in the post of ambassador. Fragmentary as it is, the picture that emerges of Sino-Soviet bilateral contacts is more consistent with coordination of policy and tactics than with abortive attempts to settle disputes. Special attention should be drawn to the prominence, in the talks with the Chinese, of two major Soviet strategists: Kuznetsov, a leading specialist in foreign policy; and Il'ichev, a specialist in ideology as well as foreign affairs, including European security.[36] Note also the presence of Andropov, a specialist on the bloc, later chairman of the KGB, and now party leader. Tikhvinskiy, an expert on disinformation, has figured in the Soviet delegations. On the Chinese side, prominent officials of the Chinese Foreign Ministry also took part in these discussions, which suggests that the subjects involved were wider than border problems.

The number of trade delegations sent by the Chinese to the Soviet Union is also striking. It is noticeable that those in 1971, 1973, and 1977 arrived in the Soviet Union in July or August, which is the time when the Crimean summit conferences are held; the possibility of secret Chinese participation in them should not be discounted.

A similar pattern of high-level bilateral contacts between the Soviets and the Vietnamese and between the Chinese and the

Vietnamese could also be documented.

Before leaving the subject of coordination within the bloc, brief reference should be made to the close working relations between specialist departments of the central committees of the bloc parties. Intensive contacts are also carried on between administrative, international, ideological, and other departments within the bloc, and outside it in the case of those nonbloc parties large enough to have similar departments of their own.

Coordination between Bloc and Nonbloc Parties

The arrangements for coordinating the bloc and nonbloc parties and achieving what Khrushchev called the synchronization of their activities and policies are so extensive that no more than an outline can be given here.

Of fundamental importance are the international conferences of bloc and nonbloc parties. The Sixty-four–party congress of November 1957 decided to work out a new long-range policy and strategy for the bloc and for the international communist movement. The Eighty-one–party congress of November 1960 formally adopted the new policy and strategy. The Chinese, Albanian, Romanian, Czechoslovak, French, Italian, and Spanish parties all took part in it. The next such congress was held in Moscow in June 1969. Seventy-five parties attended, nine from within the bloc and sixty-six from outside it. The presence of five members of the Soviet Politburo shows the importance attached to it by the CPSU. The congress reviewed the preceding ten years and adopted a program of action for the future. The French, Italian, and Spanish parties took part.[37] The preparations for the 1969 conference extended over more than four years.

In the same period other international conferences were devoted to specific aspects of policy. For example, in October 1965 conferences were held both in Moscow and in Czechoslovakia (Prague) to celebrate the thirtieth anniversary of the Seventh Congress of the Comintern, which adopted united front tactics. Representatives of forty parties attended the Moscow meeting, which produced a report on the historic significance of the Seventh Congress of the Comintern for the modern communist movement. According to the *Great Soviet Encyclopaedia*, "new strategic and tactical forms and methods" for the communist movement were formulated.[38] In January 1970 a conference in Moscow of twenty-eight European parties discussed European security. In September, in Budapest, forty-five parties discussed common actions against imperialism.[39]

There have been systematic regional conferences of communist parties in Western Europe, Scandinavia, Latin America, Central America, the Mediterranean, and in Arab and African countries. The series in Europe included the Tihany and Berlin conferences in 1976, in which the Eurocommunist parties were active. The list of conferences could be prolonged indefinitely.

The congresses of the CPSU provide important opportunities for consultation and coordination. The congresses of other bloc communist parties attract fraternal delegations in substantial numbers. It would be superfluous to enumerate them all; a few examples will illustrate the point. The Twelfth Czechoslovak Congress, in 1962, was attended by sixty-eight delegations, the Eighth Yugoslav Congress, in 1964, by thirty; the Romanian congress, in 1965, by fifty-seven. Wherever conditions permit, the congresses of nonbloc communist parties are attended by delegations from bloc parties. There are innumerable official and unofficial contacts between communist parties and national and international communist front organizations, such as the World Federation of Trade Unions and the World Peace Council.

Permanent linkage between the bloc and nonbloc parties exists through the International Department of the CPSU Central Committee under Ponomarev (this department has representatives stationed abroad) and through the headquarters of the *World Marxist Review* in Prague, where a number of representatives of bloc and nonbloc parties work together as permanent members of the staff. The *World Marxist Review* holds theoretical conferences on major policy issues.

Huge numbers of bilateral visits are paid to the Soviet Union and other communist countries every year by the leaders and functionaries of nonbloc communist parties traveling on party business.

Conclusions

Between 1958 and 1980 the scale of contact between communist parties inside and outside the bloc is without parallel elsewhere in the world. The vast majority of communist gatherings take place behind closed doors; no more is known about them than the leaders wish to be known. Deprived of authentic news and hypnotized by "revelations" about communist disunity derived from communist sources, Western commentators have tended to underrate or ignore the vast weight of the evidence of continuing systematic coordination of the bloc from 1958 to the present day. The scale, the scope, and the manner in which this coordination is conducted refute the notion that international communism is a movement that has lost its momentum, direction, and ideological sense of purpose through disunity. Furthermore, the movement has not lost its controlled, organized, and disciplined character. True, systematic dissent on the part of any one communist country could only lead to its expulsion from the communist bloc and its ostracism by all other communist countries, as was the case with Yugoslavia in 1948. What has changed since 1957–60 is not the nature of communism, but the appreciation by communist leaders of the strategic and tactical advantages of spurious dissent within the movement and the experience they have gained in exploiting it strategically in the interests of long-range policy. The old methodology resolves the contradiction between the evidence of coordination and the evidence of disunity by ignoring much of the evidence of coordination. The new methodology resolves it by demonstrating the contrived and spurious nature of the disunity. The scale of the acknowledged contact between the Soviets and the Chinese, the Yugoslavs, the Romanians, and the Eurocommunists betrays the nature of the "splits" and "differences" between them and confirms that they are no more than manifestations of strategic disinformation in action in support of long-range policy.

24

The Impact of the Disinformation Program

The Shaping of Western Assessments of the Communist World

The launching of a strategic disinformation program in 1958 invalidated the conventional methodology of Western students of communist affairs. A carefully controlled flood of information was released through the whole range of sources under communist control. As in the NEP period in the 1920s, this flood of information confused and distorted Western views on the situation in the communist world. Western analysts, lacking the ability to acquire inside information on communist strategic thinking, planning, and methods of operation, gratefully accepted the new stream of information at face value. Without their knowing it, their conventional methods of analysis were invalidated and turned back on them by the communist strategists. Because of the deliberate projection by these strategists of a false image of the dissolution of communist unity, the noncommunist world ignored or undervalued open and significant evidence pointing to bloc cooperation from 1957 onward on a new footing of equality and commitment to fundamental ideological principles and long-term policy objectives. The new dispensation allows for variation in domestic and international tactics and provides unlimited opportunities for joint efforts between bloc countries to misrepresent the true state of relations between them whenever this should be to their mutual advantage. Unnoticed by the West, communist ideology was freed from its Stalinist straitjacket and revived on Leninist lines. The change was successfully misrepre-

309

sented as the spontaneous replacement of ideology by nationalism as the driving force behind the communist world.

Noncommunist studies came increasingly to be based on information emanating from communist sources. While observers in the noncommunist world sometimes showed some awareness that information was reaching them through channels under communist control, there was virtually no recognition of the fact that the information had been specially prepared behind the Iron Curtain for their benefit. The political role of the intelligence services was ignored, and since the evidence of planning and coordination in the activities of the bloc was also overlooked, the growth of internal opposition movements and the eruption of disputes between communist states and parties were wrongly seen as spontaneous developments.

Up to 1960, and despite the Tito-Stalin split of 1948 and the Polish and Hungarian uprisings of 1956, the noncommunist world was willing to accept as fact the growth of a cohesive communist bloc and international movement. Some Western analysts, like Professor Possony, regarded the decisions of the Eighty-one–party congress in November 1960 as indicating the adoption of a long-range policy. But the acceptance at face value by Western statesmen, diplomats, intelligence services, academics, journalists, and the general public of the subsequent evidence of disputes and disunity in the communist world precipitated a new attitude that would have been unthinkable before and that caused the views of Possony and others to be regarded as anachronistic if not antediluvian. The Eighty-one–party Manifesto came to be regarded as a temporary, patched-up compromise between the parties signifying their failure to adopt a common policy, and so was brushed aside. The evidence of evolution and splits in the communist world was so overwhelming in volume and so convincing in character that none could continue to question its validity. Acceptance in particular of the Sino-Soviet split as a reality became the common basis for all noncommunist attempts to analyze present and future policies and trends in the communist world. As a result Western perception of offensive communist intentions was blunted and the evidence of coordination in the execution of worldwide communist strategies was discounted.

Because strategic disinformation was not recognized as such, Western views on internal developments in the communist world came increasingly to be shaped and determined by the communist strategists in the interests of their own long-range policy. In the

Soviet Union the dropping of the "dictatorship of the proletariat," and the introduction of market-orientated enterprises and other measures of economic reform seemed to presage a reversion toward capitalism. The gradual rise in living standards seemed to be taking the edge off the Soviet appetite for revolutionary change, generating new pressures on the regime to allow greater freedom and improve the supply of consumer goods. Apparent differences in the Soviet leadership between the liberal reformers and conservative ideologists on how to grapple with these pressures and reconcile the need for progress with lip service to ideology confirmed Western belief in the recurrence of power struggles, mainly behind the scenes but sometimes in the open, as in the case of Khrushchev's dismissal. When the liberals appeared to have the upper hand, expectations were aroused of increasing cooperation between the Soviet Union and the West. Moderation in Soviet propaganda and expressions of interest in peaceful coexistence and businesslike negotiations seemed genuine, especially when compared with the implacable hostility of the Chinese. Occasional aggressive Soviet actions were attributable to the survival within the leadership of a group of die-hard Stalinists who had to be appeased from time to time by the liberal reformers. If the Stalinists were once more to regain control, détente would be reversed and there might be a Sino-Soviet reconciliation. The West therefore had an interest in strengthening the hand of liberal reformers. Provided they survived, there were prospects of an improvement in relations owing to the existence of common interests between the Soviets and the West in avoiding nuclear conflict and confronting Chinese militancy. In the long run the technological revolution offered prospects of a gradual narrowing of the gulf between the communist and non-communist systems.

Such were the arguments of the 1960s. Despite the revival of neo-Stalinism toward the end of the decade, the arguments survived and gained weight until the later 1970s.

The apparent opening up of cracks between the communist states was assessed as an encouraging development. The emergence of a range of different brands of communism seemed to show how ideology had lost its binding force. The rivalries between the communist states appeared rooted in traditional national sentiment.

The impact of the Sino-Soviet dispute on Western thinking can be illustrated by the change in attitude of Allen Dulles, the former director of the CIA, a man of unquestionable integrity and anticommunist conviction with access at the time to all available open and secret information. In an address delivered on April 8, 1959, Mr. Dulles said: "As long as the principles of international communism motivate the regimes in Moscow and Peking, we must expect that their single purpose will be the liquidation of our form of free society and the emergence of a Sovietized, communized world order. They change their techniques as circumstances dictate. They have never given us the slightest reason to hope that they are abandoning their overall objectives. We sometimes like to delude ourselves into thinking that we are faced with another nationalistic power struggle of which the world has seen so many. The fact is that the aims of the Communist International with its headquarters in Moscow are not nationalistic; their objectives are not limited. They firmly believe, and eloquently preach, that communism is the system which will eventually rule the world and each move they make is directed to this end. Communism, like electricity, seeks to be an all pervasive and revolutionary force."[1] Only three years later, speaking on the same subject at the Convention of the American Bar Association, in August 1962 in San Francisco, Dulles, in referring to the unfolding Sino-Soviet dispute, maintained that the communist system was showing manifold vulnerabilities and weaknesses.[2]

Confirmation of this view was soon visible in the growing "independence" of Romania. Following Tito's example, Ceausescu seemed to be championing his people's cause against Soviet interference in their country. He was therefore worthy of support in concrete terms. Similar aspirations and tendencies toward independence from the Soviet Union were thought to be at work elsewhere in Eastern Europe, especially in Poland. But it was in Czechoslovakia that the newest and most exciting brand of communism burst upon the market in the "Prague spring" of 1968. This seemed more than just an assertion of Czech and Slovak nationalism; it was a rethinking of some of the basic concepts of the relations between the individual and the communist state: It was "socialism with a human face," and it opened up new possibilities of East-West cooperation. But because it threatened the foundations of the communist system, it was crushed by brutal Soviet military intervention.

Apparently shaken by rebellion outside their borders and the growth of dissidence at home, the Soviet leaders under Brezhnev reverted to repression on crude Stalinistic lines. It was therefore with reservations that the West received communist proposals for a conference on European security. Nevertheless, the Czechoslovak experience had, it seemed, demonstrated the existence of liberalizing tendencies in the communist world, a point underlined by vocal Soviet "dissidents." It was therefore worthwhile for the West to engage in discussions on European security and human rights, even if only with an eye to the future.

Tito and his Yugoslav regime were thought to be helpful in promoting liberalizing tendencies in the bloc. Yugoslav influence in the nonaligned movement was welcomed as an obstacle to the extension in the developing countries of Soviet and Chinese power.

The tendency toward disintegration seemed to have spread from the bloc to the international communist movement. The Sino-Soviet split had triggered off a splintering process in many communist parties. Soviet intervention in Czechoslovakia had been repudiated by several important parties, including the French and Italian, the two most powerful in Europe. In the mid-1970s both parties had expressed their independence of the Soviet Union and added their voices to the cry for democracy, human rights, and a Europe free of military pacts. Even if the Italian party came to power, it seemed that that might not be incompatible with the survival of democracy or even with continuing Italian adherence to the North Atlantic Treaty.

To sum up, the apparent loss of revolutionary ardor, the apparent disunity in the bloc and movement, the apparent preoccupation of the communist states with fratricidal struggles, and the advent of détente all pointed to the same conclusion: The Cold War was over. The new situation seemed to demand accommodation and a positive response to communism rather than the old forms of resistance and containment.

The Effect on Western Policy Formation

During the Cold War, when the threat of communism seemed dangerously acute, traditional national differences between the

Western powers were to some extent subordinated to the common
interest in self-defense. From 1945 to 1949 Western Europe was
recovering from the devastation of the war. American superiority
was unquestioned. Europe was dependent on the United States
to restore its economic life and protect it from Soviet attack. By
the mid-1950s the situation was already changing. Europe was on
the road to recovery and was beginning to see itself as a community
of rapidly advancing economic powers. Resentment of American
influence was growing. Especially in France, there was a demand
for a more equal partnership with the United States. In October
1958 General de Gaulle addressed a memorandum to the American
and British governments asking in effect for the creation of a trium-
virate of powers with worldwide responsibilities. The memorandum
reflected the changing economic realities in Europe. Given a clear-
sighted and realistic common assessment of the long-range communist problem, the required adjustment of relationships within the
Western alliance, based on the principle of equal partnership, might
have been achieved. As it was, the alliance was allowed to drift.
At the same time changes began to appear in the communist world
that, distorted and exaggerated by communist disinformation, indicated a reduction in the immediacy and intensity of the threat
from communism. The argument for sacrificing national interests
for the sake of Western unity in defense was weakened. If the
communist monolith was disintegrating into a set of rival national
regimes, whose national interests were increasingly overriding their
supposedly common ideology, the nations of the West could afford
to revert to the pursuit of their traditional national interests in
their particular spheres of influence. It was no longer necessary
to strengthen Western unity under American leadership. It was
more important to examine possible new alignments. The developing nations were no longer frightened into joining Western-backed
military alliances; they could pursue their independence more effectively outside, or in active opposition to, the alliances while seeking
cooperation with the communist countries.

If communist ideology was a declining force, then Western ideological anticommunism of the Cold War variety was outdated; it
would serve only to blight the growth of nationalism in the communist world and drive the increasingly "independent" communist
regimes back together. The new look in the communist world dic-

tated a reexamination of traditional Western concepts. The world could no longer be simply divided into two antagonistic blocs divided neatly along ideological lines. Given Soviet commitment to détente and peaceful coexistence and given the existence of the Sino-Soviet split, the concepts of East-West ideological competition and the global containment of communism seemed obsolete; they could endanger peace or provoke a Sino-Soviet reconciliation. Unity in Western military, political, and economic policies toward the bloc had become superfluous even before it had been achieved. The new situation called for flexibility and freedom of initiative.

Different schools of thought developed on how best to take advantage of the new situation in the communist world. If nascent differences between the communist states were to be encouraged, differentiated approaches to them were needed. Bridge-building with those East European states showing liberal or independent tendencies would help to wean them away from the Soviet Union.

At the same time it seemed necessary to encourage closer Western relations with the Soviet Union to stimulate the process of internal evolution and to exploit her differences with China—in other words, to "play the Soviet card." "History," it was said, "will not forgive us if we miss that chance."

In the United States some argued that the emergence of the Soviet Union and the United States as nuclear superpowers rendered the Western alliance less important. A unilateral approach to the Soviet Union was to be preferred as less complicated and less likely to provoke Sino-Soviet reconciliation. A sympathetic understanding was required of the position of liberal Soviet leaders. Their influence would be strengthened if they could be helped to solve their agricultural crises, industrial failures, technological backwardness, and shortages of consumer goods. Better fed, better housed communists would be more satisfied and less revolutionary.

The extent to which Khrushchev was accepted as a liberal in the West was illuminated by the widespread Western fears of a reversion to hard-line Soviet policies provoked by the news of his "dismissal" in 1964 and the relief that ensued when it became apparent that détente and peaceful coexistence would continue.

Another school of thought in the United States contended that the West should not seek actively to exploit the Sino-Soviet dispute for fear of achieving the opposite effect to that intended; the two communist giants were best left to fight it out between themselves. A passive policy on the Sino-Soviet split could nevertheless be accompanied by an active policy toward Eastern Europe. The continuing independence of Yugoslavia had demonstrated the success of Western policy toward her after 1948. An active trading policy in Eastern Europe, apart from being profitable, offered hopes of prizing other East European satellites away from the Soviet Union.

In France the Gaullist vision of a greater Europe stretching from the Atlantic to the Urals became a topic for serious discussion.

Differences over policy toward China widened. The United States clung to the view that no concessions should be made as long as the regime pursued its radical, militant line. Other countries, especially France, argued that China was embittered by its diplomatic isolation. Granted diplomatic recognition, a seat in the United Nations, and more favorable openings for trading with the West, it would evolve, like the Soviet Union, on more moderate lines.

In the 1970s the obvious Soviet military threat in Europe and open Soviet aggressiveness in Africa and Afghanistan, in contrast with China's new-found moderation, generated a new school of thought advocating closer relations with China, or "playing the China card."

In oversimplified form these were some of the arguments and considerations taken into account by the architects of Western policies in the 1960s and 1970s. The major criticism of these policies is not that they were influenced by cryptocommunists or fellow travelers, though this factor should not be disregarded. The policies were, in the main, honestly developed from certain basic premises, namely, that the Soviet system was evolving, that the Sino-Soviet split was genuine, and that the communist monolith was in the process of disintegration. The policies were wrong because the premises were false: They were the product of communist disinformation.

The Practical Effects on Western Policies

Apparent disunity in the East provoked real disunity in the West. Antagonisms and disputes between the Western allies came out into the open. For a while, they made headline news. Soon they were accepted as normal.

The trend toward the pursuit of national interest was most evident in France. It entailed a sharp decline in cooperation with the United States, the adoption of a new national defense policy, a withdrawal from France's military commitments to NATO in 1966, concentration on France's leading role in the Common Market, and the revival of interest in her traditional allies in Eastern Europe: Russia, Poland, and Romania. The deterioration in relations with some of the NATO allies was sharp. Cries were heard of France for the French, Europe for the Europeans, America for the Americans. Suspicions were fanned that the defense of Europe was not a vital United States interest. American reactions to the reassertion of French identity and interests were not always tactful or farsighted. The United States refused to share its nuclear technology with France. The Americans failed to consult the French adequately over the Cuban crisis. France was not a party to the test-ban treaty signed by the United States and Britain with the Soviet Union in 1963. The French openly flouted American policy on the recognition of communist China. As the American military commitment in Vietnam built up, so did the intensity of West European, especially Swedish, criticism of American policy there.

Franco-American hostility spilled over into Franco-British relations. Because of the "special relationship," Britain was cast in the role of an American agent in Europe. Britain's application to join the Common Market was vetoed by France. Britain focused on relations with EFTA and the Commonwealth and on cutting back her overseas commitments.

These developments were accompanied by unjustified fears of a revival of the German threat in Europe and by the questioning of the wisdom of Franco-German rapprochement, which, though desirable in the interests of Western European unity, was in itself no substitute for it.

Elsewhere, quarrels multiplied. The Austrians and Italians quarreled over the Tirol; the French and the Canadians over Quebec; Greece and Turkey over Cyprus; Britain and Iceland over fish; Pakistan and India over Kashmir and other issues. Arab-Israeli hostility reached new levels of intensity. These conflicts had their roots in historical problems that had little or nothing to do with communism. Nevertheless, the apparent weakening of the communist threat permitted a degree of indulgence in emotive nationalistic disputes that might have been more muted in the face of a common danger commonly perceived. In the atmosphere of détente NATO, which had been created to contain the obvious postwar Soviet military threat to Western Europe, lost momentum. Not only were there political conflicts among its members, but the effort to establish standardized arms and equipment languished. Joint NATO programs were stillborn or halfhearted. In 1974 Greece followed France in withdrawing from its military commitments. Tension with Turkey gravely weakened NATO's southern flank.

In 1965 a Western observer who, like everyone, accepted the authenticity of the Sino-Soviet split commented thus on NATO: "The basic Soviet blackmail strategy in the past decade has been to splinter NATO. This was the purpose behind the Berlin crisis. If the trends within NATO are not reversed, this objective may be accomplished, not by the more militant Soviet strategy, but by the temporary reduction of Soviet militancy, encouraging disarray within the alliance. How true it is that the use of force is often not the best strategy. The Soviets may in retrospect count the Sino-Soviet split more than compensated by a NATO split. As for the West, any breakup of NATO into power clusters, or a Balkanization of West Europe, could produce miscalculations or appeasement."[3]

The abandonment by the West of concerted policies toward the communist world led to changes in Western diplomatic practice. Personal contacts—including confidential talks—negotiations, and understandings between leading communist and noncommunist statesmen, even if initiated by the communist side, were welcomed in the West. A unilateral approach to relations with communist countries became the norm. General de Gaulle's visit to Moscow in 1966 revived talk of the Franco-Russian alliance of the 1890s and the Franco-Soviet pact of the 1930s. The United States agreed to conducting the SALT negotiations with the Soviet Union on a bilateral basis. Regular bilateral political consultations between the Soviets and the French and Italian governments became accepted practice. In West Germany the argument for an opening to the East gathered strength and found expression in Chancellor Brandt's Ost politik in the early 1970s. The Western response to China's détente diplomacy appeared not to be concerted. There were conspicuous examples of failure to consult; for example, the Japanese were not warned by the Americans of the Nixon-Kissinger initiative in China in 1971; President Giscard d'Estaing gave his allies little or no notice of his meeting with Brezhnev in Warsaw in May 1980.

The widening of the range of the contacts between communist diplomats and politicians in the noncommunist world was as warmly greeted as the widening of Western contacts with the communist world.

With the advent of détente Western business interests pressed for the expansion of trade with communist countries. Normally without consultation or regard for any common Western policy or interest, individual noncommunist countries took their own initiatives. Justification, if needed, was to be found in the arguments that the trade was profitable and beneficial to the economies of the noncommunist world, and that it would promote good East-West relations and stimulate pro-Western, liberal, nationalistic, and separatist tendencies in the communist world, thereby contributing to world stability and peace, and perhaps in the long run to the formation of a world common market.

Many Western firms, attracted by apparently golden opportunities, sent their representatives to explore the communist market. The British, having the greatest experience in world trade, took the lead, closely followed by the French, West Germans, Italians, and Japanese. The Germans, in particular, extended long-term credits to Eastern Europe, hoping, apart from making a profit, to promote independence from the Soviet Union. The Europeans and the Japanese increased their trade with China, hoping at the same time to take the edge off Chinese militancy.

There was a general trend in the 1960s toward easing restrictions on trade with communist countries. The policy of limiting East-West trade, underlined in the Rome agreements of 1958–59, was abandoned in favor of expansion; controls on strategic exports from the West were relaxed, and major industrial plants of definite strategic importance to the communist bloc were constructed on communist territory by Western enterprises. Longer-term credits were provided. Most favored nation status was granted to additional communist countries, including Romania and, in 1980, China. The United States, which had for long opposed the expansion of East-

West trade, began to change its ground. By 1977, as the President's State of the Union Message for that year shows, the encouragement of trade with the Soviet Union and Eastern Europe had become official American policy. Scientific and technical cooperation flourished, and the export of high-technology goods, including computers, was permitted even by the United States. All these steps were taken by Western nations acting individually, with little or no consideration of the possible long-term consequences.

Particular favor was shown to the Yugoslavs on the grounds that, having broken with the Soviet Union in 1948, they had established a precedent for Eastern European independence.

Next in favor were the Romanians, for the very reason that they appeared to have set off on the same independent course as Yugoslavia. The Romanian minister of foreign trade was received in France, West Germany, and the United States. Romania was given most favored nation status. Credit was made available to Romania more freely than to any communist country other than Yugoslavia and Poland.

By the end of the 1970s the expansion of trade and credit had allowed overall communist indebtedness to the Western world to rise to a total of about $70 billion. The growth of East-West trade had a pronounced effect on the overall Western approach to the communist world, since it built up powerful vested interests in the continuance of détente despite the growth of communist military power and other indications of aggressive communist intentions.

Détente and disinformation on communist "evolution" provided grounds for socialist parties to view with greater favor the formation of united fronts with communist parties. Apart from improving the chances of socialists' gaining power, united fronts looked like a promising device for influencing communist parties to move closer to social democracy and further from the Soviet Union. Such ideas were strong in the Italian, West German, French, and Finnish socialist parties. In general, socialist parties looked less favorably on coalitions or electoral alliances with center parties. The general leftward trend of the 1960s had a polarizing effect. It widened the gulf between conservative and progressive parties and between the reforming and revolutionary wings of socialist parties. More often than not, the moderate center suffered. The pragmatic relationship between conservative American and socialist European tendencies seemed to have outlived its usefulness.

Opposition to communism in principle became unfashionable. The basic differences between democracy and communism were lost from sight. It was considered more rewarding to seek out common interests through increasing East-West scientific, cultural, and sporting exchanges that, it was thought, would contribute to the liberalization of communist regimes. In the 1960s anticommunist writers virtually lost their admission tickets to the communications media; their attitude was deemed inimical to détente.[4] European radio and television organizations negotiated their own arrangements with their official Soviet government counterparts. The need for anticommunist broadcasts was called into question. The direct anticommunist content was drastically reduced.[5] Attention was focused instead on the Sino-Soviet split, other fissures in the bloc, and the growth of dissident movements. Official and semiofficial funding of noncommunist cultural and student organizations for the purpose of countering communist fronts was largely discontinued.

Soviet expansionism in Africa and the intervention in Afghanistan at the end of 1979 drew attention to underlying Soviet aggressiveness. Some of the more naive Western illusions about détente were shattered. At the same time Western reactions to the Soviet action demonstrated the extent to which vested interests in détente had been built up in the West, not least in West Germany and France. Despite American opposition, the West Germans and French have shown themselves determined to proceed with the construction of a gas pipeline from the Soviet Union to Western Europe. It is doubtful if the Afghan situation will alter long-term Western attitudes to détente any more than did the Cuban crisis of 1962. It has not dissipated long-term Western expectations, fostered by twenty years of communist disinformation, that the decay of ideology and the growth of internal opposition will lead eventually to the liberalization of the Soviet regime.

Meanwhile, China's vigorously expressed hostility to the Soviet Union offers apparent prospects of alliance with the West on the basis of a common interest in containing Soviet expansionism. Because there has been no understanding in the West either of disinformation or of long-range communist policy and the scissors strategy, "playing the China card" is now regarded as a serious strategic option for the United States.

Conclusion

Communist strategic disinformation has had a profound influence on international relations. Western governments and their professional advisers have remained oblivious of the problem. The fundamental purpose of the disinformation program has been to create favorable conditions for the fulfillment of long-range communist policy. The communist strategists have achieved their purpose thus far by misleading the West on developments in the communist world with three main aims in view: to relieve Western pressure on the communist regimes while they are "building socialism" and laying the groundwork for an eventual worldwide federation of communist states; to provoke the Western responses they desire to their activist diplomacy and international communist strategy; and to prepare the ground for a major shift in communist tactics in the final phase of policy in the 1980s.

The success of the communist disinformation program has engendered a state of crisis in Western assessments of communist affairs and therefore a crisis in Western policy toward the communist world. The meaning of developments in the communist bloc is misunderstood and the intentions behind communist actions are misinterpreted. Enemies are accepted and treated as though they were allies of the West. The Soviet military threat is recognized, but the strategic political threat is not comprehended and is therefore underestimated. Communist political offensives, in the form of détente diplomacy and disarmament negotiations, are seen as indications of communist moderation. Communist strategy, instead of being blocked, is unwittingly assisted by Western policies.

The first communist strategy of strengthening and stabilizing the bloc politically and economically has been assisted by Western economic aid and by the acceptance of détente and cooperation with communist governments. By responding favorably to communist initiatives on SALT and collective security in Europe, the West has helped the communist strategists to prepare the ground for the dissolution of NATO and the withdrawal of US troops from Europe. By accepting Yugoslavia as independent, the West has given her the opportunity to organize much of the Third World into a socialist-orientated bloc with a procommunist, anti-Western bias. By accepting Sino-Soviet rivalry as genuine and considering

China as a possible ally against Soviet expansionism, the West is creating opportunities for the construction of new alignments that will rebound, in the long run, to its own detriment. By engaging in SALT talks and agreements with inadequate awareness of communist long-range policy and strategy and by providing advanced technology first to the Soviet Union, then to China, the West has helped to shift the balance of military power against itself. Failing to appreciate the control over communist intellectual and religious figures and taking détente at its face value, the West has been ready to accept the notion of a long-term evolution of communism and its ultimate convergence with the democratic system. The West has assisted communist ideological strategy by its own unilateral ideological disarmament.

The spurious notion of a common interest between the United States and the Soviet Union against China in the 1960s was deliberately contrived and successfully exploited in the interests of communist strategy. The same can be said of the common interest between Eastern and Western Europe in seeking collective security against West German "revanchism" and American "interference"; or the common interest between communist and developing countries in the struggle against "imperialism"; or the common interest between China, Japan, and the West in resisting Soviet expansionism. Even the genuine common interest between the Soviet Union and the United States in avoiding nuclear conflict has been successfully exploited to swing the military balance in favor of the communist bloc.

The Western strategy of a mildly activist approach to Eastern Europe, with emphasis on human rights, is doomed to failure because it is based on misconceptions and will lead ultimately into a trap when a further spurious liberalization takes place in Eastern Europe in the final phase of long-range communist policy. Not the least disturbing aspect of the present crisis in Western assessments and policy is that, if it is recognized at all, its causes are misunderstood. As matters stand the West is acutely vulnerable to the coming major shift in communist tactics in the final phase of their policy.

PART THREE

The Final Phase and the Western Counter-Strategy

25

The Final Phase

THE CONTENTION OF THIS BOOK has been that, during the past two decades, the communist bloc has substantially achieved the objectives of the first two phases of its long-range policy. The individual communist regimes have been consolidated. The bloc communist parties, with the help of the security services, have built up their active forces within revitalized national and international front organizations, especially those concerned with trade unions, intellectuals, and young people. The importance of this drive is demonstrated by the appointment of Shelepin as head of the Soviet trade union organization from 1967 to 1975. The credibility abroad of "dissidence" as a serious internal political factor in the communist world has been established. A degree of accommodation with organized religion has been achieved. A nexus of interparty relationships, transcending the formal structure of Comecon and the Warsaw Pact, has been built up.

In consequence, the communist strategists are now poised to enter into the final, offensive phase of the long-range policy, entailing a joint struggle for the complete triumph of communism. Given the multiplicity of parties in power, the close links between them, and the opportunities they have had to broaden their bases and build up experienced cadres, the communist strategists are equipped, in pursuing their policy, to engage in maneuvers and strategems beyond the imagination of Marx or the practical reach of Lenin and unthinkable to Stalin. Among such previously unthinkable strategems are the introduction of false liberalization in Eastern Europe and, probably, in the Soviet Union and the exhibition of spurious

327

independence on the part of the regimes in Romania, Czechoslovakia, and Poland.

Western Misinterpretation of Events in Poland

Because the West has failed either to understand communist
strategy and disinformation or to appreciate the commitment to
it of the resources of the bloc security and intelligence services
and their high-level agents of political influence, the appearance
of Solidarity in Poland has been accepted as a spontaneous occur-
rence comparable with the Hungarian revolt of 1956 and as portend-
ing the demise of communism in Poland. The fact that the Italian,
French, and Spanish Communist parties all took up pro-Solidarity
positions gives grounds for suspecting the validity of this interpretation.

Western misreading of events led to predictions of Soviet intervention in Poland in 1981, which turned out to be unjustified. It
may lead to more serious errors in the future.

A New Analysis

There are strong indications that the Polish version of "democratization," based in part on the Czechoslovak model, was prepared
and controlled from the outset within the framework of bloc policy
and strategy. For twenty years the Polish Communist party had
been working on the construction of a "mature socialist society"
in which the party and its mass organizations would play a more
active and effective political role. In 1963 the party's ideological
commission was set up. In 1973 new means of coordinating the
activities of youth organizations were established. In 1976 a new
law was adopted on the leading role of the party in constructing
communism and on the party's interaction with the Peasant and
Democratic parties. In the same year all youth organizations, including those of the army, were merged into one Union of Socialist
Polish Youth.

Party membership increased from 1 million in 1960 to 3 million
in 1980. In the same period Polish trade unions increased their

membership from 5 to 13 million. The Union of Socialist Polish Youth had 2 million members in 1980. By the end of that year, 85 percent of the army's officer corps were party members. All Poles of Jewish origin had been eliminated from the army.

Throughout the twenty-year period Polish leaders have been fully involved in the coordinating mechanisms of the bloc, such as Comecon and the Warsaw Pact, as well as in bilateral meetings with other communist parties. The Polish security service took part in the conference in Moscow in 1959 of bloc security services at which their new political role was discussed and means of coordination were improved. Poland was among the countries visited by Mironov, the originator of this new political role, when he was head of the CPSU's Administrative Department.

Developments in the 1970s

Significantly two of the key figures in recent Polish events, the so-called "renewal," took up important positions soon after the "Prague spring" in 1968: Jaruzelski became Minister of Defense, and Kania became head of the Polish communist party's Administrative Department, with responsibility for the affairs of the Polish security service. In 1971 Gierek took over from Gomulka and the future leader of Solidarity, Walesa, began his political activity. Gierek and members of other important departments, including Kania's Administrative Department, consulted with their Soviet counterparts in Moscow. In the same year the Polish and Czech leaders had several meetings. In 1973 an agreement on ideological cooperation was signed between the two parties. In 1977 a delegation led by Gierek signed an agreement on the further strengthening of cooperation between them. Gierek also took part in Crimean summit meetings in the 1970s at which strategic questions were discussed.

In the course of the 1970s Kania was promoted to be Minister of the Interior and a member of the Politburo with responsibility for supervising the army and the security police. He also acted as the government's principal link with the politically active Catholic church. After the "renewal" had begun, Kania was further promoted to be leader of the party. Two other security chiefs were also promoted, Moczar to membership in the Politburo and Kowalczyk to be deputy premier. These promotions are the clearest indication of the involvement of Kania and the security services in the preparation of the Polish "renewal."

Final Preparations for the "Renewal"

There was intensive consultation between Polish and Soviet leaders and party officials in the two years preceding the "renewal." Among the more significant items, apart from Comecon and Warsaw Pact meetings, were the appointment of a new Soviet ambassador to Poland in 1978 (Aristov, a senior party official from Leningrad); a conference in Moscow of bloc officials (including Poles) on organizational matters and mass organizations; Jaruzelski's visit to Moscow in 1978; the meeting of Jaruzelski and the commander in chief of the Warsaw Pact forces in 1979; two meetings in 1978 and 1979 between Soviet and Polish party officials responsible for strategy and coordination of the communist movement, at which there were discussions on international and ideological questions; visits to Moscow by Cruchek, the chairman of the Polish trade union organization, and by Shidlyak, head of the Polish-Soviet Friendship Society, who discussed the strengthening of Soviet-Polish cooperation with his Soviet counterpart, Shytikov. This last visit is particularly interesting, since between February and August, 1980—just before the "renewal"—Shidlyak was head of the Polish trade unions.

In 1979 Gierek had two meetings with Brezhnev and separate meetings with the Czechoslovak, East German, West German, and French Communist party leaders. At the meeting with Brezhnev in the Crimea in August 1979, the discussion focused on "favorable new conditions for joint action in Europe." In February 1980 a Soviet publication referred to the strengthening of fraternal relations between the two countries resulting from agreements reached at their meetings.

A Polish party delegation attended a twenty-nine–party conference in Hungary in December 1979 that discussed relations between communists and social democrats and perspectives for European security. Suslov, the late leading Soviet ideologist and strategist, headed the Soviet delegation to the Polish party congress in February 1980. At the congress Gierek attacked NATO and the deployment of nuclear missiles in Western Europe and offered to act as host to an East-West disarmament conference in Warsaw. In May 1980 Brezhnev, Gromyko, and other senior Soviet officials attended a conference of bloc leaders in Warsaw. In his introductory speech Gierek said that the conference would open new prospects for peace and security in Europe and the world. His speech was the only part of the proceedings to be published.

There were frequent consultations between Polish party officials responsible for the press, TV, and radio with their Soviet colleagues, suggesting preparation of the Soviet and Polish media for a forthcoming important event.

Brezhnev awarded honors to Gierek and Jaruzelski in 1978 and Gierek honored Rusakov, head of the CPSU's department for bloc affairs, in February 1980. The awards can be seen as recognition of the contributions made to the preparation of the "renewal" by some of its key figures. It may also be surmised that Gierek's departure from the scene was envisaged at this stage. He doubtless had good reason for saying, shortly after his dismissal, that "proper appraisal of the Polish developments in the 1970s could only be made from a certain distance in time."

All of the foregoing evidence points to the conclusion that a major development in Poland, the "renewal," was planned thoroughly, and well in advance, by the Polish Communist party in cooperation with its communist allies and with a view to furthering the communist strategy for Europe. The conclusion is further supported by the evidence of the Polish Communist party's involvement in the formation and functioning of Solidarity.

The Polish Communist Party within Solidarity

Kania himself revealed that there were 1 million communist party members in Solidarity. Forty-two out of the 200 members of the party's Central Committee in 1981 were Solidarity members. Bogdan Lis, Walesa's deputy, was a Central Committee member. Zofia Gryzb, another Solidarity leader, was a member of the Politburo.

These leaders were not expelled from the party for their membership in Solidarity. On the contrary, Solidarity recognized the leading role of the party and the party recognized Solidarity's existence. Kania and Moczar even made statements in favor of it. Solidarity enjoyed access to the state-controlled media. Obstacles were not placed in the way of Walesa's extensive foreign travels; indeed, the Polish ambassador to Japan, who defected after the introduction of martial law, assisted in arranging Walesa's contacts with Japanese trade unions.

Stripping away the disinformation as before, it becomes clear that the changes in the leadership of the Polish party from Gierek to Kania to Jaruzelski were not the outcome of power struggles between factions in the leadership, but reflections of different stages in the "renewal" process, in the planning of which all of the leaders were equally involved.

The visits of Kania and other Polish leaders to Moscow and the visits of Suslov and Gromyko to Poland in April and July 1981 were part of the process of high-level coordination and readjustment of an agreed-upon strategic plan, not evidence of Soviet coercion being exercised over the Polish leaders.

Soviet military and naval maneuvers in the vicinity while the "renewal" was being introduced would have been planned and agreed in advance with the Polish and East German governments as a warning to the Polish and East German peoples that genuine anticommunist feeling would not be allowed to get out of hand.

Motives for the Creation of Solidarity

As with the "Prague spring" of 1968, the motives for the Polish "renewal" were a combination of the internal and external. Internally it was designed to broaden the political base of the communist party in the trade unions and to convert the narrow, elitist dictatorship of the party into a Leninist dictatorship of the whole working class that would revitalize the Polish political and economic system. The "renewal" followed the lines of Lenin's speech to the Comintern congress in July 1921. "Our only strategy at present," said Lenin, "is to become stronger and therefore wiser, more reasonable, more opportunistic. The more opportunistic, the sooner will you assemble again the masses around you. When we have won over the masses by our reasonable approach, we shall then apply offensive tactics in the strictest sense of the word."

Polish trade unions before the "renewal" were suffering from the stigma of party control. To have attempted to apply Leninist principles by creating a new trade union organization through governmental action would have failed to remove that stigma. The new organization had to appear to have been set up from below. Its independence had to be established by carefully calculated and controlled confrontation with the government. The origin of the Solidarity movement in a shipyard bearing Lenin's name, the singing of the "Internationale," the use of the old slogan "Workers of the world, unite" by Solidarity members, and the constant presence of Lenin's portrait are all consistent with concealed party guidance of the organization. Without that guidance and help, the discipline of Solidarity and its record of successful negotiation with the Polish government would have been impossible. The party's concealed influence in the Polish Catholic church ensured that the church would act as a force for moderation and compromise between Solidarity and the government.

Externally the strategic objectives behind the creation of Solidarity resemble those behind the "Prague spring." In brief, they were to deceive Western governments, politicians, and public opinion generally as to the real nature of contemporary communism in Poland in accordance with the weakness and evolution pattern of disinformation. More specifically, the intention was to use Solidarity to promote united action with free trade unions, social democrats, Catholics, and other religious groups to further the aims of communist strategy in the advanced countries, and to a lesser extent in the Third World. The name Solidarity is itself symbolic of this intention, which was made plain by Walesa's state-sponsored visits to trade unions in France, Italy, and Japan and to the Holy See.

Solidarity's effort to strengthen its international ties was part of a wider effort by the international communist movement to press forward with its strategy. In February 1981 Brezhnev spoke about the new, favorable conditions for unity of action in the world trade union movement. The communist World Federation of Trade Unions and regional European, Latin American, and Arab trade union bodies stepped up their campaigns against monopolies and in favor of disarmament. Meetings in Moscow in October 1980 and Berlin in March 1981 discussed working class solidarity and new forms of cooperation with trade unions of differing political orientation. A Soviet trade union delegation visited Italy for talks with three major Italian trade union federations. The influence of Solidarity was felt throughout the labor movement, even in the United States, where the left showed interest in Solidarity's experience. The communist intention was, and will remain, to exploit this influence for strategic ends.

The creation of Solidarity and the initial period of its activity as a trade union may be regarded as the experimental first phase of the Polish "renewal." The appointment of Jaruzelski, the imposition of martial law, and the suspension of Solidarity represent the second phase, intended to bring the movement under firm control and to provide a period of political consolidation. In the third phase it may be expected that a coalition government will be formed, comprising representatives of the communist party, of a revived Solidarity movement, and of the church. A few so-called liberals might also be included.

A new-style government of this sort in Eastern Europe would be well equipped to promote communist strategy by campaigning for disarmament, for nuclear-free zones in Europe, perhaps for a revival of the Rapacki Plan, for the simultaneous dissolution of NATO and the Warsaw Pact, and ultimately for the establishment of a neutral, socialist Europe. The revival of other elements of communist strategy for Europe—Eurocommunism and CSCE negotiations, for example—would be timed to coincide with the emergence of such a government.

Intensified solidarity campaigns between East and West European trade unions and peace movements could be expected; preparations are, in fact, already in train. In October 1980 a new all-European structure for youth organizations was set up at a conference of five hundred national youth organizations held in Budapest. A meeting of the World Parliament was held in Sofia in September 1980 in which leading communist authorities on united action took part. The Soviet and East European Committee for European Security was reactivated. A meeting of parliamentarians from communist states was held in Moscow in March 1981, at which Shytikov was much in evidence.

There are increasing signs of preparation for a communist initiative on Germany, the key to progress toward a neutral, socialist Europe. Among these were the meeting between Brezhnev and the East German leader, Honecker, in the Crimea in 1980 at which a European conference on disarmament was discussed. Similar discussions took place between the Soviet and West German peace committees in February 1980. A specialist on Germany, Czyrek, was appointed Polish foreign minister. Another specialist on Germany, Kvitsinskiy, was chosen late in 1981 to be chief negotiator for the Geneva nuclear arms reduction talks.[1] Winkelman, former head of the International Department of the East German Communist party, was appointed ambassador to the Soviet Union in March 1981. Falin, a senior CPSU official and former ambassador to West Germany, was appointed deputy head of the USSR–West Germany Society, and Zamyatin, a CPSU Central Committee official, was appointed head of the section of Soviet parliamentarians in contact with West Germany.

A revived Solidarity movement could be expected to extend its influence in Latin America, drawing together social democrats, Catholics, and progressives against military dictatorships. Here again there are signs of preparation. There was a meeting of Soviet and Latin American trade union leaders in Moscow in April 1981, and there were other, WFTU-sponsored, preparatory meetings for a World Congress of Trade Unions of Different Orientation in Cuba.

The Threat to the West from the Polish "Renewal"

A coalition government in Poland would in fact be totalitarianism under a new, deceptive, and more dangerous guise. Accepted as the spontaneous emergence of a new form of multiparty, semidemmocratic regime, it would serve to undermine resistance to communism inside and outside the communist bloc. The need for massive defense expenditure would increasingly be questioned in the West. New possibilities would arise for splitting Western Europe away from the United States, of neutralizing Germany, and destroying NATO. With North American influence in Latin America also undermined, the stage would be set for achieving actual revolutionary changes in the Western world through spurious changes in the communist system.

If in a reasonable time "liberalization" can be successfully achieved in Poland and elsewhere, it will serve to revitalize the communist regimes concerned. The activities of the false opposition will further confuse and undermine the genuine opposition in the communist world. Externally, the role of dissidents will be to persuade the West that the "liberalization" is spontaneous and not controlled. "Liberalization" will create conditions for establishing solidarity between trade unions and intellectuals in the communist and noncommunist worlds. In time such alliances will generate new forms of pressure against Western "militarism," "racism," and "military-industrial complexes" and in favor of disarmament and the kind of structural changes in the West predicted in Sakharov's writings.

If "liberalization" is successful and accepted by the West as genuine, it may well be followed by the apparent withdrawal of one or more communist countries from the Warsaw Pact to serve as the model of a "neutral" socialist state for the whole of Europe to follow. Some "dissidents" are already speaking in these terms.

Yugoslavia may be expected to play a conspicuous role in the new scenario. A display of Sino-Soviet rivalry for influence in Europe may be expected on the lines of the "struggle for hegemony" already being witnessed in South-East Asia. Its purpose would be to assist in the creation of new, false alignments between communist and noncommunist powers, and to break up the existing NATO structure and replace it with a system of European collective security entailing the ultimate withdrawal of the American military presence from Western Europe and the growth of communist influence there.

It is through flexible maneuvers such as these that the ruling communist parties, in contrast with the damaging rigidities of their performances during the Stalinist period, will provide the international communist movement with the kind of strategic backing Togliatti had in mind.

The recent travels of Chairman Hua to Yugoslavia and Romania and the closer ties between the French and Italian Communist parties and the Chinese are portents of things to come. In fact, using the new methodology, more and more signs can be detected that the onset of the final phase of communist long-range policy is imminent. The "arrest" and "exile" of Sakharov, the occupation of Afghanistan, developments in Poland, and the Iraqi attack on

Iran in the autumn of 1980 are among the pointers.

The last two are of special strategic importance. The developments in Poland look like a major move toward the final phase of communist strategy for Europe. The Iraqi attack on Iran looks like a concerted effort by radical Arab states, each of which is in a united front relationship with the Soviet Union against "imperialism," to use dual tactics (hostilities by Iraq, assistance by Syria and Libya) with the single overall objective of bringing Iran into an anti-Western alliance with them. The object of the alliance would be to gain control over a strategically vital area of the Middle East. Its success could but serve the strategic interests of the communist bloc. Despite Saddam Hussein's alleged purges of communists in Iraq and the moderation in his attitude toward the United States, he is continuing to receive arms supplies from communist sources, as are his Iranian opponents.

Certainly, the next five years will be a period of intensive struggle. It will be marked by a major coordinated communist offensive intended to exploit the success of the strategic disinformation program over the past twenty years and to take advantage of the crisis and mistakes it has engendered in Western policies toward the communist bloc. The overall aim will be to bring about a major and irreversible shift in the balance of world power in favor of the bloc as a preliminary to the final ideological objective of establishing a worldwide federation of communist states.

There are a number of strategic options at the disposal of the communist strategists that can be used in various combinations to achieve their ultimate objectives. It would be impossible to list them all but five likely interconnected options are as follows:

• A closer alignment of an independent socialist Europe with the Soviet bloc and a parallel alignment of the United States with China. Japan, depending on whether it remains conservative or moves toward socialism, might join either combination.

• A joint drive by the Soviet bloc and a socialist Europe to seek allies in the Third World against the United States and China.

• In the military field, an intensive effort to achieve US nuclear disarmament.

• In the ideological and political field, East-West convergence on communist terms.

• The creation of a world federation of communist states.

In each of these the scissors strategy will play its part; probably, as the final stroke, the scissors blades will close. The element of apparent duality in Soviet and Chinese policies will disappear. The hitherto concealed coordination between them will become visible and predominant. The Soviets and the Chinese will be officially reconciled. Thus the scissors strategy will develop logically into the "strategy of one clenched fist" to provide the foundation and driving force of a world communist federation.

The suggested European option would be promoted by a revival of controlled "democratization" on the Czechoslovak pattern in Eastern Europe, including probably Czechoslovakia and the Soviet Union. The intensification of hard-line policies and methods in the Soviet Union, exemplified by Sakharov's arrest and the occupation of Afghanistan, presages a switch to "democratization" following, perhaps, Brezhnev's departure from the political scene. [The following observations were made prior to Brezhnev's death. They are followed by comments on developments subsequent to that event, beginning on page 347. ——Ed.] Brezhnev's successor may well appear to be a kind of Soviet Dubcek. The succession will be important only in a presentational sense. The reality of collective leadership and the leaders' common commitment to the long-range policy will continue unaffected. Conceivably an announcement will be made to the effect that the economic and political foundations of communism in the Soviet Union have been laid and that democratization is therefore possible. This would provide the framework for the introduction of a new set of "reforms."

The Brezhnev regime and its neo-Stalinistic actions against "dissidents" and in Afghanistan would be condemned as Novotny's regime was condemned in 1968. In the economic field reforms might be expected to bring Soviet practice more into line with Yugoslav, or even, seemingly, with Western socialist models. Some economic ministries might be dissolved; control would be more decentralized; individual self-managing firms might be created from existing plants and factories; material incentives would be increased; the independent role of technocrats, workers' councils, and trade unions would be enhanced; the party's control over the economy would be apparently diminished. Such reforms would be based on Soviet experience in the 1920s and 1960s, as well as on Yugoslav experience. The party would be less conspicuous, but would continue to control the economy from behind the scenes as before. The picture being deliberately painted now of stagnation and deficiencies in the Soviet economy should be seen as part of the preparation for deceptive innovations; it is intended to give the innovations greater impact on the West when they are introduced.

Political "liberalization" and "democratization" would follow the general lines of the Czechoslovak rehearsal in 1968. This rehearsal might well have been the kind of political experiment Mironov had in mind as early as 1960. The "liberalization" would be spectacular and impressive. Formal pronouncements might be made about a reduction in the communist party's role; its monopoly would be apparently curtailed. An ostensible separation of powers between the legislative, the executive, and the judiciary might be introduced. The Supreme Soviet would be given greater apparent power and the president and deputies greater apparent independence. The posts of president of the Soviet Union and first secretary of the party might well be separated. The KGB would be "reformed." Dissidents at home would be amnestied; those in exile abroad would be allowed to return, and some would take up positions of leadership in government. Sakharov might be included in some capacity in the government or allowed to teach abroad. The creative arts and cultural and scientific organizations, such as the writers' unions and Academy of Sciences, would become apparently more independent, as would the trade unions. Political clubs would be opened to nonmembers of the communist party. Leading dissidents might form one or more alternative political parties. Censorship would be relaxed; controversial books, plays, films, and art would be published, performed, and exhibited. Many prominent Soviet performing artists now abroad would return to the Soviet Union and resume their professional careers. Constitutional amendments would be adopted to guarantee fulfillment of the provisions of the Helsinki agreements and a semblance of compliance would be maintained. There would be greater freedom for Soviet citizens to travel. Western and United Nations observers would be invited to the Soviet Union to witness the reforms in action.

But, as in the Czechoslovak case, the "liberalization" would be calculated and deceptive in that it would be introduced from above. It would be carried out by the party through its cells and individual members in government, the Supreme Soviet, the courts, and the electoral machinery and by the KGB through its agents among the intellectuals and scientists. It would be the culmination of Shelepin's plans. It would contribute to the stabilization of the regime at home and to the achievement of its goals abroad.

The arrest of Sakharov in January 1980 raises the question of why the KGB, which was so successful in the past in protecting state secrets and suppressing opposition while concealing the misdemeanors of the regime, is so ineffective now. Why in particular did it allow Western access to Sakharov and why were his arrest and internal exile so gratuitously publicized? The most likely answer is that his arrest and the harassment of other dissidents is intended to make a future amnesty more credible and convincing. In that case the dissident movement is now being prepared for the most important aspect of its strategic role, which will be to persuade the West of the authenticity of Soviet "liberalization" when it comes. Further high-level defectors, or "official émigrés," may well make their appearance in the West before the switch in policy occurs.

The prediction on Soviet compliance with the Helsinki agreements is based on the fact that it was the Warsaw Pact countries and the Soviet agent Timo who initiated and pressed for the CSCE process. Since the Soviets signed the CSCE agreements, they may be expected at some stage, at least, to go through the motions of complying with them. Their present ostentatious noncompliance, noted at the follow-up conferences in Belgrade and Madrid, is intended to heighten the effect of their switch to apparent compliance in the final phase of policy.

"Liberalization" in Eastern Europe would probably involve the return to power in Czechoslovakia of Dubcek and his associates. If it should be extended to East Germany, demolition of the Berlin Wall might even be contemplated.

Western acceptance of the new "liberalization" as genuine would create favorable conditions for the fulfillment of communist strategy for the United States, Western Europe, and even, perhaps, Japan. The "Prague spring" was accepted by the West, and not only by the left, as the spontaneous and genuine evolution of a communist regime into a form of democratic, humanistic socialism despite the fact that basically the regime, the structure of the party, and its objectives remained the same. Its impact has already been described. A broader-scale "liberalization" in the Soviet Union and elsewhere would have an even more profound effect. Eurocommunism could be revived. The pressure for united fronts between communist and socialist parties and trade unions at national and international level would be intensified. This time, the socialists might finally fall into the trap. United front governments under strong communist influence might well come to power in France, Italy, and possibly other countries. Elsewhere the fortunes and influence of communist parties would be much revived. The bulk of Europe might well turn to left-wing socialism, leaving only a few pockets of conservative resistance.

Pressure could well grow for a solution of the German problem in which some form of confederation between East and West Germany would be combined with neutralization of the whole and a treaty of friendship with the Soviet Union. France and Italy, under united front governments, would throw in their lot with Germany and the Soviet Union. Britain would be confronted with a choice between a neutral Europe and the United States.

NATO could hardly survive this process. The Czechsolovaks, in contrast with their performance in 1968, might well take the initiative, along with the Romanians and Yugoslavs, in proposing (in the CSCE context) the dissolution of the Warsaw Pact in return for the dissolution of NATO. The disappearance of the Warsaw Pact would have little effect on the coordination of the communist bloc, but the dissolution of NATO could well mean the departure of American forces from the European continent and a closer European alignment with a "liberalized" Soviet bloc. Perhaps in the longer run, a similar process might affect the relationship between the United States and Japan leading to abrogation of the security pact between them.

The EEC on present lines, even if enlarged, would not be a barrier to the neutralization of Europe and the withdrawal of American troops. It might even accelerate the process. The acceptance of the EEC by Eurocommunist parties in the 1970s, following a period of opposition in the 1960s, suggests that this view is shared by the communist strategists. The efforts by the Yugoslavs and Romanians to create stronger links with the EEC should be seen not as inimical to Soviet interests, but as the first steps in laying the foundation for a merger between the EEC and Comecon.

The European Parliament might become an all-European socialist parliament with representation from the Soviet Union and Eastern Europe. "Europe from the Atlantic to the Urals" would turn out to be a neutral, socialist Europe.

The United States, betrayed by her former European allies, would tend to withdraw into fortress America or, with the few remaining conservative countries, including perhaps Japan, would seek an alliance with China as the only counterweight to Soviet power. The greater the fear of a Soviet-socialist European coalition, the stronger the argument for "playing the China card"—on the false assumption that China is a true enemy of the Soviet Union.

"Liberalization" in Eastern Europe on the scale suggested could have a social and political impact on the United States itself, especially if it coincided with a severe economic depression. The communist strategists are on the lookout for such an opportunity. Soviet and other communist economists keep a careful watch on the American economic situation. Since the adoption of the long-range policy, an Institute of World Economy and International Relations, originally under Arzumanyan and now under Inozemtsev, has been analyzing and forecasting for the Central Committee the performance of the noncommunist, and especially the American, economic system. Inozemtsev is a frequent visitor to the United States and was a member of a Soviet delegation received by the U.S. Congress in January 1978. The communist bloc will not repeat its error in failing to exploit a slump as it did in 1929–32. At that time the Soviet Union was weak politically and economically; next time the situation would be different. Politically the bloc would be better poised to exploit economic depression as proof of the failure of the capitalist system.

Information from communist sources that the bloc is short of oil and grain should be treated with particular reserve, since it could well be intended to conceal preparation for the final phase of the policy and to induce the West to underestimate the potency of the bloc's economic weapons. The bloc would certainly have an interest in secretly building up reserves of oil and grain that could be used for political purposes in a time of crisis to support newly established procommunist governments in Europe or elsewhere. It is worth noting that the scale of Soviet oil exports to India is already producing political dividends for the Soviet Union.

Sino-Soviet Relations

"Liberalization" in the Soviet Union could well be accompanied by a deepening of the Sino-Soviet split. This might include a rupture in trade and diplomatic relations, an increase in spectacular frontier incidents, and perhaps deeper incursions into one another's territory on the lines of the Chinese "invasion" of Vietnam in 1979—an invasion that could well have been intended as a rehearsal for a future Sino-Soviet operation.

A deepening of the split would sharpen the scissors strategy. It would encourage an even closer alignment with China of the United States and any other surviving conservative nations against a Soviet-socialist European coalition. Military cooperation would be included in this alignment and China might go so far as to offer bases in return for help in building up her military potential. In this connection, the agreements on bases between the United States and Somalia and Egypt may be a portent.

A breach in diplomatic relations between the Soviet Union and China might complicate but would not interrupt the process of policy coordination between them. They have now had twenty years in which to build up experience and mutual confidence in handling a bogus split. The existing Sino-Soviet bilateral links—political, diplomatic, and economic—could have been used for the purpose of coordinating Sino-Soviet disinformation activity connected with the split. Interruption of those channels might be a handicap, but there has been time in which to prepare alternative solutions to the problem of coordination. The breach in Soviet-Albanian diplomatic relations in 1960 was not followed by a breach in relations between Albania and all the other East European communist states. Following this precedent, Romania and Yugoslavia at least might be expected to maintain their representation in Peking if the Soviets were to withdraw or be "thrown out." To some extent, Sino-Soviet coordination could be carried on through Romanian and Yugoslav intermediaries. Another possibility is that direct, secret communications links exist between the Soviet Union and China that are not accessible to the West. In addition there is the possible existence of a secret bloc headquarters staffed by senior representatives of the major communist states, to which allusion has been made above.

The Third World

An alignment of the Soviet Union and Eastern Europe with a socialist Western Europe would exert a powerful influence over Third World socialist parties and trade unions. Some of the remaining conservative Third World countries would be strongly drawn toward a socialist orientation. Resistance to communism from the Socialist International would be replaced by a combined communist-socialist drive for Third World influence, backed by economic aid. It would have far-reaching consequences, especially if US aid should be curtailed in response to a severe depression. Soviet oil and grain could be used to good effect.

In his article on Nicaragua, Arismendi, the leading Latin American communist strategist, envisaged international solidarity between socialists and communists in support of the "national liberation" struggle in Latin America.[2] Cuba, which might follow the Soviet example of "liberalization" (the 1980 Cuban emigration might be part of the preparation for such a move) would play an active part in the liberation struggle. Those leaders of the nonaligned movement who had close relations with communist countries would try to involve the rest of the nonaligned movement in concerted actions with communists and social democrats to promote the joint aims of procuring the disarmament of the United States and the reduction of its role as a world power; of isolating Israel, South Africa, and Chile; and of helping liberation movements in Latin America, Southern Africa, and the Middle East, especially the PLO.[3] A variety of forums—the UN, the OAU, and the Brandt commission on the North-South problem—would be used for exerting political and economic pressure, including, if possible, the denial of oil.

In apparent competition with the Soviet Union, China would step up its Third World activity. The United States could be tempted to encourage the growth in influence of China and her associates, such as Egypt, Somalia, and the Sudan, as a barrier to Soviet expansion. American support for China would greatly improve her openings for maneuver and for making false alliances with Thailand and Islamic countries, such as Pakistan, Iran, Egypt, Saudi Arabia, and other conservative Arab states. It would also open doors for Chinese penetration of Latin America.

The Soviet occupation of Afghanistan was used by the Chinese to improve their position in Pakistan. Following this pattern, more Soviet and Chinese interference could be expected in the affairs of neighbor states. Sino-Soviet "rivalry" did not impede the communist victory in Vietnam; it would not impede their Third World penetration. If the Third World were to be divided into pro-Soviet and pro-Chinese camps, it would be at the expense of the interests of the United States and any other surviving conservative Western nations. The final outcome of support for Chinese influence in the Third World would be the emergence of additional regimes there that would be hostile to the West.

Disarmament

A Soviet-socialist European coalition, acting in concert with the nonaligned movement in the United Nations, would create favorable conditions for communist strategy on disarmament. The American military-industrial complex would come under heavy fire. "Liberalization" in the Soviet Union and Eastern Europe would provide additional stimulus to disarmament. A massive U.S. defense budget might be found no longer justified. The argument for accommodation would be strengthened. Even China might throw in its weight in favor of a Soviet-socialist line on arms control and disarmament.

Convergence

After successful use of the scissors strategy in the early stages of the final phase of policy to assist communist strategy in Europe and the Third World and over disarmament, a Sino-Soviet reconciliation could be expected. It is contemplated and implied by the long-range policy and by strategic disinformation on the split.

The communist bloc, with its recent accretions in Africa and South-East Asia, is already strong. European-backed Soviet influence and American-backed Chinese influence could lead to new Third World acquisitions at an accelerating pace. Before long, the communist strategists might be persuaded that the balance had swung irreversibly in their favor. In that event they might well decide on a Sino-Soviet "reconciliation." The scissors strategy would give way to the strategy of "one clenched fist." At that point the shift in the political and military balance would be plain for all to see. Convergence would not be between two equal parties, but would be on terms dictated by the communist bloc. The argument for accommodation with the overwhelming strength of communism would be virtually unanswerable. Pressures would build up for changes in the American political and economic system on the lines indicated in Sakharov's treatise. Traditional conservatives would be isolated and driven toward extremism. They might become the victims of a new McCarthyism of the left. The Soviet dissidents who are now extolled as heroes of the resistance to Soviet communism would play an active part in arguing for convergence. Their present supporters would be confronted with a choice of forsaking their idols or acknowledging the legitimacy of the new Soviet regime.

The Worldwide Communist Federation

Integration of the communist bloc would follow the lines envisaged by Lenin when the Third Communist International was founded. That is to say, the Soviet Union and China would not absorb one another or other communist states. All the countries of the European and Asiatic communist zones, together with new communist states in Europe and the Third World, would join a supranational economic and political communist federation. Soviet-Albanian, Soviet-Yugoslav, and Soviet-Romanian disputes and differences would be resolved in the wake, or possibly in advance of, Sino-Soviet reconciliation. The political, economic, military, diplomatic, and ideological cooperation between all the communist states, at present partially concealed, would become clearly visible. There might even be public acknowledgment that the splits and disputes were long-term disinformation operations that had successfully deceived the "imperialist" powers. The effect on Western morale can be imagined.

In the new worldwide communist federation the present different brands of communism would disappear, to be replaced by a uniform, rigorous brand of Leninism. The process would be painful. Concessions made in the name of economic and political reform would be withdrawn. Religious and intellectual dissent would be suppressed. Nationalism and all other forms of genuine opposition would be crushed. Those who had taken advantage of détente to establish friendly Western contacts would be rebuked or persecuted like those Soviet officers who worked with the allies during the Second World War. In new communist states—for example, in France, Italy, and the Third World—the "alienated classes" would be reeducated. Show trials of "imperialist agents" would be staged. Action would be taken against nationalist and social democratic leaders, party activists, former civil servants, officers, and priests. The last vestiges of private enterprise and ownership would be obliterated. Nationalization of industry, finance, and agriculture would be completed. In fact, all the totalitarian features familiar from the early stages of the Soviet revolution and the postwar Stalinist years in Eastern Europe might be expected to reappear, especially in those countries newly won for communism. Unchallenged and unchallengeable, a true communist monolith would dominate the world.

Comments on the Appointment of Andropov and on Other Developments Following the Death of Brezhnev.

These predictions and analyses were made during Brezhnev's tenure in office in anticipation of his departure. Brezhnev's succession and other developments confirm, in essence, the validity of the author's views. For example, the expeditiousness of the appointment of Andropov as Brezhnev's successor confirmed one of the main theses of this book; namely, that the succession problem in the Soviet leadership has been resolved. The practical consideration of the long-term strategies has become the major stabilizing factor in this solution. The promotion of the former KGB chief, who was responsible for the preparation of the false liberalization strategy in the USSR, indicates that this factor was decisive in his selection and further points to the imminent advent of such "liberalization" in the near future.

The rise of Andropov fits into a familiar pattern whereby the former security chief becomes the party leader in order to secure the important shift in the realization of the strategy. Kadar, who introduced the so-called "liberalization" in Hungary; Hua Kuo-feng, under whom China shifted to "capitalist pragmatism"; and Kania, who initiated the Polish "renewal" and recognized Solidarity—all had been former security chiefs. This pattern reflects the crucial role of the security services in the "liberalization" of communist regimes. The appointment of Andropov also implies that Shelepin would have been the successor of Brezhnev, because of his initiation of preparation for the "liberalization" in the USSR, except for the compromise by Stashinskiy, who exposed Shelepin's role in the assassination of the émigré leader Bandera, and further, because of the exposure, by this author, of Shelepin's role in the strategic reorientation of the KGB.

Another important factor in the selection of Andropov was his leadership role in the preparation for the Czechoslovakian "liberalization" in 1967–68 and the "liberalization" in Hungary, which took place when he was the head of the Central Committee's department responsible for relations with communist countries until mid-1967. Therefore, the timing of the release of the Solidarity leader and the news of the appointment of Andropov confirm another point in the book: that the "liberalization" will not be limited to the USSR, but will be expanded to Eastern Europe and particularly to Poland. The experiment with "renewal" in Poland will be repeated again. This time, however, it will be with full strategic initiatives and implications against Western Europe and NATO. The appointment of Andropov, the release of the Solidarity leader, and the invitation to the Pope to visit Poland in June 1983, made by the Polish Government, all indicate that the communist strategists probably are planning the reemergence of Solidarity and the creation of a quasi-social democratic government in Poland (a coalition of the communist party, the trade unions, and the churches) and political and economic reforms in the USSR for 1984 and afterward.

The coming offensive of the communist strategists will pursue the following objectives:

• The establishment of a model government for Western Europe, which will facilitate the inclusion of the so-called Eurocommunist parties into government coalitions with socialists and the trade unions.

• The dissolution of NATO and the Warsaw Pacts, the neutralization of Western Europe, and the Finlandization of Western Europe in general, through the advocacy of European collective security.

• The provision of a broader basis and impetus for expansion of the antimilitary movement by a more active involvement of Catholics and other believers in the West, thereby forcing the United States into a disadvantageous disarmament.

• Influencing the 1984 United States presidential election in favor of candidates who are more likely to deal with the leaders of the "liberalized" regimes in the USSR and East Europe and are more inclined to sacrifice the US military posture.

The dialectic of this offensive consists of a calculated shift from the old, discredited Soviet practice to a new, "liberalized" model, with a social democratic facade, to realize the communist planners' strategy for establishing a United Europe. At the beginning they introduced a variation of the 1968 Czechoslovakian "democratization." At a later phase they will shift to a variation of the Czechoslovakian takeover of 1948.

Developments have accurately confirmed the prediction that the communist strategists would undertake the political initiative on disarmament, particularly against West Germany. The trip of Gromyko to Bonn, the invitation of social democratic opposition leaders to Moscow, and the statements of Andropov on missile concessions (made to influence the West German elections) are all clear indications of such a political initiative. As expected, the communist initiative revealed that its main target was the socialist parties. It also showed that there are elements in their leadership who are vulnerable to such an initiative, especially those in the West German social democratic party who have anti-NATO and anti-US views, or who like Brandt and Sweden's social democrat Palme are ready to embrace Rapacki's idea of a nuclear-free zone in Central Europe. The initiative increased also the pressure on the US for concessions to the USSR. In the opinion of the author, however, the communist initiative has not yet reached its peak. How will the Western German social democrats respond when the communist regimes begin their "liberalization" by making concessions on human rights, such as easing emigration, granting amnesty for the dissidents, or removing the Berlin wall? One can expect that Soviet agents of influence in Western Europe, drawing on these developments, will become active. It is more than likely that these cosmetic steps will be taken as genuine by the West and will trigger a reunification and neutralization of West Germany and further the collapse of NATO. The pressure on the United States for concessions on disarmament and accommodation with the Soviets will increase. During this period there might be an extensive display of the fictional struggle for power in the Soviet leadership. One cannot exclude that at the next party congress or earlier, Andropov will be replaced by a younger leader with a more liberal image who will continue the so-called "liberalization" more intensively.

Sino-Soviet Developments

It is also necessary to comment on developments in Sino-Soviet relations and their actions. The sending by China of a high level delegation to the funeral of President Brezhnev, headed by Foreign Minister Huang Hua; the conduct of talks between Huang Hua and Gromyko; and the unusual statement made by Huang Hua characterizing Brezhnev as "an outstanding statesman of the Soviet Union"—all have some significance. Especially significant and contradictory was a reference to the "loss of Brezhnev, a great statesman." This characterization ignores the fact that the worst hostilities with China—if one accepts the conventional point of view—took place under Brezhnev. Such a favorable assessment of Brezhnev seems accurate and sound, however, if one accepts Sino-Soviet hostilities as strategic disinformation. According to the analysis developed in this book, these developments add to and strengthen the validity of the author's argument that the Sino-Soviet split was a disinformation mask over their secret coordination for the realization of their common strategies. Because of the secret strategic Sino-Soviet cooperation, still according to this analysis, the primary objective for the Soviet move into Afghanistan, aside from achieving its Sovietization, was not to encircle China, but to force the United States and Pakistan into a close political and military cooperation with China. It is not inconceivable that the Soviets will make concessions on Afghanistan in order to gain new strategic advantages.

Andropov's proposals about improving relations with China are not aimed at undermining China's relations with the United States, but at stimulating a revival of an American interest in closer relations with China, which are presently perceived as weakened after the departure of such strong proponents of United States–Chinese military cooperation as Brzezinski and others. Its main purpose is to facilitate the acquisition by China of American weaponry and military technology. The Soviet occupation of Afghanistan also may be designed to create more favorable conditions for China's penetration into Moslem countries, capitalizing on China's success with Pakistan. The recent trip of China's premier to Africa, which included visits to Egypt, Algeria, and Morocco, confirms another point in the book about the existing division of labor between the Soviet Union and China. It seems that the influencing of Moslem countries has been left to China by the Soviet strategists. As for China's role in the realization of communist strategy in Europe, the Sino-Soviet rivalry might be exploited by China's intervening in European politics under the pretext of resisting "Soviet hegemony." In this case, the Chinese strategists might try to gain a Rapallo type of arrangement with some conservative governments of Western Europe.

The Attempted Assassination of the Pope

It is also necessary to comment on the attempt to assassinate the Pope. The author is not naive about the attitude, involvement, and practice of political terrorism by the KGB. Earlier in the book he expressed the view that the Soviet and other communist services were behind the political terrorism of the Red Brigade in Italy and terrorism in Western Germany. The question here, however, is not whether the Soviets control the Bulgarian services as they control other communist services, or whether the Soviets and Bulgarians are involved in terrorism in Western Europe, but whether the KGB and the Bulgarian services are involved in this particular attempted assassination. In order to make an assessment of the assassination attempt against the Pope, it is not enough to refer to Soviet control of the Bulgarian service. One must first examine the Soviet rationale for political assassinations, and then address the basic question: whether the Soviet strategists have a political interest and a real need to get involved in such an affair. The author does not share the view that the KGB and the Bulgarian service are involved in the assassination attempt against the Pope perpetrated by Agca, a Turkish gunman. This conclusion is based on the following reasons:

1. This assassination attempt does not fit into the rationale of assassinations as practiced by the KGB. According to the author's understanding, the Soviet government and the KGB would resort to a political assassination of a Western leader only under the following conditions:

A. If a Western leader, who is a recruited Soviet agent, is threatened in office by a political rival. This is based on a statement made by Zhenikhov, a former KGB resident in Finland. He stated that if his agent, holding a high office, was threatened by an anticommunist social democrat during the elections, the latter would be poisoned by a trusted KGB agent.

B. If a Western leader became a serious obstacle to communist strategy and to the strategic disinformation program, he would be quietly poisoned at a summit meeting during negotiations or while visiting a communist country, since détente provides such opportunities in abundance. The practical lesson here is that a Western leader who is involved in furthering an effective counterstrategy against the communists should not visit communist countries or take part in any summit meetings with their leaders. The technique for a poisoning was described in a statement made by a KGB general, Zheleznyakov, at an operational briefing devoted to an assassination proposal against Tito in 1953 in Moscow. Zheleznyakov stated that the major requirement for success is mere physical contact with the target, as the Soviet service has technical means (special poisons) to inflict mortal diseases without leaving traces of the poison, so that death will be attributed to natural causes.

C. If the assassination of a leader provides the opportunity for a controlled Soviet agent to take over the position. According to Levinov, a KGB adviser in Czechoslovakia, this rationale was used by both the Soviet and the Czech services in the assassination of President Beneš, thus vacating a place for a communist leader, Gottwald.

D. If a communist leader decided to eliminate his communist rival. It is a well-known fact that, based on this rationale, Stalin got rid of many of his rivals, including Trotskiy in Mexico. According to the author, this rationale is not used any longer because of the cessation of the struggle for power in the Soviet party leadership.

2. In view of the arguments and reasoning made about Polish developments in this book, particularly those concerning Solidarity as a product of "mature socialism," it is clear that there is no motive for such an assassiantion (of the Pope) by the KGB and their communist partners.

3. The author regards as erroneous the perception that the KGB is a primitive and inefficient service that would resort to the use of the Bulgarian service to recruit a killer for hire, especially one who was guilty of murdering a progressive editor in Turkey, and who had earlier escaped from prison and had somehow made a strange visit to Bulgaria. According to the author's understanding, the KGB is always apprehensive about using escapees, suspecting the possibility of their being police provocateurs. The KGB would not consider such a candidate, unknown to them and over whom they had no control, for an operation of such importance and sensitivity.

4. If the Soviet strategists had reason for such assassinations, they would not attempt to act through the Bulgarian service. More likely, the KGB would undertake such a mission through their trusted illegals or through opportunities available to the Polish service. It is well known that the Pope maintains a vast staff of secretaries and kitchen help, almost all consisting of Polish nationals. He further receives visitors from Poland. The Polish security service, through its antireligious department, would study the relatives of people on the Pope's staff and would use them as hostages in the preparation of such an operation. It would be a quiet, secret operation.

5. The author is also of the opinion that the Italian services, which are seriously weakened by recent scandals and investigations, are too inexperienced to assess the strategic complexity and implications of such an operation. This affair can be assessed and understood only in terms of communist strategies (communist liberalization and Western disarmament and its implications for the West).

6. The author is more inclined to agree with the views of the Israeli and West German services, as expressed in a December 17, 1982, *New York Times* article written by Henry Kamm, in which he states that implicating the KGB in the assassination affair is outright disinformation. The author, however, does not agree with the article as to the purpose of such disinformation. In his opinion, the purpose was not to undermine or discredit Andropov, but to confuse the strategic implications.

7. There is also a serious contradiction in the actions of the Polish and Soviet governments regarding this affair. If the Soviet government perceives the Pope as an anticommunist involved in subversive activities against Poland and other communist countries, as implied in a TASS statement, it is incongruous that the Polish government would invite the Pope to visit Poland in June of 1983, since all such matters are coordinated with the Soviets.

Another relevant comment probably should be added here. In view of the ardent public statements of some Italian socialist ministers regarding their acceptance of the communist involvement in this affair, such a position strengthens their vulnerability to an erroneous response to future Polish developments. Despite their genuine anticommunism, they would be pressured to accept the Polish "liberalization" as spontaneous.

26

———————

Where Now?

THIS BOOK HAS TRIED to give an objective assessment of the
current long-range communist policy and the threat it poses
for the West. The assessment has been based partly on secret
information available only to an insider; partly on an intimate understanding of how the communist strategist thinks and acts; partly
on knowledge of political readjustments, the use of strategic disinformation, and the extent of KGB penetration of, and influence on,
Western governments; and partly on research and analysis, using
the new methodology, of open records of Soviet and communist
developments over the past twenty years. It leaves no doubt in
the author's mind that the threat is more serious, its scope wider,
and its culmination more imminent, than scholars and politicians
in the West have led him to believe.

This is not because they have consciously played down the threat.
It is due to a genuine and, to some extent, excusable lack of understanding. They accept at face value what the communists choose
for them to see and hear. They accept the existence of communist
tactical disinformation in the form of covert political actions and
forgeries of Western government documents, but fail to appreciate
the problem of strategic disinformation in the shape of communist
forgeries of differences, splits, and independence in the communist
bloc. Tactical forms of disinformation are intended to divert attention from the onset of the communist offensive in the final phase
of policy. Strategic disinformation is a root cause of the current
crisis in Western foreign policies. Even those who recognize the
dangers of disinformation cannot conceive that it can be practiced

on so grand a scale and with a subtlety so disarming. They forget—
or perhaps have never fully realized—that their predecessors were
similarly deluded in the 1920s, and they fail to take into account
that communist penetration of Western governments and intelligence services provides an accurate early warning and monitoring
service of Western reactions to disinformation.

It is not easy, living in a democracy, to accept that total, obsessive
commitment to world revolution could survive through sixty years
and then be rekindled with fresh zeal. The West, basing itself
on its own experiences, expects splits and cracks to appear in the
communist bloc. Any hint of differences between communist states
or parties is avidly seized on, while evidence of cooperation is ignored
or misinterpreted. Diplomatic overtures, based on what the West
sees as common interests, are hastily pursued; détente and disarmament are discussed in all seriousness.

The West recognizes the communist military threat but misinter-
prets the political threat. With the best of intentions, United States
policy has labored hard to bring about a liberalization in the USSR
and Eastern Europe with its human rights policy and encouragement for the internal dissident movement; but it has failed to
realize that the dissident movement has been shaped and controlled
by the party apparatus and the KGB, and that a sham "liberalization" may well be the next major step in the disinformation program.

Pursuit of a realistic foreign policy by the United States has
been made even more difficult by the demoralization of their intelligence and counterintelligence services that followed the Watergate
exposures and the overblown campaign to restrict the functions
of the CIA and FBI. The CIA's capacity for political action was
curtailed and two thousand experienced officers were retired. Particular damage was done to US counterintelligence, whose task it
should be to analyze communist policy and tactics, forecast communist intentions, and so help to protect the nation and its intelligence
services from communist penetration, subversion, agents of influence, and disinformation.

What, at the eleventh hour, can now be done? With all due
diffidence the author feels that his book would not be complete
until he has sketched in the direction in which he feels the West
should now move. For the sake of brevity the difficulties of accom-

plishment are brushed aside. The aims are stated baldly and uncompromisingly.

Although time is fast running out, the balance of forces between East and West has not yet tilted irrevocably. It is still possible for the West to recover the initiative and to frustrate the communist strategy to isolate Western Europe, Japan, and the Third World from the United States, but it is a difficult road to travel. The initial lead must be positive, and it must come from the United States.

Reassessment

The logical consequence of the argument of this book, and of the new methodology which it introduces, is that a group of acknowledged American experts should reexamine and reevaluate communist policy, tactics, and strategy of the past twenty years. They should be drawn from the intelligence, counterintelligence, military, and diplomatic services and from the academic world. They should have the support of their heads of services or institutions in providing research facilities and should have access to all information and records relating to communist state and party affairs since the 1950s. Their report should define the communist long-range strategy, predict its course of action, estimate its time scale, assess the political strength of the communist bloc and the subversive potential of the communist movement, expose communist disinformation, and estimate the extent and impact of communist penetration of, and agents of influence within, the United States and other governments.

Having set in train its own fact-finding and mind-clearing exercise, the United States should then seek to inspire a revival of allied unity on a new basis. Since the provocation of division and friction between member nations of the Western alliance is one of the prime objectives of communist long-range strategy, it is essential that all Western governments and their peoples should have a clear understanding of that strategy, and of the disinformation which supports it, before any other remedial measures can become effective. That is why reassessment of the threat comes first. Ideally each major Western country should, like the United States, set up its own commission of enquiry into communist policy, tactics, and strategy as reflected in its own intelligence, counterintelligence, military intelligence, and diplomatic records of the past twenty years.

To counter communist strategy and regain the initiative for the West, a new Western strategy is needed, based on a true understanding of the situation, policy, and strategic disinformation of the communist bloc. Without a clear appreciation of the deceptive nature of Sino-Soviet rivalry and of "liberalization" and splits in the communist world, Western governments, whatever their political complexion, cannot recover from the crisis in their foreign policy and are at risk of sliding into false alliances with one communist state against another. If possible, a moratorium should be imposed on any form of rapprochement with any member of the communist bloc while the reevaluation takes place. The publication could then follow of an allied defense document setting out calmly and clearly the agreed overall Western assessment of current communist bloc policy and the means being used to implement it. Public discussion of the findings would be encouraged by conferences of the Western governments, of political groupings such as the Socialist International, and of the leaders of the moderate, pro-Western Third World nations; parallel professional exchanges would take place between the Western intelligence and counterintelligence services.

The effect that an exposé on this scale would have should not be underestimated. The communist bloc leaders and strategists would find, if the Western assessment were correct, that their next strategic offensives and moves in the deception plan had been preempted. The initiative would have been snatched from them. Their complicated political, diplomatic, and disinformation operations still in the pipeline would, if pursued, confirm the correctness of the Western assessment. The peoples of the communist bloc, the majority learning for the first time of the deceit on which their country's policy had been based, would—whatever their feelings about its morality—realize that it would not work in the future and that their leaders had failed. While a communist regime remains successful, the people can be coerced into going along with it. It is when failure—or, at least, lack of new successes—sets in that, as was shown in Hungary and Poland in 1956, real and radical changes may happen. Exposure of a bankrupt policy would unleash powerful political pressures on communist leaders and on their regimes, parties, and governments, perhaps forcing them to change their conduct in international relations.

It will be argued by faint hearts in the West that to proclaim publicly that the full significance of the communist threat is now recognized and that a realistic response is on its way is only to drive the communist leaders to an openly hard-line attitude and even to war. But does this argument stand up? If the threat has been correctly evaluated and properly explained, it will be clear to public opinion that, although disinformation may have concealed the intentions of communist policy, its line could scarcely have been harder. Indeed, if the Western exposé were to result in the reemergence of the communist monolith—China and the USSR "reconciled," Romania and Yugoslavia openly back in the fold— that would be no cause for alarm. For the West it would be the most advantageous of all possible outcomes, for it would mean that the communist bloc had had to retreat; and that the Western miscalculations, which the bloc had striven so long and hard to create, would be left unexploited while the innate strength of the West was still intact. It would, moreover, have a salutary effect on the peoples of the Western nations. A full-strength communist bloc, all illusions of splits and rifts removed, would inspire them to close ranks and face up to reality. It would demonstrate that their governments had made the right assessment. It would give breathing space during which past mistakes could be corrected. It would give solidarity to the alliance and heart to the whole noncommunist world to be able to say to the communist leaders: "We have seen through your disinformation and pretences; we can interpret your double-talk; we now call halt."

The cynics in the West will argue that it is an illusion to imagine that, at this late hour, the communist threat can be averted by exhortations to close ranks and unite. The peoples of the West detest uniformity; the nations of the West will never give up their traditions of independence. A common cause may bring them together, but no cause has ever held them together for long. But as Professor Goodman points out in his book *The Soviet Design for a World State* (p. 487): "The communists have acted cautiously when confronted by strong external power and aggressively when

they have been tempted by weakness. . . . If one of the principal
sources of weakness of the contemporary non-communist world is
its disunity, then the surest way to precipitate war is to provide
seemingly easy targets of Soviet conquest through dissension or
neglect on the part of the non-Soviet world to formulate unmistak-
ably affirmative policies. . . ."

For one who, like the author, was brought up in the communist
world, who in his early years worked for the communist cause only
to reject its code of ethics in maturity, it is difficult to believe
that, faced with imminent subjection to the communist way of
life, the Western nations would be unable to find lasting ideological
and political solidarity. Solidarity does not mean conformity. The
spiritual strength of the West lies in its freedom and diversity,
but freedom and diversity should not be cultivated to the point
where they become an obstacle to survival.

To achieve the lasting solidarity that can withstand the communist challenge, the West should make a number of fundamental
changes of attitude, direction, and counterstrategy. These changes
emerge logically from an understanding of the long-range communist policy; they seek to frustrate what the communist strategists
aim to accomplish. Above all, the Western alliance should refresh
its sense of common purpose, common interest, and common responsibility. The main causes of internal dissension should be removed or mollified. They are: national rivalries, originating deep
in history; the distrust that American conservatism and European
democratic socialism hold for each other; the growing hostility between conservatives and socialists inside Western Europe.

End to National Rivalries

The deep-seated national rivalries and suspicions between the
nations of Western Europe, between Western Europe and America,
and between America and Japan must somehow be controlled. Despite the tragic conflicts of the past, despite the present mutual
distrust, the advanced nations of the noncommunist world now
all share a democratic process of government, freedom of opposition
and dissent, and an economic system that relies, at least in part,
on free market competition. If the peoples of these nations would

realize that the communist threat to their way of life, far from receding as they had thought, is now at their heels; if they would see that unless they present a cohesive force in the face of the communist challenge, they will be picked off one by one; surely then they would insist that their governments sink their differences.

National interests can no longer be protected by purely national efforts. The communist threat is now so formidable that for any nation, be it France or even the United States, to stand half-aloof from the alliance is irrational and potentially suicidal. The allies themselves should establish, and then submit to, some form of supranational authority for policy coordination. Perhaps the most effective initial step would be for the United States to offer to sacrifice a measure of her own sovereignty in favor of such a body if the Western European nations would do likewise.

Ideological Solidarity

Differences between American conservatives and European social democrats in their attitudes toward capitalism should not be allowed to weaken the Atlantic alliance. Democratic socialism is now firmly entrenched in Western Europe. Its economic ideals show some common features with the communist system and differ markedly from American economic ideals. But, like Americans, European social democrats regard democratic freedoms as sacrosanct; when faced by communists, the two are natural allies. They joined together when faced by Stalin's "police socialism"; now they must join forces again to face the more insidious deception of "communism with a human face." Their common interest is overwhelming, for both Europe and America are targets of a political offensive that seeks to embrace them now only to strangle them later.

Within Europe itself, conservatives and social democrats must draw closer together, for both need to protect themselves against the growing radicalism of the far left of European socialism, which, if it is not halted soon, will inevitably lead to a united front with the communists. Both conservatives and social democrats must understand and, together, combat the communist long-term strategy; the survival of both depends on it.

Inward Heart-Searching

The West should devote the effort that it now expends on dé-tente, SALT, and European collective security (communist-style) to concentrating on its own affairs. The advanced countries are afflicted by a malaise that stems from disillusionment. Criticism of traditional values and national institutions is rife. Military forces and the military-industrial machine are held in low esteem; intelligence and security services have been savaged; private enterprise, as represented by the multinational concerns, is dubbed as greedy and power-hungry; in the United States even the presidency is belittled. Each individual nation must find its own way to recover self-respect before the Western alliance can regain the initiative. A start might be made if thinking and concerned men and women— from the political parties, the labor movement, the universities, the media—would form cross-party political alliances in defense of democratic institutions.

Widening Defense Alliances

As a major strategic goal the West should seek to widen its defensive organization by inviting other threatened countries to share the security and the responsibilities of NATO membership. Japan, Australia, Brazil, Indonesia, Singapore, Nigeria, Pakistan, Saudi Arabia, and Israel are examples, taken at random, of countries with an incentive to join the noncommunist defense alliance; by doing so, they would lift Western defense planning from regional to global dimensions. The benefits would be mutual, guaranteeing oil supplies for the West, extending beyond strict defense considerations. The case for unity of the noncommunist nations was made by H. C. Allen in his book *The Anglo-American Predicament*. It is still valid today.

Complementary to the expansion of formal alliances, closer relations should be forged with the developing nations. Public exposure of the long-term communist bloc policy toward them, and of the Trojan horse role of Yugoslavia, Romania, and Cuba, should by itself alert the leaders of these nations to the danger. But the Western objective should be not merely to frustrate communist intentions, but to strengthen the political and economic basis for their independent development. National rivalries, spheres of influence, and patronage would be replaced by joint efforts to give aid, trade, and credit to enterprising young nations not only for future commercial gain, but to mould their national traditions along democratic lines and against communist subversion.

The Western military alliance should maintain superiority in nuclear weapons—not mere parity.

Reorientation of Intelligence Services

The intelligence, counterintelligence, and security services of the Western nations should be strengthened and reorientated to match the changed direction of the communist threat. Overriding priority should no longer be given to countering traditional KGB espionage and information gathering; the main task now should be to neutralize the political damage caused by communist agents of influence and their disinformation. Appreciation of the problem of disinformation should be raised from the tactical to the strategic level.

To interpret communist actions and detect communist agents of influence, the Western services should use the new methodology. A central coordinating staff, working on behalf of the security and diplomatic services of the whole Western alliance, should be set up to exchange experience, coordinate operations, and provide research on patterns of disinformation.

Security screening should be resumed for all important recent émigrés, including "dissidents." Their background and activities should be reviewed in the light of communist long-range policy and disinformation.

Diplomatic Disengagement

To protect themselves from communist strategic disinformation and activist diplomacy, the Western powers should probe every political action for its true motive. Détente discussions, SALT negotiations, and communist proposals for European collective security should be broken off or declined. There should be no independent consultations between communist leaders and member nations of the alliance.

The number of Western missions on communist territory should be reduced to the minimum—preferably no more than two or three—and strict reciprocity should be maintained when allowing communist missions and delegations into the West.

Denial of Trade and Technology

The communist bloc is still striving to level up economic and industrial strength among its more backward members—China among them—and to increase still further its military strength. Denial of trade, credit facilities, and technological know-how delays completion of these programs; strains the economies of the more advanced members, such as the USSR and Czechoslovakia; and, in the long run, breeds public discontent. The denial of credit facilities has a further advantage in that it limits communist opportunity to damage Western economies. Economic action by the West hits the communist bloc where it is most vulnerable, and should be relentlessly pursued against every bloc country, including Yugoslavia, Romania, and Poland. A central coordinating and planning staff should be set up to conduct the economic offensive.

Isolating Communist Parties

The long-range strategy of the communist movement is to broaden its political base in noncommunist countries by forming a united front with socialist and nationalist parties; when a parliamentary majority has been won, the communists will seek, through the development of extra-parliamentary mass action, to bring about fundamental changes in the democratic system. The stratagem will only succeed if the democratic parties being wooed are either ignorant of communist intentions or imagine that they can control the outcome. Exposure of the communist long-range policy, strategy, and tactics and the coming sham liberalization in Eastern Europe, with its implications for the West—in particular, for countries with Eurocommunist parties—should warn the unwary and detach the deceived.

Addressing the Peoples of the Communist Bloc

It is not the communist leaders or the dissidents (brain children of the KGB) on whom the West should pin its hopes for genuine changes in the communist empire. It is the people—Russians, Chinese, and the Eastern European nationals—who, despite Western errors and miscalculations, are still potential allies. It is to the peoples of the communist bloc that Western foreign policy should be addressing itself.

They should be distinguished from their rulers and from the false opposition their rulers have invented. They expect to be addressed as equals and allies. They want to be told the truth in plain, unvarnished terms about both communist and Western policies, successes, and failures. They will respect a true picture, blemishes included, of the guiding moral, political, and economic principles of the West. They will listen to exposés of their own country's policies and malpractices, provided they are factual and dispassionate, but they will expect to be told, equally plainly, the implications of what the West is doing to combat them. If over a period of years the peoples of the communist bloc could be kept informed, objectively and scrupulously fairly, of what is taking place in the world around them, one day they might find ways to turn their thoughts into actions.

The Next Half Century

Suppose all that has been suggested here were to happen. Suppose the Western alliance did publicly proclaim its realization that it had been deceived by communist disinformation, that its policies of détente and arms limitation had been misguided, that the alliance was now united in its determination to face the challenge. What then? It is obvious that there can be no quick solution to an ideological struggle that has continued unabated since 1917. Perhaps there never can be a solution. Perhaps the two camps, each representing a way of life abhorrent to the other, must for all foreseeable time oppose each other. But is this so bad a thing? Is it unthinkable that ideological and political competition should become permanent? Might not open competition between two fundamentally opposed systems be the best way to sort things out? Might not the two systems, in vying with one another, improve each other?

There seem to be three possible scenarios around which the history of the next half century will be written:

In the first, communism, meeting neither ideological nor political resistance from the West, continues along its present course to disarmament, then to convergence with the West on its own terms, and so to world domination.

In the second, the West realizes in time the nature of the communist threat, solves its own national problems, unites the noncommunist world, and adopts a policy of open competition between the two systems; as a result, the peoples of the communist bloc repudiate their leaders and the communist empire disintegrates.

The third scenario resembles the second except that both systems remain intact and competition continues for a very long time.

And who shall say that unrelenting competition between two opposing systems of government, each secured by the nuclear deterrent, would not prove fruitful? But where are the statesmen who will recognize this path to possible safety and guide their peoples along it?

Glossary

AAPSO	Afro-Asian Peoples' Solidarity Organization.
CHEKA	The Soviet security service in the early post-revolutionary days under Dzerzhinskiy. See also VCHEKA.
Chekist	Member of VCHEKA staff. Also a secret KGB magazine.
Comecon	Council of Mutual Economic Assistance of Communist States.
Cominform	(*Informatsionnoye Byuro Kommunisticheskikh Partiy*). Information Bureau of the Communist Parties from 1947 to 1956.
Comintern	(*Kommunisticheskiy Internatsional*). Communist International, also known as the Third Communist International. Abolished in 1943.
CPSU	Communist Party of the Soviet Union.
CSCE	Conference on Security and Cooperation in Europe.
DVR	(*Dal'ne-Vostoch'naya Respublika*). Far Eastern Republic, established in 1920. Incorporated into the Soviet Union in 1922.
FCD	First Chief Directorate of the KGB. Soviet intelligence service.

GPU	See OGPU.
GRU	(*Glavnoye Razvedyvatel'noye Upravleniye*). Chief Intelligence Administration, the Soviet military intelligence service.
GSE	(*Bol'shaya Sovetskaya Entsiklopediya*). The *Great Soviet Encyclopaedia*.
Illegal resident	Intelligence representative operating abroad under nonofficial cover.
Izvestiya	Daily newspaper, organ of the Supreme Soviet.
KGB	(*Komitet Gosudarstvennoy Bezopastnosti*). Committee of State Security, the Soviet foreign intelligence and internal security service, created in 1954.
KI	(*Komitet Informatsii*). Committee of Information, the political and military intelligence service from 1947 to 1949 under the Council of Ministers. From 1949 to 1951, the political intelligence service under the Ministry of Foreign Affairs. From 1951 to 1957, the research and disinformation service under the Ministry of Foreign Affairs. From 1958 to the present, the research, disinformation, and special operational political service under the Central Committee of the CPSU, probably under cover of the State Committee for Cultural Ties.
Komsomol	(*Kommunisticheskiy Soyuz Molodezhi*). Communist Youth Organisation.
MGB	(*Ministerstvo Gosuparstvennoy Bezopastnosti*). Ministry of State Security, including,

from October 1946 to March 1953, the Soviet intelligence and security service.

MID   (*Ministerstvo Inostrannykh Del*). Ministry of Foreign Affairs.

MVD   (*Ministerstvo Vnutrennikh Del*). Ministry of Internal Affairs, responsible for general internal security. For one year, from March 1953 to March 1954, it was also responsible for foreign intelligence and state security.

NEP   (*Novaya Ekonomicheskaya Politika*). The New Economic Policy, initiated by Lenin in 1921 and continued until 1929.

Novosti   Soviet press agency, abbreviated as APN.

Novyy Mir   Literary and political monthly publication in Moscow.

NTS   (*Natsional'nyy Trudovoy Soyuz*). National Labor Union, an émigré political anticommunist organization in the West.

OGPU   (*Ob'yedenennoye Gosudarstvennoye Politicheskoye Upravleniye*). Federal State Political Administration, the Soviet intelligence and security service from February 1922 to July 1934.

Oktyabr'   Literary and political monthly publication in Moscow.

Politburo   (*Politicheskoye Byuro*). Political Bureau. The leading organ of the Central Committee of the CPSU. Renamed the Presidium before Stalin's death; reverted to Politburo under Brezhnev.

Pravda	Daily newspaper, organ of the CPSU.
Residency	KGB secret intelligence apparatus in a non-communist country. The KGB itself uses the term *Rezidentura*.
Resident	Chief of the KGB intelligence apparatus in a noncommunist country. The KGB term is *Rezident*.
RSFSR	Russian Federation, or Russian Republic.
SCD	Second Chief Directorate of the KGB, Soviet security and counterintelligence service.
TASS	(*Telegrafnoye Agentstvo Sovetskogo Soyuza*). Telegraph Agency of the Soviet Union, a Soviet news agency.
VCHEKA	(*Vsesoyuznaya Chrezvychaynaya Kommissiya po Bor'be s Kontrrevolyutsyyey, Spekulyatsiyey i Sabotazhem*). All-Union Extraordinary Commission for Combatting Counterrevolution, Speculation, and Sabotage, the Soviet security service from December 1917 to February 1922.
WIDF	Women's International Democratic Federation
YLC	Yugoslav League of Communists, Yugoslav Communist party. Also referred to as YCL and CPY.

Notes

Chapter 1: The Problem Facing Western Analysts

1. Recognition of this may be found in, for example, *The Communist Party of the Soviet Union* (Random House, New York, 1960), by Leonard Schapiro, p. 542: "The secrecy with which the USSR has been able to surround itself had broken down, largely as the result of the testimony which thousands of Soviet citizens who had been displaced during the war, and who did not return, were able to provide. For the first time, serious academic study of Soviet history, politics and economics was providing the non-communist countries with a basis for countering Soviet propaganda claims about itself."

2. *Great Soviet Encyclopedia*, vol. 13 (1952), p. 566 (hereafter cited as *GSE*). Publishers—"The State Scientific Agency," "Great Soviet Encyclopaedia" in Moscow. This is the second edition published at the end of the 1940s and the early 1950s. Since 1957 it has published annual supplemental volumes. The volumes will be cited hereafter as *GSE* with an indication of the year of the supplement. (Supplements are not numbered but go by the year.)

Chapter 3: The Patterns of Disinformation: "Weakness and Evolution"

1. In the eighteenth century Count Potemkin organized a river journey for his sovereign, Catherine II, and the ambassadors to her court. Anxious to display the high living standards enjoyed by the local peasantry under her rule, he had artificial mobile villages constructed on the banks of the river. Once the royal barge had passed the villages, they were hastily dismantled and reassembled for display again farther along on the barge's course.

2. Former head of Soviet intelligence in Sweden and other countries.

Chapter 4: The Patterns of Disinformation: Transition

1. These statements are supported by the official records of the speeches made by various members of the Presidium at the Twentieth Party Congress, including those of Khrushchev, Molotov, Malenkov, Mikoyan, and Kaganovich.

Chapter 5: The New Policy and Disinformation Strategy

1. See Mao's articles "On the Historical Experience of the Dictatorship of the Proletariat" and "More on the Historical Experience of the Dictatorship of

the Proletariat," published in *Pravda* on April 5 and December 29, 1956, respectively. Mao wrote: "in struggles inside as well as outside the party, on certain occasions and on certain questions he confused two types of contradictions which are different in nature—contradictions between ourselves and the enemy and contradictions among the people—and also confused the different methods needed in handling them. In the work led by Stalin of suppressing the counter-revolution, many counter-revolutionaries deserving punishment were duly punished, but at the same time there were innocent people who were wrongly convicted, and in 1937 and 1938 there occurred the error of enlarging the scope of the suppression of counter-revolutionaries. In the matter of party and government organization, he did not fully apply proletarian democratic centralism and, to some extent, violated it. In handling relations with fraternal parties and countries he made some mistakes. He also gave some bad counsel in the international communist movement. These mistakes caused some losses to the Soviet Union and the international communist movement."

2. See, for instance, the 1956 speeches of Mao, Liu Shaochi, and Teng Hsiao-píng.

3. In December 1957 party members in the KGB Institute, including the author, were given a secret briefing on the November conference of bloc countries by General Kurenkov, the head of the institute, who had been a guest at conference meetings and who had himself been briefed by General Serov. This and other hitherto unpublished information about the conference is taken from that briefing.

4. During these years the author was serving in the KGB Institute and KGB headquarters.

5. *World Marxist Review—Problems of Peace and Socialism*, (December 1960) and (January 1961).

6. The author's account of disinformation is based on Shelepin's articles in the secret KGB magazine *Chekist;* on Popov's manual; and on the author's conversations with Grigorenko, Sitnikov, Kelin, Kostenko, and Smirnov of the Disinformation Department. The author borrowed Popov's book from the library on the grounds that his work on document assessment in the KGB's Information Department required that he should be able to distinguish authentic information from disinformation. The librarian called him twice daily to ask when he would return the book.

7. *Lenin's Works*, 5th ed., vol. 45, (The State Publishing Agency for Political Literature, Moscow), p. 63. The fifth edition was prepared by the Institute of Marxism-Leninism and published by the Central Committee of the CPSU during the late 1950s and the early 1960s.

8. *Questions of History of the CPSU*, no. 4, (1962), p. 152.

9. Sun Tzu, *The Art of War*, trans. Samuel B. Griffith (Oxford University Press, London, Oxford, and New York 1963), pp. 45–56, 66, 93, 183, 190, 191.

10. See page 160.

11. The issues were dead as between party leaders. Nationalism was still very much alive in the Yugoslav Communist party. Tito admitted this in his conversations with the Soviet leaders in 1955 and promised to deal with it. He explained, however, that it would take time to neutralize and eradicate it.

Chapter 6: The Shelepin Report and Changes in Organization

1. The author read and studied the Shelepin report in the KGB Institute while a student there.

Chapter 7: The New Role of Intelligence

1. Material based on a secret lecture given KGB staff by the Soviet Deputy Minister of Defense responsible for scientific and technical research and development.

2. Information made available to the French authorities in 1962–63.

3. See Henry Hurt's article in the October 1981 issue of *Reader's Digest*, supported independently by George Lardner, Jr., in his article in the *Washington Post* of September 3, 1981. According to Hurt, the FBI reexamined the Fedora case, which concerned a KGB official whom the FBI regarded as its reliable agent from 1962 onward and some of whose information was passed on to the White House. The FBI concluded that Fedora had been under Moscow's control during the years of his association with the FBI.

If this is correct, it confirms that the Soviets were actively creating new channels for disinformation in the early 1960s and the US government owes it to the public to produce an official white paper on the activities of this Soviet plant and the disinformation he provided. Such a publication would be a revolutionary contribution to the enlightenment of Western scholars and journalists on communist affairs, and to the general public, on the little-known subject of communist strategic disinformation. It should throw light on concrete Soviet disinformation themes, particularly on intrabloc relations, and would illustrate how such disinformation shaped or influenced US attitudes and decisions during the period.

4. Material based on secret instructions, given between 1959 and 1961, from the head of Soviet intelligence to the intelligence residents in those countries.

5. Told to the author by Zenikhov himself.

Chapter 9: The Vulnerability of Western Assessments

1. Some details on the subject are available in "Interlocking Subversion in Government Departments," the *Report of the Subcommittee to Investigate the Administration of the Internal Security Act and other Internal Security Laws* to the Committee on the Judiciary of the US Senate, 83rd Cong., 1st sess., July 30, 1953.

Chapter 10: Communist Intelligence Successes, Western Failures, and the Crisis in Western Studies

1. A special secret review of Popov's case (known as "Operation Boomerang") was circulated to KGB staff after his arrest. It stated that Popov was uncovered as a result of reports from agents abroad (not named) and from surveillance over Popov and his case officer. Popov could not be arrested earlier because a GRU

colonel was "in American hands." Popov's use in an operational "game" against
the Americans was excluded because he was known to be very anti-Soviet and
would therefore be likely to disclose the game to the Americans.

2. See B. Nikolayevskiy's article on the Nineteenth CPSU Congress, *The New
Leader*, October 6, 1952. See also Franz Borkenau, *Sino-Soviet Relations*, Department of State ERS paper, series 3, no. 86, February 1, 1952; and "Mao Tse-
tung," *The Twentieth Century*, August 1952.

3. Use of the facade and strength pattern has sometimes been recognized.
See, for example, Walker's *China under Communism*, (Richard Lewis Walker;
George Allen and Urwin, Ltd., London, 1956) pp. 240–45.

Chapter 11: Western Errors

1. W. A. Douglas Jackson, *The Russo-Chinese Borderlands*, (D. Van Nostrand,
Princeton, New Jersey, 1962) p. 95.

2. "Bear and Dragon: What Is the Relation between Moscow and Peking?",
supplement to the *National Review*, November 5, 1960.

3. Suzanne Labin, *The Anthill: The Human Condition in Communist China*
(Stevens and Sons Ltd., London 1960), pp. 419–20, in which the author quotes
Dr. Tang: "The fact that in all questions basic to their survival both regimes
always agree helps us to understand that their disagreements on tactical questions
simply stem from a division of labour by which Russia and China take turns in
throwing the ball. For example, where the one makes an aggressive move, the
other comes forward to play the role of mediator, and so calm the free world's
fears. It is, I think, what is called in American slang 'working both sides of the
street.' Please remember, Madame, that until comparatively recently the Soviet
Union alone staged the international moves on behalf of the whole Communist
world, and thus the Soviet Union itself had to alternate the tough and the soft
lines according to the reactions of the West. But in recent years Communist
China has come on to the international scene as a partner, and the two of them
working together can now follow these disparate policies simultaneously—the one
from Moscow, the other from Peking. This gives the Communist powers great
advantage and increases the disarray of the West."

4. Tibor Mende, *China and Her Shadow*, (Thames and Hudson, London 1960),
pp. 162, 180–81: "There are indeed few imaginable developments in the world
today which could more completely alter the existing balance of forces than the
eventual drifting apart of the two major Communist powers. For the same reason,
there are few subjects on which, based on so little concrete evidence, so much
speculation has been built. If, at the beginning, fascination with the immense
impact of the Sino-Soviet collaboration tended to discount signs of disagreements
now the danger is rather that, under the influence of political mystery literature,
the importance of existing differences may be vastly exaggerated. . . .

"The outside world's understandable interest in the detection of the symptoms
of discord inevitably leads to a distorted picture in which dissension is magnified
at the expense of the much more important field where there is coincidence of
interests. To mistake the occasional creakings of the Moscow-Peking axis for symp-

toms of deep-seated conflict is, and is likely to remain for many years to come, a dangerous miscalculation. The image of a Russia frightened by a reckless China is a poor substitute for a coherent Western policy in Asia. The illusion that the West can thrust a wedge between the two allies is likely to remain fashionable for some time even though its victims continue to do their utmost to weld the two countries even closer together.

"When China and the Soviet Union meet it is not merely to bargain but also to concert their action."

5. Supplement to the *National Review*, November 5, 1960.

6. According to *Diversity in International Communism*, ed. Alexander Dallin (New York: Columbia University Press, 1963; p. xxxviii, note 4), the term "esoteric communications" came into use through Myron Rush's *Rise of Khrushchev* (Washington, D.C.: Public Affairs Press, 1958), which made extensive use of this technique of analysis. In his note on methodology in *The Sino-Soviet Conflict, 1956–1961*, Donald S. Zagoria wrote: "Since the time five or ten years ago when systematic analysis of Communist communications was dismissed as "Kremlinology," Western students have developed a considerable amount of sophistication in using these sources. Although this approach is still regarded in some circles as a black art, there can be no reasonable doubt that a rich body of work has grown up which provides important insights into various aspects of Communist politics. . . . [Because] factionalism and open airing of differences have been proscribed, Communists are forced to differ with one another through the employment of . . . "esoteric communication" or Aesopian language. As often as not, differences over policy or strategy alternatives are heavily veiled in doctrinal exegesis. Yet behind the seemingly arid doctrinal polemics lie real and serious political problems."

7. Edgar Snow, *The Other Side of the River: Red China Today* (New York: Random House, 1961), pp. 97–100, 431.

8. See, for example, Zbigniew K. Brzezinski, *The Soviet Bloc: Unity and Conflict*, rev. ed. (New York: Frederick A. Praeger, 1961), pp. xx, xxii, 424–25, and footnote 43, p. 514.

9. See also William E. Griffith, "The November 1960 Moscow Meeting: A Preliminary Reconstruction," *China Quarterly*, no. 11 (July–September 1962).

Chapter 12: The New Methodology

1. See *Lenin's Works*, vol. 8, p. 96.

2. An alternative possibility would be a deceptive Chinese alignment with a conservative Japan and the United States.

3. Edvard Kardelj, *Socialism and War: A Survey of the Chinese Criticism of the Policy of Coexistence* (Methuen, 1961), p. 11.

4. Ibid., p. 238.

5. Ibid., p. 229.

6. Ibid., p. 9.

7. Quoted from *Yugoslav Facts and Views* (New York: Yugoslav Information Center), no. 50 (May 5, 1958).

8. Yuriy Krasin, "The International and the National in the Revolutionary Process," *Novoye Vremya*, no. 7, February 13, 1981.

9. Denis Warner, *Hurricane from China* (New York: Macmillan, 1961), p. 123.

10. Documentary record of the Extraordinary Twenty-first CPSU Congress, *Current Soviet Policies*, vol. 3, Leo Gruliow, editor, Praeger (January 1959), p. 206 (hereafter cited as *CSP*).

Chapter 13: The First Disinformation Operation: The Soviet-Yugoslav "Dispute" of 1958–60

1. *Pravda*, June 4, 1958.

2. The author was a subordinate of Grigorenko in the Counterintelligence Department in 1951. On one occasion in December 1959 Grigorenko visited the Information Department, where the author was then working, seeking staff with expertise on Yugoslavia and Albania for service in his department. The nature of this quest obliged Grigorenko to give information on the kind of work for which the officers were required. The information on Pushkin's involvement in this operation was confirmed to the author independently by another KGB officer, Kurenyshev.

3. Georgiy Maksimovich Pushkin, Soviet diplomat since 1937, ambassador in East Germany until the beginning of 1958, with previous experience in Hungary, Sinkiang, and Middle East affairs. Listed officially as Deputy Minister of foreign affairs from 1959.

4. *Yugoslav Facts and Views*, no. 56, 1958.

5. CSP, Leo Gruliow ed., (New York: Frederick A. Praeger, 1959), vol. 3, p. 62. Khrushchev stated: "On many questions of foreign policy we speak a common language."

6. *History of the Communist Party of the Soviet Union*, English ed. (Moscow: Foreign Languages Publishing House, 1960), pp. 701–2.

7. Ibid., p. 641: "Subsequently, the Communist Party of the Soviet Union, on its own initiative, took steps to restore normal relations between the USSR and Yugoslavia.

"The policy of friendship and mutual assistance, pursued by the CPSU, triumphed. The mistakes made occasionally in the relations with fraternal countries were of a secondary, accidental character. The essence of these relations was genuinely Socialist, and accorded fully with the principles of proletarian internationalism. The CPSU directed all its efforts to strengthening friendship with People's China and the other People's Democracies, and this policy was entirely successful. The joint activities of the CPSU and the other Communist Parties standing at the helm of their respective States, resulted in the establishment of a fraternal community of Socialist countries, and no amount of intrigue on the part of their enemies could, or can, shake their solidarity and unity. This unity is a source of the strength of the Socialist camp. . . . The problem of relations between the Socialist countries was, for all its complexity and novelty, successfully solved in the interests of each country and of the entire Socialist camp."

8. *CSP*, vol. 3, pp. 68–69.

9. *GSE* (1961), p. 374.

Chapter 14: The Second Disinformation, Operation: The "Evolution" of the Soviet Regime (Part One: The Major Changes in the USSR)

1. For an example, see *Pravda*, September 9, 1962.

2. Officially introduced in 1961.

3. *Izvestiya*, May 19, 1959.

4. *Izvestiya*, January 28, 1959, p. 9: "There is not now condemnation by the courts in the Soviet Union for political crimes. It is a big achievement which speaks for the exceptional unity of the political views of the people with the Central Committee of the Party."

5. *Kommunist*, no. 11 (1960), p. 44.

6. The author learned this from Grigorenko, whose department helped Shul'gin to write and publish the brochure.

7. See, for example, the letter from Soviet Foreign Minister Gromyko to the United Nations, September 20, 1958, about a 10–15 percent reduction in the military budgets of the major powers. (*Pravda*, September 1958)

8. On June 6, 1958, *Pravda* published Khrushchev's letter of June 2 to President Eisenhower in which he forwarded to the American government the Soviet government's proposal for "joint measures for an increase in trade." The letter stated that the Soviet Union and the US, as the two most economically powerful states, could "carry on trade with one another on a wide scale."

9. See Khrushchev's report to the Twenty-second CPSU Congress in October 1961 (*CSP*, vol. 4, p. 69): "the Soviet Union is giving particular attention to the development of ties with its neighbours. The differences between our social and political systems have not been preventing the development of friendly, mutually beneficial relations between the USSR and such countries as Afghanistan and Finland. Our relations with Austria and Sweden are coming along quite well. We have been making efforts to improve our relations with Norway and Denmark and shall continue doing so. Relations with neighbouring Turkey have been improving of late. We want these relations to develop still further."

10. See, for example, Khrushchev's report to the Twenty-second CPSU Congress (*CSP*, vol. 4, p. 46): "To-day, the USA, which has become the centre of world reaction, takes the role of the chief aggressive nucleus. The US imperialists are acting in alliance with the West German militarists and revanchists and threatening the peace and security of peoples. . . ." Ibid., p. 45: "Comrades, the 20th party congress, analysing the situation in the countries of capitalism, came to the conclusion that they were moving steadily toward new economic and social upheavals. Has this conclusion been borne out? Yes, it has. In the years that have elapsed there has occurred a further sharpening of contradictions, both within the capitalist countries and among them; colonial empires have collapsed and the struggle of the working class and the peoples' national liberation movement have assumed tremendous proportions."

11. *Détente: Cold War Strategies in Transition*, ed. Eleanor Lansing Dulles

and Robert Dickson Crane (Published for the Center for Strategic Studies, Georgetown University, by Frederick A. Praeger, New York, 1965), p. 268.

12. Lazar Pistrak, *The Grand Tactician* (New York, Praeger 1961), p. 269.

13. G. A. von Stackelberg, *Bulletin of the Institute for the Study of the USSR*, vol. 7, no. 4 (April 1960), pp. 16–20.

14. A penetrating explanation of Soviet provocation of the Berlin Crisis as being based, in large part, on Lenin's *Left-Wing Communism, an Infantile Disorder* was given by Nikolay Galay, "Berlin and Soviet Foreign Policy," *Bulletin of the Institute for the Study of the USSR*, vol. 6, no. 6 (June 1959).

15. See *CSP*, vol. 4, p. 23: "Having brought about the complete and final victory of socialism, the first phase of communism, the dictatorship of the proletariat has fulfilled its historical mission and has ceased to be essential in the USSR from the point of view of internal development. The state which arose as a state of the dictatorship of the proletariat has turned into a state of the entire people, which expresses the interests and will of the people as a whole."

16. Satyukov said (*CSP*, vol. 4, p. 176): "The delegates to the 22nd congress should know that in October of this year, just before the congress opened, Molotov sent a letter to the Central Committee. Without having a word to say about his subversive, factionalist work against the Leninist party and against the decisions of its 20th congress, he tries afresh in this letter to pose as interpreter of Leninism and again attacked the Central Committee and the draft of the CPSU programme. Molotov declares in his letter that the draft programme fails to co-ordinate communist construction in the USSR with the prospects for the revolutionary struggle of the working class in capitalist countries, with the prospects for socialist revolution on an international scale. And this at a time when the draft programme has been unanimously approved not only by our party and the Soviet people but by the international communist movement. . . . His contentions lead to the conclusion that it is impossible to continue the advance to communism without the most serious political conflicts with the imperialist countries, and hence without war. We say to Molotov: no, the CPSU has been and is doing everything possible to ensure peace for the Soviet people, the people who are building communism. The Leninist principle of peaceful co-existence has been and remains our general line in foreign policy. This is plainly stated in the new programme and the party will pursue this line consistently."

17. The Soviet Academy of Sciences includes historians, lawyers, and economists as well as scientists in the conventional sense. The expression "Soviet Scientists" should be interpreted as including these additional categories.

18. Mose L. Harvey, Leon Goure, and Vladimir Prokofieff, *Science and Technology as an Instrument of Soviet Policy* (Center for Advanced International Studies, University of Miami, 1972), pp. 93–94.

Chapter 15: The Third Disinformation Operation: The Soviet-Albanian "Dispute" and "Split"

1. See *Albania and the Sino-Soviet Rift* by William E. Griffith (Cambridge, Massachusetts: MIT Press, 1963), p. 37.

2. *Izvestiya*, January 10, 1981.

3. In one article (June 1962) David Floyd in the *London Daily Telegraph* noted that "it was through Durres and . . . Vlora . . . that the Albanians received last year the grain shipments which enabled them to resist the Russian economic blockade. It was the Chinese who brought the wheat from Canada, paid for it in clearing rubles, and shipped it to Albania in West German ships."

4. *Zeri-I-Poppulit*, February 14, 1961; reprinted as Document 6 in *Albania and the Sino-Soviet Rift*, p. 207.

Chapter 16: The Fourth Disinformation Operation: The Sino-Soviet "Split"

1. Joy Homer *Dawn Watch in China*, (Boston: Houghton Mifflin Co., 1941), pp. 194–95: "from the day that I set foot in Yenan, I noticed a lukewarm attitude towards Russia on the part of students and young officials. Far more popular than Russia were America and Great Britain. At least once a day I was told very earnestly something like this: 'You must not confuse our communism with the communism of Russia. Today we do our own thinking. In your country, you would probably call us socialists. We believe in sacrifice for each other, and in hard work and love for all men. Almost it is like your Christianity."

2. An account of Harriman's interview is in *The China Tangle* by Herbert Feis (Princeton, New Jersey: Princeton University Press, 1953), p. 140.

3. Charles B. McLane, *Soviet Policy and the Chinese Communists 1931–1946* (Freeport, New York: Books for Libraries Press, Copyright 1958 by Columbia University Press, 1972), pp. 1–2.

4. Robert E. Sherwood, *Roosevelt and Hopkins: An Intimate History* (New York: Harper & Bros., 1948), p. 902–3: "[Stalin made the] categorical statement that he would do everything he could to promote unification of China under the leadership of Chiang Kai-Shek. . . . He specifically stated that no Communist leader was strong enough to unify China."

5. McLane, *op. cit.*

6. Robert Payne, *Portrait of a Revolutionary: Mao Tse-Tung* (London and New York: Abelard-Schuman, 1961), footnote, p. 175.

7. See the official announcement in *Pravda*, October 23, 1949. Tikhvinskiy was named as an intelligence officer by the former Soviet intelligence officer Rastvorov in his article in *Life*, December 6, 1954.

8. See Chiang Kai-Shek, *Soviet Russia in China* (New York: Farrar, Straus, and Cudahy, 1957), p. 369.

9. This treaty remained in force throughout the Vietnam War. On its expiry in April 1980, it was not renewed; by then, there was no discernible threat to China from any Western nation.

10. Walt Whitman Rostow in *The Prospects for Communist China* (Cambridge, Massachusetts: Technology Press of Massachusetts Institute of Technology, 1954), pp. 216–220, notes "under what circumstances, if any, is a break up of the alliance to be foreseen? In a technical sense the evidence of an alliance lies in the relative weakness of China vis-à-vis the Soviet Union. This means that

three conditions are probably required to effect a Chinese withdrawal from the Sino-Soviet alliance:

"1. Acute dissatisfaction among an effective group of Chinese leaders with the workings of the Soviet alliance, and probably with the consequences of applying Soviet technique to the problem of China's economic growth.
"2. Assurance that withdrawal would be met by more favourable terms of association with the West.
"3. The neutralization of potential Soviet strength vis-à-vis China either by severe internal Soviet difficulties or by some third power.

"In the light of this basic situation there are several conditions, now beyond the horizon of immediate possibility. . . . The Sino-Soviet tie might be definitively altered if the uneasy process of adjustment . . . in the Soviet Union created by Stalin's death should break into open conflict, resulting in either a drastic weakening of Moscow's power on the world scene or a drastic shift in its internal and external political orientation, even the present Chinese communist rulers might be prepared to rethink their relationship to Moscow and move towards a greater degree of independence from the Soviet Union or association with the non-communist world. Their precise course of action would depend on many factors, notably the character and probable duration of changes in the Soviet Union and the terms the Free World might offer for a change in [Chinese] orientation."

11. See *CSP*, vol. 3, p. 129: "in the U. S., I was asked many questions about the relations between the Soviet Union and China. I must assume that these questions derived from the revisionist anti-Chinese propaganda in the Yugoslav press which recently . . . published insinuations about incipient disagreements, if you please, between the Soviet Union and China. . . . I replied that the gentlemen questioners were evidently dreaming sweet dreams in which, lo and behold, magic could cause disagreements to appear in the socialist camp between the Soviet Union and China. But I said that . . . the dream was unrealisable. Soviet-Chinese friendship rests on the unshakable foundation of Marxist-Leninist ideology, on the common goals of communism, on the fraternal mutual support of the peoples of our countries, on joint struggles against imperialism and for peace and socialism. [Applause.] The greetings of the CPC Central Committee to our congress, signed by Comrade Mao Tse-tung . . . are a reaffirmation of the eternal, indissoluble friendship between our parties and between our countries. [Applause.] We shall cherish this friendship as the apple of our eye. Our friendship is a sacred thing, and let not those who would seek to defile it reach out with unclean hands for this purpose. [Applause.]"

12. "Imperialist, renegade and revisionist hopes of a split within the socialist camp are built on sand and doomed to failure. All the socialist countries cherish the unity of the socialist camp like the apple of their eye." (*Manifesto*)

13. "I want to emphasize our constant effort to strengthen the bonds of fraternal friendship with the CPC, with the great Chinese people. . . . the friendship of our two great peoples, the unity of our two parties . . . are of exceptional importance in the struggle for the triumph of our common cause. . . . The CPSU

and the Soviet people will do their utmost to further increase the unity of our parties and our peoples, so as not only to disappoint our enemies but to jolt them even more strongly with our unity, to attain the realisation of our great goal, the triumph of communism." (Khrushshev's speech, January 6, 1961)

14. In his speech to the Twenty-first CPSU Congress (*CSP*, vol. 3, pp. 77–78), Chou En-lai said: "The Soviet Union and China are fraternal socialist countries . . . the close friendship of the peoples of our two countries is eternal and indestructible." In an interview published in *Peking Review* on November 8, 1960, he said, "The solidarity between the two great countries, China and the Soviet Union, is the bulwark of the defence of world peace. What the imperialists and all reactionaries fear the most is the solidarity of the socialist countries. They seek by every means to sow discord and break up this unity."

15. *The Sino-Soviet Dispute*, an article by Geoffrey Francis Hudson, Richard Lowenthal, and Roderick MacFarquhar which was published by the *China Quarterly*, 1961, p. 35.

16. A timely warning against false historical analogies was given by former leading American communist Jay Lovestone in testimony before the Internal Security Committee of the U. S. Senate Committee of the Judiciary on January 26 and February 2, 1961: "We must guard against the temptation to resort to historical analogies. Since Communist Russia and Communist China are bound together by this overriding common objective [communist conquest and transformation of the world], it would be dangerously false to equate their differences or jealousies with the hostility and clash of interests between Czarist Russia and pre-World War I China."

17. *Kommunist*, no. 5 (1964), p. 21.

18. *Party Life*, no. 10 (1964), p. 65.

19. Ibid., no. 7 (1964), p. 9.

20. *Problems of Philosophy* (October 1958).

21. See his speech at Leipzig on March 7, 1959, reprinted in *World without Arms, World without Wars* (Moscow: Foreign Languages Publishing House, 1960), vol. 1, p. 198: "Broad co-operation is developing between the sovereign countries of the socialist camp in every sphere of economic, public, political and cultural life. Speaking of the future, I believe that the socialist countries' further development will in all likelihood follow the line of consolidating the single world socialist economic system. The economic barriers that divided our countries under capitalism will be removed one after another, and the common economic basis of world socialism will be steadily strengthened, eventually making the question of boundaries pointless."

22. *CSP*, vol. 3, p. 188: "The thesis in Comrade N. S. Krushchev's report that "from the theoretical standpoint it would be more correct to assume that by successfully employing the potentialities inherent in socialism, the countries of socialism will enter the higher phase of communist society more or less simultaneously" will be of tremendous interest not only to Communists of the Soviet Union but also to Communists of all the socialist countries as well as Communists of the entire world. This is the first formulation of the new thesis that the law of planned and proportional development applies not only to individual socialist

countries but also to the economy of the socialist camp as a whole. This is a new pronouncement in the theory of scientific communism. It expresses the profound truth of Leninism that the world socialist camp constitutes a single economic system. As time goes on, the economic plans of these countries will be more and more co-ordinated and the more highly developed countries will help the less developed countries in order to march in a united front toward communism at an increasingly faster pace."

23. Mende, *China and Her Shadow*, pp. 175–76, 338–39.

24. The following is an extract from this letter: "It is not only at present that the Soviet leaders have begun to collude with US imperialism and attempt to menace China. As far back as 20th June 1959, when there was not yet the slightest sign of a treaty on stopping nuclear tests, the Soviet government unilaterally tore up the agreement on new technology for national defence concluded between China and the Soviet Union on 15 October 1957, and refused to provide China with a sample of an atomic bomb and technical data concerning its manufacture. This was done as a presentation gift at the time the Soviet leader went to the US for talks with Eisenhower in September."

25. For an example, see *Trud*, August 31, 1963: "The 10 MW pilot nuclear power plant and the 24 million electron volt cyclotron commissioned in 1958 were another aspect of Soviet aid to China which was too many-sided to be mentioned in all the details."

26. See *Peking Review*, April 26, 1960: "A new nuclear particle—anti sigma minus hyperon—has been discovered by scientists of the socialist countries working together at the Joint Nuclear Research Institute in Dubna, outside Moscow (established in 1956 by representatives of 12 governments of the socialist states). In addition to the Soviet physicists who led in obtaining this remarkable result, Professor Wang Kan-chang, prominent Chinese scientist who is the vice-director of the Joint Institute played a big part. He has long been a figure of world reknown in the field of physics. Speaking of the new success, Professor Wang described it as the first discovery of a charged anti-hyperon ever made, marking another step forward in man's knowledge of the basic particles of the microworld. Professor Wang attributed this triumph first of all to leadership and support by the Soviet director of the Institute and to close co-operation in work by scientists of other socialist countries. It is truly, he said, a fresh testimony to the superiority of the socialist system."

27. Snow, *Other Side of the River*, p. 642.

28. See Mende, *China and Her Shadow*, pp. 182–93.

29. *Military Strategy: Soviet Doctrine and Concepts*, ed. Marshal V. D. Sokolovskiy (Moscow, 1962).

30. For an instance, see *Pravda*, August 27, 1963, on the alleged Chinese objection to the admission of the Soviet delegation to the Afro-Asian Solidarity Conference in 1963 in Moshi on the grounds that the Soviet delegates were neither black nor yellow.

31. See Douglas Jackson, *Russo-Chinese Borderlands*, p. 91: "Salisbury also attributes the Khrushchev virgin and idle lands programme which in 1954–56 resulted in the ploughing of millions of acres of unused land in Western Siberia

and Northern Kazakhstan and the settling of several hundred thousand Russians and Ukrainians there, as proof of Soviet concern for its vast empty Siberian spaces. The Khrushchev programme unquestionably has political overtones, but more compelling reasons for its implementation may be found in domestic conditions in the Soviet Union than in the Chinese population problem."

32. In Moscow on September 2, 1980, the Chinese Friendship Association celebrated the anniversary of the Japanese defeat in Manchuria. A report was delivered by the association's deputy chairman, Tikhvinskiy.

33. *New York Times*, November 22, 1966.

34. *Kommunist*, no. 5 (1964), p. 21.

35. See Douglas Jackson, *Russo-Chinese Borderlands*, p. 110: "As events have unfolded their role has changed with circumstances. From zones of tension between Imperial Russia, Imperial China, Soviet Russia and Nationalist China, the borderlands have become, since the Communist revolution in China, zones of co-operation and stabilisation. Their further economic development will undoubtedly strengthen the hold that the Communists have over them—and in turn, they will contribute much to the overall Communist strength. Indeed, the role of the borderlands in future Sino-Soviet relations may in some ways be as dramatic as that played in preceding centuries of Russo-Chinese competition and distrust. Whatever the future may bring, the lands of Asia, where Russia and China meet, will continue to fascinate us, and what is more, demand our awareness and understanding."

36. For examples, see the speeches of Mao, Liu Shaochi, Peng Te-huai, and Teng Hsiao-p'ing at the Eighth CPC Congress in September 1956. (*Jen min-Jih-Pao*, September 1956)

37. See Field-Marshal the Viscount Montgomery of Alamein, *Three Continents* (London: Collins, 1962), p. 40: "Chou emphasized again and again that China must have peace, although she will always fight to resist aggression against her own territory. . . . Marshal Chen Yi, the foreign minister, had given me exactly the same views during my talks with him." See also Chou En-lai's emphasis on China's recognition of the policy of peaceful co-existence in the article in *Peking Review*, November 8, 1961.

38. See Khrushchev's speech of January 6, 1961: (the war in Algeria) is a liberation war, a war of independence waged by the people. It is a sacred war. We recognize such wars; we have helped and shall continue to help peoples fighting for their freedom. . . . is there a likelihood of such wars recurring? Yes, there is. Are uprisings of this kind likely to recur? Yes, they are. But wars of this kind are popular uprisings. Is there the likelihood of conditions in other countries reaching the point where the cup of the popular patience overflows and they take to arms? Yes, there is such a likelihood. What is the attitude of the Marxists to such uprisings? A most favourable attitude. These uprisings cannot be identified with wars between countries, with local wars, because the insurgent people are fighting for the right to self-determination, for their social and independent national development; these uprisings are directed against the corrupt reactionary regimes, against the colonialists. The Communists support just wars of this kind wholeheartedly and without reservations."

39. "The interests of the struggle for the working-class cause demand of each communist party and of the great army of communists of all countries ever closer unity of will and action." (Manifesto)

40. *Kommunist,* no. 13 (1964), p. 21; and *Jen-min Jih Pao* and *Huntzi,* February 4, 1964.

41. *World Marxist Review—Problems of Peace and Socialism,* no. 6 (1964), p. 33.

Chapter 17: The Fifth Disinformation Operation: Romanian "Independence"

1. See, for examples, David Floyd, *Rumania: Russia's Dissident Ally* (New York: Frederick A. Praeger, 1965).

2. *Ibid.*

3. Ibid., pp. 119–20.

4. Ibid., p. 108.

Chapter 18: The Sixth Disinformation Operation: The Alleged Recurrence of Power Struggles in the Soviet, Chinese, and Other Parties

1. In the author's opinion, Robert Conquest and Myron Rush both misinterpreted the change of leadership from Khrushchev to Brezhnev in their books, respectively, *Russia after Khrushchev* (New York: Frederick A. Praeger, 1965) and *Political Succession in the USSR* (New York Research Institute on Communist Affairs, Columbia University Press, 1965).

According to Conquest's interpretation, Khrushchev was removed as the result of a sudden secret coup in accordance with Kremlin traditions for his mistakes in domestic and foreign policy, the "conservatives" uniting with "modernizing moderates" and "defectors from Khrushchev's own faction" (Brezhnev) to oust him. The reasons were objections to his ill-prepared schemes. It is very notable that by far the most powerfully urged complaints were the fact that he acted without consulting them, that he turned Central Committee meetings into crowd scenes to carry his proposals by acclaim, that he used his son-in-law, Alexey Adzhubey, as a personal agent in foreign affairs without informing the Presidium, and so on. But the crucial point was reached when Khrushchev openly proposed to them the installation of Adzhubey in the machinery of power. Here was a threat to old Khrushchevites and non-Khrushchevites alike. The former must have remembered how Stalin, too, had replaced his old followers with men of his personal entourage."

Conquest bases his interpretation on the parallel with the struggle for power after Stalin's death. "The present situation differs in many important respects from that which followed Stalin's death in March 1953. However, the events of that time are the only parallel we have and some further examination of them must certainly prove fruitful. For the more the structure of power depends on one man, the more it is likely to be shaken when that one man is removed. On Khrushchev's departure, as after Stalin's, a power vacuum came into being. . . . There were then a number of figures of the second rank with long experience at the top and high prestige in the apparat ready to move."

Accordiing to Rush's interpretation, struggles for power in the Soviet Union continue as after Lenin's and Stalin's deaths, since the problem of the political succession has not been solved. Rush's interpretation also accepts Khrushchev's dismissal as the result of a conspiracy. "Khrushchev's surrender of the posts that made him the effective ruler of the Soviet Union, announced on October 15, 1964, came as a surprise to the West and to Khrushchev as well. The coup d'etat prevented him from attending a celebration for Soviet space-men he had just announced over radio and television. Khrushchev's overthrow was the result of a conspiracy, not the culmination of a series of moves aimed at reducing his power." Rush sees Khrushchev as a dictator. "A conspiracy was necessary to remove Khrushchev because sovereignty resided in no collective but in Khrushchev's person."

According to Rush's view, an arranged political succession in the Soviet Union is impossible and the ruler's demise or removal begins the succession crisis. "In the USSR the ruler evidently cannot inherit authority but must win it, and it is difficult to see how such vast powers can be seized against the certain opposition of rivals without producing a political crisis. Its depth and effects, however, are variable, according to the scope and intensity of the struggle and the manner of its resolution. Succession is initiated by the political or physical demise of the ruler. The circumstances in which this event occurs may significantly affect the course of succession, yet even the ruler who attempts to arrange his succession cannot know with confidence what these circumstances will be. The ruler's demise may be a political rather than a physical event as when he is removed in a palace revolt, as Khrushchev was in fact, in which case his person and politics immediately become a central issue in the succession. . . . However it begins, the succession crisis is at the outset largely colored by the personal rivalry of the most ambitious of the former ruler's heirs. In their efforts to inherit his power, they are compelled to manoeuvre and compromise, forming factions in the top leadership according to the shifting calculation of personal interest and political principle."

Rush recognizes Khrushchev's concern over the succession problem: "if, as we shall argue, Khrushchev tried to deal with the problem of succession, his dispositions did not lose significance because he was ousted before he could achieve his purpose. On the contrary, his succession arrangements shaped the situation that resulted from his fall, and even helped to bring it about. Khrushchev was deeply aware of the Soviet succession problem, although Marxism contributed little to that awareness. Preoccupied with the problem of the transfer of power from one class to another, it has relatively little to say about the transfer of power between rulers. Khrushchev learned of the succession problem through experience—not theory. He was already in his thirties during Lenin's succession and he in some measure relived that experience in his campaign against Stalin's memory."

2. See Lenin's letter of 1923, published in *Kommunist*, no. 9 (1956), pp. 11–17: "Comrade Stalin, having become General Secretary, has concentrated enormous power in his hands and I am not at all certain that he is capable of always utilising this power with sufficient caution."

3. Rush's analysis of the succession problems after Lenin's and Stalin's deaths, given in *Political Succession in the USSR,* is in general accurate. See pp. 39–43: "Lenin's effort to influence the succession with respect to personalities, policy, and organization met complete defeat. His advice, offered after serious deliberation and with due gravity, was disregarded even while he lived by men who professed to serve him. They not only failed to act on Lenin's recommendations; they also failed to learn from the arguments by which he justified them. Stalin, however, may be an exception to this; Lenin's testament may have taught him caution and dissimulation even beyond what was natural to him. Lenin's last writings had not exhausted their historical significance in 1930. A third of a century later, they were finally handed over to the Party's Congress by a new pretender to Lenin's mantle, who had learned that his ambitions could be advanced by attacking Stalin. Khrushchev's use of Lenin's testament in 1956 serves as a reminder that it remained an important part of the Soviet political scene even after the XIII Congress decided to suppress it. . . . [Stalin's] chief preoccupation was assuredly the continued exercise of his own authority rather than arranging its transfer to his heirs, so that the need to preserve his own vast power intact narrowly limited his succession arrangements."

4. See his concluding remarks to the Twenty-second CPSU Congress (*CSP,* vol. 4, p. 200): "It is wrong, comrades, it is simply impossible to permit the inception and development of instances when the merited prestige of an individual may assume forms in which he fancies that everything is permissible to him and that he no longer has need of the collective. In such a case this individual may stop listening to the voices of other comrades who have been advanced to leadership, just as he was, and may begin suppressing them. Our great teacher V. I. Lenin resolutely fought against this, and the Party paid too dear a price for not heeding his wise counsel in good time. So let us be worthy disciples of Lenin in this important matter."

5. Ibid.: "But each leader must also understand the other side of the matter—never to plume himself on his position, to remember that in holding this or that post he is merely fulfilling the will of the Party and the will of the people, who may have invested the greatest power in him but never lose control over him. The leader who forgets this pays heavily for his mistake. I would add that he will pay while he is alive, or even after his death the people will not forgive him, as has happened with the condemnation of the cult of Stalin. A person who forgets that he is obliged to fulfill the will of the Party and of the people cannot, properly speaking, be called a true leader; there must be no such 'leaders' either in the Party or in the state apparatus."

6. Ibid., p. 198: "In the conditions of the cult of the individual, the Party was deprived of normal life. People who usurp power cease being accountable to the Party, they escape from under its control. Herein is the greatest danger of the cult of the individual. The situation in the Party must always be such that every leader is accountable to the Party and its agencies, and the Party can replace any leader when it considers this necessary."

7. Ibid., p. 200: "I would like to say a few words about the following question. In many speeches at the Congress, and not infrequently in our press as well,

when mention is made of the activity of our party's Central Committee, a certain special emphasis is placed on me personally and my role in carrying out major Party and Government measures is underlined. I understand the kind feelings guiding these comrades. Allow me however to emphasise emphatically that everything that is said about me should be said about the Central Committee of our Leninist Party, and about the Presidium of the Central Committee. Not one major measure, not one responsible pronouncement has been carried out upon anyone's personal directive; they have all been the result of collective deliberation and collective decision. And this concluding speech, too, has been considered and approved by the executive collective. Our great strength, Comrades, lies in collective leadership, in collegial decisions on all questions of principle."

8. Ibid., pp. 199–200: "The 22nd Congress is confirming this beneficial course. The Party Programme and Statutes and the resolutions of the congress set forth new guarantees against relapses into the cult of the individual. The role of the Party as the great inspiring and organising force in the building of communism is rising higher still."

9. Stenographic records of the Twenty-second Congress (Moscow, 1962), vol. 3, pp. 356–60.

10. The information about the relationship of these leaders to Khrushchev was obtained from KGB officials in the Ukraine and Moscow (Kolesnikov and Kochurov) and was partially confirmed in Zhukov's attack on Khrushchev at the meeting of the Politburo in the fall of 1957.

Chapter 19: The Seventh Disinformation Operation: "Democratization" in Czechoslovakia in 1968

1. The Soviet leaders contributed to the promotion of this analogy. For instance, while visiting Sweden in the summer of 1968, Kosygin three times made a slip of the tongue confusing Czechoslovakia and Hungary.

2. GSE (1962), p. 458.

3. GSE (1962), p. 16.

4. GSE (1963), p. 18.

5. See Prague Notebook: The Strangled Revolution (Boston: Little, Brown & Co., 1971), p. 30. M. Salomon, however, misinterpreted this evidence attributing Khrushchev's proposal not to long-range bloc policy, but to the example of President Kennedy's "brain trust."

6. Ibid., p. 30, note 1. Salomon overlooked the significance of the close relations between Barak and Sik.

7. Ibid.

8. Ibid., pp. 101–10.

9. Ibid., p. 69.

10. Ibid., p. 229.

11. See the following extract from the Czechoslovak communist party letter to the five Warsaw Pact powers, dated July 20, 1968, quoted in [Salomon], Prague Notebook, p. 121: "The manoeuvres of the armed forces of the Warsaw Treaty on Czechoslovakian territory constitute a concrete proof of our faithful

fulfilment of commitments of alliance. In order to assure the success of these manoeuvres, we have, on our side, taken all necessary steps. Our people as well as the members of our army have welcomed the Soviet army and the allied armies to our territory in a friendly way. The supreme leaders of the party and the government, by their presence, have testified to the importance we attach to these manoeuvres and the interest we take in them. The confusion and certain doubts expressed in our public opinion appeared only after the reiterated changes in the date of departure of the allied armies from Czechoslovakia at the end of the manoeuvres."

12. See the Czechoslovak party's letter of July 20, 1968, quoted [Salomon], in *Prague Notebook*, pp. 120–21: "We will never accept that the historic achievements of socialism and the security of the nations of our country should be threatened or that imperialism, in a peaceful manner or by violence, should shatter the socialist system and modify the balance of power in Europe in its favour. The principal content of our evolution after January is just this tendency to increase the internal strength and the stability of the socialist regime and thus that of our relationships of alliance."

13. *Prague Notebook*, Michel Salomon, p. 243.

14. See the Czechoslovak party letter dated July 20, 1968, quoted in *Prague Notebook*, pp. 118–19: "Our alliance and our friendship with the USSR and the other socialist countries are deeply rooted in the social regime, in the traditions and the historical experiences of our nations, in their interests, their sentiments and their thoughts. . . . We behave in such a way that friendly relationships with our allies, the countries of the world's socialist community, will deepen on a basis of mutual respect, sovereignty and equality of rights, and international solidarity. In this sense, we contribute more actively to the common activity of [*Comecon*] and the Warsaw treaty."

15. Here, while maintaining that "democratization" was on the whole controlled, one can allow for the existence of genuine antiregime individuals either inside or outside the country, who, without realizing what was really going on, acted completely independently during the last months of the crisis, thereby revealing themselves to the regime as counterrevolutionary elements. No doubt they were registered as such.

Chapter 20: The Second Disinformation Operation: The "Evolution" of the Soviet Regime (Part Two: The "Dissident")

1. Andrey D. Sakharov, *Sakharov Speaks*, ed. Harrison E. Salisbury (London: Collins & Harvill Press, 1974).

2. Leon Goure, Foy D. Kohler, Richard Soll, and Annette Stiefbold, *Convergence of Communism and Capitalism—The Soviet View* (Miami, Florida Centre for Advanced International Studies, University of Miami, 1973), pp. 44–46; *Sakharov Speaks*, pp. 107 et seq.

3. *Sakharov Speaks*, p. 108, gives these dates as 1968–80.

4. *Sakharov Speaks*, pp. 107 *et seq.*

5. See note 3. Ibid.

6. It is not clear why Sakharov and Kapitsa, who are both so outspoken, have not been expelled from the Soviet Academy of Sciences, although Sakharov, at least, was allegedly stripped of his state honors and awards. For some unexplained reason, this did not occur until January 1980.

Chapter 21: The Eighth Disinformation Operation: Eurocommunism

1. Leonard Schapiro, *The Soviet Union and "Eurocommunism,"* Conflict Study no. 99 (London: The Institute for the Study of Conflict, 1978). Some Spanish socialists also seem to regard Eurocommunism as a deceptive device.

2. See, for examples, *World Marxist Review—Problems of Peace and Socialism,* no. 6 (1974); *Pravda,* August 6, 1975; and *Novoye Vremya,* no. 9 (1976).

3. Schapiro, *Soviet Union and "Eurocommunism,"* p. 2.

4. Ibid., p. 5.

5. B. N. Ponomarev, "The World Situation and the Revolutionary Process," *World Marxist Review—Problems of Peace and Socialism,* no. 6, (1974): "Détente strengthens the realistically minded elements within the bourgeois camp and helps to isolate the more reactionary, imperialist forces, the 'war parties' and the military-industrial complexes."

6. Paul Wilkinson, *Terrorism: International Dimensions,* Conflict Study no. 113 (London: The Institute for the Study of Conflict, 1979).

7. See Kevin Devlin, "The Challenge of 'Eurocommunism,' " *Problems of Communism* (Washington, D. C.), January–February 1977.

8. *GSE* (1968), pp. 480–481.

9. Devlin, "The Challenge of 'Eurocommunism,' " p. 3.

10. Schapiro, *Soviet Union and "Eurocommunism,"* p. 8

11. *World Marxist Review—Problems of Peace and Socialism,* no. 7 (1964), pp. 1–2.

12. *Rabochiy klass i sovremennyy mir,* 1976, no. 4, as quoted in Schapiro, *Soviet Union and "Eurocommunism."*

Chapter 22: The Role of Disinformation and Intelligence Potential in the Realization of the Communist Strategies

1. *GSE* (1969), p. 52.

2. *GSE* (1972), p. 269.

3. *GSE* (1974), p. 278.

4. See, for example, the Chinese *People's Daily,* September 6, 1963: "The leadership of the CPSU has become increasingly anxious to strike political bargains with U.S. imperialism and has been bent on forming a reactionary alliance with Kennedy even at the expense of the interests of the socialist camp and the international communist movement."

5. *GSE* (1977), p. 294.

6. Sun Tzu, *The Art of War,* p. 77.

7. Boris Ponomarev, "Topical Problems in the Theory of the World Revolutionary Process," *Kommunist,* no. 15 (October 1971).

8. The award of an Order of Lenin to Timo followed the award earlier of an Order of Friendship.

9. *GSE* (1965), p. 374.

10. *GSE* (1969), pp. 388–89.

11. Aliyev became the Soviet Premier under Andropov.

12. Information from Kirilin, deputy head of the KGB religious department, and Lapshin, officer of the religious section of the KGB émigré department. See *Izvestiya*, November 26, 1960.

13. *Izvestiya*, December 16, 1960.

14. *GSE* (1970), p. 318.

15. *GSE* (1971), p. 323.

16. See "Political Shifts in the Middle East: Roots, Facts, Trends," World Marxist Review—*Problems of Peace and Socialism,* no. 2 (1980). The article is a summary of a discussion on events in Iran and Afghanistan; participants included a Soviet Afghan scholar. It notes: "Albeit difficult, it is fully realistic (and the experience of Soviet Central Asia is highly instructive in this sense) in some way to enlist Islam into serving the revolution and the building of a new life."

17. *Journal of the Moscow Patriarchate,* no. 9 (1976).

18. Yuvenaliy was replaced, allegedly for reasons of health, in April 1981.

Chapter 23: The Evidence of Overall Coordination Between the Communist Governments and Parties

1. See *CSP* vol. 4, p. 44.

2. *GSE* (1962), p. 460.

3. *GSE* (1963), p. 451.

4. *GSE* (1966), p. 52.

5. *GSE* (1967), pp. 447, 472–73.

6. For Prague, *GSE* (1973), p. 491, for Warsaw, *GSE* (1975), pp. 502–503.

7. *GSE* (1971), p. 55.

8. *GSE* (1976), p. 487.

9. *GSE* (1974), p. 6.

10. *GSE* (1975), p. 502.

11. *GSE* (1976), p. 42.

12. *GSE* (1977), pp. 18, 44.

13. *GSE* (1977), p. 454.

14. See, for example, *GSE* (1967), p. 35.

15. *GSE* (1966), p. 598.

16. See the section on the development of communist contacts in *GSE* each year from 1958 onward.

17. *GSE* (1969), p. 468.

18. *GSE* (1962), p. 283.

19. *GSE* (1964), p. 15.

20. *GSE* (1965), p. 285.

21. *GSE* (1965), pp. 47, 69, 75, 459; also *GSE* (1970), p. 63.

22. *GSE* (1966), pp. 26, 51.

23. *GSE* (1967), pp. 473, 475.

24. *GSE* (1970), pp. 53, 62.

25. *GSE* (1970), p. 53.

26. *GSE* (1971), p. 80.

27. Ibid.

28. *GSE* (1971), p. 66.

29. *GSE* (1974), p. 310.

30. *GSE* (1975), p. 64.

31. *GSE* (1976), p. 59.

32. *GSE* (1977), pp. 65, 295.

33. *GSE* (1978), p. 56.

34. *GSE* (1980), p. 64.

35. *New York Times*, March 25, 1982.

36. In 1980–81 he led the Soviet delegation to the CSCE conference in Madrid.

37. *GSE* (1970), pp. 9–22.

38. *GSE* (1966), pp. 466–67.

39. *GSE* (1971), p. 34.

Chapter 24: The Impact of the Disinformation Program

1. Quoted in Alvin Z. Rubinstein *The Foreign Policy of the Soviet Union* (New York: Random House, 1960), p. 405.

2. *New York Times*, August 10, 1962.

3. David M. Abshire, 'Grand Strategy Reconstructed: an American View,' in *Détente: Cold War Strategies in Transition*, ed. Eleanor Lansing Dulles and Robert Dickson Crane (New York: Frederick A. Praeger, 1965), p. 269.

4. "The New Drive Against the Anti-Communist Program," hearing before the Subcommittee to Investigate the Administration of the Internal Security Act and Other Internal Security Laws of the Senate Committee on the Judiciary, Washington, D. C., July 11, 1961, p. 10.

5. R. Strausz-Hupe, W. R. Kintner, J. E. Dougherty, and A. J. Cotrell, *Protracted Conflict*, (New York: Harper Brothers, 1959) pp. 115–16: "It is no exaggeration to say that in recent years the Western governments have shown neither enthusiasm for, nor skill in, the conduct of their official "information programs" which are a poor substitute for ideological-political warfare. Western peoples, in general, are hardly exercised about the future of the free way of life. So defensive has the Western mentality become that many intellectuals devote most of their time to apologizing for the institutions and the processes of liberal society. Paradoxically, even those intellectuals who are most dedicated to the cause of individual freedom within their own nations do not manifest as profound a concern over the threat which communist expansion poses to human freedom."

Chapter 25: The Final Phase

1. *New York Times*, December 1, 1981.

2. *Questions of History*, no. 2 (1980).

3. The involvement of socialists with "national liberation" movements can already be seen, for example, in relation to El Salvador and the meeting in 1979 between the Austrian socialist leader Kreisky and Arafat of the PLO.

Index

Abshire, David M., 129
"Actions Against American Institutions," 53
"Active coexistence," 111–12
Administrative Organs Department, 48, 50
Adzhubey, Alexey, 55, 202–3, 384
Afghanistan, 164, 179, 256, 267, 274, 316, 321, 336, 338, 345, 350, 351, 377, 390
Africa, 129, 176, 178, 179, 263, 267, 293, 316, 321, 345
  KGB in, 290, 291
  national liberation movements in, 116
  see also South Africa; South-East Africa
Afro-Asian Solidarity Conference, 382
Agabekov, 61
Agayants, Colonel, 51, 53
Agca (Turkish gunman), 352
Agents of influence, 265–66
  and intelligence potential, 282–91
Agriculture, collectivization of, 121, 134, 168–69
Ai Sy-tsi, 181
Akhmedov, 61
Albania, 40, 87, 88, 107, 110, 124, 139, 174, 287, 303, 379
  accusations of, 130–31, 132, 135
  denounced by Khrushchev, 81, 99, 138, 143, 146, 149, 150, 161, 164
  and Yugoslavia, 53, 144–45, 150, 152, 268
  see also Soviet-Albanian "dispute"
Albanian party, Fourth Congress of, 148
Aleksiy, Patriarch, 291
Algeria, 351, 383
Aliyev, 290–91, 390
Allen, H. C., 362
All Union Ministry of Internal Affairs, 124
All-World Conference, 294
Andropov, Yuriy, 133, 286, 297, 302–3, 305, 349, 353, 390
  appointment of, 347–48
  and China, 350–51

Anglo-American Predicament, The (Allen), 362
Angola, 267
Anticommunism, international, 25–26
Anticontraband Department (KGB), 121–22
Anti-Stalinism, 26–28
  controlled, 39–40
Antonov, Sergey, 290
Arab countries, 110, 190, 267, 297, 317, 337, 344
  KGB in, 290, 291
Arafat, Yasir, 391
Arbatov, G., 291
Arismendi, 344
Aristov, 202, 330
Armenia, 11, 16
Aron, 238
Art, socialist realism in, 125
Artists, 339
Artobolevskiy, 140
Art of War, The (Sun Tzu), 42–43
Arzumanyan, 342
Asia, 129, 176, 263, 267, 293
  see also Central Asia; South-East Asia
Asian republics, 16
Assassination
  attempted, of Pope, 351–54
  and KGB, 55, 126
Atlantic Alliance, 246, 258
Atlantic Charter, 69
Atomic Test Ban Treaty, 275, 303
  see also Nuclear Test Ban Treaty
Australia, 171, 280, 362
Austria, 317, 377
Azcárate, 248, 251
Azerbaydzhan, KGB in, 291

Babakhanov, 293
Bagdad pact, 28, 37

393